Brexlit

21ST CENTURY GENRE FICTION SERIES

The *21st Century Genre Fiction* series provides exciting and accessible introductions to new genres in twenty-first-century fiction from credit crunh literature to Steampunk to Scandinavian crime fiction. Exploring the history and uses of each genre to date, each title in the series will analyse key examples of innovations and developments in the field since the year 2000. The series will consider the function of genre in both reflecting and shaping socio-political and economic developments of the twenty-first century.

Also available in the series:
Crunch Lit by Katy Shaw
Apocalyptic Fiction by Andrew Tate
Scandinavian Crime Fiction by Jakob Stougaard-Neilsen

Brexlit

British Literature and the European Project

Kristian Shaw

BLOOMSBURY ACADEMIC
LONDON • NEW YORK • OXFORD • NEW DELHI • SYDNEY

BLOOMSBURY ACADEMIC
Bloomsbury Publishing Plc
50 Bedford Square, London, WC1B 3DP, UK
1385 Broadway, New York, NY 10018, USA
29 Earlsfort Terrace, Dublin 2, Ireland

BLOOMSBURY, BLOOMSBURY ACADEMIC and the Diana logo are trademarks of
Bloomsbury Publishing Plc

First published in Great Britain 2021
This paperback edition published 2023

Copyright © Kristian Shaw, 2021

Kristian Shaw has asserted his right under the Copyright, Designs and Patents Act,
1988, to be identified as Author of this work.

For legal purposes the Acknowledgements on pp. viii–ix constitute an extension of this
copyright page.

Cover design by Alice Marwick

All rights reserved. No part of this publication may be reproduced or transmitted
in any form or by any means, electronic or mechanical, including photocopying, recording,
or any information storage or retrieval system, without prior permission in writing from
the publishers.

Bloomsbury Publishing Plc does not have any control over, or responsibility for,
any third-party websites referred to or in this book. All internet addresses given in this
book were correct at the time of going to press. The author and publisher regret any
inconvenience caused if addresses have changed or sites have ceased to exist,
but can accept no responsibility for any such changes.

A catalogue record for this book is available from the British Library.

A catalog record for this book is available from the Library of Congress.

ISBN: HB: 978-1-3500-9083-5
PB: 978-1-3502-2581-7
ePDF: 978-1-3500-9084-2
eBook: 978-1-3500-9085-9

Series: 21st Century Genre Fiction, Volume 4

Typeset by Deanta Global Publishing Services, Chennai, India

To find out more about our authors and books visit www.bloomsbury.com and
sign up for our newsletters.

For Bombadil and Lúthien (who couldn't care less about Brexit)

Contents

Acknowledgements	viii
Introduction: The European question	1
1 An imperfect union: British Eurosceptic fictions	35
2 This blessed plot: The English revolt	59
3 The disunited kingdom: Politics of devolution	101
4 Fortress Britain: The great immigration debate	141
5 L'espirit de L'escalier: Post-Brexit fictions	167
Conclusion: Life after Europe	215
Bibliography	221
Index	251

Acknowledgements

In early 2016, I became convinced that the UK would vote Leave in the EU referendum, chancing a rather large bet on this result coming to fruition. It was my belief that the referendum was not responsible for dividing the UK, but merely revealed the inherent fissures already existing within society. This study, and the development of the term 'Brexlit' during 2016 more specifically, was born out of those experiences. My heartfelt appreciation goes out to those researchers and journalists who cited my initial work in this area (academic publishing can often be a painfully slow and agonizing process). Certain established journalists who got in touch to ask for guidance on the emerging genre, but failed to acknowledge the work of academics in their subsequent articles, shall remain nameless.

A number of academics offered generous reflections on specific areas of the study. Tremendous gratitude is extended to Bob Eaglestone, Sara Upstone, Eva Urban-Devereux, Caroline Lusin, Scott Hames, Dawn Miranda Sherratt-Bado, Joanna Rostek, Sibylle Baumbach and Geoff Rodereda – a European constellation of superb researchers. I am also indebted to several prominent writers for permitting interviews and discussing their thoughts on Brexit and literature. Particular thanks go to Adam Thorpe, Niall Griffiths, Sarah Moss, James Hawes, Sam Byers, Glen James Brown, Anthony Cartwright, Fiona Shaw, John King and Marina Lewycka. I'm grateful to the publishers of the fictions cited by this study, for their kind permission to reproduce sections of the works here.

The professionalism of the editorial and production teams at Bloomsbury has been exemplary. I am especially grateful to Ben Doyle, Lucy Brown and David Avital for their guidance and belief in (what eventually became) an extremely long and complicated project. The anonymous reader reports were overwhelmingly positive and encouraged me to broaden the interdisciplinary scope of the study. Thanks also to the University of Lincoln for a sabbatical award during the early stages of the writing process.

Over the last three years I have presented various ideas within this study as keynote speeches or invited talks at several universities, including Georgetown University, University of Stuttgart, University of Goettingen, Royal Holloway, Keele University, Manchester Metropolitan University, Northumbria University and the University of Lincoln. The insightful suggestions of attendees at these conferences and symposiums undoubtedly strengthened my core argument. Working on my special issue for the OLH journal (co-edited with the indomitable Ann-Marie Einhaus), 'Writers and Intellectuals on Britain and Europe 1918–2018', has reinforced my belief that academics have an active role to play in shaping national narratives. Generous funding from the British Academy and Alexander von Humboldt Foundation also allowed me to gain insight into wider European perspectives on this moment of political rupture.

Brief comments on British fiction's response to the referendum were published as 'BrexLit', in *Brexit and Literature: Critical and Cultural Responses*, edited by Robert Eaglestone (Routledge, 2018: 15–30). Elements of Chapter 4 were reworked for the essay 'Refugee Fictions: Brexit and the Maintenance of Borders in the European Union', in *Borders and Border Crossings in the Contemporary British Short Story*, edited by Barbara Korte and Laura Lojo-Rodríguez (Palgrave, 2019: 39–60).

My greatest debt is to Joy, Mike and Katy for their support and kindness, as always. My two cats, Tom Bombadil and Lúthien Tinúviel, were just kittens when I began this study. Their constant companionship and arrogant disregard for current political events has been the best antidote to the horrors of the last few years.

Introduction

The European question

We cannot recreate the past but we cannot escape it. It is in our blood and bone. To understand the temperament of a people, a statesman must first understand its history

(Bryant 2001: n.p.)

The more one looks at the problems of modern Britain and the problems of the European Union, the more the one seems to be a kind of warped mirror of the other

(Marr 2000: 243)

Britain's decision to leave the European Union on 23 June 2016 signalled an unprecedented historic moment for the nation and has resulted in a form of political isolationism unthinkable at the turn of the millennium. The years leading up to the EU referendum witnessed a sudden and violent shift towards right-wing populism, hostility towards supranational forms of cosmopolitical democracy and global interdependence, extensive opposition to open-border policies, discontent with the cultural implications of globalization and a xenophobic resistance to both immigrants and transnational mobility in general. Financial markets went into panic and media commentators immediately began to question existing party allegiances and debate the emergence of a global populist revolt. The reverberations of the vote resulted in a critical restructuring of the European political landscape and a transformation of Britain's planned domestic agenda. Few issues have divided successive governments, interest groups, communities and families as European integration. Many initial academic responses to Brexit suggested a clear oppositional struggle between the forces of cosmopolitanism and nationalism – mapped onto the Remain and Leave camps, respectively. However, this study will question such a simplistic and politically reductive framework, noting the complex intersections of race, class, sovereignty and devolutionary developments (as well as several idiosyncratic causal factors) to interrogate the multidimensionality of the Brexit result.

As the current post-Brexit negotiations have proven to be so mercurial, a more historical approach is required, casting an eye back to the initial foundations of the European project and considering the key factors that shaped the EU referendum. It is only when we consider both Britain's internal struggles and its historical stance towards European integration that we can comprehend the reasoning behind the fateful events of 2016. In the post-war period, for example, Britain witnessed the loss of Empire, a decline in industrial supremacy, a drive towards national and regional devolution and rapid changes to its cultural demographic. This study – the first monograph to chart the literary response towards European integration from the creation of the European Coal and Steel Community to Britain's eventual withdrawal from the EU – will attempt to *read Brexit backwards* by acknowledging how Britain's long-standing antipathy to the European project, as well as the tactics of various oppositional groups aligned against repeated attempts at membership, often projected a misplaced external rage when faced with internal ailments affecting the body politic. The subsequent chapters will consequently echo Ben Wellings in treating Brexit as a 'protracted' and 'extended' political event with deep historical roots that pre-date and post-date the referendum (2018: 147). That being said, the study has been mindful of Michael Oakeshott's warning of 'the false emphasis which springs from being over-impressed by the moment of unmistakable emergence' (1962: 13). The following analysis not only engages with academic debates surrounding Brexit, but draws on British media accounts, government reports, opinion polls, public surveys and social attitudinal studies to demonstrate the wide-ranging influences on public perceptions of the European project from 1945 onwards. In considering the beginnings of European membership and the implications of Britain's decision to exit the union, the study aims to provide a comprehensive multifaceted analysis of the historical background and future implications of Brexit in order to indicate how literature both comments upon and feeds into such debates.

As Menno Spiering points out, tensions between Britain and Europe are often analysed and explained in terms of party political considerations and economics, but there is a vital 'cultural component' that is overlooked (2015: 74).[1] It is in literary studies, for Lyndsey Stonebridge, 'where we do the thinking it seems that our political culture can no longer support' (2018: 10). There is, however, something telling in the *absence* of literature about the various incarnations of the European project, which is perhaps symptomatic of the fact that Britain has never really *felt* European, nor has the European Union stimulated the public imagination in the same manner as the Commonwealth or Empire. This lack of engagement with Europe is evident in critical surveys of the post-war literary period which touch upon national identity such as *The Cambridge Introduction to Modern British Fiction, 1950–2000* (2002) by Dominic Head or *Reading the Novel in England, 1950–2000* (2005) by Brian W. Shaffer.

The novel was, after all, once a key tool in the production of national identity – a socially transformative instrument in the shaping of public consciousness. As Benedict Anderson explains in his seminal text *Imagined Communities: Reflections on the Origin and Spread of Nationalism* (1983), works of literature are integral to the construction of imagined national communities. Imagined communities are formed through storytelling and shaped by language as the 'idea of the nation, though a potent one, belongs to the realm of the imaginary rather than the real. It occupies a

---

[1] To say 'Britain and Europe' suggests that the British are somehow set apart from troubles of the Continent due to geographic felicity. Existing accounts on Britain's troubled history in the European arena, including *An Awkward Partner* (1998) by Stephen George, *Reluctant Europeans* (2000) by David Gowland and Arthur Turner, and *Continental Drift* (2016) by Benjamin Fitz-Gibbon, stand testament to British truculence and intransigence towards integration.

symbolic rather than territorial space' (Samuel 1989: 16). For Timothy Brennan, such national 'imaginary constructs [. . .] depend for their existence on an apparatus of cultural fictions in which imaginative literature plays a decisive role. And the rise of European nationalism coincides with one form of literature – the novel' (1990: 49). Accordingly, although responses to Brexit are clearly evident in British poetry and theatre, it will be suggested that the causal factors and motivating impulses of Brexit are best captured in the medium of the British *novel*. The selected fictions in this study testify to the ongoing conversation Britain is continuing to have with itself through this literary form: the novel as a potent resource which both comments upon and feeds into existing cultural imaginaries and patriotic attachments. Yet the novel can also serve as a significant, socially constitutive form for challenging monolithic constructions of national identity, heightening public consciousness of political events and advancing an outward-facing global outlook in defiance of prevailing political discourses. To echo Pheng Cheah (2008), the dialogic novel opens up cosmopolitan optics, capable of challenging established structures and raising awareness of global inequalities. Literature thus operates as a tool of empathetic identification, enabling readers to cross established lines of nationality, ethnicity, class and gender to identify and understand the views of others.

The study will pose several questions on the role of the novel in an environment of increasing public anti-intellectualism and collapsing historical consciousness. What is the purpose of 'national' literature in a divided cultural landscape? How can literature help to make sense of political and social realities? Can literature point towards new models of community and identity? What role, if any, does literary studies have to play in responding to recent cosmopolitical events? Literature has always been a significant influence on the perception of Britishness (or narrower Englishness), shaping the markers of national identity in the popular cultural imagination. Martha Nussbaum writes it is only by 'looking at ourselves through the lens of the other, [that] we come to see what in our practices is local and nonessential, what is more broadly or deeply shared' (2010: 159). With these questions in mind, there is a history of Eurosceptic British fiction, relating specifically to the supranational project, dating back beyond Britain's first attempt at joining the European Economic Community (EEC), as authors addressed the nation's diminished post-war role on the world stage from a dominant player to a disempowered European member state. It is worth noting this study will use the term 'Britain' as shorthand for the United Kingdom of Great Britain and Northern Ireland; as Geoffrey Evans acknowledges in *Brexit and Politics* there is a widespread historical preference in both academia and the media to do so.[2] Further, Linda Colley notes that constitutionally our country is the United Kingdom, but the UK 'has never proved a very compelling identifying name' and nobody refers to themselves as a 'UKanian' (2014: 6).

---

[2] There are, of course, numerous problems with reading the nation in this manner. There will inevitably be a selection bias and certain works may contradict arguments made; moreover, separating English, Scottish, Welsh and Northern Irish texts into distinct sections and chapters may assist in highlighting their cultural and political differentiation yet neglect what they have in common and what is shared between voters across Britain.

In a post-Brexit landscape, literary works are already appearing that could claim the tag of Brexit fiction, which I label *Brexlit*, reflecting the divided nature of the United Kingdom as well as both the motivations for, and ramifications of, the referendum. I developed the term 'Brexlit' in the months leading to the EU referendum, when Britain's fate was still unknown.

In my previous study *Cosmopolitanism in Twenty-First Century Fiction* (2017), I noted the recent surge in right-wing nationalism across Western Europe and North America culminating in Brexit and the inauguration of Donald Trump, arguing that literature 'must set itself the task of imagining new narratives [. . .] representative of the sociocultural changes such historical events inspire' (Shaw 2017: 90). *Brexlit* concerns fictions that either directly respond, or imaginatively allude, to Britain's exit from the EU, or engage with the subsequent sociocultural, economic, racial or cosmopolitical consequences of Britain's withdrawal (see Shaw 2018). However, many pre-Brexit Eurosceptic fictions anticipate the thematic concerns encapsulated by this proposed literary term, including the nostalgic appetite for (an admittedly false) national heritage, anxieties surrounding cultural infiltration and a mourning for the imperial past. Re-evaluating these pre-Brexit fictions from the vantage point of the contemporary moment ensures their political undertones attain a fresh piquancy and assume a new topical relevance.[3] *Brexlit* examines the work of over a hundred British writers from a range of cultural backgrounds, including established names such as Julian Barnes, Kazuo Ishiguro and Ali Smith, to newer literary voices yet to receive widespread critical attention such as Sam Byers, Sarah Moss and Mohsin Hamid. In so doing, *Brexlit* will gesture to literature's capacity to engage with emergent political realities in an increasingly inward-looking British society and anticipate potential futures for 'life after Europe'. The introduction will begin with a brief chronological analysis of the key political events that preceded Brexit, indicating Britain's shifting relationship with the EU, from the signing of the Treaty of Paris in 1951 to the end of the post-Brexit transition period in 2020, before moving on to evaluate the response of literature to European integration.

The foundations of the European project, 1945–70

If we are half ruined, we have done it ourselves, without any sinister plotting abroad.
(Priestley 1977: 81–2)

This brief overview will suggest that a prevailing institutionalized Eurosceptic tradition within British politics (coupled with an underlying cultural disdain for the Continent)

---

[3] Birte Heidemann produces a misreading of the term 'Brexlit', suggesting the term purports 'finitude or closure' and ignores 'a continuing sense of crisis'; in so doing, she neglects that the original term also includes the *legacy* of pre-Brexit Europhobic fictions that anticipate the thematic concerns encapsulated by this term (2020: 679). She also wrongly suggests that Brexlit and post-Brexit fictions are used interchangeably and inconsistently; post-Brexit fictions clearly refer to texts produced *after* the EU referendum but are part of the Brexlit genre.

hindered any real attempts to support integration from the outset, preventing more Europhilic politicians from advancing a more positive case for EU membership. In short, while the study does not suggest a *post hoc ergo propter hoc* explanatory logic, the causal seeds of Brexit had already been sown. British public and political opinion towards the European community was highly influenced by transient, tangential and often unforeseen events. It is also important to note that the various developments impacting British Euroscepticism are of a national and domestic, as opposed to international, nature. Klaus Armingeon and Besir Ceka highlight the tendency for citizens 'to use the national context in evaluating the EU', claiming 'low levels of support for the EU merely reflect how citizens evaluate the performance of domestic governments or even their distrust of national elites' (2014: 86; 85). According to Robert Lister Nicholls, there was a general absence of debate over the European question in the period from 1959 to 1984, coupled with a failure to recognize the long-term possibilities offered by membership, resulting in Britain's eventual departure from the EU (2019: 1). Current EU debates have their roots in the foundations of the ECSC and in Britain's historical relationship with Europe (not to mention Britain's historically rooted suspicion of external cultural influence more generally). We must therefore look to Britain's past to understand the present crisis and to consider life after Brexit.

The European project has undergone a continual process of revision since the Second World War and it is impossible to understand why Britain voted for Brexit without appreciating a number of concerns from this period onwards, including the rise in British Euroscepticism, the politicization of EU migration, the resistance towards devolutionary dispensations, the persistence of substantial regional inequalities, and the struggle over the perceived dilution of national and parliamentary sovereignties. British exceptionalism was animated by a proud and melancholic rootedness in the glories of the nation's past, allowing Eurosceptics to cite the nation's irreconcilable differences with the Continent. Indeed, a noticeable continuity exists between the British exceptionalism and Euroscepticism of the immediate post-war years and that found in twenty-first-century British politics. For other Continental powers, such as France, the experience of occupation and the bitter cultural memory of two world wars was a significant factor in their desire to formulate a European community. James Kirchick deems the European project 'the greatest experiment in political cooperation in human history', yet notes that for 'all of its utopian trappings', it is founded on 'negative lessons' and destructive nationalisms of violent European aggression that defined early twentieth-century international relations (2017: 5; 226). The Second World War stands as a pivotal historical landmark when the British last retained a clear and positive sense of their national identity and role in the world. As Krishan Kumar notes, 'nothing sustains a nation, or at least nationalism, like war' (2003a: 38). Unlike its Continental neighbours, Britain had never suffered the ignominy of occupation and defeat; however, in the following decades the wartime memories were utilized both as a rationale for, and a warning against, greater European integration. Such thinking was embraced by those for whom Britain's 'finest hour' was a patriotic expression of nationalist strength rather than a tacit reminder of the value of multinational alliances to face global threats. Robert F. Dewey argues that the war was a key 'mitigating factor against early British participation in the European project and the absence of a more *communautaire* spirit'; Britain's wartime experience was thus 'insular despite the global dimensions of the conflict, because of the symbolic values attached to "the Blitz" and the Battle of Britain [. . .] That "Britain alone" triumphalism buttressed a sense of national uniqueness' (2009: 35–6).

In 1948, the Labour government boycotted the Hague Congress of Europe where early ideas for a federal Europe were floated. Clement Attlee would go on to decline the invitation to join early discussions regarding the Schuman Plan, avoid the Treaty of Paris in 1951 which established ECSC, and remain ambivalent about American calls for a European Defence Community (EDC) in a post-war landscape despite the foreign aid provided under the Marshall Plan. Britain also failed to attend the 1955 ECSC Messina conference 1955 to discuss the formation of a customs union – the beginnings of a process that would result in 'the Six' (France, Germany, Belgium, Italy, the Netherlands and Luxembourg) ratifying the Treaty of Rome in 1957 and conceptualizing the EEC. For political commentator Andrew Marr, Britain's reluctance to attend this conference was a 'lost opportunity' for the nation: the 'moment when Britain could probably have created the European Union it wanted' (2000: 176). The subsequent creation of the EEC (or the Common Market as it would be referred to in British discourse) on 1 January 1958 failed to excite British interests, with the Conservatives doubting the potential of the enterprise, fearing that it might undermine British parliamentary democracy. Wolfram Kaiser (1994) goes so far as to suggest that Britain was not simply a pensive or reluctant partner, but rather demonstrated an unconcealed disdain for their Continental counterparts; a strategy of 'using Europe and abusing Europeans' that they would continue to employ over subsequent decades.

In the immediate post-war years, Europe was simply not a salient issue for Conservative or Labour leaders. Churchill, despite initially advocating a United States of Europe in his 1946 Zurich speech and voicing a faint hope 'to see a Europe where men of every country will think as much of being a European as belonging to their native land', had little interest in strengthening a European economic entity (Churchill 1950). Hugo Young defines him as 'a grandiloquent map-maker' who may genuinely have wanted 'to dissolve the divisions between warring continental countries' but envisaged Britain to be 'a facilitator, even a mere spectator, of the process' (1999: 17). For Churchill, who fluctuated between promoting the European project and flagrant Europhobia, Europe was at the back of the queue in terms of international allegiance: 'The first circle for us is naturally the British Commonwealth and Empire [. . .] Then there is also the English-speaking world [. . .] And finally there is United Europe' (Churchill 1950). Europe's relegation to the 'subordinate circle' in this model 'reinforced the British view of European integration as a zero-sum game' (Gowland and Turner 2000: 26). Clement Attlee (who set down his thoughts in 'I Say "Halt!" Britain Must Not Become Merely a Part of Europe') claimed 'outsiders' failed to understand Britain and its ties to the Commonwealth due to their vague 'Continentalism' which was incompatible with the British way of life, while Anthony Eden cast his eye westward towards the United States (Attlee 1963). Harold Macmillan strived to direct attention towards the less successful European Free Trade Association (EFTA), comprised of Britain, Austria, Switzerland, Portugal, Norway, Sweden and Denmark. This strange association, referred to as the 'Outer Seven', proved a poor substitute for the superior EEC. In its attempt to preserve and foster a special relationship with the United States, Britain instead became woefully ignorant of important geopolitical connections being cultivated within the European community and remained disengaged from the emerging multinational bloc.

Yet it would be inaccurate to claim Britain was against *any* form of European engagement in this period (participation in the European Payments Union, for example), simply that Westminster wanted integration to proceed on an intergovernmental not supranational basis. British resistance to the European project had both *inward-looking* and *outward-facing* considerations. If the desire to preserve and maintain the national culture and parliamentary sovereignty was evidence of an insular mindset resistant to external influence, then the historical experience of Empire and lingering attachments to the Commonwealth were forwarded as reasons why a Global Britain should be afforded a paternal role in European affairs, overseeing the political and economic affairs of lesser nation states. This British preference for intergovernmental associations over federal designs had long persuaded Churchill to conclude: 'We are with Europe, but not of it. We are linked but not compromised. We are interested and associated but not absorbed' (Wolff 1976: 184). Britain's history of Empire is, of course, significant to the discussion; British psychological detachment from Europe due to its more global interests was undoubtedly reinforced during this era.

For Gowland and Turner, the Commonwealth in particular, 'with its mixture of tradition, sentiment and interest, symbolized British power and independence in the world' and had served 'as a major source of economic and military assistance' in the war, serving as 'the focal point of British interests, identity and emotional appeal [...] in ways that could not be matched by Europe' (2000: 13; 83). The political class advanced the notion that Britain enjoyed more organic and historic cultural ties to 'English-speaking Peoples' as opposed to a forced relationship with European neighbours, whose separate cultures were too diverse for a common bond of unity or fellowship to be cultivated. Research by Knight, Niblett and Raines (2012) demonstrates that public opinion clearly agreed with this assessment. Ben Wellings and Helen Baxendale outline how the notion of the 'Anglosphere' – a development of ties with Commonwealth nations – was consistently 'adopted on the Eurosceptic right of British politics as an alternative to European integration', often when no alternative vision to greater integration seemed viable (2015: 123). Britain's reluctance was perceived as aggressive intransigence by their European counterparts: a futile attempt by anti-Marketeers (early Eurosceptics) to arrest the development of a federal heart by maintaining national autonomy through intergovernmental relations. The subsequent success of the EEC placed greater strain on a nation that was already becoming unsure of its role in an unstable post-war landscape, suggesting an increasingly fragile British identity was somehow at odds with the changing face of European relations. The widespread belief that Britain had 'missed the bus' in the movement towards European integration resulted in rapid policy changes and unforeseen paradigm shifts towards the end of the decade.

By the early 1960s EEC economies were outperforming Britain with Commonwealth exports in decline, leading Dean Acheson, former US secretary of state, to famously remark: 'Great Britain has lost an empire and not yet found a role' (Acheson 1963: 163). These developments, coupled with emergent economic crises within Britain, forced Harold Macmillan to reconsider his stance on Europe. Despite Britain's unwillingness to accept the prospect of its reduced standing as a mere European member state, the risks of exclusion were simply too great and remaining British motivations for delaying membership further wilted under close scrutiny. Macmillan's subsequent application to join the EEC in 1961 was a key moment which impacted UK–European relations for decades. Andrew Gamble correctly identifies the application as 'part of a more general reassessment of Britain's place in the world, and the need to modernise British institutions' (1998: 16). During negotiations, Macmillan believed he could secure key concessions relating to agriculture and the Commonwealth, but he failed to recognize that the real battle was being fought over the more abstract and volatile concerns of national identity and parliamentary sovereignty. As Dewey argues, the most relevant aspect of opposition to the EEC during this period was the 'notable success in grafting a host of emotive and enduring patriotic meanings to a foreign policy issue for the purposes of domestic consumption' (2009: 214). Later claims by the 2016 Vote Leave campaign that independence from the EU would result in a more 'Global Britain', as opposed to an act of Little Englander isolation, has its precedent in the rhetoric of anti-Marketeers and a Eurosceptic press during Britain's attempts at entry into the EEC. The much-touted slogan 'Commonwealth not Common Market' encapsulated the stubborn anxiety that an abandonment of the British imperial past signalled the end of Britain's global relevance and the submersion of British national identity by an unwelcome European culture – surrendering our national voice and assuming the role of a fifth-rate power.

Macmillan's decisive application led Hugh Gaitskell, leader of the Labour Party, to famously proclaim that British entry to the Common Market amounted to submission to a shadowy federated polity and spelt 'the end of Britain as an independent nation; we become no more than Texas or California in the United States of Europe. It means the end of a thousand years of history' and 'the end of the Commonwealth' (despite Britain only becoming a state in 1707) (Gaitskell 1962). For anti-Marketeers, any potential benefits of membership was marred by fears surrounding the resultant reduction in democratic control, the (admittedly accurate) belief that it would be difficult to extract Britain from European agreements once it had already joined, and a reduction in parliamentary decision-making regarding fiscal and monetary policy. Dewey notes 'symbols of nationhood were conveniently mobilized or manipulated to serve the anti-Market cause'; in harking back to nostalgic notions of imperial Britishness, anti-Marketeers hoped the public would be unable to judge the EEC on its own merits, but rather consider it a poor substitute for a once-proud Empire (2009: 7). In a Conservative Party political broadcast, Macmillan argued:

> Some people will think that if you enter into one of these alliances or groupings, you will lose your identity. Well of course if you enter into any kind of contract, a treaty, if you join a club [...] you hand over to the common pool something of your own liberty. But that doesn't mean that if we join one of these, that Britain will cease to be Britain or British people to be British. (Macmillan 1962)

The statement was not only directed at anti-Marketeers but delivered a strident response to public fears that the proposed EEC membership naturally entailed a loss of national sovereignty. Nevertheless, by letting anti-Marketeers shape the political agenda, the government ensured public opinion was hardened towards the merits of accession (David Cameron's government was to make the same fatal error decades later).

Unfortunately for Britain, once it had formally applied for membership, European political attitudes (particularly in France) towards what was perceived as British exceptionalism and an assumed superiority began to matter more than Britain's Europhobic antipathy, dictating the manner and timing of entry and affecting UK–EU relations from the outset. In 1963, French president Charles de Gaulle vetoed Macmillan's application, declaring the nation was not *communautaire* ('community-minded'). His evaluation of post-war England would prove to be rather prescient: 'England in effect is insular, she is maritime [...] She has in all her doings very marked and very original habits and traditions. In short, the nature, the structure, the very situations that are England's differ profoundly from those of the continentals' (de Gaulle 1963). De Gaulle's conflation of England with Britain here is indicative of how strongly Westminster dictated Britain's overall stance towards European integration in the period. He perceived Britain's application for membership to come not from a driven desire to embrace Europe, but from economic and political vulnerability: '[Britain] feels the profound need to find some sort of framework, even a European one if need be, which would enable her to safeguard her own identity, to play a leading role' in light of recent economic downturns (qtd. in Gibson 2011: 288). Gowland and Turner recognize there is a 'certain irony' in that the arguments proffered by de Gaulle echoed the self-same reasons British politicians had provided for Britain's exceptionalism in the past (2000: 138). Yet there is no denying de Gaulle's grievances and insecurities, stemming from France's occupation and surrender during the war in comparison to Britain's island defence, intensified British antipathy towards what was perceived as a Franco-German endeavour. Macmillan went so far as to claim that 'if Hitler had danced in London we would have had no trouble with de Gaulle' (Horne 1989: 319). De Gaulle may have done great long-term damage in this respect; his selfish motivations ensured that when Britain did finally enter the EEC it was on less favourable terms which would be a matter of contention for decades. From the early stages of integration, then, Britain desired an exceptional role at critical junctures in the creation of the European project, leading other member states to believe that Britain lacked a commitment to integration and resulting in de Gaulle's resistance to their delayed accession.

Harold Wilson also held a personal preference for the Commonwealth and Anglosphere over European attachments, alluding to Britain's established links with Australia, Canada and New Zealand in a debate on potential accession to the EEC: 'We are not entitled to sell our friends and kinsmen down the river for a problematical and marginal advantage of selling washing machines in Dusseldorf' (Wilson 1961). Nevertheless, he begrudgingly planned a second application in 1967. If the application was approved, he would have succeeded where the Macmillan had failed; if it was rejected, he would have at least appeased pro-European factions within his party. According to Young, for Wilson 'the government itself would benefit from a revivalist project: that "Europe", however regrettably, was becoming the only place to look' (1999: 191). His remarks are echoed by Andrew Geddes, who argues Britain's application 'was born from a lack of alternatives' (2005: 122). But Britain was once again rebuffed by a bitter de Gaulle. These various attempts at entry merely revealed the weakening of Britain's assumed dominance of the Continent and the psychological impact of surrendering the Empire left clear traces of lingering resentment in British society in the immediate post-war period. Although it is not quite fair to say, as Acheson remarked, that Britain had failed to find a 'role', it is undoubtedly the case that imperial ideology continued to shape and define British self-perception in the 1960s.

Wilson's unexpected defeat in the 1970 UK general election led to the surprise appointment of Conservative Ted Heath. Whereas previous post-war leaders had been ambivalent towards the Common Market, Heath was a staunchly pro-European premier. He perceived his electoral victory as a mandate to try and take Britain into Europe for a third time. Yet a Gallup opinion poll in October 1971 found only 32 per cent of respondents favoured entry, with 51 per cent against; the British public still viewed accession as *concession* (Gallup 1976). Heath's personal guarantee to de Gaulle's successor, French president Georges Pompidou, that the 'Britain was genuine in its desire to enter the European family' rang sadly hollow (Heath 1998: 372). By proceeding along the path to accession regardless, Heath contradicted his assertion that 'the bedrock of European union is the consent of the people' and reinforced the perception that, when it came to the European question, public consent was not the primary consideration (1998: 359).

Belated entry, 1973–92

Ultimate sovereignty has been handed back through the ballot box to the sovereign people.

(Wilson qtd. in Nicholls 2019: 85)

On 1 January 1973, Britain eventually entered the EEC as a unitary state alongside Ireland. Heath's lifelong desire to take Britain into the Common Market was thus achieved by downplaying the domestic concerns of the electorate. As John Turner recognizes, 'the level of understanding of developments in Europe has been low and public perceptions have often been manipulated for party advantage' (Turner 2000: 10). Heath's government capitulated on many issues in order to gain membership, including on the EEC's Common Fisheries Policy and Common Agricultural Policy (CAP); the latter was especially geared against British interests and would re-emerge as a Eurosceptic bone of contention for decades to come. Britain's disproportionate contribution to the EEC budget would also plague British membership under Thatcher. Delayed entry was widely perceived as a defeat – a retreat from leading the world to being led by lesser powers – but the British press attempted to position accession as a success. In 1971, the *Daily Mail* ran with the headline, 'Now we can lead Europe!', while *The Sun* promised its readers that membership offered 'an unrepeatable opportunity for a nation that lost an empire to gain a Continent' (qtd. in Saunders 2019).

While out of office, Wilson had argued against membership, criticizing Heath's negotiation tactics, yet Labour's subsequent election victory in the 1974 general election came with the promise of a referendum on continued membership. Wilson's pledge was ostensibly designed to heal festering wounds within his party but he was supported in his efforts by large numbers of pro-European Conservatives. All sides of the political spectrum contained Eurosceptic factions creating strange alliances that complicated traditional left/right divides, but Labour's internal divisions were particularly apparent. For leading left-wing figures, like Tony Benn, the 'capitalist club' of the EEC was not only antidemocratic but also bureaucratic, elitist and monopolistic in design. He claimed the encroaching 1975 referendum placed Britain 'on a federal escalator [. . .] towards a federal objective we do not wish to reach', fundamentally threatening the fate of working-class Britons, and ensuring a surrender of sovereignty to faceless bureaucrats 'projecting an unjustified optimism about the Community, and an unjustified pessimism about the United Kingdom, designed to frighten us in' (Benn 1975). Wilson's successor James Callaghan did not share many of Benn's reservations, but still suggested any ongoing alliance with the EEC should amount to nothing more than a 'business arrangement' (Glencross 2016: 8). Neil Kinnock was also initially an anti-Marketeer, claiming the EEC was depriving the British people of true sovereignty.[4] Even at this early stage, Britain's approach to European integration was 'characterized by a pragmatic and utilitarian element – stripped of a normative commitment to a European ideal of ever closer union' (Glencross 2016: 7). As would be the case again in 2016, Labour's position towards Europe in the early 1970s was arguably 'a surrogate issue, of more importance to the struggle over the ideological direction of the Labour Party, than the question of Britain's future per se' (Forster 2002: 40).

A range of oppositional pressure groups emerged helped to shape and influence popular opinion during the referendum campaign, including the National Referendum Campaign, the Anti-Common Market League (ACML) and the Forward Britain Movement (FBM). The Britain in Europe and Get Britain Out campaigns in particular, advocating for continued membership and an exit from the Common Market respectively, were clear precursors of Vote Remain and Vote Leave. Further parallels with the 2016 referendum are evident; the role of the British press in swaying public opinion was crucial and cannot be underestimated. Nicholls notes the political elite often employed 'the rhetoric of sovereignty, expressed in populist terms' to advance their personal agendas, revealing that in the 1975 referendum, like the subsequent EU referendum forty years later, 'the issue of Europe was subordinate to matters of party management' (2019: 93; 129). To secure a Yes vote, Wilson positioned the vote as a national conversation on sovereignty, claiming that the holding of a referendum ensured the people's voice was finally dictating Britain's post-war direction. When Wilson initially called the referendum, opinion polls indicated that public support for the EEC was worryingly low; however, by the day of the vote the public had swung strongly behind membership, demonstrating the power held by the British press and political elites in swaying public opinion.

On 5 June 1975, 67.2 per cent of voters favoured continued membership – a majority of almost 9 million votes – but only 65 per cent of the electorate voted on the

---

[4] There were some pro-European Labour voices during this period, including Shirley Williams, Roy Hattersley and Roy Jenkins, who went on to serve as European Commission President.

issue. It was strongly suspected Scottish voters would reject European integration due to firm opposition from the SNP (in a stark contrast to 2016 where Scotland was the constituent nation most fervently attached to continued membership) but all counting areas, including in Scotland, Wales and Northern Ireland, returned substantial Yes votes except for the Western Isles and the Shetland Islands. The sizeable two-thirds Yes vote arguably strengthened the case for European integration and dealt a harsh blow to anti-Marketeers. Whereas the 2016 EU referendum result bitterly divided the nation, the 1975 referendum dampened the salience of Europe as a provocative political football for a brief period. The result also signalled a fundamental shift away from the dreams of Empire. Crucially, however, this shift only materialized following an extended period of economic decline, the break-up of the Commonwealth and process of decolonization, and the reluctant acceptance of a diminished global standing. Britain simply had no other options that appeared so economically viable. If continued membership was an embrace of Europe, it was a begrudging embrace devoid of enthusiasm or fidelity. As Andrew Glencross argues, after 1975 there followed a '40-year "neverendum"' on EEC/EU membership, with repeated calls for another referendum in the intervening years (2016: 7). Despite Wilson's apparent success, the referendum result would go on to divide an increasingly Eurosceptic Labour Party and result in the formation of the pro-European Social Democratic Party (SDP) in 1981. Following the 1975 referendum, Britain entered a period where it attempted, albeit begrudgingly, to adjust to unfavourable terms of membership, most notably the issue of net contributions to the EEC budget. In 1978, Callaghan faced internal party revolts over a proposed European Monetary System (EMS) and Britain ultimately refused to participate in the Exchange Rate Mechanism (ERM). Wellings and Baxendale note that this national emotional distancing from the EEC continued well into the 1980s, attributing the resistance to 'a lack of media coverage of matters European' and 'a lack of education in schools about the EEC'; to this we can add the absence of a concentrated literary effort to engage with the European project (2015: 128).

The election of Margaret Thatcher's Conservative government in 1979 provoked new developments in UK–EU relations. Thatcher herself became a key player in Britain's chequered history within the European community; her mercurial stance towards Europe encapsulates the unpredictable shifts in British public opinion during the 1980s. As Michael Kenny and Nick Pearce detail, having 'started her premiership as an undoctrinaire supporter of the UK's membership, she finished in a position of open conflict with the architects of a changing Europe' (2018: 113). Thatcher's volte-face from a passionate (if cautious) pro-European – responsible for approving the Single European Act – to one of the EU's most vehement critics, mirrored the personal stance of Churchill, himself an early advocate of European integration. Thatcher's main bone of contention was Britain's grossly high budgetary contribution to EEC expenditure – a consequence of delayed accession after the Six had already established rules to suit their own economies. She realized that the British support for EEC membership would fall even further if a rebate was not secured and calls to leave Europe may resurface. Her success in this endeavour and recognition of its significance was acutely prescient; the deployment of the Leave campaign's red battle bus in the 2016 referendum campaign testifies to the legacy of public feeling that Britain was contributing too much to the European project while neglecting domestic inequalities. Thatcher reiterated a pronounced British exceptionalism during her time in office and her desire for intergovernmental cooperation in place of undiluted supranationalism continued to cloud political judgements until the notion of pooled sovereignty became unthinkable. Whereas Euroscepticism in several European countries was predominantly fuelled by populist discontent, British Euroscepticism in this period was also stimulated by a political elite intent on restoring Britain's former imperial glory or preserving national sovereignty.

After Jacques Delors' appointment as president of the European Commission in 1985, plans to deepen European integration took on a new impetus. Delors proposed a Single European Act, increased structural funds and sought to create an Economic and Monetary Union (EMU). The Single European Act significantly deepened the integration process but provoked Thatcher into a series of attacks on Delors and reawakened earlier forms of British Eurosceptic discourse. For Kenny and Pearce, Thatcher's 'main political legacy in this area was to create the impetus for a more full-throated scepticism towards European integration to take root in the UK party system'; her 1988 Bruges speech at the College of Europe not only 'became the template for an emerging wave of Euroscepticism in British politics', but sowed 'some of the seeds that were harvested' in the Brexit campaign (2018: 117; 118). Opposing federal designs for what staunch Eurosceptics feared would become a United States of Europe, she fought for Britain to retain its own national identity and traditions: 'Europe will be stronger precisely because it has France as France, Spain as Spain, Britain as Britain, each with its own customs, traditions and identity. It would be folly to try to fit them into some sort of identikit European personality' (Thatcher 1988). Although Thatcher's own demise was triggered by her newly assumed Eurosceptic stance, her passionate defence of British interests in the face of apparent Brussels bureaucracy (which she labelled the 'Belgian Empire') detracted attention away from her disastrous social policies and a continued failure to arrest post-war decline. This would not be the last time the European question was utilized by British leaders to cover up for domestic failings at home. Thatcher also strongly opposed the proposed introduction of a single currency, fearing that monetary union would naturally lead to full political union, once again resurrecting the spectre of national sovereignty to signal her opposition. Despite her reservations, Britain did reluctantly enter the ERM in 1990. Upon leaving office, Thatcher (like so many of her predecessors before her) turned back towards the Anglosphere as an alternative future for a disillusioned Britain: a nation for whom retreat now seemed to be the only form of advance. The spectre of Thatcher's late-period Euroscepticism was to haunt British politics for the next thirty years.

Maastricht to referendum, 1992–2016

We have not successfully rolled back the frontiers of the state in Britain only to see them reimposed at a European level with a European superstate exercising a new dominance in Brussels.

(Thatcher 1988)

The signing of the Maastricht Treaty by members of the European communities on 7 February 1992 was a seminal moment in UK–EU relations and its significance should not be underestimated. Maastricht, more than any other development in this period, reignited the Eurosceptic fear that British national sovereignty was being corroded by a dominant Brussels. Once again, the influence of Delors was instrumental in proceedings; under his Presidency Maastricht renamed the EEC as the European Union (to indicate the movement beyond economic policy alone), introduced the notion of European citizenship, established a common foreign and security policy and led to the eventual adoption of the single currency Euro under the convergence criteria of the EMU. The goal of the treaty was to further 'an ever closer union' between member states; but Maastricht transformed the EU into a much more threatening and insidious institution, with radical implications for free movement, citizenship, border checks and asylum, criminal justice, environmental policy, transport and industry. Robert Ford and Matthew Goodwin find that in 1992 'only 14 per cent of the electorate placed Europe among the three most important issues facing Britain', but following the Maastricht Treaty the climate changed; by 1997, the 'share of voters ranking Europe among the three most important issues had tripled, to 43 per cent' (2014: 28). Moves were also made to strengthen and institutionalize European citizenship, despite the fact that many British citizens remained largely unaware of, or ambivalent towards, symbolic European attachments. As Anderson accentuates, 'in *themselves*, market-zones, "natural"-geographic or politico-administrative, do not create attachments. Who will willingly die for [...] the EEC?' (1983: 53).

The evolution of the economic Common Market into a political union led British voters to question the EU's institutional structure and a more focused and vehement opposition to a federal superstate began to emerge. These fears were not unfounded; political rhetoric from within the burgeoning EU often hinted towards further supranational synthesis, ensuring that right-wing Eurosceptic resistance to the implied loss of parliamentary sovereignty would continue to be a vital and volatile issue, while those on the far-left complained that the EU only benefited the political elite (a common refrain first uttered during Britain's application to the EEC). In the years immediately following Maastricht, it was difficult to perceive how Britain would ever leave the EU. For Eurosceptics, Europeanization in general seemed an irreversible process geared towards the needs of a 'core' group of member states. Political sociologists Ulrich Beck and Edgar Grande, despite being supportive of the notion of 'cosmopolitan sovereignty' in Europe, point towards the 'asymmetrical political order' of the EU (which they term a 'European Empire'), that fails to 'subordinate the multitude and variety of different national cultures and identities to a standardized "European" culture' (2007: 63; 65). The transferral of national sovereignty to the European level (evident in the creation of such multilateral institutions as the European Commission) initiates a form of 'institutionalized cosmopolitanism' so despised by certain sections of the British political class and media, and can degenerate into a '*deformed* cosmopolitanism', with the acknowledgement that 'what empowers the governments and supranational actors disempowers the parliaments and democratic processes of citizenship participation' (2007: 17–20). Peter Mair concurs, conceding that 'even if [the EU] is not anti-democratic, it is nevertheless non-democratic [...] there is a lack of democratic accountability, there is little scope for input-oriented legitimacy and decision-makers can only rarely be mandated by voters' (2013: 138).

Less than a year after Maastricht became law, on 20 July 1993, the Channel Tunnel was officially opened, drawing more public attention to the European issue and introducing anxieties of territorial encroachment. The opening of the 'Chunnel' was soon followed by the implementation of the Schengen Agreements from 1995 onwards. First signed in 1985, during a period in which the core EU member states had been driving for deeper integration, Schengen attempted to establish a Europe without borders, allowing for free movement between Belgium, France, Germany, Luxembourg, the Netherlands, Portugal and Spain. By the early 2000s, Schengen would eventually grant visa-free travel within twenty-six of the EU member states, but Britain and Ireland opted out. While Britain cited its historic status as an island nation and its role as a popular host state (in comparison to member states who were traditionally sources of out-migration such as Greece or Portugal) as explanatory grounds for exemption, Ireland pointed to the crucial need to retain the common travel area it shared with Britain (concerns that would once again raise their heads following the EU referendum). Select EU member states grew increasingly vexed at what they correctly perceived to be the emergence of differentiated integration in a multi-speed Europe due in no small part to British obstructionism. These tensions exposed the conflicting agendas and aspirations of certain member states, suggesting a time would come when arguments for British exceptionalism would no longer prove justifiable.

Britain became paradigmatic for its anti-immigrant outlook: a stance mutually reinforced by its entrenched Euroscepticism. The British media and political class sustained and intensified these links in the minds of the electorate over the following decades. The swift succession of rapid European developments led to the emergence of more Eurosceptic, right-wing populist parties in British politics like the United Kingdom Independence Party. UKIP emerged out of the Anti-Federalist League in this period, which was established in 1991 in response to the impending Maastricht Treaty. Although the growth of UKIP was slow, it would go on to have later success by contesting European elections and tapping into side issues which proved divisive with the electorate such as criminal justice and the protection of sterling. By conflating Englishness with Britishness, suggesting the primacy and dominance of the former, the party recognized early an emergent English nationalist sentiment forming in certain regions. UKIP leader Nigel Farage put it bluntly, 'the fact is we just don't belong in the European Union. Britain is different. Our geography puts us apart. Our history puts us apart' (Farage 2013). Writing in 1996, Stephen Haseler predicted, 'Twenty-first century Britons will see the British Isles as being a part of Europe [. . .] British sensibility will expand to encompass continental European history as part of its own' (1996: 185). The subsequent fusion of anti-EU immigration with wider xenophobic intolerance in intervening years by UKIP and other nationalist parties, coupled with heightened fears of pooled sovereignty, ensured Haseler's vision remained a bleak prospect.

In the early 1990s, John Major had attempted to distance himself from Thatcher's anti-EU rhetoric; his 1992 Conservative election manifesto proclaimed 'Britain is at the heart of Europe' (qtd. in Gowland and Turner 276). Yet Britain's humiliating withdrawal from the European Exchange Rate Mechanism, just two years after entry following a collapse in the pound sterling, led to further internal squabbles over Britain's reticent participation in the developing European project. By the mid-1990s, following a radical deepening of European political union, it was the Conservatives who were the party most divided over Europe, perceiving the expansion of the EU as a threat to national sovereignty and responsible for the over-regulation of the British economy in direct opposition to Thatcherite free-market ideology. More importantly, identity-related factors concerning the erosion of local traditions became powerful motivating factors in determining public attitudes towards the EU. Liesbet Hooghe and Gary Marks (2009) identify the shift in the 1990s from a state of 'permissive consensus', whereby the British public were content to let successive governments dictate EU relations, to a position of 'constraining dissensus', whereby public Euroscepticism began to dictate the responses of political leaders.

While the Conservatives tore themselves to pieces over the European question, New Labour emerged as a potent threat. The landslide victory of Tony Blair in the 1997 general election marked the end of eighteen years of Conservative government; Blair's forward-looking approach to Europe and more inclusive sense of Britishness proved extremely attractive to the electorate. As Gowland and Turner point out, unlike previous post-war British premiers, Blair's formative years were less impacted by the Second World War (2000: 332). For Blair, Britain's post-war relationship with Europe was one of 'hesitation, alienation, incomprehension'; he endorsed a more Europhilic approach to integration: a dramatic shift from stubborn isolation to generous cooperation (Blair 2000). Yet following his appointment clouds were already appearing on the horizon; in the immediate fallout of the 1997 Treaty of Amsterdam the Conservatives accused Blair of capitulating on immigration and asylum policies. The treaty did little to allay the fears of Eurosceptic voters, transferring further powers from national governments to a now muscular European Parliament as well as preparing the ground for further EU expansion for new member states. Blair considered pooled sovereignty to be a necessary evil 'in order to extend the reach of democratic action', but his tentative embrace of Europe still contained echoes of his more Eurosceptic predecessors: 'We fear that the driving ideology behind European integration is a move to a European superstate, in which power is sucked into an unaccountable centre' (Blair 2002). For his Chancellor Gordon Brown, too, an intergovernmental rather than federal approach was still preferable. Blair's foreign secretary, Robin Cook, summed up the problem facing pro-European British politicians in positioning the EU as a force for good in the public imagination: 'We have not yet developed the vocabulary to get this complex idea across forcefully and to show why supporting the EU should be the natural reaction of patriotic British citizens' (Cook 2000: 25). This conundrum would continue to puzzle successive British governments for the next two decades.

Despite New Labour's suggested turn towards Europe, Britain continued to opt out of undesirable EU policies and frameworks and the persistence of British exceptionalism continued to have a corrosive effect on European relations. Blair initially argued Britain should adopt the euro if it could pass the 'five economic tests' criteria set out by Gordon Brown but the government eventually ruled out joining the EMU and Blair avoided a referendum on the euro, proclaiming 'I am not going down in fucking history as the prime minister who took Britain out of Europe' (qtd. in Macshane 2019: 42). When it came to British exceptionalism, the past was not a foreign country. Consequently, Britain watched from afar once more as the EU introduced the single currency Euro on 1 January 1999: the final stage of economic union. Public and political opinion was strongly against the euro, and implied devaluation of the pound, continuing Britain's historical distaste for closer monetary union. However, much bigger internal developments were occurring which would have more far-reaching consequences for British membership within the EU.

The concentration on Anglocentric Westminster politicking up to this point gestures to the ways by which the economic fortunes of Scotland, Wales and Northern Ireland were shackled to those of Britain. But under New Labour legislation was enacted from 1998 onwards to introduce new constitutional arrangements and devolutionary dispensations to Wales, Scotland and Northern Ireland: a tacit acknowledgement that the United Kingdom was a multinational state. Bogdanor identifies how these initial reforms would have an indirect impact on Britain's eventual decision to leave the EU: 'Brexit comes in the wake of a long period of constitutional reform which began with Tony Blair's government in 1997' (2019: 258). Devolution may have granted substantial powers and freedoms to Wales, Scotland and Northern Ireland (turning away from Westminster's long-standing attempt to maintain the illusion of political unity by submerging these constituent territories under a dominant Anglo-centrism), but the move further undermined the unitary state of a United Kingdom. Reforms exacerbated an ongoing English identity crisis evident in the groundswell of support for far-right political parties, indicating a fresh opposition to Europeanization, and failing to heal existing intra-UK divisions. For Sean Carey, the EU posed an existential threat to England's dominant position in the union, whereas Scotland and Northern Ireland perceived the EU as a protective force in the expression of their respective identities (2002: 406). The Scottish enthusiastically embraced greater devolution of powers, perceiving the reforms as a viable first step towards independence, but the creation of a Welsh Assembly was only approved by a slim majority, reflecting the deeply divided public opinion within Wales on the British union. In Northern Ireland, devolutionary dispensations coincided with the signing of the 1998 Good Friday Agreement, putting in place a power-sharing arrangement that marked the end of much sectarian, inter-community violence. The EU played an integral role in negotiations, supporting the peace process and providing social and economic development funding. For Eurosceptics, any splintering of the union or increased support for a 'Europe of the regions' would encourage the EU to deepen the integrationist project and weaken the parliamentary sovereignty of Westminster. As a result, it became 'increasingly difficult to see the politics of European integration and British disintegration as separate and distinct processes' (Wellings 2015: 33).

Existing tensions regarding EU membership were exacerbated on 1 May 2004, when the EU witnessed the largest enlargement in its history, expanding to include ten Central and Eastern European (CEE) states. The influx of Eastern Europeans was initially considered a boost to the national economy in providing a cheap source of labour; however, enlargement accelerated concerns that the accession of less financially stable member states would threaten the economic stability of the union, lead to unprecedented immigration levels and have a damaging economic impact to working-class citizens. The 2004 expansion provoked a substantial rise in electoral support for far-right and nationalist political parties which all placed immigration and Europe at the forefront of their respective manifestos; their provocative tirades naturally struck a chord with economically insecure working-class voters and the squeezed middle class. By 2007, following a subsequent further enlargement to accept Bulgaria and Romania as member states, a 'New Europe' had been created in which Britain was an increasingly recalcitrant and peripheral member.

The EU was placed under further intense pressure following the 2007–2008 global financial crisis and struggled to avoid collapse; the subsequent economic downturn precipitated the European debt crisis. While Britain was not a member of the Eurozone, the financial crisis deeply affected British society, precipitating a fresh Eurosceptic backlash and the contributing to the subsequent success of UKIP in the 2009 and 2014 European elections; their billboards during the campaign, concentrating heavily on immigration and utilizing Churchill as the defender of the English tradition, were the precursor to Leave.EU's billboards in 2016. In the 2014 elections they forced the Conservatives down into third place, securing 26.6 per cent of the vote.[5] Fragmented left-behind communities in the North and Midlands, already weakened by decades of deindustrialization, began to push for political-economic change and directed their ire at immigration and the London bubble. British voters increasingly perceived the EU to be an imperfect union offering more risks than rewards. The 2009 parliamentary expenses scandal compounded the situation, eroding the public trust in the British political elite and their capacity to govern truthfully and equitably. When the Conservative-Liberal Democrat coalition came to power in 2010 it adopted the approach of earlier post-war governments towards Europe: offering support and advice while remaining semi-detached. Claims from core EU member states that greater integration with regards to economic governance was required to confront the crisis increased the likelihood that an eventual withdrawal from Europe may be on the cards. While the EU struggled to save the Eurozone from collapse the British government rallied to protect its banking sector, vetoing plans for greater monetary integration in the Eurozone. The financial crisis thus shattered trust in national governmental institutions, while the Eurozone crisis weakened faith in European bodies by association, fanning the flames of Eurosceptic unrest.

If Brown had won the 2010 UK general election, Britain would arguably still be a member of the EU. In 2007, he issued a Green Paper which communicated a deep sensitivity to the crisis of national identity in Britain, accentuating the 'need to ensure that Britain remains a cohesive society, confident in its shared identity' in order to 'provide a clearer articulation of British values [. . .] which have not just to be shared but also accepted' and 'articulate better a shared understanding of what it means to be British, and of what it means to live in the UK' (Brown 2007: 10). David Cameron's election victory put an end to any potential refashioning of inclusive British values and ensured Euroscepticism endured as a talismanic issue for the Conservatives, opening up divisions that would not fully emerge until 2016. Cameron adhered to the long

---

[5] UKIP received 2,498,226 votes in the 2009 European Elections compared to just 150,251 votes in 1994 (Etheridge 2014: 174).

British political tradition of positioning European identity as antithetical to British national identity, invoking the Shakespearean image of the nation as 'a fortress built by Nature for herself':

> We have the character of an island nation: independent, forthright, passionate in defence of our sovereignty. We can no more change this British sensibility than we can drain the English Channel. And because of this sensibility, we come to the European Union with a frame of mind that is more practical than emotional. For us, the European Union is a means to an end – prosperity, stability, the anchor of freedom and democracy both within Europe and beyond her shores – not an end in itself. (Cameron 2013)

Support for UKIP also increased significantly following the election and played a key role in Britain's decision to leave the EU; their success in the 2014 European elections, and strong showing in the 2015 general election, represented a tangible shift in the British political system towards greater support for populist, anti-establishment figures and parties. Initially a single-issue party focused on withdrawal from Europe, UKIP matured into a broader populist organization, launching attacks on various failings within contemporary Britain; the tactic tapped into the concerns of disparate groups within the electorate and across the political spectrum. A YouGov poll on 3 May 2013 showed UKIP support was primarily driven by opposition to immigration (76%) with only 59 per cent of respondents citing a desire to leave the EU (Jordan 2013). As psephologists Matthew Goodwin and Caitlin Milazzo (2015) argue, UKIP did not simply redraw Britain's political map but also channelled the deep reservoir of anger stemming from financial insecurity and perceived cultural marginalization. UKIP became the mouthpiece for voters left behind by economic transformation, fearful of economic instability in Europe, disillusioned with Labour's new careerist political class (who mocked contemporary modes of patriotism) and frustrated with the lack of social mobility outside the south-east. Under such overlapping conditions, it is not surprising that a worrying concoction of strident nationalism emerged in areas such as Boston in Lincolnshire, Clacton in Essex or Dudley in the West Midlands. UKIP became a protest party for voters concerned less with the EU than the overall disenchanting state-of-the-nation; and yet, EU membership 'provided UKIP with a lifeboat into which the warring camps could climb' (Goodwin and Milazzo 2015: 300). It is important to note there were also strident pro-European voices in this period. Pauline Schnapper correctly identifies that the temptation to concentrate on a pronounced Euroscepticism neglects the Europhilic stance of politicians within Labour, the Liberal Democrats and the Green Party; nevertheless, such parties 'faced an uphill struggle trying to convince the electorate of the merits of the EU', particularly given Labour remained out of power and the Liberal Democrats were very much the junior partner in the Coalition (2015: 118).

Within the Conservative Party, opposition to the EU was split between those who perceived the political union as a threat to Britain's historic identity and those who believed the union arrested the economic development of Britain as a major trading nation in the twenty-first century. Cameron's infamous Bloomberg speech on

23 January 2013 was a last-ditch attempt to move beyond Euroscepticism as a defining party issue and 'settle this European question in British politics' (Cameron 2013). Cameron committed his party to an in/out referendum on Britain's EU membership. The decision was motivated by a desire to fend off an incipient challenge from UKIP and to appease disaffected backbenchers: a gross miscalculation designed to alleviate internal party insecurities. That being said, the promise was the by-product of forty years of British Euroscepticism. Cameron recognized that support for the EU had grown 'wafer thin' and gave voice to the 'growing frustration that the EU is seen as something that is done to people rather than acting on their behalf' (Cameron 2013). Despite conceding the Continent constituted 'our geographical neighbourhood', Cameron went on to emphasize the clear distinction between 'Britain' and 'Europe' as separate cultural and political entities (Cameron 2013). In the same year Cameron delivered his Bloomberg speech, an IPPR poll (taken from a 'Future of England' survey) found Euroscepticism to be a distinctly English, as opposed to British, phenomenon: '72 per cent of those who say they are exclusively English and 58 per cent of those who say they are more English than British would vote to leave the EU respectively' (IPPR 2013). Conservative voters were also found to possess a far stronger sense of their English identity, revealing the opening up of a political space for an English nationalist party willing to tap into underlying cultural grievances. Euroscepticism and Englishness were thus symptomatically entwined.

Scotland had long recognized this fact; the 2014 Scottish independence referendum channelled a frustration with the paternalistic nature of Anglocentric political governance. Although 55.3 per cent of Scottish voters went on to reject independence, the Scottish National Party (SNP) accused the Better Together campaign of what they labelled 'Project Fear', issuing dire warnings of the economic consequences should Scotland dismantle the union. Scotland may have stayed in the fold, then, but the referendum result failed to reinforce the vision of a harmonious reunited kingdom and prompted Scottish voters to turn towards the EU as a potential future partner in securing greater political autonomy. Numerous other poly-crises functioned as causal factors for a resurgent Euroscepticism, hindering and destabilizing the image of the EU as a stable entity during the run-up to the referendum, including the after-effects of the banking crisis and unprecedented 2015 refugee crisis, coordinated terrorist attacks in European capitals, the Tata steel crisis, and geopolitical tensions between Russia and Ukraine. Arguments pertaining to national and parliamentary sovereignty served as a useful conduit for a variety of anti-European sentiments – a guise under which to hide or camouflage personal xenophobia or distaste of multiculturalism – that had very little to do with the political idiosyncrasies of the EU. At the Munich Security Conference in February 2011, Cameron proclaimed 'state multiculturalism' had failed within Britain, criticizing 'segregated communities behaving in ways that run completely counter to our values' (Cameron 2011). In the process, he formed dangerous associations between the values of multiculturalism and terrorist acts of Islamic radicalization in the wake of 7/7. Farage echoed these sentiments regularly, blaming the Paris attacks in January 2015 on multicultural dynamics and implying an insidious Islamicization was infecting British communities. Such thought was not just employed for political purposes; the historian Niall Ferguson considered the European continent to be 'experiencing fundamental demographic and cultural changes whose long-term consequences no one can foresee [. . .] A youthful Muslim society to the south and east of the Mediterranean is poised to colonize – the term is not too strong – a senescent Europe' (Ferguson 2004). Turkey's ongoing negotiations for accession to the EU amplified these concerns and UKIP foregrounded the issue as a key reason for British withdrawal from the European arena.

Free movement of people has been integral to designs for the European project since the Treaty of Rome. However, the EU struggled to develop a Common Policy (especially policies concerning visas and asylum seekers) and, even following Schengen, certain exclusionary border restrictions remained firmly in place with migrants continuing to run up against the brute force of state policies. The very issue of illegal migration problematized post-Maastricht Europe's perception of itself as a coordinated community; this absence of a unified stance with regards to the movement of individuals from outside the EU into European member states was amplified by Eurosceptics in the years leading to the EU referendum. An increase in migration numbers to 333,000 in 2015 reinforced the concern that Britain was not a member of a stable and secure organization but trapped within a union undergoing a constant state of flux, with the geographic and symbolic borders separating European member states becoming more porous and the focus of intense scrutiny. The figures revealed Cameron's pledge to reduce immigration 'back to the levels of the 1990s – tens of thousands a year, not hundreds of thousands' to be nothing more than empty rhetoric, further weakening public trust in governmental institutions (Dennison and Goodwin 2015: 169). The 2015 Syrian refugee crisis intensified the already fraught issue of immigration and its potent capacity as an emotive political resource, resulting in an immediate public desire to 'Take Back Control' of Britain's external borders. Rather than perceiving the refugee crisis as a humanitarian disaster, affecting citizens from war-torn nations and requiring the empathetic responses of European member states such as Italy and Greece, dominant voices in the British press ignored cross-border commonalities and deemed the crisis to be a burden unfairly placed upon the British public. National security was increasingly employed as a justification for political isolationism and severe asylum policies, with Muslims often forced to the forefront of debates regarding immigration within Britain. As home secretary, Theresa May diverted £15 million of funds to strengthen control checks and police presence within Calais, an approach maintained by Cameron in 2016. Fears regarding the refugee crisis were thus attached to the ongoing symbolic effort by a Eurosceptic Britain to reinforce its separateness from Continental Europe: immigration and the EU were fused in the minds of the electorate.

The 2015 UK general election prepared the ground for the much-anticipated EU referendum the following year. The Conservatives, having promised the referendum to dampen Eurosceptic revolts within the party, won an overall majority, while in Scotland the SNP claimed 56 of 59 seats, gesturing to an ever-widening Anglo-Scottish political rift. Cameron had made it clear the referendum would only take place following renegotiations on the long-contested terms of British membership, but was unsuccessful in securing significant concessions on British membership; having established he would campaign for Britain to remain in the EU, his efforts to obtain a reform package which would place an 'emergency brake' on EU migrant benefits and a symbolic opt out from ever closer political union were ultimately futile and failed to quell public disquietude. German chancellor Angela Merkel (who stated Britain continued to be Europe's 'problem child') and other European leaders would not budge on what they considered cornerstones of EU policy, particularly the principle of free movement (qtd. in Seldon and Snowden 2015: 268). In spite of Cameron's best efforts to stop his party 'banging on about Europe', recent memories of the Eurozone crisis and refugee crisis gave succour the Eurosceptic right in his party.

The referendum became the means by which anger and grievances towards the state-of-the-nation (not simply EU membership) could be channelled and communicated, opening up bitter divides between generations. During the campaign, British society witnessed the politicization of intra-EU migration, aggressive debates on socioeconomic regional inequalities and a violent backlash against the political establishment. The EU itself became almost a peripheral issue as the campaign descended into a bitter dispute on regional imbalances. A cross-party group Britain Stronger in Europe secured the right to be the official Remain campaign, but Eurosceptics were split between Vote Leave, consisting of high-profile Conservatives, and Leave.EU, founded by Farage and his donor Aaron Banks. The Electoral Commission granted the more professional Vote Leave the official designation, but the rivalry between the two camps would define the tenor of the campaign. While Vote Leave concentrated their efforts on positioning the EU as a threat to national sovereignty and a drain on the NHS – employing an omnipresent red battle bus which bore the falsehood that Britain sent the EU £35 million a week – Leave.EU zeroed in on immigration, utilizing UKIP's tactics from the 2014 European elections. Farage's most incendiary act was to erect a controversial billboard with the headline 'Breaking Point: the EU has failed us all'; the billboard photo depicted a stream of weary non-white refugees ostensibly heading for Britain (the photo was actually of refugees along the Croatian-Slovenian border). Just hours later the pro-European Labour MP Jo Cox was tragically murdered by a far-right supporter, Thomas Mair, who during the subsequent trial gave his name as 'death to traitors, freedom for Britain', signifying the febrile culture war Leave.EU had inflamed during the campaign by espousing the worst kind of demagogic and xenophobic nationalism.

The vocal Leave campaigns were undoubtedly more proficient at constructing a coherent national narrative, accentuating that authority should be placed in the hands of 'the people' as opposed to the shadowy agreements of political elites. Indeed, selected media outlets also positioned Vote Leave as consonant with a proud history of British autonomy and the Stronger In camp as enemies of the British people, while John Fitzgibbon (2015) also points to the oft-forgotten role of extra-parliamentary Eurosceptic groups, such as the Bruges group, in mobilizing Eurosceptic support. As with the 1975 referendum, the British press played a key role in swaying public opinion. While *The Telegraph* and *The Times* often assumed a Eurosceptic stance, *The Guardian* was overtly pro-European. Roy Greenslade's assertion that the 'British newspaper is a nationalist enterprise, beset by the realisation that its own power is threatened by greater European integration' seemed to bear weight (qtd. in Nicholls 2019: 12). On 8 March 2016 *The Sun* went so far as to claim the Queen backed Brexit, a claimed denied by Buckingham Palace but apparently reflective of her Majesty's mild Euroscepticism.

By appealing to the public mood and drawing on patriotic idealism, Vote Leave was absolved from the responsibility to define or expand upon their post-truth policies. In response, the Remain camp warned of a further economic downturn if Britain left the EU and argued that promises to 'Take Back Control' were not reflective of an outward-facing, future-oriented 'Global Britain' but instead betrayed an innate cultural insecurity when faced with the shifting landscape of contemporary globalized life. Chancellor George Osborne utilized numerous warnings from the broad array of respected institutions, including the Treasury and IMF, that any withdrawal would negatively impact British household budgets and living standards and effect a post-Brexit devaluation of the pound. Dismissing the opinions of economic experts, the electorate appeared to associate the shadowy actions of a bureaucratic EU with the Conservatives' austerity programme: a conflation of a cruel and unaccountable political elite. Even the intervention of Barack Obama, who advised against withdrawal and dismissed the idea that any US–UK special relationship would override economic pragmatism after a Leave vote, backfired; voters resented his interference in a national referendum and Leave went up in the polls after his visit. The failure of the Remain camp's economic message, stifled by vocal sections of the Eurosceptic British press, ultimately suggested the EU was still perceived by the electorate as a political project first and foremost.

Referendum to exit, 2016–2020

I don't want Europe to define my premiership.
(David Cameron, qtd. in Seldon and Snowdon 2015: 165)

Britain voted to leave the EU by a narrow margin of 1,269,501 votes from a total electorate of 46,500,001. The overall turnout was 72.2 per cent – the biggest nationwide vote since 1992. England and Wales returned solid Leave votes; in England, the Remain vote was limited to university towns outside London. The electoral map reflected this clear divide, leaving small islands of Remainia, adrift in the Great Leave sea. The divide was not perforated down traditional Labour-Tory loyalties or left-right lines, but rather determined by a range of local, national and international grievances and impulses, complicating existing class alignments – a bifurcation of the electorate along a new axis. The result also threatened the internal integrity and continued existence of the United Kingdom as a coherent state. Majority Remain votes in Scotland and Northern Ireland pointed to underlying devolutionary energies which would only become more pronounced in the post-Brexit period. The EU referendum thus marked a critical moment at which the politicized narratives surrounding devolution, immigration, Englishness, austerity and Euroscepticism reached breaking point, bringing to the surface tensions which had been bubbling under the surface of British society for decades. Unlike in 1975, the politicization of EU immigration played an integral role and was arguably the crucial factor tipping the balance in favour of a Leave vote. Glencross argues 'the novelty of 2016 was that traditional Euroscepticism [. . .] tapped into a groundswell of anti-immigration sentiment determined to see the end of the free movement of people principle' (2016: 3). The success of UKIP at the 2014 European elections demonstrated that the principle of free movement was a central issue for voters. As Blair's government had overseen the 2004 EU enlargement, Labour also came under fire and its working-class support began to evaporate. Political commentators were quick to note the Leave vote was particularly high in traditional Labour heartlands (neglecting to mention the strong support for Leave in southern Tory suburbs of Middle England).

In holding the referendum, Cameron possessed a false confidence following two successful referendum campaigns and a strong showing in the 2015 UK general election; however, his failure in renegotiating the terms of British membership and determined focus on the economic risks of Brexit alone – as opposed to an acknowledgement of fears surrounding national identity and sovereignty – sealed a Leave victory. Further, while in 1975 the British press were strongly in favour of EEC membership, in 2016 a hostile Euroscepticism was evident in both tabloid and broadsheet reporting. On the morning of the result, Cameron tendered his resignation, becoming the fourth Conservative PM forced out of office over the European question. Despite Cameron's early aside to his director of communications Craig Oliver that even holding a referendum may 'unleash demons of which ye know not' – a comment which would prove to be acutely prophetic – he would later admit he fundamentally underestimated 'the latent Leaver gene' (Oliver 2017: 10; qtd. in Bush 2019). For Robert Saunders, Cameron presided over 'the most significant policy reverse since decolonisation' (2018: 382). The charge remained that he had trapped Britain in a constitutional quagmire simply to dampen a domestic matter within his own party. Home Secretary Theresa May, who had backed Remain and assumed a submarine strategy of silence during the campaign, arose amid bitter Tory backstabbing to become the new PM. The two oppositional campaigns in the EU referendum offered competing and irreconcilable visions of the nation's future: for Remain, a passive future tempered by economic realities and global responsibilities; for Leave, a redemptive future free of European control and full of political possibilities, resurrecting a national self-determination associated with Victorian imperialism.

It was not until after the referendum result that due attention was given to the most contentious issue affecting withdrawal from the EU – the Northern Irish border. Debates over the Single Market and Customs Union heightened the threat of a 'hard border' across the island of Ireland – effectively a UK–EU border. Any border posts or customs checks threatened to unravel the hard-won negotiations of the Good Friday Agreement and re-activate underlying tensions along the Northern Irish border. Moreover, in underestimating the socioeconomic and psychological consequences of dragging Northern Ireland out of the EU against its will, Westminster increased the likelihood of the province aligning itself with the Republic of Ireland, creating the conditions for re-unification. May's DUP deal after failing to secure a majority also raised fears that the pro-Union Conservatives were willing to stay in power at the risk of destabilizing peace. The government were faced with the challenge of creating a frictionless border, eventually proposing a backstop: keeping Britain in the Customs Union until some future agreement could be reached to avoid a hard border. After facing an aggressive backlash from her 'hard Brexit' backbenchers, who wished to sever all ties with the EU, May was forced to find alternative arrangements for the backstop.

The difficulties in enacting Brexit were evident in the years following the vote: Britain entered a state of parliamentary paralysis involving a series of torturous struggles between government and the Supreme Court. Sold 'as a fantasy of national liberation', the referendum 'simply could not survive contact with reality. It died the moment it became real' (O'Toole 2020: 301). Between 2016 and 2020, Britain thus experienced what MacShane (2019) terms a 'Brexistential crisis' as EU withdrawal could only occur after tense and arduous negotiations with Brussels which threatened to run on indefinitely. Further, the Conservatives were divided between hard-line Leavers and more Europhilic metropolitan MPs. Labour's electorate problem was also compounded by ongoing internal divisions. Britain's negotiations with the EU led to tensions and eventual civil war within the Conservative Party in late 2018, with several right-wing factions unwilling to accept any form of compromised Brexit in which Britain continued to adhere to EU regulations. As Marr astutely observes, the fight was really about alternate visions for the nation: 'If you think Britain needs a further bout of Thatcherite radicalism [. . .] then Brexit is the necessary – but, of course, not sufficient – first step [. . .] their real aim is a different kind of Britain' (Marr 2018). Speaking on the death of Jo Cox, Gordon Brown acknowledged that the referendum vote itself

> was always about more than Europe. It was about what kind of Britain we are and what we aspire to be. And the tragedy is that the discourse on the referendum too easily descended from a vote on the future of Britain in Europe into a vote on immigration into Britain. (Brown 2016)

The election of Jeremy Corbyn as Labour leader in 2015 was problematic for pro-European in the party; Conservatives pointed out that Corbyn had submitted a No vote in the 1975 referendum, consistently voted against all EU treaties since beginning his parliamentary career in 1983, and held a position towards integration which seemed ambivalent at best. Pro-European parties (along with Supreme Court judges) were constantly attacked by the pro-Brexit press, including the *Daily Mail*, *The Sun* and *The Daily Telegraph*, for being 'enemies of the people' by not respecting the 'spirit of democracy' or the symbolic articulation of popular sovereignty. Labour MPs in pro-Leave voting seats were, naturally, reticent to question the legitimacy of the result and a number of internal conflicts arose between the London-centric Labour cabinet and their grassroots support. Early momentum for a People's Vote on what form of withdrawal Britain should take – with the ultimate aim of achieving a 'soft Brexit' which allowed Britain to remain in the Single Market and Customs Union – petered out as negotiations ran on indefinitely. The negligence of Labour to advance a progressive patriotism ensured the politicization of Englishness was seized upon and defined by the reactionary right. For MacShane, Labour, correctly surmising the Brexit fallout was the result of an internal Tory conflict, 'preferred to watch from the stand

and not get down onto the pitch and fight to defeat the Trump–Farage–Johnson vision of a Europe in which Britain ceased to be a major partner, player and leader' (2019: 64).

As the post-Brexit aftermath has evidenced, political parties acknowledged the necessity of immediately responding to disillusioned and neglected voters. Theresa May's first speech as British prime minster on 13 July 2016, addressing the concerns of 'ordinary working class family', bore strong parallels to President Donald Trump's inaugural address, directed to the 'forgotten men and women of our country', threatened by globalization, immigration and the dismantling of industrial and manufacturing industries. Trump's campaign soundbite 'Make America Great Again', after all, stemmed from the same nationalist impulse as 'Take Back Control'. For her party-conference speech in October 2016, while tensions were still running high following the referendum result, May announced that she had 'a vision of a country that works not for a privileged few but for every one of us', ostensibly aiming to open up communication channel between political elites and the left behind (2016b). In vowing to 'stand up for the weak and stand up to the strong' and put her government squarely 'at the service of ordinary, working people', May cut an anti-establishment Robin Hood figure, attempting to distance herself from her predecessor and profit from the mood of disillusionment still blanketing the nation (2016b). Her comments were almost an admission that Brexit was not a protest vote against the EU, but against the London-centric British establishment. The repeated insistence on a 'hard Brexit', coupled with her decision to install outspoken Leave-supporting Conservative MPs in her cabinet, testifies to her immediate attempt to monopolize on a lingering Euroscepticism within traditional Labour heartlands.

Nonetheless, in May's now infamous Lancaster House speech on 17 January 2017, she doubled down on her commitment, promising to address the hardships felt by working-class communities while indicating that under her guidance Britain would continue to be an outward-facing nation seeking new free-trade agreements with the rest of the world. The speech signalled an immediate attempt to draw working-class voters in the North and Midlands, disillusioned with the liberal multiculturalism of a London-led Labour Party, towards the Conservatives. May's insistence on controlling 'the number of people who come to Britain from Europe' encapsulated a symbolic return to the British exceptionalism of the post-war year, treating Britain and Europe as separate and incompatible entities. The pronouncement that 'no deal is better than a bad deal' angered MPs in her own party who perceived the Single Market as a safer option than crashing out of all economic unions. May gestured to her (albeit ambivalent) inheritance of the Eurosceptic victory, citing Britain's instinctive urge to 'get out into the world and rediscover its role as a great, global, trading nation' (May 2017a). Over the next following months, she espoused a range of adjectival options for Brexit – soft, hard, red-white-and-blue – which failed to adequately explain the various forms of withdrawal Britain might pursue. On 29 March 2017 May finally sent a letter to the European Council triggering Article 50, starting the stop-clock on Britain's final two years within the EU unless some unforeseen agreement could be reached. In spite of her inclusive political rhetoric, May failed to establish a cross-party response to post-Brexit negotiations and lost support from her own backbenchers. Her oft-repeated mantra, 'Brexit means Brexit', became a needless piece of obfuscation designed to conceal the lack of forward planning conducted by the British government. May's subsequent failure to secure an overall majority in the 2017 UK general election following a lacklustre campaign weakened her ability to dampen internal dissent over withdrawal. As a result, the first 'meaningful vote' on her Brexit deal in January 2019 was firmly rejected by a record majority of 230 MPs: the heaviest defeat of any serving prime minister.

Although May went on to survive a vote of no confidence in her leadership, she swiftly promised to step down having failed to unify the party or the country; Britain's initial departure date did not come to pass. In the 2019 Conservative leadership contest, Boris Johnson swept to victory running on a Eurosceptic, 'hard Brexit' platform. Following the 2019 European elections, in which Farage's newly formed Brexit Party romped home to victory, Johnson recognized the Brexit vote had failed to quell fears surrounding immigration; Leave voters continue to believe the government has failed to 'Take Back Control', while supporters of a 'hard Brexit' considered the loss of Single Market access a small price to pay for reduced EU immigration and tighter border controls. The 2020 general election saw the Conservatives secure a convincing majority while their opposition remained internally divided. The result may have secured Johnson a stronger mandate for his EU withdrawal bill, but robust anti-Brexit sentiments in Scotland and Northern Ireland gestured to the ongoing splintering of the union. On the issue of the backstop, Johnson agreed to a border in the Irish Sea while Northern Ireland remained in the Customs Union for a limited period. Once in power, Johnson went so far as to prorogue parliament – suspending any discussion of his Brexit plans in an effort to leave the EU even without an agreed deal. During post-Brexit negotiations Johnson exuded a bulldog patriotism associated with his hero Churchill, reiterating a desire to rekindle faded relationships with the Commonwealth, which he deemed a 'weirdly harmonious family' in comparison to the alien alliances with the Continent (Johnson 2018a). His coarse political rhetoric pointed to a clear lineage between Powellite xenophobia, Thatcherite authoritarianism and Johnsonian bluster, particularly in an eccentric articulation of a virulent strain of Euroscepticism (first articulated in his 1990s *Telegraph* articles), which only became more coherent over time. Britain officially left the EU at 11 pm (GMT) on 31 January 2020 – more than three and a half years since the referendum – starting an eleven-month transition period to confirm all future UK–EU trading relationships.

Chapter summaries

Fiction seeps quietly and continuously into reality.

(Anderson 1983: 36)

Given this long and arduous history, British authors have certainly not engaged with Europe in the same way they have engaged with the legacy of empire. In the first chapter it will be argued that post-war literature recognized the early warning signs of Europhobic antipathy inherent in society long before the events of 2016. The post-war years were undoubtedly a period of introspection for a British society that endeavoured to be fiercely and defiantly insular, yet became increasingly aware of its isolation on the fringes of a European community, overlooked and marginalized as shifting geopolitical relations reshaped the war-torn Continent they were supposed to be paternally overseeing. The study will propose Britain's role as a reluctant partner derives from unique national circumstances, leading to a perception of arrogant British exceptionalism by European member states. Accordingly, although protagonists in several of the selected fictions visit the Continent, immersing themselves in foreign cultures and leaving their comfort zone, they fail to establish a dialogue with their European interlocutors. Instead, an overt and paradigmatic 'us' versus 'them' dichotomy emerges: a comparative differentiation aligning proud British (or more often than not, specifically English) protagonists against the undesirable characteristics of their Continental counterparts. The chapter does not suggest these specific authors are themselves Eurosceptic, nor that their novels contain only Europhobic sentiments, merely that through their works they give voice to this underlying sense of lingering resentment towards the Continent: a resentment provoked and reinforced by a political class and British press who encourage a destructive nostalgia for a factitious national past. As several of the fictions in this study will suggest, the resultant public resistance to European integration during the post-war decades was not simply a response to the specificities of post-Maastricht policies but also informed by the emotionally charged cultural memories of decisive national moments and constructed notions of British heritage.

The first chapter begins by considering the contrasting opinions of a range of prominent writers and intellectuals on Britain's proposed entry into the European community in 1962, before moving on to discuss fictions which engage with a range of developments and concerns including the English Defence Community (EDC), the 1987 Single European Act, the Maastricht Treaty, the neoliberal implications of the European integrationist project and dystopic visions of a federal superstate eroding patriotic attachments. Even at this early moment in the move towards economic integration, it is clear the European question problematizes and cuts across established political divides of left and right, tangled up in much more complex concerns relating to national identity and parliamentary sovereignty. The fictions in this chapter indicate that from the very inception of the ECSC, the European community (in its various forms) has been positioned as a scapegoat for internal ailments affecting the body politic, alluding to the ways by which the British press and political class have negatively impacted public perceptions of European unity. The Common Market was perceived as a vehicle for the political ambitions of key Continental member states rather than simply the means of improving post-war economic instabilities. Geddes' assessment that British identification with the European project was 'based on pragmatic calculations about costs and benefits, rather than any attachment to European ideals' seems well grounded and is directly reflected in the response of British fiction (2013: 11). The preservation of outdated cultural imaginaries and identities points to the inability of Eurosceptics to offer alternatives to the European project or imagine new directions for a nation in decline.

Outside of London, England voted to leave the EU by 55.4 per cent to 44.6 per cent, resulting in Brexit being perceived as an 'English revolt'. As the fictions in the second chapter will demonstrate, Brexit arguably concerned England's own identity crisis rather than an adjudication of its relationship with the EU or the wider world. Internal national struggles became a convenient proxy for perceived external threats. Wellings goes so far as to argue Euroscepticism has become 'in all but name English nationalism' (2010: 503).[6] Calls for a resurgent English national identity became a recurrent rallying cry for those disenchanted with the state of the nation and generated a potent reactionary nostalgia which resurfaced with a vengeance in the years leading to the EU referendum, marking a devaluation of British's prospective future in favour of a political discourse that foregrounded a distinct imperial fantasy. An analysis of Brexit would not be complete without an appropriate consideration of Britain's troubled imperial legacy. By exiting the EU, Brexiteers envisioned a means of rebuilding people's patriotic attachments to traditional institutions, misrepresenting their desperate retreat into indulgent imperial dreaming as the pursuit of national self-determination. Fintan O'Toole interprets their political manoeuvring as a continuation of the national desire for 'heroic failure', defining Brexit as 'imperial England's *last* last stand' (2018a: 73). Understanding the commanding Leave vote in England is impossible without an appreciation of the legacy of imperial rule and its privileged nostalgic position in the national imaginary.

Although Englishness and Britishness are often employed interchangeably in popular discourse (despite the more inclusive sentiments of the former, not to mention the contradictory positions held by Scottish, Welsh and Northern Irish governments), this chapter will draw attention to texts in which the two terms are clearly not coterminous and mark a more general resistance to redefine national identity in relation to emergent European frameworks. In his 1964 essay 'On Being English but Not British', the author John Fowles recognizes how the two terms jostle against one another, indicating Britishness is employed as a 'slogan word' when the nation wants to appear powerful, resulting in 'jingoism at home and arrogance abroad' (1998: 82). The second chapter will therefore begin with an analysis of novels in which antiquated notions of imperial or quintessential Englishness haunt the present and become fruitful sources of parody – to demonstrate how contemporary manifestations of post-imperial melancholia were evident in British literature long before the referendum. As author Julian Barnes himself points out, 'Books travel strangely through time, sometimes remaining just themselves, sometimes picking up an extra charge and weight from the circumstances in which they are read' (Barnes 2017). The ironic treatment of nostalgia in these selected fictions also registers what would come to be perceived as the dismissal of traditionalist English ideals by the Remain camp, which only exacerbated the existing grievances of those citizens 'left behind' and disillusioned by cultural change.

However, although imperial nostalgia was undoubtedly a core subliminal message of the Vote Leave campaign (and addressed urgent concerns relating to England's diminished status both within the union and on the global stage), it was not the primary motivating factor in activating and influencing citizens to leave the EU. The Leave vote was a broad church containing a strange alliance of establishment figures,

---

[6] Admittedly, Northern Irish unionist parties have also expressed pronounced Eurosceptic sentiments (evident in the breakdown of the referendum result).

disenfranchised working-class voters and disillusioned Middle Englanders. The second half of the chapter will examine texts which anticipate the rise of English nationalism and its crucial impact on the EU referendum, indicating how anti-EU protestations and more general racial logics were to be fused in the minds of the electorate for the purposes of national protectionism. The chapter will conclude by concentrating on the deepening economic inequalities related to English deindustrialization alongside the emergence of right-wing parties and their impact on the political arena. These selected fictions mark an early attempt to establish a literary conversation about contemporary England – an attempt that was not reciprocated by the major political parties (or at least did not consolidate into a progressive dialogue) given the mounting restlessness and simmering resentment of English voters. By shutting down debate and ignoring fears regarding English identity and the sense of socioeconomic decline, established parties enabled the far right to colonize the political landscape, exploit patriotic sentiments as antithetical to European integration and cast the EU as the scapegoat for a variety of cultural ills. The second chapter will therefore address key catalysts that laid the groundwork for the fateful Leave vote, excavating the deep-rooted anxieties and historical origins of the so-called English revolt.

Prior to Brexit, Britishness was 'already engaged in a fraught attempt to centrifugally define itself against a series of overlapping but distinctly different national identities: Englishness, Irishness, Scottishness and Welshness, each of which is contested and historically contingent' (Bentley 2015: 69–70). Although it is often stated that the *United* Kingdom voted to exit the EU, its four component nations were not of one mind. The breakdown of the Brexit vote reveals a clear territorial differentiation: England and Wales voted Leave, while Scotland and Northern Ireland voted Remain. For Tom Mullen, Brexit consequently 'presents a major challenge to the territorial governance of the UK' and, despite devolutionary strategies in recent years, unresolved issues have been reopened 'in fraught political circumstances which make them harder to resolve' (2019: 276). Bogdanor rightly identifies that the EU and devolution 'offer complementary challenges to the profoundly unitary nature of the British state' (1999: 2). Eurosceptics are often hostile to emergent devolutionary strategies, for while the EU submits the notion of external power-sharing with member states, devolution introduces the idea of internal power-sharing (both processes threatening the sanctity and stability of the unitary state). As the historic legacies influencing Brexit and the struggles of post-Brexit negotiation play out differently in each nation, it is important to consider Wales, Scotland and Northern Ireland in turn. The third chapter will therefore consider the impact of Brexit, and its potential seismic shift on intra-UK and UK–EU relations, by documenting the multiple and diverse perspectives of writers within its component nations.

The first section of the chapter will examine pre- and post-Brexit fictions that evaluate devolutionary strategies, as well as industrial decline and structural unemployment affecting 'left behind' regions in Wales, to provide potential answers for the Welsh Leave vote. The chapter will then turn to the fractious Anglo-Scottish divide opening up in contemporary politics and Scottish literature's response to the EU from the 1975 referendum onwards. The second section of the chapter will first position Scotland's literary figures as key cultural figures in the struggle against the hegemonic control of Westminster. Through their discussions of political devolution, these Scottish authors construct what Michael Gardiner terms a 'sub-British' discourse which challenges Anglo-centric conceptions of constitutional hierarchy. This resurgence of Scottish literature in the 1980s 'had less to do with patriotic ethnonationalism than with a national voicing of constitutional criticism', encapsulating the ongoing frustration of being the disenfranchised weaker member of a larger union (Gardiner 2012: 141). The creation of the Scottish Assembly and devolutionary dispensations went some way to readdressing existing imbalances, but the indyref and EU referendum exposed the perceived lack of constitutional voice within post-devolutionary Scotland and its ideological antagonism with Westminster. As O'Toole notes, 'When Scots and Welsh were asked to identify which layer of government had most influence over their lives, just 8 per cent and 7 per cent respectively cited the EU', compared to 31 per cent of English respondents (2018a: 190). The post-Brexit climate has undoubtedly stimulated (if not exacerbated) existing nationalist demands for Scottish independence following devolution and the failed 2014 indyref. It will be suggested that certain Scottish fictions engage with such constitutional debates to indicate an ethical commitment to alternate political realities and a rejection of prevailing Eurosceptic discourses.

If Britain enjoyed a reputation of being an awkward partner in the European community, then historical relations between Westminster and the island of Ireland have been marked by conflict and mistrust. Ever since the 1920 Government of Ireland Act partitioned the island into Northern Ireland and the Republic of Ireland, the relationship was one of acrimonious neighbours tied into a tense political arrangement. Brexit, however, marks a critical moment with wide-ranging social, cultural, economic, political, ideological and psychological consequences for the island of Ireland, threatening to undo the hard work of the peace process and fatally corroding the future integrity of the UK. The third section of the chapter will attend to works of post-Agreement Northern Irish literature, which respond to the tentative equilibrium that has been reached, before engaging more substantially with post-Brexit works which acknowledge the re-politicization of historical feuds, exposing the key electoral divides which informed Northern Ireland's Remain vote. The chapter concludes by returning to the troubled state of England, suggesting political devolution was a significant contributing factor in the English identity crisis of the 1990s and led to calls for greater regional representation. The Future of England Survey, for example, listed 'devo-anxiety' as a major contributing factor in politicizing Englishness as an electoral issue (alongside immigration and Euroscepticism); an anxiety heightened by an increasingly multicultural landscape under New Labour (Wyn Jones et al. 2013). The 'English revolt' was arguably influenced by the perception that devolutionary dispensations and decentralization was giving greater power to Scotland and Northern Ireland (including higher public expenditure under the Barnett formula) than citizens in less affluent Welsh and English regions, resulting in the introduction of 'English Votes for English Laws' (EVEL) in October 2015 and a resurgence in calls for an English parliament. The third chapter will therefore assert that an evaluation of the internal struggles within the UK's component nations and their separate relationships with the EU is crucial to an understanding of the Brexit vote.

Countless polls, studies and surveys conducted both during and following the EU referendum campaign confirmed immigration was the key emotive issues for the electorate (Owen and Walter 2017; Glencross 2016). Political studies of the period indicate those voters who felt their national identity to be threatened by immigration were naturally more Eurosceptic (Hooghe and Marks 2005). Anti-immigrant sentiments began to escalate from 2004 onwards, especially in constituencies which returned a Leave vote. Marcel Lubbers concludes that 'Euroscepticism is to a large extent related to attitudes toward immigrants', anticipating a 2016 BSE survey where many respondents cited national sovereignty and immigration alongside one another, signifying their fusion in the minds of the electorate as a single issue (2008: 81; Prosser, Mellon and Green 2016). Jackie Hogan and Kristin Haltinner suggest the threat of immigration can be divided into two categories: 'interest-based threats (economic and security threats) and identity-based threats (principally threats to culture, democracy and "traditional" ways of life)' (2015: 528). Accordingly, British political and public discourses during the referendum involved a disproportionate and irrational concentration on two main groups: Eastern Europeans and Muslims. While economic anxieties were attached to Eastern Europeans (particularly after the 2008 economic crisis), security concerns were associated with Muslim immigrants. The more general public demagoguery of Muslim communities within Britain became increasingly ethnically coded and such discursive prejudice was driven home by the right-wing press during the referendum campaign. As Homi Bhabha recognizes, narratives and discourses of 'nationness' involve a consideration of both 'the *heimlich* pleasures of the hearth' – a psychological assessment of what defines our national community – and 'the *unheimlich* terror of the space or race of the Other' (1990: 2). Bhabha's imperial analogy not only resonates with the English revolt but the immigration debate that preceded the vote. The fourth chapter therefore begins with a discussion of significant anti-immigrant legislation, before examining the 2004 EU enlargement which exacerbated existing tensions relating to benefit migrants and the depreciation of the British workforce. Given the conflation of EU and non-EU immigration by both the media and political class during the referendum, the chapter will then examine the Syrian refugee crisis, evaluating the impact of the crisis on the Brexit vote and shining a light on the lives of those who came from beyond the margins of the European imaginary. The act of border-crossing was utilized during the EU referendum campaign as a scare tactic and instrument of control in the formation of a Fortress Europe (with particular reference to the Schengen immigration zone); accordingly, key works of contemporary British literature question the *progressiveness* of EU immigration policies and comment on enforced immobilities characterizing the contemporary moment. The fourth chapter will argue that the post-Brexit novel moves beyond the cultural insularity of pre-Brexit Eurosceptic fiction and gestures towards the need for cosmopolitan hospitality in the twenty-first century. By comparing works which engage with the plight of Eastern European economic migrants with contemporary refugee narratives that respond to the brutal injustices of forced migration, it will be suggested that a heightened political climate of atavistic nationalism and widespread xenophobia was already well established in the years leading to the Brexit vote.

When the British people voted to leave the EU on Thursday 23 June 2016 it had been over forty years since the electorate were last asked about their ongoing relationship with continental Europe. Brexit is a moment of rupture that is not readily translatable, but creative examinations of Britain's exit from the EU have been widely explored in literature, particularly through the novel form. Twenty-first-century writers and artists seem to be diverging from the prevailing anti-European political opinions of the post-war period and moving towards a more cosmopolitan embrace of alterity. The first wave of post-Brexit fiction reveals a deep concern regarding social inequalities, ethnopolitical injustices and immigration, recognizing that the sudden shift towards populist revolts emerges as a desperate reaction for those 'left behind' by globalization or *squeezed* by recent economic developments. The term 'post-Brexit' involves a sense of continuation and inheritance as well as a backward-looking impulse. The protracted UK–EU negotiations which seemed to run on indefinitely encapsulated the contradictions inherent in the prefix 'post', aligning with Wendy Brown's notion of that which is '*temporally after but not over* that to which it is affixed' in conjunction with 'a present whose past continues to capture and structure it' (2010: 21). It would, given that Britain did not officially leave the EU until 31 January 2020 (with the Withdrawal Agreement specifying a subsequent transition period until 31 December 2020), be more accurate to name these works *post-referendum fictions*. Naturally, there is a temptation to conflate the referendum result with the actual moment of exit. Indeed, the phrase 'Brexit means Brexit' has become an empty declaration of patriotic nationalism; its popularity protected by its ambiguity. As Thomas Docherty succinctly puts it, 'In a striking rhetorical paradox, the formulation states truth and meaning in the clearest possible linguistic manner while simultaneously occluding truth and meaning completely' (2018: 181). Beginning with a brief analysis of Brexit and its immediate consequences, the fifth chapter will therefore provide a timely and original close reading of post-Brexit fictions, demonstrating literature's potential to engage with emergent political realities in an increasingly fragile and uncertain climate.

The chapter begins by commenting on the rise in political thrillers by media commentators and political figures before discussing the presence of post-truth rhetoric and political whiteness in recent fictions. The chapter then engages with the contention that Brexit was the product of London-centric power plays and political in-fighting. After all, while the capital was the centre of Remain support, it was 'England-without-London' (as Anthony Barnett puts it), which tipped the balance in favour of a Leave vote (Barnett 2017). A range of fictions have emerged which accentuate the fundamental disconnect between the capital and the rest of the country from resentment towards the Westminster bubble, to the abandonment of the industrial order, to deep-rooted structural and geographical inequalities of access and opportunity. Regional landscapes often become spectral sites of memory disturbed not only by recent disappearances but by national anxieties which haunt the margins of the narratives. The selected fictions in this chapter indicate how the Leave vote coagulated disparate groups and united their grievances under the same broad banner, capturing the feeling that, for many voters, 'marking Leave on the ballot paper in June 2016 was a way of scratching the name of England on their arms to prove their love' (O'Toole 2018a: 128). The fifth chapter concludes by considering hauntological fictions which dig into Britain's turbulent national past to expose the historical roots of the Leave vote, suggesting that although Brexit operates as a national epiphany for some, for others it is simply an ignoble vision that falls well short of the sublime. Just as Patrick Parrinder (2006) identifies the vital role of British fiction in altering and registering alternate conceptions of national identity in the twentieth-century (a period in which Britain's geopolitical standing was radically reduced), post-Brexit fictions indicate a heightened sensitivity to the value of European integration and a renewed attempt to engage with the social divisions affecting British society. In this way, these selected fictions signal a movement away from the pronounced cultural Euroscepticism in post-war British literature and gesture to ways by which Britain may resist an inward-looking political landscape.

Brexlit will therefore provide the first monograph-length analysis of British fictions that either anticipate or respond to the political and social anxieties surrounding the EU referendum. While Britain's withdrawal was certainly not predictable or predetermined by prior events, *Brexlit* argues literature anticipated many of the debates that would erupt during the referendum campaign, from immigration and working-class alienation, to fears surrounding the splintering British union and the weakening of national sovereignty. The study does not suggest Euroscepticism to be a recently instituted phenomenon; it merely sketches the contours of British Eurosceptic discourses from the formation of the post-war European project onwards. Britain's decision to leave the European Union was motivated by numerous conflicts that had been festering within British society from the post-war period onwards. The study will conclude by assessing what role literature might play in contributing to the future relationship between Britain and Europe. If nations are 'imagined communities' as Anderson attests, then the task of British literature is to find ways in which the nation can be *re-imagined*. Drawing on recent events such as the Black Lives Matter movement and the Covid-19 crisis, the conclusion argues that the key divides and conflicts that erupted in 2016 have not been adequately addressed in the post-Brexit moment.

1

An imperfect union

British Eurosceptic fictions

May I say how pleased we are to have some Europeans here, now that we are on the Continent? I didn't vote for it myself, quite honestly, but now that we're in, I'm determined to make it work.

(Cleese and Booth 1975)

A symposium in the literary journal *Encounter*, 'Going into Europe', communicates the views and concerns of a range of prominent writers and intellectuals on the merits of European integration. Within its pages we can discern early anti-Common Market leanings that would go on to characterize an underlying Euroscepticism in British literature for decades. As the editors of the journal identify, however, it has always been difficult to forecast the assumed stances of writers and literary scholars on European integration:

> What has been a constant source of surprise to us has been the unpredictability of almost everyone's attitude – not merely to the 'pro' and 'con' of the relatively technical questions of Common Market entry but more interestingly to the deeper emotions involved. 'Regional poets' have turned out to be internationalists; cosmopolitan travellers to be 'provincials'; the idea of 'little England' appears suddenly to be both virtue and vice. (1962: 56)

For C. S. Lewis, the fear of European integration was not that it made a federal superstate inevitable, but rather that any supranational arrangement would be 'built out of units far smaller than the existing nations: units like Wessex and Picardy, not like "Britain" (a horrid word) and France', neglecting the local and regional idiosyncrasies of culture, language and local customs (1962: 57). Iris Murdoch adopted a related stance, emphasizing that attention should be focused on the political protection and maintenance of the Commonwealth which was surely going to be marginalized in favour of a greater concentration on European economic attachments. E. M. Forster shared this fear that the Common Market was a foil for the 'Europe of Big Business', wavering on the merits of entry (1962: 64). Playwright John Osborne concurred, declaring '[I] am proud to settle for a modest, shabby, poor-but-proud Little England any day. I'd gladly say goodbye to those hordes of grasping businessmen and technocrats, and see the lot off to the Rhine' (1962: 59). Playwright and screenwriter Robert Bolt reasoned that while the Tories desired an entry into Europe due to their opportunistic 'greed' for such economic growth, Labour's reluctance was due to 'inertia', concluding 'the Tories have the best of it. Greed is at least an active principle' (1962: 58). 'Going into Europe' is particularly significant in revealing the vast number of writers and intellectuals for whom European integration was simply a non-issue. J. B. Priestley (2015), who later called for a protection of the English national character and dismissed the merits of Common Market membership, was an early detractor on EEC membership and cast doubts on public enthusiasm for such an endeavour. In his 1962 novel *The Shapes of Sleep*, a reporter charged with ascertaining the public stance towards integration merely concludes: 'Britons are not thinking about the Common Market' (182).

Priestley's remarks are shared by historian A. J. P. Taylor, who opined 'we have never belonged political to Europe and I see no reason why we should begin now' (Encounter 1962: 62). He concludes: 'There is no British opinion about "going into Europe" [. . .] [It] is the greatest non-question of all time' (Encounter 1962: 62). Harold Pinter echoed his remarks, briefly stating 'I have no interest in the matter and do not care what happens' (Encounter 1962: 59). Moreover, some contributors were acutely prescient in doubting the validity or suitability of a referendum to determine the European Question. T. S. Eliot, for example, conceded a slight personal bias for greater cultural integration, yet deemed the matter should not 'be decided by a plebiscite' (Encounter 1962: 65). Anthony Powell, despite his personal antipathy towards the EEC, went further, asserting that writers or artists should not even be consulted on matters for which they were not informed, pre-empting the thoughts of several Leave-supporting politicians in the 2016 referendum.

As the introduction discussed, there has been a notable absence of engagement with Europe in post-war British literature, as authors concentrated instead on the legacy of Empire or internal developments affecting Britain's economic stability and structural integrity. However, this chapter will identify a range of disparate novels which depict a diminished and fearful Britain, belatedly and belligerently limping into the European arena. A particular strain of wartime resistance often seeps into these various narratives, as characters are forced into new European spaces in which their national identity (and enforced Europeanized identity) must be negotiated.

In his 1976 essay 'Englands of the Mind', Seamus Heaney characterized the post-war period as a time of national self-reflection (1980: 150–69). Nick Bentley rightly identifies that such concerns take on literary expression, with fictions of the 1950s revealing 'a deep concern with the nation's changing identity, its international status and role, and the reconstruction of Englishness' (2007: 36). Ongoing decolonization and mass immigration threatened existing constructions of national identity and resulted in 'a sense of existential crisis in national terms' as Britain sought to safeguard its splintering identity and imperial authority (2007: 37). While society struggled to adapt to post-war life, with the subsequent political, social and cultural upheavals, British authors also struggled to engage with changing European relations. In comparison to the deep literary engagement with the Commonwealth and Britain's postcolonial condition, the question of European influence and integration has attracted far less critical attention.

The awkward partner

A demoralised nation tells demoralised stories to itself.

(Okri 1995)

Kingsley Amis was an early opponent of British membership yet his opposition is arguably more nuanced. In his contribution to 'Going into Europe', Amis reflects on the condition of post-war England and determines that a 'closer economic union relation with the Continent seems desirable, even necessary', conceding he 'can contemplate closer cultural ties without shuddering' (1962: 56). It is the 'inevitable progression to political unity' that Amis finds 'disturbing', as well as the suggestion that a 'Continentalised Britain' would have to surrender its close 'special' relationship with the United States and the Commonwealth (1962: 56).[1] Instead, Amis considers the privileged 'English-speaking' realm of the Anglosphere to be Britain's 'future' destination while Europe remains 'a place we have spent much of our history trying to extricate ourselves from' (1962: 57). His Anglocentric comments seem to align with the views of poet W. H. Auden, who succinctly captures the psychological separation preventing a close cultural alignment with the Continent: 'If I shut my eyes and say the word Europe to myself, the various images which it conjures up have one thing in common; they could not be conjured up by the word England' (Encounter 1963: 53).

Amis' engagement with the question of Europe as a literary theme is crystallized in his 1958 novel, *I Like It Here*. The novel follows Garnet Bowen, a freelance journalist and lecturer, as he travels to Portugal on an assignment. Tired of relying on tenuous contracts, Bowen begrudgingly accepts a commission for an article on European culture despite his abject disdain of 'going abroad', in return for the promise of a key position in publishing. *I Like It Here* conforms to the narrative style of the travel novel but employs a seriocomic stance in order to deconstruct British perceptions of post-war European engagement. Bowen shares similarities with Amis' earlier protagonists such as John Lewis and Jim Dixon in his self-deprecating acknowledgement of his pretentious social attitude but retains a staunch resistance against those who attempt to alter his isolationist posture: 'he suffered from acute prejudice about abroad. Some of this he thought he recognised as unreasonable, based as it was on disinclination for change, dislike of fixing up complication arrangements' (1968: 23). After all, Bowen does not decide to travel to Europe of his own volition but rather is sent there for business, interpreting the telegraph offering him the trip as 'a deportation order' (1968: 5). The proffered trip is a fictionalized account of Amis' own visit to Portugal, after receiving a £500 financial reward for winning the Somerset Maugham Award for *Lucky Jim* (1954), and Bowen is arguably employed to voice Amis' own Europhobic sentiments (he even has two sons and a daughter like his author). As Philip Gardner has observed, Garnet Bowen's initials appropriately allow him to become the mouthpiece for Great Britain; initials which he proudly displays on his number-plate when driving

---

[1] In an article entitled 'What's Left for Patriotism?' (1963), Amis reiterates his defence of the Anglosphere and rejects the assumption that Britain is now a quaint relic consigned to history.

abroad (1981: 50). Upon arriving in Portugal, 'hoping not to be addressed in a foreign tongue', Bowen remains thankful that the Portuguese 'had not tried to knife him or rob him', and discovers that 'trying to pronounce even a few syllables of French set off [. . .] a most complex and deep-seated network of defensive responses' (1968: 11; 20; 157). Like Roger Micheldene – the protagonist of Amis' 1963 novel *One Fat Englishman* – Bowen revels in the distinctive privileges and national eccentricities that mark him apart from his European interlocutors.

By concealing semi-autobiographical elements under the guise of social satire, critics interpreted *I Like It Here* as evidence of Amis' own Europhobic anxieties and sneering condescension towards the Continent, and heavily criticized the novel in early reviews. Fellow author Margaret Drabble deemed the novel 'xenophobic and slight' and declared the novel among his weakest works (2006: 25). Yet many critics also fail to note how Amis consciously satirizes both his own bitter vitriol and the Angry Young Man movement. The title of the novel itself is not so much a reflection of the protagonist's own defiant Euroscepticism but an exaggeration of Amis' own parochial and insular aesthetic evident in his early fiction. Amis privately called the novel 'a very slipshod, lopsided piece of work that has very little to say about anything', but defended himself against accusations of Euroscepticism: 'In *I Like It Here* people thought I was attacking Europe, but I was attacking the people who like it' (Barber 1975: 48; qtd. in McDermott 1989: 89). Bowen's defiant parochialism in the novel is often directed towards the 'upper-middle-class traveller' who insolently believe they have 'the right to knock the English', promoting the value of foreign culture and bemoaning 'the spirit being chilled and restricted in the foggy atmosphere of Anglo-Saxon provincialism' (1968: 32).

As Cecile Leconte identifies, such 'cultural anti Europeanism is a key dimension of Euroscepticism' within Britain (2010: 69). Yet Andrew James qualifies Amis' personal fear of 'abroad', suggesting it is 'best viewed as a further manifestation of his poetic provincialism and not xenophobia', noting that Amis so enjoyed his time in Portugal that he began to travel widely after the publication of the novel; his experiences shaping his subsequent novel *One Fat Englishman* (James 2013: 59). That being said, given *One Fat Englishman*'s concentration on American society this merely serves as further evidence for Amis' continued attachment to both the Anglosphere and the 'special relationship' in place of any burgeoning Continental attachments: 'let [European relations] be ties, not bonds' (Encounter 1971: 20). Further, the denouement of *I Like It Here* does not bring a shift in Bowen's cultural outlook and we are still left with a protagonist who resents lecturing on the work of French nationalists for Modern European literature course, mocks the English mispronunciations of his foreign students and only takes pleasure in Harry Bannion's recital of Charge of the Light Brigade, before retreating to the relative safety of British soil convinced of the futility of European relations. The satirical commentaries on Europeans and their cultural idiosyncrasies, rather than the EEC directly, hints at 'a disconnect that goes much deeper than mere frictions between a member state and an institution [. . .] we are dealing with two opposing concepts. The one is called Britain, the other Europe' (Spiering 2015: 2).

The novel is certainly anti-cosmopolitan in tone, regardless of Amis' satirical stance. Bowen is not what Anthony Appiah would term a 'cosmopolitan patriot', incapable of entertaining 'the possibility of a world in which everyone is a rooted cosmopolitan, attached to a home of his or her own, with its own particularities, but taking pleasure from the presence of other, different, places that are home to other, different, people' (1998: 91). But in Bowen's mind Europe is a homogenized space of cultural otherness and he is unable to discount 'the essential abroadness of the place, the things it must share with millions of square miles between here and Istanbul', inhabited by elitist Europeans who subscribe to a stereotyped pattern, deployed to aggrandize the superiority of the British national character (1968: 157). His distaste for faux-cosmopolitan attachments (captured by the character of Celia Welch in *Lucky Jim* who perceived herself as 'Western European first and an Englishwoman second') offers a veiled commentary on Britain's brief forays into European political arrangements: 'Going and standing on the touchlines of other chaps' ways of life and telling yourself you're joining in isn't very self-aware. Just like going through foreign poetry with the dictionary and telling yourself you're reading it (1968: 16).

In 'Going into Europe – Again?', published a decade on from his initial article on British membership of the EEC, Amis has become more staunchly opposed to the question of membership, citing his distaste of the extortionate entry fee – which merely benefits 'French and German farmers who are even less efficient than our own' – and the concerning aim of monetary union (1971: 19). More importantly, he offers an early critique of the implied loss of national sovereignty which was to characterize British Eurosceptic fiction for the following decades: 'Let us not submit ourselves to "harmonisation" – that new and dreadful euphemism for the projected ironing-out of national differences in every department of life' (1971: 20).[2] *I Like It Here* ultimately remains sceptical of the merits of European integration, privileging national attachments and espousing a form of British exceptionalism which places it in line with other provincial Little Englander texts of the decade:

> the place is located abroad and the people are foreigners, which [. . .] means that they and I belong to different nations, so we can't understand each other or get to know each other as well as chaps from the same nation can. I'm all for international co-operation and friendship and the rest of it, but let's be clear what we mean by it. (1968: 185)

Imagined threats to Britain's post-war European security find fertile ground in Nancy Mitford's humorous novel *Don't Tell Alfred*. Published in 1960, the narrative places a satirical spin on the cultural hostilities and tensions of the 1950s when 'Anglo-French relations have never been worse' (1963: 184). Events unfold in the British embassy in Paris – a recreated little England cut off from foreign ground – as the novel's protagonist, Lady Fanny Wincham, accompanies her husband Alfred to France when he is appointed British ambassador. Fearing threats by the United States in 1954, that if a European Defence Community (EDC) did not materialize alongside the ECSC to

---

[2] Such political reasoning for the rejection of the European Project is arguably indicative of Amis's gradual political shift from left-wing to right-wing during his literary career (see 'Why Lucky Jim Turned Right' in Amis 1970).

counter the growing influence of the USSR it would be forced to consider an 'agonizing reappraisal' of its defence commitment to Western Europe, Alfred is subsequently charged with the task of promoting the benefits of a pan-European defence force against the wishes of a highly Eurosceptic British press who scorn 'foreign countries' and 'cultural bodies' (1963: 25). Mitford's Europe remains a foreign environment to be exploited for comedic effect in British literature – evinced by the entrepreneurial schemes of Fanny's son Basil who organizes budget package-tours around Spain and Italy for those tourists who are fearful of venturing beyond the safe sanctuary of their English towns and cannot digest European fare.

Despite Alfred's fictionalized endeavours to persuade France that the EDC was an inevitability, in reality the British government under Churchill and Eden remained convinced of its unacceptability and only encouraged greater military coordination in order to placate American interests, safeguard their own post-war financial stability, and maintain the semblance of the 'special relationship'. Plans for the EDC eventually collapsed due to French concerns over the latent erosion of national sovereignty, but the novel does capture a rare instance in the recent history of the European project where the British were more willing than their French counterparts to consider greater integration. As Kevin Ruane identifies, the British approach to the EDC 'was a great deal more positive and constructive than often allowed in the historiography of Britain and Europe', yet Britain's potential role remained conditioned by its continued desire for intergovernmental cooperation as opposed to supranational surrender, strengthening Anglo-American bonds by whatever means necessary (2002: 176). While Mitford draws on real events to confront the urgent nature of post-war supranational alignment, the narrative adopts a rather backward-looking and outmoded stance towards European relations, reinforced by her personal comments that 'it is impossible for [Britain] to join any sort of federation' and should practice a political strategy of 'non-cooperation' (1988: 86). Selina Hastings notes that *Don't Tell Alfred* was Mitford's last novel as she began 'to feel out of tune with the times' and 'her nostalgia for the past grew stronger' (1986: 230). Following the economic crises of the 1960s, however, she shifted her stance on European integration and conceded a preference for joining the Common Market:

> since it appears that [England] can no longer stand alone. We are Europeans [...] *We* have more in common *with* the other founders, our neighbours, than with ex-colonial powers across the oceans. We should form a United States of Europe with the nations whose philosophic and geographic positions we share. Otherwise, may we not become a neglected appendage of North America. (Encounter 1962: 64 – emphasis in original)

In *The Situation of the Novel*, Bernard Bergonzi identifies how Wilson's *The Old Men at the Zoo* (1961) 'echoes, in a more sinister way, the gallophobia of Kingsley Amis' *I Like It Here,* no doubt motivated by de Gaulle's repeated rejection of British accession throughout the 1960s (1970: 155). Published the same year that Britain attempted to join the EEC, the novel draws heavily on Wilson's personal memories of the Second World War, but imagines a non-nuclear war between European powers set in 1970. Rather tellingly, Wilson states he had originally intended for the novel to be set in

1940 following 'a triumphant German invasion of England [. . .] but I was told that I would be laid open to libel law' (McDowell 1972: 90). The novel's narrator, Simon Carter, administrative secretary for the Regent's Park Zoological Gardens (now the London Zoo), dutifully serves under three male directors, each with his own vision of how the zoo should be managed. The parallels between the running of the zoo and the governmental approach to European integration are glaringly transparent as Carter demonstrates a distinct British obstinacy in ensuring the organization is run according to established customs. The zoo arguably serves as a microcosmic analogy for British society more generally, with characters forced to re-evaluate their post-war identities in the face of European unification and national economic decline, while characters are reduced to their zoomorphic traits in coordination with both the deterioration of the zoo and European relations. Wilson even directly alludes to the tendency for British politicians in the 1960s to slip into 'pan-European phases' by espousing Francophilic sentiments before retreating back into their Victorian dreaming (1992: 52).

The first director, Dr Leacock, perceives the claustrophobic Victorian atmosphere of the zoo to be evidence of its dead spirit, and intends for the animals to roam free on a National Zoological Reserve. Leacock is ignorant of rising European tensions surrounding economic trade agreements and disregards developments from the outside world; his naïve and misguided outlook leaves the zoo vulnerable to sudden shifts in geopolitical relations and exposes the introspective stance of British post-war society: 'the impression we formed in our anthill was an ever clearing sky outside' (1992: 87). Lord Godmanchester, president of the zoological society and newspaper magnate, reports in his Eurosceptic press that a pan-European war is imminent but his warnings go unheeded. When certain animals escape and attack members of the public, a new director, Sir Robert Falcon, takes over control and aims to restore the zoo to its imperial days of grandeur. For Falcon, the zoo is a vehicle to both celebrate Britain's proud imperial legacy and a means of promoting a renewed British identity attuned to the fractious post-war landscape. In his jingoistic speeches he decrees that 'strictly European animals or those creatures [. . .] whose species had never known the glories of British rule' should be cast out to the furthest sectors of the zoo, while those animals associated with Britain, either through domestication or their links to Empire, are awarded pride of place (1992: 254). In an attempt to drag the zoo back to its Victorian heyday, Falcon organizes a theatrical 'British Day' – an allusion to the colonial celebrations of British Empire Exhibitions and the Festival of Britain in 1951 – designed to create a sense of post-war reconstruction and recovery. Falcon's exhibition contains key set pieces: 'a British lion and an Indian elephant', 'tulips and wallflowers that spelt "God Save the Queen"', and 'birds from every corner of the earth that was now or ever had been British' (1992: 253; 254). The zoo becomes a constructed fantasy containing both a nostalgic vision of Britain's imperial prestige and the illusion of uninterrupted cultural dominance, offering a safe space of 'deep nostalgia' in which disillusioned post-war citizens can 'surrender [themselves] to the prettiness and die' (1992: 267). The opening of the patriotic event, however, is marred by the unexpected invasion of Federated European Forces, who bomb the zoo and enforce a naval blockade from Glasgow to Southampton. Falcon is blown unceremoniously – in an appropriate piece of comic symbolism – onto the bronze lion statue during the bombing campaign.

While the zoo has been deludedly tending to insular affairs and reliving past glories, the European Alliance, consisting of Germany, France and Italy, has systematically invaded Britain's ally Portugal, then the British sovereign territory of Gibraltar, before coercing Britain to submit its industries to European control.[3] In retaliation, the British government release the Melbourne Declaration, citing the nation's continuing ties with their Commonwealth allies Australia and New Zealand and alluding to the natural Anglosphere relationship that exists outside of European *belonging*. The declaration beseeches Britain's allies to break the naval blockade and halt the deepening food crisis, but no nation dares to risk the wrath of the Uni-Europeans and a new pro-European government is inaugurated. Despite the obvious allusions to ongoing developments in the EEC, the origins of the pan-European war are not made explicit. It is suggested that the preference for the British to trade with rebellious countries during the early stages of the novel leads to a Continental embargo on British goods, indicative of the nation's post-war trade agreements and delayed reappraisal of the ECSC as an economic alternative for Britain's faltering economy.

Following the successful invasion, a third director, Dr Englander, is installed. Englander's designs exemplify the previous director Falcon's accusation that the 'English government lets everything go in order to kowtow to the commercialism of France and Germany' under the banner of 'Modern Europeanism' (1992: 31). His support of the Uni-Europeans seems to stem from commercial interests rather than a profound belief in political union. This desire to 'substitute prosperity for patriotism' alludes to Britain's delayed accession into the EEC, perceiving the organization to simply be a capitalist venture hidden behind the seemingly benevolent guise of European cooperation: 'if this country had come to its senses sooner [. . .] events would never have brought such men to the fore' (1992: 305–6). While the invading Federated European Forces eradicate those animals associated with British rule, Englander's reptiles – with all the explicit connotations of treachery and betrayal anthropomorphically attached to the Uni-Europeans – are evacuated to the Hebrides. Englander himself is influenced by an incipient Uni-European movement, led by Hilary Blanchard-White, who wishes for the zoo to be reopened under a 'continental' design, implementing a series of violent public spectacles pitting animals against political prisoners. This so-called European Day – a forceful repudiation of Falcon's British Day – involves a 'Russian Bear' torn down by dogs and an 'American Eagle taught a lesson' to accentuate the ascendancy of the multinational bloc (1992: 325). Blanchard-White explains such spectacles are orchestrated to demonstrate the supremacy of the Uni-Europeans and move 'closer to the rich vein of Mediterranean brutality on which our European legacy so much depends' (1992: 310). The denouement's development of a national resistance movement of patriotic Britons, holding placards calling for 'a London Zoo and a free England', strengthens this direct parallel between the microcosmic power struggles of the zoo and the wider analogy of declining post-war British sovereignty (1992: 322).

Carter switches allegiance from one director to the next throughout the novel, reflective of the changing public mood towards the European question across the

---

[3] Kingsley Amis described these three countries, the major players of the EEC in the 1960s, as 'potentially very wicked' (Encounter 1962: 56).

decade, deluding himself into believing Englander is merely 'putting sense before self-indulgent sentiment' and reasoning that 'the British people [. . .] never objected to Federation with Europe' (1992: 312). The denouement of the novel sees Carter finally recognize the need to engage more deeply in European affairs and rely on informed personal conviction in place of his prior detachment, conformism and subservient collaboration, rebelling against Blanchard-White and subsequently being detained in a concentration camp. Yet Wilson does not celebrate the strength or determination of British post-war spirit. Even Liberation Day, the overthrowing of the Uni-European movement, is sanctioned by the French and German governments rather than a patriotic British insurgency, in recognition that European integration has mutated from its original idealistic aspirations. Wilson's novel concludes before a new director can be installed, leaving the fate of the zoo (and Britain more generally) unresolved, but a suggestion remains that Carter's plans for a British Reserve will be restored and an insular organizational framework enforced once more. As Peter Faulkner notes, the uncertain denouement could signal 'a newer, more realistic attitude', with the modest plans for the zoo indicating 'a warning to the English reader to accept a realistic view of his country and its place in the modern world' (1980: 125). The novel ends, then, by endorsing a diminished future for England sensitive to the shifting power dynamics at play in post-war Europe.

In Wilson's essay 'Evil in the English Novel', an evaluation of the post-war literary scene, he declares himself concerned that the English novel is 'becoming provincial' and identifies 'once more an attempt to build up a citadel that will protect us from a changing world' (1967: 167; 190). And yet, Wilson's claim that this symbolic defensive 'citadel' is once again a key characteristic of the post-war English novel can arguably be attributed to *The Old Men at the Zoo* with its outdated stereotypes which conflate misconceptions of Continental culture with the European question. Spiering perceives in the novel a strong tendency to 'link the negative with the foreigner' (specifically the figure of the European) and considers the depictions of pro-Europeans to be brutal and hostile caricatures, concluding that the novel ultimately sides with a 'Little England' mentality (1988: 50). James Gindin concurs, noting how in Wilson's body of work more generally the 'principal villains [. . .] have usually immigrated from foreign countries' and import their contagious degeneracy into hallowed British space (1962: 163). While Wilson is certainly no isolationist (being a vocal supporter of the EEC) neither is he an unwavering disciple for European integration. In an interview from 1963, Wilson accentuates how he views 'England's increasing insularity with alarm', but also warns that 'there is a little-Europeanism as narrow and pretentious as little Englandism. If entry to the Common Market frees us from false provincialism, well and good. If it reinforces an arrogant European contempt for American or other non-European cultures, so much the worse' (Encounter 1963). Wilson's words betray Britain's veneration of its ties with the Empire and Commonwealth and its special relationship with the United States. The humiliation of the American eagle by the Uni-Europeans captures his distaste for 'little-Europeanism' and rejects the implication that European integration should necessitate an abrogation of wider global trading ties.

Ironically, the Uni-Europeans (with their pan-continental alliance) assume an oppressive stance, while the nationalistic British characters are portrayed as the victims of this drive for European dominance. There are subtle fascist undertones in the depiction of the Uni-Europeans, 'march[ing] in groups' and holding flags of their various European districts (1992: 321). As Hammond recognizes, Wilson's novel avoids the speculative dystopian trend in Eurosceptic British fiction, evident in the later fiction of Andrew Roberts, Brian Aldiss and Rob Grant, which challenges 'Europeanist fervour with right-wing calls for a return to isolationism', and instead adopts a left-wing stance, calling for 'a socialist basis for continental unity' (2016: 205). Wilson's authorial critique of Englander, with technocratic and commercial interests motivating his desire for a united Europe, attests to the fact that forceful opposition to the European question also came from the left. Political figures such as Tony Benn and Michael Foot held strong reservations against the neoliberal capitalist designs of the EEC which operated in contrast to the support for socialism and industrial democracy espoused by the Labour Party in the 1970s and 1980s.[4] Although the novel was poorly received, *The Old Men at the Zoo* diagnoses the various cultural and economic factors which would influence British antipathy towards Europe for decades to come. In her biography of Wilson, Drabble reasons that the tepid response to the novel could stem from the British not wanting to see 'the besetting sins of themselves and their old men' exposed – citing this 'obstinacy, vacillation, wishful thinking or even plain blindness to change' – particularly 'when they were still congratulating themselves on having won the last war' and could not face Britain's diminished role in Europe (1995: 280). Indeed, as Drabble drily notes, many critics found Wilson's prophetic vision of 'a Europe torn apart by local nationalist violence and simultaneously occupied [. . .] by nostalgic theme parks' implausible: 'Such things had not yet come to pass' (1995: 281).

Countless post-war British novels have plunged into the memory of the Second World War and the grand rhetoric of wartime resistance as a sublimated response to European developments. From a post-Brexit perspective, the 're-engineering of the Second World War as the defining national event marks out the nation's moral telos in a particularly tidy but thickly textured manner, a story of progress that culminates in an isolated Britain spearheading the fight for good against a historically transcendent evil' (Valluvan 2019: 115). Eaglestone builds on Lauren Berlant's (2011) notion of 'cruel optimism' – when the object you desire is actually harmful to your advancement or well-being – to position Brexit as a form of 'cruel nostalgia' (2018: 92). Whereas Berlant's affect theory focuses on the future (and is tied to the forward-looking impulse of the American Dream), cruel nostalgia is a form of 'deeply felt affect-memory'; for the British this is wrapped up in memories of the Empire or the Second World War and the desire for shared national narratives which overcome the inferiority of the present (2018: 97). These heroic reminders of national pride provide a comforting resource from which the populace can draw when faced with economic or cultural uncertainty; however, they are also 'a set of easily accessible affective cues which politicians and others can manipulate' in times of national crisis (2018: 103). This particular strain of nostalgic wartime resistance combined with anti-European anxiety, glaringly evident

---

[4] The 'Lexit' stance of socialist figures during the 2016 EU referendum campaign has its roots in this left-wing resistance to the EEC before Labour adopted a more sympathetic approach to the vision of a 'Social Europe' under Blair in the 1990s.

in Wilson's novel, seeps into a number of later post-war British fictions. David Lodge's semi-autobiographical *Out of the Shelter* (1970) depicts a child fantasizing over the protection of Britain from external Continental influence, 'His back was to England, and his face, set in an expression of watchful defiance, was turned towards Europe' (1985: 32). The scene not only hints at the ways by which such wartime rhetoric was almost pedagogically ingrained in the next generation, but conflates the Nazi threat with a more general Europhobia. Len Deighton's *SS-GB* (1978) presents a counter-factual history of the Second World War in which Germany has overcome its enemies and demands the unconditional surrender of Britain in 1941. Published after Britain's first entry into the EEC, the novel responds to initial fears surrounding European federalism, uniting wartime resistance and Euroscepticism under the same defiant banner. Plans for a European trading bloc in the novel mask Germany's true intentions; namely, the furthering of Nazi ideology by neoliberal means: 'at the European Parliament [. . .] flags of the twelve member nations were lit by spots. The swastika which flew above them was twice the size of the other standards' (2016: 163). The anti-Europe movements of the early 1970s were also heavily reliant on wartime rhetoric and imagery. The Common Market was styled a 'new Munich' by Christopher Frere Smith, founder of the Get Britain Out campaign, while Europhobic Conservative politician Nicholas Ridley claimed the European Monetary System was 'a German racket designed to take over the whole of Europe' (Ridley 1990). This perception that relenting to the pressures of the EEC was somehow betraying the memory of those who had given their lives in the Second World War would re-emerge in the 2016 EU referendum.

Robert Harris' *Fatherland* (1992) posits a similar counter-factual past and furthers this fear of Germanic domination. Harris' novel alludes to the new threat posed by Germany's central economic role in the European Union, corralling other Western European nations into a trading bloc under their control (Harris wrote the novel immediately after the reunification of Germany following the fall of the Berlin Wall). The EU thus becomes a more subtle means for the Germans to further their cultural and territorial ambitions, until swastikas, 'twice the size of the other [flags]', are flying outside the European Parliament (1992: 163). Owen Sheers' *Resistance* (2007) paints an even bleaker picture of British wartime defeat in which the inward-looking conservatism of Britain is exposed by ruthless German efficiency leading to the formation of an SS Albion division devoted to furthering Hitler's territorial designs. While these novels often rely on lurid perceptions of supranational relations, their anticipatory energy was vindicated in comments made by Boris Johnson just a month before the referendum campaign: 'Napoleon, Hitler, various people tried [unifying Europe], and it ends tragically. The EU is an attempt to do this by different methods' (Johnson 2016). Farage reinforced these views, commenting, 'It is an irony, is it not, that a project that was designed to contain German power has now given us a totally German-dominated Europe' (European Parliament 2015). Ironically, the xenophobic pronouncements of Brexiteers came perilously close to echoing the tenets of National Socialism in the drive for a racially pure *Volkskorper* to protect the English body politic.

More nuanced comments concerning the Europeanization of English culture are evident in the fiction of Anthony Burgess. For Burgess, an avowed Europhile who relocated to Europe in the late 1960s (living in several countries including France, Italy and Switzerland), the 'great dream of a united Europe with England as part of it has been fulfilled by the Common Market' (Ingersoll and Ingersoll 2008: 76). While Burgess considered European integration to be an admirable ideal, he voiced doubts over the viability of a truly Europeanized monoculture, citing the parochial tendencies of the (specifically English) national mindset:

> The history of England, from the time of the Roman occupation until twenty years ago, has been about the insistence of a very insular people on cutting itself off from that huge and dangerous continent that lies to its east and is separated by a mere twenty miles of sea. (qtd in Crumbie 2018)

His 1985 article, 'England in Europe', revealed misgivings about the bureaucratic federalism at the heart of the European project, claiming Europe should instead strive for greater linguistic communication strategies. Early signs of such views were evident in 'Here Parla Man Marcommunish' (1966), Burgess' tongue-in-cheek commentary on Britain's unsuccessful attempts to join the Common Market, in which he imagines Harold Wilson delivering a speech to his new political partners in a modish lingua franca, which kickstarts 'a new wave of Europeanising English':

> He can tell the europeans that the britannic nation has emerged from a *mauvaise époque* in which the *Lumpenproletariat*, rendered torpid by *la noia* of the *ancien régime*, with its *Unrealpolitik* of *il faut cultiver notre jardin*, possessed of no viable *Weltanschauung* [is] becoming *au fait* with the *nouvelle vague* politique. (1966: 674–5)

The intensification of the multinational bloc in the 1980s saw Burgess communicate further fears over the exact form European supranationalism may take. His Orwellian novel *1985* (1978) details how the 'decimilizing of the 1960s' was intended 'to force Britain into line with rest of the European Community' and resulted in 'one hundred new pence (called with proper contempt *p*)', while his 1986 article 'Chunnel Vision' casts doubts on the merits of the proposed railway tunnel between England and France (2013: 132). And yet, beneath his reservations Burgess retains an underlying enthusiasm for the process of Europeanization, acknowledging that any integrationist project represents a movement away from the horrors of nationalism and provides an alternative political future for a monolingual and inward-looking post-war Britain. In this regard, at least, he shares Jean Monnet's belief in the potential for European cohesion to overcome nationalist ideologies.

Ever closer union

We shall perish as we tear each other's guts out and shout 'unity' in a dozen different languages.

(Pickles qtd. in Dewey 2009: 112)

The Single European Act of 1987 envisioned 'an area with frontiers' in which 'national and regional cultural traditions flourish, whilst reinforcing the sense that despite their differences European citizens share a common cultural heritage and common values' (European Commission 1997: 1). In response to this attempt to install a pan-European outlook, Britain continued to augment its national characteristics and emphasize its separation and distinctiveness from the continent. The ascendancy of Margaret Thatcher marked a new phase of British exceptionalism in the 1980s. In her Bruges speech, Thatcher staunchly defended Britain from perceived threats to its cultural and political position: 'We have not successfully rolled back the frontiers of the state in Britain only to see them reimposed at a European level, with a European superstate exercising a new dominance from Brussels' (1993: 744–5). While national identity can be strengthened through the allusion of a common past, a Europeanized identity was less tangible, leading Britons to question whether they shared cultural memories with their continental neighbours. Malcolm Bradbury's *Rates of Exchange* (1983) playfully deconstructs these proposed mutual bonds by exposing the legacy of political turmoil at the heart of the European project, documenting the efforts of a fictional eastern European state, Slaka, to secure EEC member status in the foreseeable future despite their fundamentally unstable economy.[5]

Rates of Exchange shares a similar geopolitical focus with Julian Barnes' *The Porcupine* (1992), set in a nameless eastern European country in a post-communist period, and Bradbury's later novel *Dr Criminale* (1992), at a time when Western Europe was re-evaluating the geographical parameters of its union and considering expansion. As Bradbury asserts, 'Europe was a continent that lacked any fixed or comprehensible borders or limits, a firm eastern perimeter. It had no acknowledged common existence [. . .] Hence Europe was an idea less of peoples than of elites' (1995: 7). He consequently envisions a fictional nation which has 'seen its borders expand, contract and on occasion disappear from sight' (1983: 2), compounding his fears that 'Europe could soon be a very large entity indeed, and some of it not in Europe' (1991b). Bradbury describes how he conceptualized and concocted Slaka 'like a cocktail: a mixture of [. . .] Bulgaria, Romania, Yugoslavia, and Hungary' (CEE countries which eventually became new member states of the EU following the 2004 and 2007 Eastern enlargements despite their penurious economic records) (1994: 21). The novel thus anticipates the fragile economic interdependence and disarray of encroaching monetary union in the 1990s and 2000s, alongside the breakdown of the Exchange Rate Mechanism, and Britain's own vociferous opposition to greater economic and monetary integration with new member states. In so doing, Bradbury acknowledges the 'totally transformed political climate and organisation of the postwar world' while displaying how Europe remains 'a place of extreme historical anxiety' for British citizens (1983: 38; 39).

Bradbury sets his narrative in 1981, against a backdrop of British deindustrialization, rising unemployment, falling sterling and labour unrest, as

---

[5] Bradbury's novel *Why Come to Slaka?* (1986) marks a return to his satirical swipe at the EEC and serves as a pastiche guidebook to the eastern European state.

Britain comes to terms with its declining cultural currency on the world stage and the Thatcherite government faces widespread public dissatisfaction with European budgetary obligations. The novel's protagonist Angus Petworth, a mild-mannered British linguistics professor, travels to Slaka for a lecture tour on behalf of the British Council. A comic caricature who manifests Britain's insular mentality, he clings to his 'Helpful Hints for British Businessmen' to navigate the foreign environment where transactional systems and cultural values are alien: he is 'a man in a chair in the air over Brussels, perhaps, or Paris, trying to understand what the difference is' (1983: 17; 28). Slaka's own perpetual economic upheaval ensures he never ascertains the 'rate of exchange' required to understand his foreign environment, monetarily, linguistically or culturally; in the neutral space of the airport announcements appear as 'a confusion of languages', an 'endless web of multilingua', with 'signs turning toward redundancy' (1983: 302). Anglo-Slakan relations thus parody Britain's reductive cognizance of EEC affairs. Petworth, like Amis' Bowen, resists the embrace of European culture during his sojourn, resenting the need to confront a homogenous 'state of foreignness, which is a universal country' and opting to remain in his hotel room to prepare for his lectures rather than partake in the disorienting itineraries prepared for him by 'Cosmoplot', the eurosceptically inflected state tourist board (1983: 37). *Rates of Exchange* mimics the narrative structure of *I Like It Here*, charting the protagonist's journey to the Continent before his decidedly provincial retreat to home soil and domesticity, his European sojourn failing to disturb a decidedly nostalgic nationalism.

As Robert A. Morace notes, the rate of exchange metaphor not only alludes to the 'literal exchange of currencies' as Europe inches towards monetary union, but 'the figurative exchanges of various kinds – economic, cultural, diplomatic, linguistic', that govern and obstruct harmonious European relations (1989: 88). At a dinner party hosted in his honour, Petworth toasts the power of language to draw European peoples together; the irony of his speech compounds both the failure in communication that has characterized his stay in Slaka, and the naïve assessment that linguistic comprehension can overcome the cultural and economic concerns governing cynical perceptions of the Eastern bloc. His most famous piece of academic criticism titled 'The English Language as a Medium of International Communication' conceals how his linguistic competence concerns only dead languages, being of no pragmatic use and relegating Petworth to 'that conventional, minimal polyglotism that has, for centuries, taken the English, stammering and nodding [. . .] into every corner of the world' (Bradbury 1983: 42; 33). His European counterparts and interlocutors share a similar quandary, their slapstick mispronunciations of his surname implying his purported cultural superiority is a farcical notion, leaving him a signifier without a signified. Petworth's repeated insistence that he works for the British Council is itself redundant, as the British Council does not operate in Slaka, and thus becomes a 'sterile sign, a meaningless meaning' indicative of Britain's insularity (1983: 54). Despite his linguistic prowess, by the end of his visit he remains unable to establish a system of signification to understand his European environment. Rather than the English language bridging divides between European member states, compounding the cultural levelling and horizontality of EEC bodies, Bradbury's sardonic linguistic deconstruction of keywords ensures both parties are left in a constant state of misunderstanding and mistrust.[6]

Following the release of *Rates of Exchange*, Bradbury remarked that in the future he hoped for 'imagination instead of politics' to influence future international relations denouncing the 'Sadomonetarism' at work in both Western and Eastern Europe (qtd. in Haffenden 1985: 27). As Bradbury outlines in *The Gravy Train Goes East*, a politician 'is someone who invents a fiction and tries to tell the world it is a reality', whereas a writer 'is someone who invents a reality and tries to tell the world it is a fiction' (Bradbury 1991c). The Slakan novelist Katya Princip, who rejects the isolationist 'fictions' of her post-Communist state and determines to liberate the country through her imaginative postmodern works, thus gives voice to Bradbury's liberal humanism, indicating literature's capacity to overcome national insularities: 'reality is what happens if you listen to other people's stories and not to your own. The stories become a country, the country becomes a prison, and the prison comes in your mind [. . .] Soon it is the only story, and that is how comes reality' (1983: 204). Bradbury's extensive commentary on Europe throughout his career, however, betrays his personal aversion to greater integration. In his article 'All Aboard for the New Europe', he reiterates fears concerning an EEC which 'is beginning to feel like an international federation, with a political vision', detailing how the question of Europe has not simply contributed to Thatcher's political demise – whose anti-European stance he (in part) seems to share – but will prevent John Major playing 'his proper part in Europe' as 'no one in Britain is sure what it is' (Bradbury 1991b). Nonetheless, Nicoletta Pireddu argues *Rates of Exchange* operates a dual critique, ensuring Bradbury's savage opprobrium on the 'impersonal, hierarchical and undemocratic' bureaucracy of the EEC is counterbalanced by 'the Euroscepticism of a self-absorbed, haughty Britain' (2017: 629). Princip's recurrent condemnation of Petworth, claiming he is 'not a character in the world historical sense', could equally serve as a rebuke of Britain's cynical retreat from post-war European collective policies: 'You come from a little island with water all round' (1983: 139). Following Thatcher's resignation in 1991, as the EEC reached the final stages of negotiation for EMU – an intensification in the coordination of European fiscal policies – Bradbury reluctantly concludes: 'like it or not, Europe is in motion' and Britain must decide 'whether it wished to be in the driver's cab or the rear compartment' (Bradbury 1991b).[7] In his 1990 article 'Frontiers of Imagination', Bradbury articulated specific concerns about the pace of European integration and the shift towards a predominantly political rather than economic union, predicting that novelists would begin to respond to such fears as Britain entered uncharted waters. Elizabeth Wilson's dystopic novel *The Lost Time Café* (1993) and Tim Parks' 1997 Booker-shortlisted novel *Europa* provide clear examples

---

[6] Bradbury dispenses a more direct commentary on the EEC in his 'television novels' for Channel 4, *The Gravy Train* (1990) and *The Gravy Train Goes East* (1991), which confront ongoing calls for greater integration and continue Slaka's attempt to join the EEC in spite of their economic instability and questionable governance. As Sheridan Morley comments, *The Gravy Train* 'manages to make of the Common Market an even greater satire than has already been achieved by its own functionaries' (1990: 18).

[7] Bradbury showers derision on the numerous political bodies and councils formulated by the EEC, claiming 'the New Europe has brought acronymery to a fine art' (1991b).

of literature's immediate response, revealing internal fears and commenting on the political stance Britain subsequently adopted as the European project gathered speed.

The Lost Time Café (1993), set at the turn of the millennium, documents how British resistance to deepening integration also came from those on the left of the political spectrum (as discussed in the introduction's evaluation of Labour's contradictory policies towards Europe during the post-war period). Published in 1993, the release of the novel coincided with the Treaty of Maastricht, the ratification of which was to fundamentally impact Britain's future involvement in the European project. As Hammond notes, Wilson captures a '[l]eft wing melancholy' towards the integrationist project; the decline of Britain's welfare state in the novel delivering a staunch critique on both Thatcherite social policy and a 'post-welfarist European Union, with its commitment to marketisation and security [. . .] and its culturalist plans for ensuring mass loyalty' above the level of national community (2016: 198; 199). The novel's narrator, Justine Unwin, returns from California to discover a Britain suffering under a pro-European right-wing government which is only too willing to forfeit British sovereignty in the pursuit of economic gain. The erosion of political autonomy is reinforced by a decline in cultural heritage: the European institute has become the main entertainment complex, the pound has been replaced by the ecu (the European Currency Unit, a forerunner of the euro), and British culinary presence on restaurant menus is reduced to 'roast beef and all the trimmings (a dish no one ate anymore)' (1993: 165). The titular café itself, staffed by poor migrant workers and designed as a refuge to escape the current dystopic state of the nation, is no monument to a forgotten British period, but rather exposes the extent to which processes of Europeanization have transformed post-war British society.

As the implications of the pro-Europeans become clear, the anti-federalist Patriotic Party emerges in response, convinced that the integrationist project is destroying democratic governance. The party soon spawns a militant wing, 'Albion', whose nationalist agenda and push for home rule results in a series of terrorist attacks on London. The opportunity for Britain to reclaim its political sovereignty, however, seems to be lost as the politician tipped for future leadership, the Brussels-centric Roland Rodgers, curtails the aspirations of the appropriately titled Alex Kingdom, Minister of the Interior (responsible for funding Albion's terrorist activities in order to fuel public unrest). The denouement details Rodgers elevation to prime minster as the elusive 'search for a more socialist basis for European integration [. . .] in the face of the EU's intensifying neoliberalism' continues unabated, signalling increasing fears of the impending implications of the Maastricht Treaty on Britain's economic and political future (Hammond 2016: 31).

On 10 October 1997 in Strasbourg, the Second Council of Europe Summit launched a year-long campaign to raise awareness of a shared European cultural heritage between member states, 'promoting the fundamental values of our common culture' and 'preventing an ill-conceived reference to cultural heritage from giving rise to xenophobic and ultra-nationalist behaviour' (Kruger 1998). This ongoing attempt to construct a pan-European identity is central to Tim Parks' *Europa*. Set over forty-eight hours, the narrative follows a delegation of lectors and students from the University of Milan as they travel by coach to the European Parliament in Strasbourg

– the supposed centre of European cultural heritage – to protest against the treatment of foreign lectors by the Italian government, following a reduction in their salaries and amendments to teaching contracts (a violation of a key clause in the Treaty of Rome). Parks, a British novelist and former English language lecturer who relocated to northern Italy in 1980, offers an oblique and sardonic commentary on the enlargement of the EU post-Maastricht and its intrusive symbolic impact on British national sovereignty. *Europa* is inspired by real events, when Parks and his fellow lectors at the University of Verona travelled to the European Parliament in February 1993 to petition for a change in employment legislation. Curiously, as in Amis' *I Like It Here* and Bradbury's *Rates of Exchange*, a university academic serves as the focal point in the discussion of British engagement with the European project. The shared occupation of these various insular protagonists, seemingly isolated and protected within their aloof academic spheres, complements their nation's attempt to avoid the complex realities of post-war European interdependence. *Europa*'s protagonist, Jerry Marlow, functions as an authorial mouthpiece for Parks' own reservations regarding the nebulous qualities of a European identity, his interior monologue providing a sustained critique of the EU's seemingly naïve attempt to forge an abstract European identity in the face of rising support for populist and nationalist forces. The novel's title is more than simply an allusion to the abducted Phoenician of Greek mythology (after whom the continent of Europe is named), but also a forthright rejection of what Marlow considers the myth of Europe: a wider cultural community to which he feels no allegiance.[8] His sentiments resonant with many voters in 2016, where citizens with a stronger attachment to a proposed European identity were far less likely to support for Brexit than those who possessed a strong British (or specifically English) identity (Goodwin and Milazzo 2017: 458).

While *Rates of Exchange* offered a satirical and critically detached perspective on British insularity, Parks' own personal reluctance to endorse the neoliberal socioeconomic vision of a post-Maastricht EU is more transparent. Despite the author's defensive remark that he is 'not the typical English sceptic', he does admit to being 'suspicious of the process' of EU expansion in the 1980s and 1990s (Parks 2010). In *Adultery and Other Diversions* (which documents the real events of the 'ridiculous excursion'), he reiterates: 'we desire to feel European and cannot. We cannot be enthusiastic' about integration and instead implies member states are influenced by 'a certain weary economic opportunism' which enables the EU to proceed 'sceptical and crabwise from one compromise to the next' (2011: 21; 55). Similarly, Parks notes how the spectre of the Second World War continues to motivate sovereign nations to surrender more of their independence: 'Scared of another war between ourselves, we had to tie ourselves together in a mesh of commercial rules and regulations governed by tier after tier of bureaucracy' (2010).[9] Appropriately, the narrative is punctuated by

---

[8] The continent of Europe itself is built on a myth; its name is taken from the story of Europa, abducted by Zeus and taken to Crete against her will. The very story of Europe, then, involves the violation of national sovereignty and the contravention of established borders.
[9] *The Capital* (2019) by Robert Menasse contains a similar critique of the workings and machinations of the European Commission: 'Brussels, a hive of tragic heroes, manipulative losers, involuntary accomplices. No wonder the European Commission is keen to improve its image' (Menasse 2019).

the sporadic, haunting reappearance of the number 45 gesturing to the horrors of that fateful history that necessitated such cultural entanglement and subsequently impelled the initial formation of the EU.

Marlow's seating location for his journey to Strasbourg, on the back seat of the coach – 'the only place left unoccupied on my late (stupidly late) arrival' – communicates both Britain's own ideological position on the European political spectrum and the nation's belated, antipathetic involvement in post-war European integration (1997: 14). His sense of entrapment and estrangement in the delegation embodies the spirit of Europe, a forced participation in a group where 'the supposed desires of the majority are now foisted upon everybody' and infringe upon 'splendid isolation' (1997: 3; 53). Over the course of the journey, Marlow himself begins to acknowledge and formulate parallels between the lectors' crisis, the sordid antics of the Euro-trip and the process of European integration more generally, even referring to his fellow passengers as 'key members of our union' (1997: 239). Joining the coach party against his better instincts, he quickly realizes 'the moment you commit yourself to some joint project, some communal enterprise, circumstances are always well and truly beyond your control', as some members will follow their 'sovereign urges and desires' to 'grab more power and responsibility in our little group' and will ultimately 'mythologize' the journey to claim 'now we are safer' (1997: 19; 20; 21).

The interior monologue gives voice to Britain's reluctant membership in the period (echoing the bitter tensions within the Conservative Party in the 1990s), coerced into appealing to an institution many citizens do 'not support, nor subscribe to in any way' and believe 'perhaps should not exist at all' (1997: 4). Indeed, Marlow possesses an ulterior motive for joining the delegation, hoping to covertly shadow his French ex-mistress who has penned an essay on the theoretical construction of European identities and the formation of a united Europe in the hope of securing a scholarship in Brussels. Marlow shares the assumed cultural superiority of Amis' Bowen, merely desiring a superficial aesthetic experience of 'authentic' European life, practising cultural consumption and engaging in social interactions without strengthening his connections or personal attachment to European culture in the process. In fact, Article 128 (later Article 151 after the Amsterdam Treaty) became the first piece of EU policy to suggest that culture has an integral role to play in the integration process: 'The Community shall contribute to the flowering of the cultures of the Member States, while respecting their national and regional diversity and at the same time bringing the common cultural heritage to the fore' (qtd. in Foster 2002: 45). Whereas his fellow lectors harbour an entrenched Europhilic optimism, Marlow remains thoroughly unconvinced by the notion of pooled sovereignty, which he considers a paradoxical expression and reminds him of his ex-mistress's accusation that British Euroscepticism derives from a lack of cultural flexibility required to forge more negotiable forms of national identity (an accusation that can equally serve as a condemnation of post-war British policy towards Europe more generally).

On reaching Strasbourg, Marlow (sharing a surname with Conrad's infamous narrator) finds a darkness at the heart of the European experience and questions the shared values that supposedly tie member states together. Parks also directs his ire towards the decision-making centres of the EU, such as the European Commission and European Monetary Institute, which are shielded from scrutiny and enjoy little democratic accountability to the British public, evident in Marlow's aversion to a multinational bloc seemingly run by the German Bundesbank and centred around their own financial interests. During the coach journey from Milan to Strasbourg the Italian Lira plummets in value against the French franc and German Deutschmark, critiquing the unstable and tumultuous nature of currency markets just a few brief years before European monetary unification. The cultural devaluation of the EU is reinforced by his comparison of the Parliament building to a 'Euro-architecture' of a Swiss service station, with its flagpoles promoting some neutral form of 'fraternity among nations' to hide its true purpose: 'exacting the maximum price (in whatever currency)' from its patrons (1997: 5; 72).[10] The building, 'isolated' and 'set apart [...]' in its own abstract space', suggests the artificial construction of the supranational arrangement, designed to countermand the nationalist claims to territory that necessitated its inception; its circular design, ensuring 'no nation should feel they have been pushed into a corner', suggests the faux-cosmopolitan and inaccurate notion that all member states are equal components in the running of the institution (1997: 190). Rather than interpreting the architectural design of the building as evidence of a functioning cosmopolitical democracy, Marlow determines: 'any meaning here expressed must lie in the absence of meaning, in the absence of any hierarchy' between nation states, espousing the 'perfect indistinction and equality which can only come, perhaps, in the absence of any real relationship, only exist for people, countries, thousands of miles apart' (1997: 191).

Parks shares Bradbury's judgement that the multinational bloc, 'whose exact functions and powers [...] none of us understands', suffers from problems of legitimacy and its economic, administrative and cultural policies are often perceived as counterproductive by the British populace (1997: 21). The controlled, homogenized and neutral EU architectural space may override national forms of identification but fails to offer any cultural meaning in exchange and simply serves as a centre for opaque bureaucratic control and arbitrary decision-making processes which attempt to render every issue 'soluble, from cross-border immigration to the size of a condom and the quality of a mushroom and the strength of a perfume' (1997: 197).[11] Parks implies that such an egalitarian arrangement conceals the financial dynamics that govern EU operations in a post-Maastricht environment, granting stronger voices to those member states with a more secure economic footing, enforcing austere fiscal policies on weaker members of the union, and thus installing a hierarchy within what ostensibly should be a multilateral democratic union. Dismissing his students' naïve and idealistic desire to experience life at 'the heart of Europe [...] to see that Europe wasn't just an idea but a concrete entity', his narrator refuses to perceive the European flag as an emblem of unity, solidarity and harmony, but rather 'twelve identical yellow nebulae encircling a

---

[10] The constant repetition of Euro-neologisms in the narrative conveys how the inchoate concept of Europe has been diluted and stripped of meaning.

[11] Parks' caustic critique echoes W. G. Sebald's *Austerlitz* (2001) in suggesting that the architectural design of EU buildings betray the international organisation's cultural vacuity. Sebald's protagonist, Jacques, deems the EU Palace of Justice a 'singular architectural monstrosity' with 'corridors and stairways leading nowhere, and doorless rooms and halls where no one would ever set foot, empty spaces surrounded by walls' (2001: 39).

void' (1997: 134). In satirically deconstructing the symbolic emptiness at the heart of the EU project, Parks' novel also exposes the shortcomings of postnational projections which fail to acknowledge the continuing relevance of the nation state paradigm to globalized life.

While not sharing Garnet Bowen's insular stance and assumed cultural superiority towards European culture, Marlow nevertheless betrays a 'typically Anglo-Saxon, and above all *un-European*' perspective on federalist designs, seeing no reason to surrender their national allegiance in favour of a tenuous symbolic identification with an indeterminate European community (Parks 1997: 72). His meditations on failed past relationships, with his French ex-mistress and Italian wife, symbolize both the deficiency of his own European relations and those of his diminished nation state. While conceding John Donne proposed a 'false dichotomy' by declaring 'every man is an island', he maintains the sovereign implications of this statement do not necessitate the dissolution of one's individual and national bearing: 'That is the paradox, I thought, that one is not entire unto oneself, and yet still not a piece of the continent, still not a part of the main' (1997: 246). As Sylvie Gambaudo affirms, 'the suggestion that identity can be undone at the national level and recreated or displaced onto a European level exposes identity as a construct' and an 'illusion masked by a tacit, collective agreement that identity is stable and inherent'; there remains 'a collective hesitation' to undo the national attachments which protect citizens from the instability of the globalized world (1999: 226).

Marlow's reluctant engagement is at odds with the hybridity of his colleague Vikram Griffiths, an 'Indian Welshman' and spokesman for the delegation on the basis of his fervent belief in the European cause, whom he dismisses as a 'feckless fragment of the British Empire' on account of his ethnicity, exposing the cultural alterities already transforming British society irrespective of EU influence (1997: 253). After unwittingly usurping Vikram's role as spokesman, Marlow finds himself before the EU Parliament Petitions Committee, forced to launch into an insincere defence of the supranational organization he so vehemently resists. Robbed of his leadership role, Vikram decides to hang himself in the European Parliament building; Pireddu argues, however, that 'not even this turning point in the novel establishes the affective and political sovereignty of Europeanness' (2017: 645). Marlow callously defines Vikram's suicide as mere theatrics which lack any real potency. Vikram's marginalization in the narrative (and the negligible power of a cohesive European identity) is reinforced by the absence of a Welsh flag at the Parliament building of the institution he so idolizes: 'he wasn't even properly represented, didn't even turn up, as the Scottish and Irish did, as decorative elements, trophies really, within the British flag, the Union Jack, which anyway Europeans notoriously refer to as English' (1997: 192).

Parks offers little discussion of the key issues affecting British membership at the turn of the millennium, only briefly alluding to fluctuating currency markets prior to the introduction of the Euro. Rather, he imparts one man's psychological perception of the Europeanization of national identity – views shared by the majority of the electorate and vast swathes of the political class. Marlow's patriotic tirade, insisting that a sovereign state should always exercise 'all the power it had at its disposal to get, so far as was possible, what it wanted, what it perceived, that is, was in its, and only its, best interests' succinctly encapsulates British Euroscepticism in this period, and brings into sharp focus the national mood that would shake the foundations of European unity twenty years later (1997: 71). Admittedly, Parks positions the EU as an ongoing political project, as opposed to an end-product, yet Marlow's decision not to return on the coach and instead work for the European Parliament cannot overturn the sense that the protagonist remains 'lost in this foreign country [. . .] this Europe that may or may not exist, and we wouldn't know what to do if we had to go home' (1997: 26).

A range of dystopic political thrillers emerged in the mid-1990s onwards which hammered home the message that the British electorate had effectively been manipulated into accepting EU membership at the behest of some pro-European quislings.[12] Examples of this trend include Andrew Roberts' *The Aachen Memorandum* (1995), Graham Ison's *Division* (1996) and Terry Palmer's *Euroslavia* (1997). A common element of Europhobic fiction during this period is the conflation of Englishness with Britishness, with the former coming to overwhelm any intra-UK cultural idiosyncrasies associated with the latter. For Lisa Bischoff, novels such as *The Aachen Memorandum* depict a 'dys-EUtopia', drawing on depictions of Orwellian state control, in which pro-European federalist will go to any lengths to secure the future of the integrationist project (2020: 181). Set in 2045, Britain is no longer a major player in the European arena but merely an insignificant outpost of a dominant Europe ruled not by Brussels but Berlin. Following an In/Out referendum, the result of which was manipulated by pro-European agents, the British public find themselves locked in a surveillance state where all historical markers of national identity, including historical figures, landmarks and events, are gradually eroded.[13] Trafalgar Square is renamed 'Delors Square' with Nelson's statue replaced by that of Robert Schuman, one of the key architects of the European Union, while Buckingham Palace is transformed into the 'European bank for Reconstruction and Development' (Roberts 1995: 25). This reinscription of the landscape is intended to suppress any nostalgia for the national past and instil a new euro-patriotism in a backward-looking populace. To further their aims, the EU regime encourages British citizens to abandon the English tongue for the language of their German oppressors as a harmonization strategy, positioning their integrationist project as a peaceful enterprise and thus succeeding by 'stealth in doing what we British twice stopped them doing by force last century' (1995: 143). As Wellings notes, 'linking peace and European integration is a key component of the EU's legitimacy and forms the bedrock of its foundational mythology' (2015: 44). For O'Toole, Brexiteers also perceived the 'new German invasion, cloaked in the guise of peaceful co-operation' to be 'more damnable' than the threat of the Third Reich, 'because it does not give the English Resistance a proper physical target' (2018a:

---

[12] These thrillers inherited autocratic and rapacious visions of German culture from post-war novels such as R. J. Minney's *Carve Her Name with Pride* (1958), Adam Hall's *The Quiller Memorandum* (1966), Daphne du Maurier's *Rule Britannia* (1972) and Michael Stewart and Peter Jay's *Apocalypse 2000* (1987). Du Maurier's prescient satire describes the economic difficulties faced by Britain after leaving the European Community and forming a new transatlantic alliance, USUK, in defiance of the emergent European order.

[13] Kingsley Amis' *The Alteration* (1976) serves as a precursor for this dystopic Eurosceptic vein, envisioning an alternate history in which the British Isles which has lost its independence and parliamentary sovereignty to a dominant European empire.

52). Roberts terms the new German-dominated European project a 'fourth Reich in disguise', anticipating Boris Johnson's same wording (1995: 12; Johnson 2016).

Seditious activities continue in *The Aachen Memorandum*, despite the regime's federalist propaganda and surveillance methods, as the British public prove unwilling to abandon the 'territorial, tribal symbol' of the Union Jack in favour of 'that golden halo of twelve stars', and reading 'subversive' national works of literature by Shakespeare, Dickens or Kingsley Amis (1995: 215). The novel's protagonist, Horatio Lesto, joins the English Resistance Movement (ERM) with a paramilitary wing dedicated to the restoration of Britain's parliamentary sovereignty, rejecting the Europeanization of their culture and the historical revisionism of the national mythology. The novel's denouement sees King William IV, now living in New Zealand following the dismantling of the Commonwealth, decrying the political tactics and Brussels directives by which the EU has managed to subjugate his people: 'this great country was tricked, conned, cheated into joining a Union which has been disastrous for her economy, her world standing, her true interests and her God-given independence' (1995: 269). The language of the novel anticipates the re-energized Eurosceptic discourse employed during the referendum campaign; as Bischoff details, David Cameron and Michael Gove, as well as hard-line Eurosceptics such as Bill Cash, were present at an event celebrating the publication of the novel on 5 October 1995 (2020: 196). By launching stunning attacks on EU integrationist policies, Roberts aims to hammer home the pluck and determination of the Churchillian 'bulldog breed', which must unite if it is to confront a newly reformed German Empire intent on masterminding the United States of Europe. Roberts' novel is, of course, frighteningly prescient, portending a referendum on Complete Union which passes by the familiar margin of 52 per cent to 48 per cent; however, his valorization of staunch Eurosceptics such as Iain Duncan-Smith, John Redwood and Michael Gove, fictionalized as the wise seers of a noble anti-federalism, betrays an authorial partisan bias towards the Europhobic elements gaining traction in British politics following Maastricht. Ison's novel *Division* reinforces this suggestion that the British public might rise up against their European oppressors and reclaim their once-proud national sovereignty; the British traitor of the novel is a Europhilic spy trained and educated in Germany. These Eurosceptic political thrillers reflect O'Toole's insightful analysis of the English cultural imaginary, which encapsulates a 'desire to have *actually been invaded* so that one could – gloriously – resist' (2018a: 44).

The Eurosceptic reticence of post-war British fiction did not simply fade following the political shift to Blair's pro-European New Labour government from 1997 onwards, evidenced by novels such as Brian Aldiss' *Super-State* (2002), Ken Jack's *United States of Europe* (2011) and Dave Hutchinson's *Europe in Autumn* (2014).[14] John King's *The Liberal Politics of Adolf Hitler* (2016), published just a month before the EU referendum, is the best example of how the dys-EUtopic tendencies of post-war British fiction continue into the twenty-first century. King's novel echoes *The Aaachen Memorandum* by projecting fears regarding the dilution of national sovereignty and the bureaucratic overreach of 'Eurofascist poodles' within a post-Maastricht EU (2016a:

---

[14] Jack's novel echoes Wilson's *The Old Men at the Zoo* in projecting fears of a future attack by a Euro-army intent on punishing Britain for its desire to withdraw from the integrationist project.

226). In 'The Left Wing Case for Leaving the EU', published by New Statesman in 2015, King draws attention to the words of former European Commission president José Manuel Barroso, who conceded the EU possessed 'the dimension of empire', positioning the formation of the current EU to be 'a very corporate coup' orchestrated by big business (King 2015). For King, a fervent Leave supporter whose earlier works shall be discussed in greater detail in the next chapter, EU membership was the most significant issue affecting the 2015 UK general election and the Conservative majority reinforced the overwhelming public support for the subsequent referendum. Set in a near-future where the nations of Europe have been abolished and the UK dissolved in favour of a United States of Europe (USE) run from Brussels and Berlin, *The Liberal Politics of Adolf Hitler* voices King's own concerns with the extent to which political power is now centralized under EU councils with European harmonization merely a cover for a neoliberal dictatorship hiding behind liberal rhetoric. A divided kingdom emerges in which the Free English towns outside London retain the hard pound while cosmopolitan USE cities adopt soft euros. King's distaste for the process of cultural Europeanization – 'which was so often married to a disgust for all things British' – is particularly evident in his concentration on the incorporation of the English Premier League into a European division, marking a return to the Anglocentric football-focused themes of his earlier novels such as *The Football Factory* and *England Away* (2016a: 10). In defiance of the rapid harmonization process, resistance groups such as GB45 emerge which honour the Britain's heritage and denounce the larceny of English symbols as markers of racist dissent (with related radical networks operating in Free Welsh, Scottish and Irish regions). In 'The People Versus the Elite', an article published to coincide with the release of the novel, King reveals how closely his personal animosity towards the EU aligns with the English resistance fighters of his novel: 'where is the EU leading? My belief is that it has the potential to become a new sort of dictatorship' suggesting the dystopian novels of Orwell, Huxley and Bradbury act 'as guides to its nature' (King 2016b).

Once installed as the dominant political structure, the corporate European superstate indoctrinates British citizens with their post-truth propaganda and historical revisionism, inculcating the falsehoods that British terrorists murdered European idealists in the First World War, Churchill instigated the Final Solution against German and French democracies, and the USE saved Britain from the 'cult of the Commonwealth' (2016a: 56). The Churchill war rooms themselves are only preserved 'as a testament to the perils of Englishness, the bigotry of a Britain that had for so long rejected integration' (2016a: 30). Good Europeans, wrapping themselves tight in the lies of the USE, strive to eradicate the remaining traces of Englishness to ensure the smooth homogenization of Europe's rough edges. By utilizing USE Controller Horace to quote directly from Jean Monnet's infamous declaration on the aims of European integration (also utilized as the novel's epigraph), King insinuates the end designs of the EU to be a deceitful manoeuvre akin to the Orwellian designs of his fictional USE: 'Europe's nations should be guided towards the superstate without their people understanding what is happening. This can be accomplished by successive steps, each disguised as having an economic purpose, but which will eventually and irreversibly lead to federation' (2016a: 162). King predicts a similar movement to *rejoin* the EU may emerge at some point in the future, validating the fears raised in his novel (Personal Correspondence 2020). Although the eventual assassination of Controller Horace by GB45 temporarily stalls plans to infiltrate and destabilize the remaining Free English areas in Wessex, the sense of powerlessness and impotent rage persist, and King's novel speaks as much to the present moment as it does to the entrenched Euroscepticism of the post-war decades, when Britain strived to resist the inevitable process of ever closer political union.

The post-war fictions examined in this chapter capture an image of Britain as the recalcitrant European, the belligerent neighbour, peering over the Channel with disdain at the Continent. Hammond correctly identifies that as British fiction moves into the 1990s, it begins to demonstrate a stronger inclination to engage with Project Europe yet remains 'unable to express either political support or political alternatives' to post-Maastricht expansion (2017: 22). The grand unifying idealisms of the integrationist project are increasingly regarded as a cause for concern, eating away at the national sovereignty and territorial integrity of a fragile and disunited kingdom. The EU gradually becomes the scapegoat towards which voters can channel their anger and resentment, encapsulating a more general disillusionment for the ways by which remote financial bodies and indifferent political elites promulgate unnecessary regulations, undercut workers and undermine traditionalist national identities and values. As the next chapter will demonstrate, English fiction in particular communicates a growing self-destructive nostalgia for a lost period of national ascendancy which jostles uncomfortably with the gathering pace of ever closer European political union and devolutionary dispensations, gesturing to an underlying crisis of confidence which would result in the forceful Leave vote of 2016.

2

This blessed plot

The English revolt

Confronted with the nation's degradation, a degradation written also on his or her own person, the citizen laments. Unable to mourn (because the nation is not dead – better it were dead – only diminished), unable to abandon this object of desire, unable to return to the nation's lost time of accomplishment, the citizen can only brood. Turning longingly to the past, the citizen sees the portrait of lost perfection; turning resentfully to the present, he or she sees diminishment.

(Baucom 1999: 185)

In 2016, England voted to exit the EU by 53.4 per cent to 46.6 per cent, returning the highest Leave vote of the UK's constituent nations. Of the 17.4 million votes cast for Leave, 15.2 million came from England. Brexit is therefore often referred to as an English revolt or English nationalist movement, dominating the overriding perception of a Eurosceptic *Britain*. Because England is the largest country in the United Kingdom (both in terms of population and landmass), and given London's international financial centrality, it is understandable that much attention has been concentrated on English antipathy towards the Continent. Stephen Haseler considers debates surrounding Englishness to be principally responsible for Britain's awkward history with Europe and its subsequent lacklustre approach to European integration, diagnosing the combination of the 'twin pressures of global capitalism and European union' as the cause of a 'potentially terminal crisis' for the English (1996: vii). Recent political events indicate these pressures have also served as a catalyst for the English to reaffirm and obstinately defend their national identity in stubborn resistance to cultural globalization, which so often paves the way 'for a more open connection of place and culture challenging the bounded spaces of nation states' (Hopper 2007: 115). Focusing on the 1990s onwards, when an emergent English identity crisis was triggered by devolutionary movements, the legacy of Thatcherite deindustrialization, the multicultural inclusiveness of Blair's New Labour government, and the post-Maastricht acceleration of ever closer union, it is possible to offer revitalized readings of late-twentieth-century texts and identify the early animating energy of the Brexit vote. A critical examination of Englishness will also be conducted to diagnose the imperial nostalgia underlying the Brexit debate, involving the reconstruction of Anglospheric designs to combat undesirable European futures.

Despite Macmillan's assurance to de Gaulle in June 1962 that 'the England of Kipling is dead', a deep vein of imperial Englishness lingered on in the public imaginary as conservative forces resisted a historical closure of Britain's illustrious past (Peyrefitte 1994: 301). As Sara Upstone explains, 'Rather than focusing our attention on immediate sociopolitical contexts, cultural imaginaries ask us to consider how places and communities have been represented over time and to ask how attitudes to national and international identities and alliances exist as a result of a long process of representation' (2018: 47). With this in mind, this chapter will suggest certain English texts contribute to, or reveal, an underlying structure of feeling which goes some way to accounting for the high Leave vote in England. This chapter will also map how these political visions of England and Englishness are articulated in literature and the crucial role played by cultural nostalgia, whiteness and socioeconomic inequality, respectively, in generating support for the Eurosceptic cause. It will be suggested that the project of English nationalism is decidedly at odds with the project of European integration.

In 2012, the Institute of Public Policy (IPPR) released a report entitled 'The Dog That Finally Barked', which identified early the emergence of 'a different kind of Anglo-British identity in which the "Anglo" component is increasingly considered the primary source of attachment for the English' (Wyn Jones et al. 2012: 3). The IPPR's 2013 follow-up report, 'England and its Two Unions' went further, examining the regional and intra-national tensions within the UK, qualifying that 'It is English, rather than British, hackles that rise in response to Europe' (2013: 22). The reports proved to be exceptionally prescient with their arguments borne out in the 2016 EU referendum results. The BBC's recent English Question project in June 2018, one of the largest and most comprehensive surveys of its kind in England, revealed that 80 per cent of respondents continue to 'strongly identify as English'. There were considerable variations in relation to age, political affiliation and regional location. Nearly 75 per cent of over sixty-five-year olds stated they were proud to be English compared to less than half of eighteen to twenty-four-year olds, while Leave voters were far more likely to support the statement that England was 'better in the past' than Remainers (however, half of all those surveyed supported this contention with only one in six stating England best days were yet to come) (Easton 2018). Respondents were also far more likely to identify as English or with their regional identities the further away they lived from London. The survey substantiated established divides that had been apparent long before the EU referendum and reinforced the perception of the English as a nostalgic, backward-looking people, paralyzed by uncertainty when forced to consider the current state-of-the-nation. As Susan Bassnett argues, this 'nostalgia hardly accords with the image of a forward looking nation moving into the twenty-first century'; instead, it encapsulates 'a nostalgia that says: sometime in the past there was something known as Englishness and it was good. But now it has changed, it has vanished and we can no longer find it. This view [. . .] unites all kinds of people in England in a sense of loss' (1996: 342). May's proposal for a £120 million national festival to commemorate Britain's departure from the EU – swiftly dubbed the 'Festival of Brexit' and redolent of the 1951 Festival of Britain – testifies to the nostalgic cultural paradigms which powered the Brexit vote, as opposed to simply socioeconomic precarity or fear of immigration. The strange bedfellows united under the Leave banner, from political elites to disillusioned northern working-class voters to squeezed Middle Englanders, lends credence to Bassnett's identification of the deep-rooted emotional attachments associated with English identity.

Conservative theorist Roger Scruton, in his sentimental *England: An Elegy* (2000), goes so far as to suggest 'England has been forbidden' in the contemporary national imaginary: 'any activity connected with the hierarchy and squirearchy of Old England is now likely to be persecuted [. . .] even the keeping of national customs and the display of a national flag' (2000: 247). Such persecution not only stems from 'the transfer of sovereignty to European institutions', but 'progressive intellectuals' who 'regard national loyalty as a crime', devote their efforts towards 'undermining the authority of Old England [. . .] making it faintly ridiculous in the eyes of the young' and dismiss those who oppose the 'tinpot tribunals of the European Union' as 'Little Englanders' (2000: 252). Scruton's rather extreme views notwithstanding, he tapped into the sense of loss felt by vast swathes of the British populace and such rhetoric was visibly widespread during the EU referendum. As Scruton identifies, 'the official map of the European Union, issued by the European Commission in Brussels [. . .] makes no mention of England. England has been finally disposed of', reinforcing fears that the integrationist project aimed to transcend national spheres of interest and threatened the internal integrity of the UK (2000: 253). Marr concurs, stating 'conservative writers have been slowly burnishing and practising the language of Englishness' precisely because 'the centre and left of politics have shied away from the very question of whether English consciousness exists' (2000: 230). It is rather revealing that Scruton immediately diagnoses England's ailing condition to be the result of European integration; Benjamin Grob-Fitzgibbon (2016) suggests that post-imperial nostalgia became virtually inseparable from Euroscepticism, operating as mutually reinforcing discourses. The EU, as a supranational entity, operates in opposition to what traditionalists perceived as the more *natural* image of an imperial England leading not only the UK, but a global Commonwealth and Anglosphere.

There is much merit in Richard Rose's assertion that England 'is a state of mind, not a consciously organised political institution' (1982: 29). What exactly this intangible, vanishing Englishness involves or *demands* is hard to define, yet such nostalgic historicization is important to note, as it resurfaces time and again in British fiction's confrontation with European integration. Several writers and commentators in the twentieth century compiled eccentric lists, attempting to pin down the idiosyncratic spirit and character of England. For Jeremy Paxman, Englishness evokes 'brass bands, Shakespeare, Cumberland sausages, double-decker buses, Vaughan Williams, Donne and Dickens' (1999: 23). Orwell's infamous imagery of 'old maids biking to Holy Communion through the mists of the autumn morning' in his 1941 essay 'The Lion and the Unicorn' reverberated through the decades and was seized upon by John Major during this period of identity crisis (Orwell 2018). Englishness thus emerges as an elusive and historically weighted concept resistant to cultural change: both an innate and constructed concept. The rise in Eurosceptic hostility noted in the first chapter was complemented by a corresponding increase in support for nationalist parties, particularly in English politics, supporting Anderson's assertion that 'nation-ness' remains 'the most universally legitimate value in the political life of our time' (1983: 3). Crucially, Goodwin and Milazzo find that those more strongly attached to the concept of a European identity were more likely to vote Remain in 2016, while those who strongly identify as English were much more likely to vote Leave, underpinning the argument that Brexit was driven by concerns surrounding national identity (2017: 458).

English literature has a long and varied history of excruciating national introspection. As Ian Baucom notes, this tendency to turn 'a resentful back on the present and a teary eye toward the image of a dying England' has been taken up by successive generations of English writers, from Ruskin to Conrad to Naipaul, suggesting that 'to be English is, often, to be a member of a cult of the dead, or, at the very least, a member of a cult of ruin' (1999: 175). These lamentations over England's diminished role on the global stage become more pronounced throughout the twentieth century, from George Sturt's *Change in the Village* (1912) onwards. Bentley notes that 'Literary expression of national identity is [. . .] one of the most powerful ways in which the nation has been constructed, reinforced and challenged', yet Englishness 'was undergoing a period of crisis and transformation in the fourth quarter of the twentieth century' (2015: 70; 83). The 1990s in particular witnessed a heightened concern with the fate of England and Englishness, marking a return to the literary Euroscepticism of the immediate post-war period. Representations and examinations of this anxious Englishness in literature of the period tend to be the domain of predominantly white male authors whose interests are geared towards economic assessments of the country and its conservative attitudes. A *muscular* Englishness emerges which draws from a sacred symbolic repertoire to reinforce traditionalist conceptions of English identity. But the end of the 1990s also witnessed an abundance of critical surveys which heralded the demise of England and lambasted the growing tendency for Englishness to serve as a synonym for a broader Britishness (the title of Clive Aslet's 1997 study *Anyone for England? A Search for British Identity* exemplifies how the narrow parameters of English identity are often conflated with a more inclusive British identity).[1] Whereas some texts such as Paxman's *The English: A Portrait of a People* (1998) eulogized over the timeless qualities of the national character, Simon Heffer's *Nor Shall My Sword* (1999) and Peter Ackroyd's *Albion* (2002) prophesized the passing of English culture or bid farewell to a rural idyll, adopting a distinctly melancholic tone. Paxman wryly notes, 'it is typical of the English to ignore the silver lining and to grasp at the cloud' (1999: 17). John Redwood's *The Death of Britain* (1999) and Peter Hitchens' *The Abolition of Britain* (1999) struck a darker note, accentuating the loss of English political sovereignty that EU membership would bring, directing anger and frustration at the integrationist project as the root cause of cultural decline. Moreover, the similar publication dates of these texts point towards the identity crisis underway at the turn of the millennium

---

[1] Author John Fowles, in his essay 'On Being English but Not British', communicated early fears that a more instinctual and cherished English identity was at risk of being superseded by a more inclusive and less tangible Britishness: 'I see my Britishness as a superficial conversion of my fundamental Englishness, a recent facade clapped on a much older building' (1964: 80). As Fowles neatly puts it, 'We have to be British and we want to be English' (1964: 82).

as politics witnessed the emergence of nationalist parties such as UKIP, dedicated to the protection of English sovereignty. Nationalism is, after all, 'episodic, triggered by a sense of crisis that the nation is in decline or under threat' (Hutchinson 2005: 135).

As the selected fictions in this chapter demonstrate, Englishness did not become a more accommodating identity to incorporate the Europeanization of the nation; rather, the bitterness of English cultural anxiety was displaced and transposed onto the EU, which became the institutional embodiment of all external threats to an instinctual English heritage. A combination of an extended period of socioeconomic decline, the inability of existing political institutions to defend English interests, the growing autonomy of a post-Maastricht EU and the progressive cosmopolitanization of society led to the politicization of Englishness by conservative forces. Further, the 1998 Good Friday Agreement and creation of the Scottish Parliament and Welsh Assembly in 1999 reinforced the perception that the English were becoming 'left-overs' of the devolving union and gave impetus to an emergent victimhood nationalism which exacerbated cultural anxieties concerning the *death* of England and threatened the stability of existing institutional arrangements. As Kenny (2014) finds, many English voters were growing frustrated and disillusioned with the twin unions – the United Kingdom and the EU – and were looking for a means of communicating their displeasure. For Wellings, this politicization of English identity in the years leading to the referendum played a significant role on the result, symbolizing a desperate attempt to maintain patriotic credentials in the face of a burgeoning EU: the 'political project to withdraw from the EU combined material and political grievances with ideational narratives conditioned by the historical construction of English nationalism' (2018: 155). Wellings captures the 'peculiar Englishness' of Brexit as 'an elite project aimed at an economic reorientation away from the EU', 'informed by the Anglosphere tradition in British politics' and 'sustained by popular English disaffections', creating a 'temporary alliance [. . .] united briefly but decisively by the device of a referendum' (2018: 155). Given that calls for a revival of English fortunes struck a powerful, nostalgic chord with voters in 2016, reports of England's death have been greatly exaggerated.

The English sublime

At the heart of the ridiculous, the sublime.

(Mahon 1985)

In his 1996 short-story collection, *Cross Channel*, Julian Barnes, an avowed Francophile and strong supporter of European cohesion, echoes the opinion of fellow author Tim Parks by labelling Britain 'the problem child of Europe, sending its half-hearted politicians to lie about their obligations' (2007: 207). The elderly narrator of 'Tunnel' (identified by Barnes as a fictional representation of himself) undertakes a journey from St Pancras on the Eurostar, reflecting on the 'surprising banality' with which globalization and Europeanization have altered English culture: 'Paris had become closer than Glasgow, Brussels than Edinburgh [. . .] All he needed was his European identity card' to permit access across the Channel 'without even a flap of his passport' (2007:

191). However, while the two capitals are increasingly culturally and infrastructurally connected, the political stance of their respective countries could not be further apart. Barnes utilizes his narrator to voice concerns regarding the restrictive remit of national identity, the impediments of patriotism, and the unquestioning veneration of cultural heritage, warning: 'It was unhealthy to be idealistic about your own country' as national memories often rely on 'a nostalgia as runny as old Camembert', containing 'a quality of cancerous growth' muddied by 'faint historical detritus' (2007: 207; 197; 210). In his Bloomberg speech in 2013, David Cameron re-emphasized that Britain's geographical positioning as an island nation, and separation from the Continental landmass, is symbolic of the divide and potential incompatibility between European cultures. Dewey argues, 'For the Little England tradition in particular, the Treaty of Rome amounted to the violation of natural order pre-ordained by the physical geography of the English channel' (2009: 30). For Barnes' narrator, France and the Channel Tunnel – a structural and metaphorical link to Continental Europe – become 'the symbol of all that is foreign; everything, not just Frenchness, begins at Calais' (Barnes 2002: xv). Given that the main architects of European integration were Jean Monnet and later Charles de Gaulle, it seems appropriate that 'Francophobia remains our first form of Europhobia' in his short story, threatening a fortified England 'bound in with the triumphant sea' (Barnes 2002: xv). Barnes' comments echo Labour minister Barbara Castle, for whom resistance to the building of the tunnel was 'not only anti-Common Market prejudice. It is a kind of earthy feeling that an island is an island and should not be violated' (qtd. in O'Toole 2018a: 167). Through his satirical dissection of the eccentric corners of the English cultural imagination, Barnes clearly indicates the country must overcome its deeply entrenched Channel complex.

Although much has been written on Barnes' postmodern deconstruction of nationhood, his subsequent novel *England, England* (1998) demonstrates clear anticipatory power in foreshadowing emergent fears surrounding devolution, a resurgent crisis of Englishness, and Britain's growing desire to exit the EU. The novel charts the construction of a theme park, entitled England, England, on the Isle of Wight by the neo-Thatcherite businessman Jack Pitman, which maps out a bounded performative space of historical English accomplishment. Driven by the fear that the UK no longer 'live[s] up to its adjective' in a post-war era, Pitman is intent on proving that glorification of 'the capabilities of the present' should not necessitate a corresponding 'disdain for the past' (1999: 38; 28). He plans for a reformation of English identity to counter the attitudes of 'historical depressives' who believe England's geopolitical function is 'to act as an emblem of decline' due to its 'lingering imperial guilt' (1999: 48). The imperial nostalgia at work during the 2016 referendum was similarly distorted, deliberately selective and culturally biased, erasing England's brutal colonial practice from the political conversation and historical record, resulting in a form of imperial *amnesia*, as opposed to imperial nostalgia.

To determine the master-signifier which encapsulates England's identity, Pitman conducts a national survey, resulting in the '50 Quintessences of Englishness'. For Berlant, such 'cultural expression of national fantasy is crucial for the political legitimacy of the nation', establishing the significant role of landmarks and historical figures in the nation's cultural consciousness and the public's diachronic engagement with these very signifiers (1991: 21). In the process, dominant nationalisms 'provide the empty signifier of the nation, which symbolizes an empty fullness, with a precise substantive content that people can identify with' (Torfing 1999: 194). The final authorized list, however, consists of English historical figures and antiquated practices – an accumulation (and authorial mockery) of ossified national signifiers and products of a *vanishing* Englishness – which bear no relation to the contemporary moment, offering a hollow reminder of the nation's triumphant past and current ailing potency. As Bhabha reminds us, 'writing the nation as narration' involves this veneration of 'historical objects' to sustain a unified nationalist pedagogy (1990: 305). Pitman discovers the public's rudimentary knowledge of their national history and culture to be limited to a scattering of key dates and place names, exposing 'patriotism's most eager bedfellow' to be 'ignorance, not knowledge' (1999: 82). Appropriately, suggested items linked to British political unions or the continent more generally are swiftly excised: 'Welsh rarebit, Scotch eggs and Irish stew were not even discussed' (1999: 91). Rather than recovering and preserving an instinctual and essentialist form of Englishness, the theme park instead monumentalizes the loss of that very identity. A cruel nostalgia emerges that testifies to the impossibility of recapturing these fetishized artefacts and traditions – their very presence betrays their absence.

Pitman creates what Pierre Nora (1989) terms a *lieu de memoire*: a memorial space that metonymically encapsulates the heritage of a community, populated by material objects, venerated cultural traditions and renowned landmarks associated with a perceived national history. For Nora, such sites of cultural memory are often social constructions and work in fundamental opposition to the authenticity of historical representation, resulting in a special significance being attached to 'invented traditions' that fail to accurately render visible the hallowed past (Hobsbawm and Ranger 1983). Patrick Wright concurs, noting how memory can often mark 'the defeat and disconnection of history. The styles and potentials of the past are finished with: their persistence as residue only testifies to the fact that they lack any leverage or active historicity in the present', ensuring the ghosts of English history return to haunt the living and prevent the nation from turning towards the future (1985: 243). Pitman's postmodern simulacrum of national space therefore unsuccessfully demonstrates the merits of an outward-facing and future-oriented global England; instead, the 'repositioned patriotism' engenders 'a proud new insularity' and the park merely represents a static narrative of national inauthenticity and cultural loss, its inhabitants indulging in a purposeful immersion of their imperial history (1999: 203). A parodic English imaginary emerges characterized by melancholy, loss and an inflated sense of self-worth. This memorial refashioning of a once-great nation, monetized, repackaged and laid bare for the consumption of the globalized marketplace, becomes a recuperative, performative space in which citizens may recover and reform their national identity following a period of sociopolitical instability and demographic transformation. Imagined communities, for Anderson, rely on this mutual understanding of the nation's past, with nations themselves operating as 'cultural artefacts' (1983: 4). The narrative mechanism of Jack's theme park establishes what Anderson terms a 'simultaneous temporality', formulating a conception of national community which transcends temporal limits, offering a vision of a secure and timeless Englishness (1983: 24). Although the park aims to preserve a collective memory of cultural supremacy, it imprisons the national character in an archaic and backward-looking nostalgic construct. The repetition (and thus reinforcement) of a quintessential English character as a substantive entity produces a refurbished mausoleum suspended in inertia, subject to temporal displacement, and built upon the ramparts of continuity, heritage and racial hierarchy.

A similar heritagization is evident in Kazuo Ishiguro's *The Remains of the Day* (1989) whereby insular English spaces become ceremonial museums within which individuals have little awareness of external cultural developments. Shaffer argues Ishiguro's novel is 'aimed at an entire nation's mythic self-identity', as the protagonist Stevens, a butler for Lord Darlington, 'equates the significance of events in Darlington Hall with those in England generally, and 'confuses "house knowledge" with world knowledge' (2006: 174). Rather than casting a nostalgic eye over Britain's imperial legacy, however, *The Remains of the Day* 'exhibits only a mock nostalgia' that criticizes both England's heritage industry and the nation's proud cultural insularity which 'mask[s] a paralyzing emotional and political disengagement' (2006). Ishiguro considers his novel to be 'more English than English' in evoking 'a harmless nostalgia for a time that didn't exist. The other side of this, however, is that it is used as a political tool [. . .] It's used as a way of bashing anybody who tries to spoil this "Garden of Eden"' (Vorda and Herzinger 1991: 139). For Bentley, if we accept Anderson's positioning of national identities as nostalgic, 'artificial' constructs, this naturally 'also implies that they can be manipulated by interested parties (cultural, aesthetic and political) to support particular versions, each with their own implied and modelled ideologies' (2015: 69). The nationalist discourses invoked during the EU referendum betrayed a similar nostalgic celebration and valorization of an inauthentic English past as a bulwark against the cosmopolitan incursion of modernity, tapping into that public psychological need for a renewed sense of secured authenticity and cohesive grand narrative of national community. Leave.EU regularly utilized images of the Second World War and drew on quotations by Churchill to tie their campaign to a more specific defence of English culture and identity – a *political* lieu de memoire. While such historical reframing was predominantly the work of Nigel Farage than Dominic Cummings, even the rival Vote Leave campaign drew on inaccurate historical juxtapositions with figurehead Boris Johnson comparing the EU to Hitler and a potential Fourth Reich. Vote Leave successfully positioned its campaign so it signified a sense of change as well as appealing to traditional conservatives and marginalized voters disillusioned with the state of the nation, ensuring Brexit cut across the established values and divisions of British politics.

By advancing an anachronistic and mythical reading of English history – foreshadowing the post-truth tactics implemented during the referendum – Jack Pitman operates as a theoretically flawed Little Englander misguidedly promoting the values of a Global Britain, his face turned definitively towards the past rather than the future. Although English national identity underwent considerable revision in the post-war period, the theme park exhibits a stubborn resistance to ongoing shifts in the cultural demographic. The elision of more contemporary or non-Caucasian characters from the theme park's imaginary not only exposes the extent to which the park operates as a brake on modernity, but how it functions as an ornamental memorial to England's foundational myths, governed by a false belief in national autochthony and the inauthentic recoding of ethnic purity. Pitman thus embodies Gilroy's formulation of a *postimperial melancholic*, one who not only resists cultural change, but refuses to accept his society has undergone such change, demonstrating an outright refusal to embrace contemporary society in favour of a cruel nostalgic longing to recapture the past (2005: 104). His own imperious position as a custodian of English culture is shrouded in doubt; it is rumoured he conceals his Hungarian heritage to appear 'one hundred percent British' (1999: 33). By instilling a national pedagogy that relocates Englishness away from recent post-war cultural transformations to society, the theme park proselytizes a wilful amnesia built around fixed racial codes. The '50 Quintessences of Englishness' equate to what Berlant refers to as the 'National Symbolic': a series of discursive practices which 'transforms individuals into subjects of a collectively-held history. Its traditional icons, its metaphors, its heroes, its rituals, and its narratives provide an alphabet for a collective consciousness or national subjectivity that attains the status of natural law, a birthright' (1989: 15). As Berlant expounds, 'disruptions in the realm of the National Symbolic', epitomized by England's diminished reputation in the narrative, 'create a collective sensation of almost physical [. . .] vulnerability because s/he has lost control over physical space and the historical time that marks that space as a part of her/his inheritance' (1989: 18–19). Although literature offers a means of reconceptualizing the 'National Symbolic', Pitman sabotages any cultural evolution of his national character by advancing a market-driven, mythologized heritage which simply gratifies an empty nostalgic desire and marks a resistance to sociopolitical transformations destabilizing the national fantasy: a populist ownership of English national symbols.

According to Baucom, while the English nation may be 'a community in mourning', this predisposition for nostalgia not only emerges 'as a sentimental attitude' but also operates 'as an injunctive politics of *return*, as an allegorical historiography of loss *and redemption*' (1999: 176 – emphasis added). Indeed, Pitman is not intent on rebuilding the British empire, simply to revere England's historic import before late-twentieth-century cultural and political developments undermined the nation's global standing. Boris Johnson echoes such sentiments, insisting the Brexiteer vision is 'not to build a new empire – heaven forfend – but to use every ounce of Britain's power, hard and soft, to go back out into the world in a way that we had perhaps forgotten over the past 45 years' (Johnson 2018b). However, Pitman's attempt to connect England's triumphant past to a redemptive global future neglects the recent multicultural transformations that have altered Britain's demography, staging a symbolic spatialization of white purity. As Mark Fisher succinctly puts it, 'A culture that is merely preserved is no culture at all' (2009: 3). Pitman's patriotic project also resists the imposition of EU regulations. Despite initially reporting his preference for England, England to gain political independence from Westminster and thus gain accession to the EU as a ratified nation state, he has no intention of allowing EU influence to pollute his Shakespearean 'precious jewel set in a silver sea, Mark II', merely affecting a desire for a 'New Europe' in order to prevent financial interference from Westminster (1999: 86; 172). His selfishly motivated exploitation of the EU gives voice to Barnes' own interpretation of Britain's role in the European constellation. For Barnes, negative perceptions of the EU stem directly from the economic motivations of the political class: 'Politicians never tried to sell

Europe to the British people as anything other than an advantageous commercial joint venture. Ours has been an entirely pragmatic membership, never an idealistic one. We never bought into Europe as a *grand projet,* or even an expression of fraternity' (Barnes 2017). Again, the EU appears to act as a bogeyman for a range of national ills, resulting in a very specific form of Europhobic melancholia, whereby shifting European power relations not only threaten discourses of Englishness but England's hallowed history within the popular cultural imagination.

By exploiting enduring symbols of national memory – potent ciphers that encapsulate how the English view both themselves and their territory – Pitman indicates the ways by which nostalgia may be exploited as a political tool: not a nostalgia 'for what you knew, or thought you had known, as a child, but for what you could never have known' (1999: 260). Pitman's employee, Martha Cochrane, swiftly perceives the theme park to be a postmodern counterfeit of Englishness, confronting the inauthenticity of her own national identity in the process. Martha realizes she has been indoctrinated into the cult of mythical Englishness from childhood, taught to 'worship' the seminal events of English history from the Battle of Hastings to the Treaty of Rome, even perceiving her Counties of England jigsaw puzzle to be dispensing Europhobic sentiments: 'Kent pointing its finger or its nose out at the Continent in warning – careful, foreigners over there' (1999: 11; 5). The theme park's imagined community exposes both the invented nature of Englishness, equally apparent in V. S. Naipaul's *The Enigma of Arrival* (1987) and Raymond Williams' *The Country and the City* (1973), and the process of 'continuing self-deception' through which a nation memorializes its sacred origins (1999: 6). Following his death, Pitman is resurrected as an immortal icon, suspending the English national character out of any historical moment – an asynchronous empty time protected from modernity – and preventing its dissolution. Extolling antediluvian symbols which no longer speak to the present, the park acts as an impediment to the process of national *becoming*.

In the final section of the novel, Albion, the theme park continues to redirect capital and investment away from the devalued English mainland: the map effectively replaces the territory. In a hauntingly familiar act of self-sabotage, Old England resolves to extract itself from the EU, 'negotiating with such obstinate irrationality that they were eventually paid to depart', declaring a 'trade barrier against the rest of the world' and reducing a once 'great trading nation to nut-eating isolationism [. . .] the last realistic option for a nation fatigued by its own history' (1999: 253). Barnes captures the sense that England is suffering from cultural exhaustion – operating as a nation in imperial decline, receding into the recesses of the past and awaiting its imminent demise – and must pin its hopes on the recalcitrant preservation of a national fiction in the face of rapid cultural transformations. Within Old England, a period of brutal austerity ensues and citizens looking to emigrate suddenly discover they are low on other's countries' lists of 'desirable immigrants' (1999: 252). Scotland and Wales, resurgent in the face of English decline, purchase large tracts of territory in the North and Midlands and are free to enter the EU as sovereign states, unshackled by English autonomy. Europe's support of Scotland in the political restructuring of the British landscape reveals related fears surrounding the fate of post-devolutionary England and is perceived as a form of 'historical revenge' towards 'a nation which had once contested the primacy of the continent' (1999: 251). Leaked documents from Brussels confirm European officials are inclined to let Old England serve as 'an economic and moral lesson [. . .] a disciplinary example to the overgreedy within other countries' (1999: 252). To inflame the humiliation, the EU begin to enact symbolic punishments which exacerbate the effacement of English cultural influence from contemporary global society: 'Greenwich Meridian was replaced by Paris Mean Time; on maps the English channel became the French Sleeve' (1999: 252). The novel thus provides a frighteningly accurate foreshadowing of the post-Brexit fallout, giving voice to those European politicians who feel England 'cut its own throat [. . .] its only function as a dissuasive example to others' (1999: 251). Although Old England continues to exist in the narrative as a retitled Anglia, it does so in a reduced form: a heritage site to a time now lost. As Wright identifies, national heritage sites promise 'that momentary experience of utopian gratification in which the grey torpor of everyday life in contemporary Britain lifts and the simpler, more radiant measures of Albion declare themselves again' (1985: 76). Where once 'there was active historicity there is now decoration and display; in the place of memory, amnesia swaggers out in historical fancy dress' (1985: 78). Yet even in this diminished state we are not afforded the glimpse of an England reawakened from its slumber, forced to acknowledge the constructedness of its self-definition and intent on redefining its global standing, but rather a country that persists in its illusory and nostalgic national performance. Anglia, too, is in danger of becoming its own past, feeding on a diminishing repository of regressive nostalgic sentiments which no longer hold contemporary potency.

Whereas Scruton argues the novel 'contains a strangely moving evocation of the old tranquillity' of England, the narrative's closing images arguably accentuate this vision of an English people uncertain of their 'authentic' national identity and cultural history, adrift in a globalized world (2000: ix). Local villagers perform a conga, 'national dance of Cuba and Anglia', to a repeated rendition of 'Land of Hope and Glory' (believed to be 'an old Beatles song from the last century'), until the conga line 'reduced to three, circled the weakening fire' (Barnes 1999: 265). Elgar's renowned anthem, a celebration of British imperial dominance, is stripped of its national grandeur and serves as a mournful and ironic elegy for a tattered and rudderless people looking forwards by misremembering their own past. No longer shall the English be rulers of the waves nor their bounds be set 'wider still and wider'; instead, the narrative depicts a land not of hope and glory but of fear and nostalgia. Barnes leaves the reader with a melancholic rendering of a nation in decline, documenting the specific frailties and parochial trivialities of an insular and diminished small island and its isolation from Europe. Pitman's postmodern celebration of archaic tradition ultimately proffers a constructed hauntology of the national past with no corresponding vision for England's future, relying on the continual redeployment of increasingly impotent national signifiers to define an intangible Englishness and advance free-market ideologies. *Britannia Unchained* (2012), a political text authored by five Conservative MPs who would (rather revealingly) go on to serve in Boris Johnson's post-Brexit cabinet (Kwasi Kwarteng, Priti Patel, Dominic Raab, Chris Skidmore and Elizabeth Truss), sets out a similar (if unironic) vision for Britain's future, claiming that the nation must support free-market economics and look beyond Europe to the Tiger economies of Singapore, for example, to ensure that Britain once again becomes a leading economic player. Appropriately, responding to post-Brexit developments for the *London Review of Books* in 2017, Barnes refers to the hypocritical ideology of his fictional theme park, declaring 'the Brexiteers' vision of our future, purified nation [. . .] to be a mixture of Merrie England, Toytown and Singapore. Outward-looking in the sense of "open for business", which tends to mean "up for sale". Inward-looking in other senses. Morally depleted by cutting ourselves off from Europe' (Barnes 2017). And yet, even a Europhilic author such as Barnes resists the temptation to forthrightly endorse the EU. Drawing on Barnes' personal remarks in *Something to Declare*, Pitman's vision could also be interpreted as a veiled broadside against neoliberal strategies at work in the European project, with harmonization merely a smokescreen to create 'an ever-bigger pool of docile customers for transnational corporations' (2002: xvi).

Barnes therefore cuts a complicated and contradictory figure, arraigning the Little Englander mentality while expressing fears of the EU's federalist designs and the erasure of national idiosyncrasies; a complex position of which he is well aware: 'So what's your position, Monsieur Barnes? Europhile but *Bureausceptic*, internationalist but *culturally* protectionist' (Barnes 2002: xvii). Looking back at the motivating factors for founding a European community, he ultimately reasons '[s]urely a bit of globalisation and European homogenisation is a small price to pay for [. . .] the last half-century of European peace', determining that opening a channel of European dialogue is infinitely preferable to the mid-twentieth-century horrors of ultranationalism (Barnes 2002: xvi). His anti-Brexit stance is mediated by an ambivalence towards the EU, concerns regarding the cosmopolitanization of British culture, and a distaste towards the technocratic machinations driving European integration. Nonetheless, when considered in light of the political events of 2016, Barnes' narrative plainly forecasts the dangers of consecrating national heritage and the restraining grip tradition can hold in regulating a nation's state of becoming. The fate of Old England, much like the fate of post-Brexit England, is indeterminate, leaving the reader to speculate:

> if a nation could reverse its course and its habits. Was it mere willed antiquarianism [. . .] or had that trait been part of its nature, its history, anyway? Was it a brave new venture, one of spiritual renewal and moral self-sufficiency, as political leaders maintained? Or was it simply inevitable, a forced response to economic collapse [. . .] and European revenge? (Barnes 1999: 257)

For Nadine El-Enany, 'Brexit is intricately connected to Britain's unaddressed and unredressed colonial past [which] haunted the recent EU referendum and prophesied its outcome' (El-Enany 2017). Spectres of Empire certainly loom large in the national rear-view mirror, retaining a feverish hold on the popular cultural imagination. Johnson's comments on the Queen's visit to Commonwealth countries back in 2008, claiming she was greeted by 'flag-waving piccaninnies' with 'watermelon smiles', draws from the same pool of imperial discourse that sustained the Empire (Johnson 2002b). A YouGov poll in January 2016 reported that 43 per cent of British people still perceived the British empire to be 'a good thing' and only 19 per cent saw it as 'a bad thing', while 44 per cent of respondents agreed Britain should be 'proud' of its history of colonialism with only 19 per cent agreeing Britain should regret its past actions (Dahlgreen 2016). James Hawes' *Speak for England* (2005) contains a clear strain of post-imperial melancholia, forcing an acknowledgement of lingering imperial ideologies within English culture and the political expressions they assume.² EFL teacher Brian Marley (his surname evocative of Dickens' tormented spectre) is haunted by his loosely defined Englishness in a devolutionary era, embodying the identity crisis facing an England which has lost its voice: 'if only he was Irish. They knew how they sounded. Or Scots' (2005: 164). After heading into the jungles of Papua New Guinea to compete in a reality TV show, he becomes disoriented and falls from a steep ledge, awakening to the quintessential sounds of an English cricket match. As Valluvan points out: 'Cricket is often raised in the conservative imagination as evocative of a country idyll where the virtues of village England are twinned to the edifying influence of elite establishment custodians', a vision 'that is gradually dissipating amid the assault of commercial and sensationalist televisual culture', represented by the reality TV show (2019: 93). Indolent and debilitating in equal measure, Marley's vision – a memorial to an Englishness seemingly lost to time – summons Orwell's infamous descriptions of an intangible Englishness: 'a warm homecoming to something we have never truly known but yet missed all our lives, the end of all that strange, shadowy homesickness and yearning that haunts us all our years like the long, still shadows on a lonely summer evening' (Hawes 2005: 28). This invocation of a sentimental, Conservative English idyll was later revived during the EU referendum campaign, drawing from a common stock of stereotypical national images and symbols.

Marley soon discerns he has stumbled upon a hidden colony consisting of survivors from a 1950s English plane crash, steered by the authoritative Headmaster, an archetypal image of a steadfast, masculine and pragmatic Victorian gentleman. Isolated and contained, the Colony has remained frozen in an immobile wartime state, serving as a monument to a bygone English era and supplying a reassuring nostalgic security. The Colonists' desire to return *home*, coupled with their veneration of the Dam Busters and Churchillian oratory, captures a symbolic desire to overturn the fundamental developments of post-war cultural decline and fend off the modernity of the outside world.³ Despite Marley's 'awakening', he is effectively experiencing what Orwell has termed 'the deep, deep sleep of England': a destructive nostalgia which fuels the running of the Colony (2000: 196). Rather than rejecting the Colony's superannuated practices, Marley experiences a 'pride and emotion which he had never known before' while contemplating a faded Union Jack flying in the jungle, pronouncing the Colony a Shakespearian 'fortress made by Nature [. . .] Against infection' (Hawes 2005: 170). Whereas back in contemporary England he had never known 'the unreflective joy of unthinking [national] union', watching in bemusement at footage of 'mass, indiscriminate copulation in the bars of Edinburgh and Cardiff when the Devolution votes were declared', in the Colony pulsed the 'oneness of us,

---

[2] During negotiations with Brussels before the referendum, the *Daily Mail* compared Cameron to the great appeaser Neville Chamberlain, with the pleading editorial headline 'Who Will Speak for England?' (*Daily Mail* 2016).
[3] In 1955 Churchill suggested 'Keep Britain White' as a potential election slogan.

of we, of home at last', ensuring 'all the barriers of Englishness tumbled away' (2005: 222). The national character of the Colonists is reaffirmed by the performance of repeated discursive practices, rituals and inherited perceptions of life back in England. The Colony thus modifies and relocates Wright's conception of 'Deep England', which imagines the nation as an endangered space centred on pastoral fantasies and Second World War imagery, founded 'on an imagined participation immemorial' (1985: 79). George, Marley's potential love interest, shouts out the names of famous English locations during copulation, reaching an orgasmic state by reciting 'the book-read names of England, her chant to her unknown homeland': 'Shepherd's Bush, Holland Park, England, oh England!' (Hawes 2005: 150; 151). While Marley represents 'real' England to George due to his birthplace, George in turn embodies an iconic Englishness – 'some place he had never been but knew well' – from which Marley has always felt estranged, allowing him to finally identity as 'really and truly English' (2005: 117; 170). Despite his occupation as an EFL instructor, Marley fails to 'speak for England'; by submitting to the Headmaster's Anglospheric vision, he ensures England's national voice remains firmly rooted in the past.

After questioning Marley regarding the ongoing downturn in England's fortunes in comparison to the jubilant and patriotic mood following the Second World War, the Colonists are outraged that the country has been rebranded in their absence, reduced to an inferior multicultural space where even poppies are losing their symbolic wartime resonance: an 'overpopulated, once-mighty country plonked halfway betwixt the widowly caution of oft-raped Europe and the bumptious, newly outraged virginity' of the United States (2005: 97). The Headmaster laments the fate of 'poor old England' faced with high unemployment rates, riots in London and liberal intellectuals who effectuate the discontinuation of the patriotic wartime bonhomie in favour of a postcolonial self-hatred: 'people with beards taught us that nothing actually meant anything and everything that was world with the world was because of White Anglo-Saxon Protestant men' (2005: 180). In listing the various forms of societal decline haunting and destabilizing an English idyll, Hawes addresses the dangerous misconception that England has succumbed to a soft, liberal disease which revels in depriving the country of its imperial grandeur. In so doing, the novel echoes Orwell's blistering critique of left-wing intellectualism: 'England is perhaps the only great country whose intellectuals are ashamed of their own nationality' (1968: 75). Hawes' novel evokes what can be termed the *English sublime*: a nationalist fable founded on a haunting and destructive jingoism which aggressively mourns the illustrious past, offers redemptive traces of former imperial glories and laments the cultural heterogeneities of the inferior present.

For Gardiner, 'Brexit England' contains this potent 'mix of hauntological melancholia – the desire for past collective political potential – and postcolonial melancholia – the desire for lost imperial privilege' (2018: 115). Hawes' colonists take psychological refuge in the English sublime to maintain some semblance of continuity and tradition, inhabiting an English *lebensraum* denied to them in the present. The Headmaster reveals he has held the Colony together for over fifty years in the hope they can return home, teaching the youth 'that England would pull through one way or another, even if it was only in Canada or New Zealand', alluding to the benefits of the Anglosphere and Commonwealth over the failed attachments of the EU or racial mixing of everyday multiculture (2005: 130). Calls for an alliance of 'English-speaking peoples' have permeated British politics since the nineteenth century; however, the advent of economic globalization and growing disillusionment with the post-Maastricht EU during the 1990s enabled the idea of an Anglosphere to be 'taken off the historical shelf, dusted down, suitably remodelled, and presented as an attractive garb for a new current of free market Euroscepticism' (2018: 171). Kenny and Pearce argue the Anglosphere 'forms an important, if overlooked, pre-history to Brexit', conjuring an imaginative neo-imperial landscape on which Britain's global future outside of the EU could be successfully mapped. Its political appeal deriving from its 'inherently flexible, ambiguous and often elusive reach in geographical terms' (2018: 2; 6). As a multinational bloc with (what the Headmaster considers to be) restrictive and bureaucratic judicial and regulatory constraints, the EU operates in opposition to the nation's 'natural' position: leading a global Commonwealth and Anglosphere.[4] Writing for *The Telegraph*, Boris Johnson demonstrates how this proposed Anglosphere remained a central political narrative into the twenty-first century:

> When Britain joined the Common Market, it was at a time when the establishment was defeatist, declinist and obsessed with the idea that we were being left out of the most powerful economic club in the world [...] it was enough to be European. Well, it is perfectly obvious, in 2013, that that is no longer enough – and that we need to seek a wider destiny for our country. (Johnson 2013)

Enthusiasm for an Anglosphere arrangement provided hard Eurosceptics with an excuse to hold principled opposition to EU membership. As Johnson concludes, 'The problem is not that we were once in charge, but that we are not in charge anymore' (Johnson 2002b).

By adopting a pedagogical approach adapted from the schoolhouses of Empire, the Headmaster establishes a public-school system with its educational ethics firmly rooted in nineteenth-century ideals of race and class. The fabricated school system, containing its own antiquated rituals and adherence to established customs, offers a clear durable loyalty to which national imaginaries can be attached, marking a return to outdated modes of Englishness based on public-school codes of obedience and diligence. Younger members of the Colony are indoctrinated into a mythical understanding of their national history and a system of racial stratification that positions the Englishman as the superior specimen. For Dorling and Tomlinson, Britain's educational system is responsible for the historic intolerance of contemporary elites 'who are often descended from the architects of empire, and who too often make claims for British exceptionalism', romanticizing the halycon days when Britain ruled the waves and was

---

[4] As the introduction argued, the rise of UKIP as a political force was a key factor behind Cameron's decision to hold a referendum on EU membership. During the 2010 general election UKIP styled itself 'the Party of the Commonwealth'; then, in their 2015 manifesto, declared: 'Britain is not merely a European country, but part of a global community, the Anglosphere' (UKIP 2015).

assured of its cultural, financial and racial dominance (2017: 9).[5] The political sphere witnessed the same cultural strategies, evident in Gordon Brown's admission that he himself had been part of an attempt 'to construct a post-imperial story' (2017: 22). Hawes himself identifies how the novel communicates 'a very specific kind of English [. . .] a nexus built out of the great public schools, Oxbridge, [and] the military/political/legal establishment in London' (Personal Correspondence 2020). Within the fictional Colony we witness the transmutation of the imperial project, with historical acts of racial oppression repositioned as national heroism and history manipulated and conscripted for urgent political purposes. Alerted to Marley's disappearance, television crews discover the Colony and the survivors return to a radically altered England, expressing outrage and confusion at being addressed by a 'black bugger' at passport control (typifying those white citizens who feel they possess a proprietary claim to national identity): 'what on earth could we be *but* English?' (Hawes 2005: 269 – emphasis in original). Hawes thus launches a veiled attack on ethnonationalist paradigms of Englishness that aim to rescind recent demographic changes and displace the politics of multiculturalism (a forced spatial alignment of race and place) in an effort to restore an imagined national history. A *vampiric* Englishness emerges, which can only be sustained by feeding off the glories, misconceptions and insecurities of the past.

While Marley has been stranded in Papua New Guinea, back in England an ineffectual PM, determined to be 'Top of the Table in Europe', has failed to speak for the country and instead promoted the union: 'plug *British, British British* [. . .] just dinnae mention *England*' (2005: 62; 172). Facing an upcoming referendum on monetary union (which offers a prophetic vision of the Brexit vote), he discovers the English public is strongly against the imposition of the euro but Scotland, Wales and Northern Ireland support the motion in the hope they will receive large EU subsidies. The breakdown of the vote enables the PM to assert 'Britain *as a whole* clearly voted for Monetary Union' and 'whatever happens in England won't matter', confirming fears surrounding the reversal of English dominance in a devolutionary-era union (2005: 61 – emphasis in original). Confronted with threats to the sanctity of the English state (and, like Pitman, seeking to whitewash the post-Windrush cosmopolitanization of society in order to preserve a monocultural English identity), the Headmaster assumes control of the Conservative Party and displaces the sitting Labour PM in a landslide victory by running on a platform of Thatcherite individualism, Churchillian resilience and (most significantly) a Powellite return to ethnic heritage as a marker of Englishness. Kenny and Pearce discuss how Powell's political speeches, like those advanced by the Leave campaign, melded 'Melancholy, loss and decline' with 'notions of redemption, emancipation and renewal', evident in his assertion that 'It's really collective memory that makes a nation, its memory of what its past was, what it has done, what it has suffered and what it has endured' (2018: 97). Powell's manufactured alignment of the

---

[5] Tomlinson (2019) details the failure of British educational structures to address Britain's cultural xenophobia, identifying the imperial values engrained in public-school systems and the extent to which education continues to be governed by racial logics. Robert Verkaik concurs, describing public schools as 'cheerleaders for colonialism' in controlling the narrative of Empire' and often imbuing the national narrative with class superiority (2018: 45).

past and present may fail to secure a legitimate cultural heritage, but it succeeds in mobilizing an electorate suffering from what Gilroy terms 'postcolonial melancholia': 'an unhealthy and destructive post-imperial hungering for renewed greatness' (2004: 331). As Nairn identifies, Powell's political project constituted a 'conservative dreamworld founded on an insular vein of English romanticism' imbibing the present with the qualities and values of the past (2003: 250). Like Powell, the Headmaster relies on the security of imperial history to mask the spectrality and fragility of the national fantasy and signals an intense desire to 'get back to the place or moment before the country lost its moral and cultural bearings' (Gilroy 2005: 89–90).

Upon learning that France has created a United Europe ('Run by them, of course') and Britain has 'joined, sort of', the Headmaster immediately enforces new cultural protectionist policies which limit the mobility of national citizens and their engagement with Europe (2005: 202). Such restrictions are considered a natural duty to ensure public security and the maintenance of a national character by 'dealing with our own sort in our own language, not with the ruddy frogs through wop interpreters' (Hawes 2005: 302). Once again, the EU is castigated as the primary threat to political legitimacy and sovereignty, epitomizing a backward and technocratic form of supranational governance: 'The dream of a Continental Empire, encompassing all of Europe, dominating all the world. That is the foe [. . .] England was once more fighting' (2005: 291). England exits the EU with red passports discontinued in favour of an English-only ID card, triggering Scotland and Wales to mount a constitutional objection to the withdrawal and eventually becoming independent states. The analysis of former Liberal Democrat Leader Vince Cable, who claimed the Brexit vote was driven by a 'nostalgia for a world where passports were blue, faces were white and the map was coloured imperial pink' is rather prophetic in this regard (Jamieson 2018). With the British union now dissolved, Ireland is reunited to the dismay of Northern Irish Loyalists, negotiating with Scotland and Wales to form the 'Federation of the Anglo-Celtic Archipelago' (Hawes 2005: 304). The Celtic Fringe, naturally, evinces less enthusiasm for a revitalized Anglosphere. Rather than activating a Brexit-style economic downturn, however, England appears to flourish and other European countries follow suit. Germany swiftly secedes from the EU, realizing it would financially responsible for supporting weaker EU states, and countries begin to look westward to the United States for trade deals and global governance. Following the break-up of the EU, England becomes the largest state in a reformulated American Union, switches currency to the dollar and (in a move reminiscent of Barnes' novel) rebrands itself as Old England.[6] Hawes' narrative thus reiterates the comments of several post-war politicians such as Clement Attlee, who suggested post-war Britain should operate 'not as a European power looking towards the East, but as the eastern extension of a Western block centred on North America' (qtd. in Hawes 2005: 281).

This cosmopolitical restructuring works alongside the dissolution of the British Commonwealth and introduction of an English Language Community in which Canada, Australia and New Zealand follow Old England's immigration and asylum laws, 'which

---

[6] The Colony remains open as an England, England-style tourist attraction for those wanting an 'authentic' experience of quintessential England.

is to say, taking none of the buggers at all', effectively curtailing the freedoms of those who mistakenly believe the European Court of Human Rights will serve as protection (Hawes 2005: 321). The Headmaster recognizes his policy of zero immigration, with male refugees conscripted into military service before eventual deportation, holds real populist appeal, satisfying post-imperial fantasies of control: 'It's as if no one's actually been *listening* to what people *want* for years, in England' (Hawes 2005: 309 – emphasis in original). Although the policy marks an inherent contradiction in that England is apparently striving for both national isolationism, on the one hand, and a reconstitution of empire, on the other, in attempting to restore 'the good old days. The whole tribe pulling together again', the Headmaster emerges as a twenty-first-century architect of a rejuvenated Anglosphere (Hawes 2005: 321). Championed by British politicians in the post-war period as offering a clear alternative to a United Europe and the possibility of a reconstituted empire, the future-oriented Anglosphere played a subordinate role to immigration in the referendum campaign, supplying 'a horizon of possibility and affective ideological content for many Brexiteers' and offering alternate futures for a post-EU Britain (Kenny and Pearce 2018: 157).[7] Appropriately, Liam Fox's initial Brexit plans – indicating a desire to reconnect the Anglosphere and Commonwealth in a rival trading empire to the EU – were nicknamed 'Empire 2.0' by civil servants, while in early 2016 Johnson and Davis endorsed a 'Global Britain', with its more expansive political outlook reproducing this Anglospheric vision.[8]

O'Toole's concept of 'zombie imperialism' is relevant here, referring to the reproduction of outdated imperial paradigms and behaviours, alongside the reconstruction of Empire 2.0, long after Britain's global prestige has faded (2018b). Conservative political rhetoric is dependent upon this constant evocation of the relics of empire: a reclamation of the living past. Although arguments for a rejuvenated Anglosphere reach beyond a simple vision of Empire 2.0, Johnson, Gove and Davis cited Anglosphere countries as potential models for a post-Brexit Britain, indicating how Anglospheric visions are both intimately connected to, yet distinct from, political systems associated with Empire (see Kenny and Pearce 2018). Dismissing the Leave vote as misguided (built upon this inaccurate historicization of the imperial legacy) undoubtedly does a disservice to the legitimate anxieties of those voters disillusioned with the rapid pace of cultural change, yet there was an undeniable monocultural nationalism at work in the appeal to the white working classes. Political factions sought to reconjure the Empire in the public imagination in more outlandish and dubious forms, whitewashing the brutality of imperial rule. Unable to lead the EU, imperially minded political factions looked elsewhere for Britain to forge a new role in the world, aiming to rekindle the buccaneering spirit of imperialism. During post-Brexit negotiations, Jacob Rees-Mogg, Daniel Hannan and Johnson all recoiled from the prospect of remaining tied to the EU in a customs union, claiming Britain would be no better than an EU colony. Cameron himself revealed a desire for Britain

[7] As Wellings identifies, England 'lay trapped between the receding memory of empire and the waking reality of deepening European integration' (2019: 96).
[8] Raheem Kassam has noted the similarities between the Brexit campaign and North American populism, claiming 'the whole Trump narrative is about the Anglosphere, about free-trade agreements with all the English speaking nations' (qtd. in Kenny and Pearce 2018: 163).

to become 'a swashbuckling, trading, successful buccaneer nation of the twenty-first century', admittedly while remaining part of the EU (qtd. in Gildea 2019: 234). In forecasting a return to a more nationalistic political landscape, Hawes thus anticipates the argument that Brexit will restore the nation's fortunes, while expressing a clear authorial critique of those who subjugate the past to political manipulation in order to invoke a revitalized and reimagined imperial history. The novel's concluding stages reveal a burgeoning resistance to Britain's slide into Anglospheric isolationism – 'We British are Europeans' – suggesting the need for England to relinquish, rather than reconjure, outdated national paradigms and warning of the danger in resurrecting old ghosts to confront new and disorienting political realities (2005: 334).

Following Hobsbawm's theory of 'invented traditions', Pitman and the Headmaster's attempts to 'structure at least some parts of modern social life around invariant and unchanging tradition' represent an ideological need to recover a stable sense of national 'self' in a period of global upheaval (1983: 2). Their nationalist designs are racialized projects – metonymic battlegrounds for the defence of Englishness – but they are also projects frozen in time and unwilling to acknowledge either the dark underbelly of imperial practice or the recent transformations within contemporary society, resulting in a culturally narrow Englishness. Both novels were written following the 1997 New Labour victory, which sought to reclaim and reposition Britain as more outward-looking. A militant Englishness, reliant on an ethnically homogenous identity, thus equates to an escape from the more inclusive conceptions of multicultural Britishness entering the cultural imaginary. The post-Brexit moment witnessed a dramatic increase in similar exclusionary practices conducted under the banner of English nationalism to justify the apparent defence of the realm.

Philip Murphy contends Johnson's reported desire to re-establish ties with burgeoning Commonwealth economies (betrayed by Britain's initial entry into the EEC) was aimed directly at white English-speaking Dominions rather than India or Africa, simply dressing the empire in 'new clothes': 'Eurosceptics [. . .] are implicitly rehabilitating the racialized, early twentieth-century notion of the Commonwealth as a cosy and exclusive Anglo-Saxon club' (qtd. in Gildea 2019: 245). Pitman and the Headmaster's respective attempts to 'make Britain great again', primarily by advancing a fortified and refurbished English nationhood, is evidently a more global impulse; the twenty-first century marked the return of authoritarian figures in the style of Donald Trump, Turkey's Recep Tayyip Erdogan, Russia's Vladimir Putin and China's Xi Jinping. Although Barnes and Hawes are often considered to be honouring traditional English values and customs, their novels deconstruct and unsettle nostalgic stereotypes associated with the English national identity. Neither novel casts a nostalgic glance back at a lost period of cultural dominance, but instead critiques and demystifies the notion of an essentialist English identity, satirizing those who believe England should continue bathing in the afterglow of its imperial dominance. As Linda Hutcheon explains, the power of nostalgia stems from its 'structural doubling-up of two different times, an inadequate present and an idealized past': 'If the present is considered irredeemable, you can look either back or forward. The nostalgic and utopian impulses share a common rejection of the here and now' (2000: 198; 204). Within the imaginations of Pitman and the Headmaster lives another England – an imaginative reconstruction of the present in which the English people retain their former glory – supporting Wright's contention that 'a simplifying nostalgia can replace any principled democratic consideration' (1985: 244). We can recognize in their actions the motivations and desires of Brexiteers who long to restore England's prime hierarchical position within both the union and the global order, yet neither of their political projects offers a clear solution for ways in which a diminished England may redefine itself in relation to its partners in the UK and the EU.

Hawes' satirical vision of a devolutionary-era England and its fear of sociopolitical decline is shared by several texts of this period. Ian McEwan's *The Innocent* (1990) alludes to this psychological anxiety concerning Britain's post-war role in relation to Europe and the United States, depicting a nation coming to terms with its reduced political capacity. As the novel's protagonist, Leonard Marnham, discerns his 'Englishness was not quite the comfort it had been to a preceding generation. It made him feel vulnerable' (McEwan 2016: 7). Alex Martin's *The General Interruptor* (1994), published immediately following Maastricht, concerns a narrator who gradually surrenders his Englishness in favour of a hybrid, Europeanized identity. His metamorphosis is a clear rebuke of an insular and hostile Britain facing a diminished future while Italy and other Continental nations concoct more supranational designs. Adam Thorpe's *Ulverton* (1992), Graham Swift's *Last Orders* (1996) and Nigel Williams' *East of Wimbledon* (1993) also critique prevailing notions of Englishness to be outdated and inadequate, positioning England as an enervated cultural space bereft of political import.

Muscular Englishness

They must have a clear notion of their own destiny and not listen either to those who tell them that England is finished or to those who tell them that the England of the past can never return [. . .] England can still fulfil its special mission if the ordinary English in the street can somehow get their hands on power.

(Orwell 1970: 55)

J. G. Ballard's work in particular responds to a perceived loss of anglicized prestige revealing an imperial inheritance which continues to haunt the impoverished present. Ballard's assertion that England 'has lost its direction, lost its purpose' is evident in the prophetic *Kingdom Come* (2006), which examines the fragility of the English psyche and charts the gradual emergence of a violent populist backlash that was to emerge a decade later (Sellars 2006). Protagonist Richard Pearson bemoans the increasingly intimate connectivity between ethnonationalism and anti-immigration fervour to a narrower conception of Englishness, with the St George's cross becoming a sacred symbol of cultural resistance to any external attempts to incorporate England within larger circles of institutional identification. Apathetic, flag-waving racists conduct attacks on Asian businesses, turning to the collective enterprise of consumerism as an inferior substitute for a civic communality once supported by a stable sense of nationhood. The novel's indictment of the state of the nation foreshadows the aggressive emotive mood which seized the country in 2016, with a populace willing to accept post-truth political strategies rather than confront their own diminishment: 'They knew they were being lied to, but if lies were consistent enough they defined themselves as a credible alternative to the truth. Emotion ruled almost everything, and lies were driven by emotions that were familiar and supportive, while the truth came with hard edges that cut and bruised' (2007: 204). Ballard's prescient remarks encapsulate the identity crisis England was to face as the country continued to undergo 'a huge transformation, changing beyond recognition into something we haven't yet figured out', yet he dismisses the politicized manipulation of imperial ideologies and nostalgic stereotypes to reclaim some semblance of national quintessence:

> The problem is that we still think we're a great nation, but we're not [. . .] We're wondering what exactly being English is about, and no one can provide an answer. Poor old John Major used to try to define Englishness with talk of village greens, warm beer and flannelled fools in the dusk. (Wakefield 2001)

For Ballard, such national navel-gazing was converted into an 'irrational antipathy towards Europe' and a little Englander mentality which compromises the potential for a re-energized Englishness to emerge: 'we should go into Europe regardless of any temporary financial problems. There's new life for us there, a larger canvas to paint ourselves upon. But we won't [. . .] [W]e react with xenophobic terror to the thought of losing our national identity. If only we had an identity to lose' (Wakefield 2001).

Jez Butterworth's 2009 play, *Jerusalem*, also attains new relevance in the post-Brexit moment, giving voice to the disenchanted and unacknowledged English voter. Set on St George's Day (often overlooked in the contemporary English social calendar) and the day of the local Flintock country fair, *Jerusalem* reiterates *England, England*'s exposure of the haunting spectral nature of English nationalism, charting the ways in which national identity becomes a commodified source of cultural protectionism for those citizens left behind by a rapidly changing world. Butterworth, who refused an OBE following Cameron's pledge to hold an in-out referendum on EU membership, explains *Jerusalem* is a play about the hunger and anxieties of Englishness, concerned with his own 'sense of loss and [. . .] attitudes towards change' (Butterworth 2011). Facing eviction from his woods by county officials to make way for a new estate, protagonist Johnny 'Rooster' Byron is forced to recognize the static nature of his diminished existence. Dawn, his ex-partner, addresses his nostalgic cultural inertia and personal stagnation, accusing him of operating like 'a stopped fucking clock': 'the world turns. And it turns. And it moves on and you don't. You're still here' (2009: 66). Butterworth's play takes its title from William Blake's anthemic and melancholic poem (cited by David Cameron as the literary encapsulation of a distinctive English nationhood), which is often considered to bemoan the passing of England's soul and a patriotic call to arms against external influences, neglecting Blake's distaste for nationalist sentiments.

The curtain opens on a faded cross of St George, revealing Byron's mobile home replete with an Old Wessex flag and railway sign reading 'Waterloo': markers of a vanishing, nostalgic and disturbingly regressive English identity. Emerging from his home wearing Second World War regalia, Byron serves as the embodiment of a depleted but defiant England where 'Nothing changes' (2009: 82). For Gardiner, the play represents 'a proactive recuperation of English place'; the woods, existing on the fringes of the new town and excluded from the centre, serve as a defensive little realm in which Byron can fortify his hallowed Englishness (2012: 157). The English character itself is effectively under siege and considered worthy of conservation. In this sense, we can certainly recognize the return of the English sublime with its nostalgic veneration of a pastoral 'green and pleasant land' suspended in a form of cultural stasis. However, although Byron appears powered by the ancient energy of 'English soil' in the 'holy land' of his woods, his liminal edgeland is increasingly endangered by excessive regulation; the material English body politic is at odds with rapid cultural change and bureaucratic interventionism (2009: 9; 72).

In analysing Byron's disenfranchisement, it is possible to understand the rise of nationalist parties as a response to political exclusion, socioeconomic precarity and the manifold resentments of Little Englanders raging against the system. Butterworth is not simply narrating the backward-looking melancholia of an isolated Englishman but critiquing a fractured country which fails to address its inherent political divides. While the EU is not explicitly named as a source of Byron's discontent, there are subtle allusions to the Europeanization of English culture. Over the course of the play, Spitfires begin to fly overhead, suggesting post-war England is once again faced with an invasive force, while BBC Points West, which used to provide local news, is now 'too busy merging with BBC Belgium' (2009: 60). This latter critique is particularly relevant, as the national media neglect to cover the events of the local county fair in favour of more international content, anticipating charges directed at the media during the EU referendum concerning the unrepresentative, London-centric nature of news programming. The county fair is responsible for securing a tangible sense of communitarian identity and localized belonging, validating an established national identity; but the instinctual Englishness of the fair has, rather like Pitman's theme park, become enslaved to neoliberal corporate interests, offering an inauthentic and commodified distortion of the national tradition. In turn, whereas once 'Bryon *was* the Flintock Fair', in the contemporary moment he is reduced to regaling others with his former glories, the external threat to his woods becoming a synecdoche for the imperilled global standing of England more generally (2009: 31). Mike Bartlett's play *Albion* (2017) communicates similar national concerns, concentrating on the historic gardens of a once-great country estate and the desire to reinstate that which is fading from memory.

Despite the evident political undercurrent of *Jerusalem*, Byron does not express a clear political position; he is simply the English spirit of rebellion, vilified by the town folk and mobilized by the necessity to defend an idyllic pastoral Albion. That being said, he communicates several grievances later articulated by Leave voters, giving voice to disenfranchised citizens nursing lingering sociopolitical and cultural resentments against elected officials and public bodies. His unequivocal distrust of the establishment and subsequent revolt brings to mind the 2.8 million 'silent' voters of England who did not traditionally vote in general elections but instigated an anti-establishment uprising, believing their protest votes could reverse the nation's declining fortunes and nullify their political alienation. By summoning figures of national mythology to rise up and prevent his *eviction* at the close of the play, coupled with his adulation towards a mystical England that never was, Byron typifies a relevant manifestation of the English revolt. It is not specifically Byron's economic precarity which is the issue, but the erosion of the intangible *magic* of England. Following the EU referendum, Butterworth's play enjoyed a major revival as commentators acknowledged its prescient power in recognizing the smouldering, latent power of English nationalism and sense of marginalization felt by working-class communities. As Katy Shaw recognizes, Butterworth 'mobilizes the spectral to show how the past continues to inform the politics of the present', uncovering the hauntological pathways by which the 'ignored, surprised, or forgotten [are] coming back' (2018: 56; May 2011: 3). *Jerusalem* thus emerges as a crucial text which profiles emergent anxieties of frustrated English voters before the referendum, offers insight into motivating catalysts of Brexit, and delivers a timely dramaturgical rendering of the English identity crisis.

As Michael Goldfarb argues, Butterworth's '*Jerusalem* is one expression of nostalgia for England', but 'Football hooliganism is a much darker expression of nostalgic nationalism [. . .] more connected to real-world politics' (Goldfarb 2019). During the run-up to the EU referendum, novelist John King, a staunch opponent of EU integration and outspoken Leave supporter, acknowledged how his football-focused fiction captured an early sense of this ongoing struggle between the political class and the English public, defining the impending Brexit vote as 'the most important issue of our twenty-first-century history' (King 2016b). In a series of articles for *New Statesman*, he presented the left-wing case for exiting the EU, blaming the multinational bloc for prolonged austerity and the direction of funds away from the welfare state. King emphasizes UKIP's concentration on poorer voters, combined with the instant dismissal of Leave voters as racists and bigots by factions of the London intelligentsia, as a key factor in their rapid political influence and ability to colonize Englishness for their own ends. King's novels, including *The Football Factory* (1996), *Headhunters* (1998), *White Trash* (2002) and *Skinheads* (2008), capture this festering anger towards political elites and record an early sense of marginalization and stigmatization reported by working-class English citizens during the run-up to the EU referendum. In 'The People Versus the Elite', published in 2016 to mark the twenty-year anniversary of his Football Factory trilogy, King recognizes how the politicization of English identity and the sense of democratic deficit within his novels 'feel much more relevant and urgent now' than in the 1990s (2016b). Linking the powerlessness and Europhobic hatred of his football supporters to the political impotence of Leave voters, apoplectic at the perceived loss of sovereignty to a European body, he identifies the roots of Brexit within the climate of late-twentieth-century British society: 'These are the same cultural connections that would see them reject the EU today' (2016b).

England Away (1998), the final component of the trilogy, considers the broader impact of European integration and post-war decline on white male identity formation in the 1990s, utilizing the highly performative figure of the football hooligan to channel this cultural and political disenfranchisement. The novel contrasts Bill Farrell's memories of Europe during the Second World War with the drink and drug-fuelled exploits of England supporters Tommy Johnson and Harry Roberts as they travel to Berlin via Amsterdam to watch the national team play Germany. Although the match was arranged by politicians to communicate a 'show of unity between the two nations [. . .] laying firm foundations for a united Europe', the fixture descends into a 'rerun of the war. Tapping into the spirit of the Blitz' (1999: 256; 271). Juxtaposing Bill's traumatic experiences with football hooligan culture, *England Away* indicates the significance of wartime imagery on contemporary conceptions of Englishness and demonstrates how the national game serves as a microcosmic performative space for the powerful articulation of defiant cultural imaginaries often grounded in racial homogeneity and anti-European rhetoric.

England Away opens by documenting the movements of England football fans across the channel, conflating their rough crossing with the wartime events of Normandy. Held up by 'Customs cunts' intent on 'nailing us with the European tag' and holding his 'shitty red passport close, the proud old British version ripped up and brunt by the invisible scum in Brussels', Tommy immediately defines himself against deepening European integration, re-establishing the national exceptionalism evident in the immediate post-war years (1999: 3). Having abandoned the political arena – 'politics is shit [. . .] We're English and that's it' – and casting about for alternative forms of national identification following a period of post-war imperial decline and cultural transformation, King's hooligans cling to football as the battleground on which debates over Englishness can be fought, operating as a First World War-inspired 'Expeditionary Force' designed to make 'Franz Foreigner nervous' (1999: 68).[9] The football grounds themselves become sites of contestation in which disillusioned English citizens are granted the opportunity to take out their frustrations on Europeans. Miguel Mota writes that 'hooligan support for England at away games' during this period 'became a kind of defensive patriotism in the face of wider national decline', with football providing a refuge to 'deeply insecure and highly aggressive' violent masculinities (2009: 265). Disenfranchised males in the narrative, fuelled by impotent rage, re-enact wartime rivalries to recover a form of contemporary relevance and overcome their perceived lack of representation and political agency: a palpable anger which resulted in a fervent backlash against the system in 2016. For Paul Beaumont, it is precisely this nationalist defiance that fuels both football hooliganism and Euroscepticism: 'football gives us something to fight over, an environment in which to experience triumph and tragedy, without actually fighting; without actually going to war' (Beaumont 2016). King has repeatedly indicated a desire to give voice to English citizens 'who are not liberal or trendy left, but anti-EU and patriotic, proud of their culture and sick of being told they are shit by our social controllers in politics and the media' (Ciesla 2006). For the character of Tommy, football offers the possibility of re-establishing England's place at the top of the European order, allowing hooligans to transcend local divides and experience a sense of cultural identification. Losing themselves in this shared endeavour, the hooligans can locate their experiences within a national narrative from which they feel otherwise estranged: 'Any lingering club grudges disappear. We're England, united, we'll never be defeated' (King 1999: 141).

---

[9] Silvia Mergenthal identifies a clear correlation between key historical events, which have threatened Britain's cultural or political reputation, and a heightened nationalist response to football tournaments, including Britain's early failed attempts to join the EEC (2002: 262).

As Hobsbawm observes, football became an intrinsic expression of national struggle following the Second World War, justifying King's intricate juxtaposition between wartime comradeship and sporting glory: 'The imagined community of millions seems more real as a team of eleven named people. The individual, even the one who only cheers, becomes a symbol of his nation himself" (1992: 143). Accordingly, Tommy ardently denounces the 'fucking mentality of those media cunts' for questioning whether patriotic citizens flying the St George's cross were 'automatically Nazis', yet many of King's hooligans espouse strong ethnonationalist sentiments (foreshadowing political opinions later expressed by parties such as the BNP and UKIP) and view themselves as guardians of the nation's heritage (1999: 44). Ford and Goodwin have argued, for example, that New Labour's attempt to appeal to younger, university-educated voters through a pro-European platform resulted in older, working-class white voters looking elsewhere for a political party to represent their communities (2014: 18). The performative nature of the hooligans' visceral Europhobia communicates their belonging and loyalty to the English *tribe*, which they perceive to be at threat from external forces: 'England's being ripped apart by Europe. None of us wants to be ordered about by Berlin. That's what the last war was about' (King 1999: 13). By also attacking 'pro-queer, pro-black, anti-white cunts chipping away at England', Tommy resists the internal infringement of liberal multicultural models threatening the primacy of white English exclusivity, ensuring Europhobia and a wider xenophobia become easily interchangeable (1999: 216). His insecure advocacy of English values signals a broader defence against efforts to destabilize the hallowed symbolic order of white Englishness and the 'Bulldog breed' (with Englishness often operating as a normative code for white Britishness). In *British White Trash*, Mark Schmitt argues King's characters operate as figurations of 'tainted whiteness' involving the semiotic practices and performances which determine whiteness as a cultural position, sustain racial privilege, and conflate ethnicity with national belonging (2018: 13). *England Away* thus confronts the spectre of racialized hierarchies and whiteness which haunts contemporary political debates surrounding the shifting conceptions of Englishness and national belonging.

The novel also reiterates the Eurosceptic arguments of mid-twentieth-century authors discussed in the first chapter, connecting England's decline to the deepening of European collectivities. King's characters effectively operate as authorial mouthpieces for his own various anxieties regarding the creation of a neoliberal superstate. Interpreting the EU as 'one more attempt to crush England', Tommy anticipates Boris Johnson's comparison of the EU to Hitler in May 2016: 'Europe's a plot by big business to centralise power [. . .] Hitler had the same idea' (1999: 48). Bill and his friends also foreshadow Johnson's deployment of Euromyths in the British media, bemoaning the bureaucratic actions of 'some faceless wanker in Brussels banning bitter' replacing pint glasses 'with some metric rubbish' (1999: 174). While Tommy articulates an outright hatred of the EU and Bill expresses outrage at how the Commonwealth has been betrayed in favour of European harmonization, Harry offers a more qualified critique of the English antipathy towards deepening integration. While acknowledging a distaste for the neoliberal-leanings of the 'money-motivated Euro-dictatorship' and its 'unelected bureaucrats', Harry appreciates his nation's cultural Europhobia 'was part of being an island race. The English channel was built into everyone' (1999: 71; 274). In a tribute to his father, King wrote of his sympathy for the older generation of voters, fictionalized by Bill in *England Away*, who disagreed with Britain's initial entry into the EEC and believed the 'Germans couldn't beat us in two World Wars so they are going to do it through the Common Market' (King 2018). Condemning the current EU as 'a slow-motion coup' which only 'works for the corporations and the wealthy', King claims these inherent vices were evident in its origins: 'Heath and his backers in the establishment knew the EEC represented the foundations of a European superstate, and this Big Lie has underpinned our forty-six years' membership of an organization that has adjusted its name as its tentacles have tightened their grip on our economy and law-making' (King 2018). King's football-focused novels do not simply celebrate the vulgar trappings of banal nationalism, but reveal how the emergent 'critical deconstruction of whiteness' operates in correlation with 'the crisis of European identity' and evince a critical awareness of the burgeoning issues and mechanisms shaping English political debates (Schmitt 2018: 18).

Following the outcome of the Brexit vote, King immediately lambasted 'bubble-living bubbleheads' within London for their political deviation from the rest of England, launching a scathing attack on the writing industry for its 'pro-EU bias' and the reluctance of authors to challenge the organization (King 2019). King goes so far as to claim that 'If George Orwell and Aldous Huxley were writing now I firmly believe they'd reject the EU, but would today's publishers print Nineteen Eighty-Four and Brave New World if they were seen to be targeting the EU? Probably not' (King 2019). His frustration led to the formation of Artists for Brexit: a national network for Leave-supporting arts workers who feel democracy is being traduced and subverted. Yet pro-Brexit creative voices such as Paul Kingsnorth and John King are largely drowned out by the predominantly Europhilic chorus of British authors in the twenty-first century. Alan Moore's multi-layered, century-spanning *Jerusalem* (2016), for example, also retains a purposeful concentration on the local to comment on the nation but on an ideological level appears to substantiate its author's claim that the Leave campaign (while founded on 'valid reasons') ultimately amounted to 'a wildly misguided protest' (qtd. in Marchese 2016). As the final chapter will demonstrate, Artists for Brexit provides a clear counterpoint to the pro-EU sympathies of most contemporary British authors and their post-Brexit fictions.

As Baucom recognizes, a sense of loss is not the most accurate way to describe the changing face of the nation: 'England has endured less the vanishing of Englishness than the dispersal of its locations of identity' (1999: 220). Unlike the flagrant hooliganism of King's work, Anthony Cartwright's fictions, including *The Afterglow* (2004), *Heartland* (2009) and *Iron Towns* (2016), detail the subtle and insidious forging of a resurgent English nationalism within the deindustrialized landscape of the Black Country, charting the profound socioeconomic changes wrought by globalization on these communities and the difficulties in representing working-class masculinities rooted in regional and local traditions.[10] Sherry Lee Linkon accentuates

---

[10] As Phil O-Brien rightly notes, the use of the term 'deindustrial' is more appropriate to a discussion of Cartwright's novels than 'post-industrial' as it suggests the ongoing restructuring of these communities as opposed to a sense of finality (2020: 232).

that 'Deindustrialisation did not simply put many working-class men out of work [. . .] it undermined the resources that they relied upon to construct their identities' (2014: 150). The physicality of the spectral industrial terrain in Cartwright's narratives forces an acknowledgement that nations are not simply imagined communities but lived historical spaces of people, practices and traditions. As Wright summates, 'where so much contemporary existence in this period of economic and imperial "decline" can only disappoint or frustrate, the symbolism of the nation can still provide meaning [. . .] to re-enchant a disenchanted everyday life' (1985: 24).

Heartland engages with the multicultural clashes within Cinderheath, a fictional ward in Dudley, its name holds connotations of disintegration and burnt-out industry. Dudley, a town in which Cartwright was born and to which he continues to hold a deep affection, is often referred to as the capital of the Black Country and was at the centre of the Industrial Revolution, renowned for its engineering, steelworks and coal mining industries. Yet *Heartland* reveals a Dudley in decline; the landscape is haunted by the legacies of 1980s Thatcherite ideology and the traces of deindustrialization that irrevocably altered the fabric of working-class communities. Widespread socioeconomic precarity ensures that Cartwright's hometown becomes a fertile breeding ground for English nationalism, which thrives on political disenfranchisement and lack of social mobility, forcing citizens to find security in more parochial forms of cultural identification. Cartwright's work can be read as almost diaristic, documenting the processes of erasure and loss that influence the cultural and political mindsets of his characters; the 'landscape of decay [. . .] fed into the psychology of the place', contributing to a collective sense of alienation and dislocation as the town was 'boarded up' around its inhabitants (Arnot 2009). Accordingly, his characters inhabit spaces of loss in which they attempt to not only locate their identity but recover their white nationhood and come to terms with the lasting psychological effects of industrial decline.[11]

In his study of English nationalism, Jeremy Black argues that political elites at the post-millennial turn avoided 'confront[ing] the issue that England exists' (2018: 194). Set against the backdrop of the demise of New Labour (resulting in millions of disenfranchised floating voters with no political home), *Heartland* identifies this failure of major political parties to address either English identity or socioeconomic inequality, allowing xenophobic elements within the BNP to draw sympathetic voters into their fold. The far-right extremism of the BNP attempts to divide the community according to ethnicity thus curtailing the emergence of an inclusive class politics. Early signs of the marginalization of the working class from the political system, a major factor buttressing the 2016 Leave vote, are evident from the outset. Rob Catesby, a former Aston Villa trainee, is sent home from his teaching job for wearing an England football shirt which could be considered offensive to members of the racially divided community due to 'the connotations of it [. . .] the message it gives' (Cartwright 2010: 231). Cartwright allows such politico-cultural tension to bleed into the fabric of the

---

[11] For Gardiner, Laura Oldfield Ford's hauntological *Savage Messiah* (2011) is another literary text whose characters appear to 'have nothing to do with 2016 Leave voters' but 'looks for the fragments of collectivity' in the 'ghostly search for lost futures in the ruins of development' (2018: 110).

novel, narrativizing the early manifestations of nationalist resistance that were to later erupt during the EU referendum campaign. The Brexit vote provided disempowered and disenfranchised voters the opportunity to direct their collective anger towards an external organization that could become a scapegoat for their socioeconomic deprivation, engendering a sense of solidarity which has been noticeably absent following the deindustrialization of these communities. Cartwright notes, 'Extremism flourishes [. . .] when people have a perception that they've been abandoned and bypassed by the pace of change. There's always a temptation to look around for simple answers to complex questions' (Arnot 2009). The English revolt can be read as a result of the inability of established political parties 'to articulate, and respond to, deep-seated and long-standing social and political conflicts in Britain' (Ford and Goodwin 2014: 12). In turn, the English vote is the end-product of systemic causation: a pathological symptom of emotional and fiscal austerity.

Jim Bayliss, a veteran Labour councillor and local resident canvassing for the 2002 local elections, is under no illusions why his Cinderheath seat is threatened by BNP candidate Philip Bailey and Glenn, his resident enforcer: 'How could there be a Labour Party when there was no labour left for it to represent? [. . .] Even the call-centre jobs were going to Bangalore. This was the town's position in the new world order' (Cartwright 2010: 51). Despite his disparaging characterization of the BNP as 'far-right crackpots', he recognizes the far-right 'would get out all sorts of characters who hadn't been bothered to vote before' by capitalizing on 'a strength of feeling, an undercurrent, a lingering resentment [. . .] throbbing from the streets all around him' (2010: 50; 110). His remarks not only anticipate Cameron's sneering dismissal of UKIP as 'loonies and fruitcakes', but unintentionally foreshadow the 'silent' voters who would fundamentally subvert media predictions prior to the referendum. Residents of the once fabled 'workshop of the world' are cognisant of 'the usual line about the BNP coming in from outside to exploit the vulnerabilities' of their ward yet retain an unease towards New Labour's multicultural vision for England (2010: 240). As Ford and Goodwin remind us, white, older, less educated men in areas of economic decline formed the basis of BNP support in this period, while citizens voting for nationalist parties were much more likely to list the economy as a pressing concern (2014: 274). Michael Sandel identifies how working-class voters not only feel as if 'the economy [has] left them behind, but so has the culture, that the sources of their dignity, the dignity of labour, have been eroded and mocked by developments with globalisation, the rise of finance' (qtd. in Cowley 2016). It is important to note, however, the limitations in applying the label 'white working-class' to these communities; as O'Brien points out, it is often 'a construction which deflects from the political ideology which caused the problems in the first place' (2020: 17).

Fearing the rewriting of their neglected landscape, the resistance of residents to plans for a new mosque to be built over the abandoned Cinderheath steel works site is immediately evident in the scrawled BNP slogans on the canalside wall. Jim comes to understand that his task of rejuvenating the Cinderheath ward is less about the practical implementation of social policies and more of a symbolic endeavour: 'To undo the rust. To heal all wounds. To raise the dead' (Cartwright 2010: 261). After sneaking a marginal victory over the BNP, he ruminates on why it feels more like an electoral defeat given the rising racial and class-based tensions in the area. The release of *Heartland* in 2009 coincided with a surge in support for the BNP at the European elections ensuring Cartwright's fateful vision of a 'new extreme-right West Midlands heartlands', emerging 'in reaction to terrorism, political correctness and multiculturalism', fictionalizes the origins of the burgeoning populist revolt (2010: 30). Forewarning of the democratic deficit beginning to emerge, coupled with a general disillusionment with politics and a decline in institutional trust, the novel illuminates the activation of a dormant anger which, as the final chapter will demonstrate, was set to erupt in destructive ways.

Although Cartwright charts the rise of the BNP in this period, it would be UKIP (emerging from the vacuum left by the BNP) that would exploit this animosity more acutely in the run-up to the referendum and position themselves as a more respectable anti-immigration party in comparison to the far-right movements of the English Defence League and Britain First. Drawing from a pool of disaffection and marginalization, and summoning a Churchillian wartime spirit, UKIP challenged the English to repossess their country, giving political purpose to a disillusioned electorate seeking new governing frameworks for the expression of the English national consciousness. The surge in support for UKIP in the 2014 election demonstrated that British Euroscepticism remained a decidedly English affair. In their analysis of UKIP and the European far-fight, Goodwin and Milazzo (2017) argue a deeper anxiety lies behind this surface fear of immigration and EU membership: namely the erosion of national identity and traditions that define the cultural imaginary. Appropriately, while *Heartland* engages with the BNP's brief and geographically limited electoral success in the early 2000s, Cartwright's *Iron Towns* documents the key sources of voter frustration that created the determining conditions for the English revolt and motivated the surge in electoral support for UKIP in the West Midlands. The anger and nationalist resentment inherent to Cartwright's earlier novel has mutated into melancholy and loss, attaining a more hauntological edge: 'Nostalgia has replaced fear' (2016: 68). Whereas once the Black Country was the centre of England industrial heartland, the 'fires are all out now' and the region 'leans in on itself', with its abandoned works sites and disused factories symbolizing 'the long slow drift into silence' of the 'great ruined cities in the north and west' (2016: 81). Characters haunt deindustrialized spaces resonating with the spectral memories of long-extinguished furnaces, while warehouses sport tattered St George's flags amid stretches of abandoned wasteland. Speaking on his fixation with the industrial heritage of the Black Country, Cartwright acknowledges 'it is a really strong identity, but then it is a problem when the source of that no longer exists. It risks being backward-looking and nostalgic'; accordingly, his characters continue to uphold 'aspects of industrial society, but instead of it being affirming and something to be proud of, it is corrupting and corroding' (qtd. in O'Brien 2015: 410; 411). The novel reinforces the extent to which Cartwright writes the histories and cultural concerns of the local community onto the contours of the landscape and architecture of the Black Country, summoning the spectre of Thatcherite social policy and the fault lines of 1980s class warfare. The smouldering fires of the Iron Towns, representative of the lingering anger and resentment of the inhabitants, exposes how the landscape is intensely politicized.

The narrative revolves around the fate of Irontowns football club, which is facing relegation and liquidation following the dark days of the 1980s. Unlike Cartwright's earlier novel, *How I Killed Margaret Thatcher* (2012), the lack of an outright authorial assault on Thatcherite socioeconomic policy is more damning for its absence: Thatcher remains a visceral spectre haunting the deindustrialized landscape. *Iron Towns* marks Cartwright's return to football as a viable source of local communion which has been erased by managed decline, with Anvil Yards football ground haunted by 'the ghost cries of great crowds [. . .] the clang of metal, the roar of a furnace' (2016: 5). Liam Corwen, a former professional footballer, is a relic of a better time, finishing his professional days as a journeyman for his local club. Confronted with an inheritance of loss in his region, Liam negotiates his past by securing himself in communal memories of the Black Country's past industrial strength. The titular Iron Towns thus become a symbolic space for the hauntological persistence of working-class nostalgia and a metonymic landscape for the structural unemployment and widespread austerity affecting twenty-first-century England.

At times the novel reinforces *Jerusalem*'s Blakean lament for a forgotten and mythic England, suggesting deindustrial melancholia to be a motivating factor in reanimating the populist resurgence. UKIP's downmarket, pub-corner patriotism drew on the disenfranchisement of many citizens who felt marginalized or ignored by mainstream politics. Cartwright's characters, 'living here in the ruins, in the shadows [. . .] becoming invisible' (2016: 263), search for some form of redemption, some means of assuring their restoration and renewal, while navigating the machinations of far-right parties only too willing to exploit the nostalgia and bitterness of 'Albion: the White Land' (2016: 84). In fictionalizing the decline of the Black Country, Cartwright's elegiac novels are saturated by the blighted hopes of forgotten men – threnodies for the broken promises and cancelled futures of England.[12] Yet, as Cartwright warns, his Black Country characters are not impotent spectres haunting a diminished terrain, but capable of finding new political allegiances and sources of identification to give voice to their socioeconomic and political marginalization: 'the iron towns rust, and you might think them all ghosts if you think of them at all, but do not be mistaken, they will not die, they take new forms' (2016: 272). His deindustrialized landscapes prove to be fertile ground for psychogeographical introspection, revealing not only what the community once was, but what it could be again.

This threat of political revolt as a response to geographic economic inequality and the decline of industry is even evident in his debut novel *The Afterglow*: 'Yow tek these thousands o blokes, working, mekkin summat [. . .] An yer just crush it. Just like tha. An yow expect everything to goo on as normal afterwards. Well, things doh work like tha' (Cartwright 2004: 118–19). Excavating these roots of deindustrialization and its psychological impact on the inhabitants, *Iron Towns* finds renewed and

---

[12] Novels of deindustrialization and national identity (given the demographic of the industry) have tended to focus on men. Nick Hubble has also drawn attention to the reduced focus on working-class women's experience in British fiction, identifying Pat Barker's *Union Street* (1982) and Zadie Smith's *NW* (2013) as disparate examples where female characters attempt to 'escape the lure of nostalgia' affecting their communities, to which Livi Michael's *Under a Thin Moon* (1992) and Catherine O'Flynn's *What Was Lost* (2007) can be added (2018: 285).

urgent expression in the form of Brexit, forcing the reminder that 'whatever comes afterwards simply amplifies the past' and necessitating a re-evaluation of how English nationalism was understood prior to the fateful vote (Cartwright 2016: 42). Much like post-imperial melancholy, contemporary English nationalism tends to look to the past for its distinctiveness and animating energy, particularly given that the erosion of established touchstones of Englishness has not been accompanied by the formation of viable sources of identification. Cartwright's persistent return to Dudley as the focus for his prescient realist narratives of working-class life betrays a personal desire to address how his left-behind community can overcome the dominant neoliberal forces that have created a divided Britain. As the final chapter will demonstrate, with a close reading of Cartwright's post-Brexit novel *The Cut*, Brexit would become the most salient means for these working-class communities to 'take back control' of their culture, their neighbourhoods, and their identities, voting for 'outsider' parties who most accurately voiced their valid concerns: 'We are the iron roar that you thought you'd silenced. We sing of better days. Better days to come' (2016: 274).[13]

Nicola Barker's *The Yips* (2012) anticipates a related sociopolitical anxiety, gesturing to the strong undercurrent of pre-Brexit xenophobia within English communities. As discussed in the previous section, the image of a white imperial nationhood persists in the cultural imaginary; immigration consequently poses a direct threat to the dominant discourses of national identity. Set in Luton in 2006, which enjoys a history of EDL support and anti-Islamic aggression, Barker's novel anticipates how anti-EU protestations and more general racial logics were to be fused in the minds of the electorate for the purposes of national protectionism. This fusion is encapsulated in the haunting and overt racism of Reggie, a recently deceased, local white supremacist and football hooligan. Reggie not only holds a reputation as 'Luton's premier Nazi', but leads a local campaign in protest against the imposition of the EU metric system, earning him the title 'Upholder of the Sanctity of the Great British Pint' (2013: 141). Such banal Euroscepticism was linked in obscure ways to anti-immigrant discourse in British politics. Returning from negotiations following the 1975 referendum, Wilson claimed to have saved Britain from 'Eurobeer': 'An imperial pint is good enough for me and the British people, and we want it to stay that way' (qtd in O'Toole 2018a: 105). During his time at *The Telegraph*, Boris Johnson invented anti-EU invectives which manufactured a spurious struggle for English culinary independence, composing 'foam-flecked hymns of hate to the latest Euro-infamy: the ban on the prawn cocktail crisp' (Johnson 2002c). He was to revive similar fictitious allegations in the referendum, accusing the European Commission of placing a ban on bendy bananas.

Sara Upstone identifies Nicola Barker's Luton as a counterpoint to London's multicultural status with the Bedfordshire town's British Asian community relegated to the margins of the narrative and subjected to racial abuse. Despite its close proximity to the capital, which imposes itself on surrounding areas with its 'enduring imaginary physicality', Luton is 'always consigned to an imaginary immateriality' and the novel continues Barker's record of setting her works in 'less documented places' (2018: 51).

---

[13] The Leave vote was twenty points higher in towns which had suffered economic decline (Jennings, Stoker and Warren 2018).

If Brexit was a protest vote by those excluded from positions of social power and an attempt to reverse this sense of political disenfranchisement, then Barker's Luton becomes representative of this belligerent backlash against both Westminster and the media by marginalized communities. Given Luton's subsequent decision to leave the EU (returning a 56% Leave vote), *The Yips* indicates how the existing reinforcement of ethnic divisions and racial hierarchies in the town – hidden under the guise of patriotic nationalism – were already ideologically set against the more cosmopolitan orientations of the EU.

Tales of Brexit past

Once we ruled over an empire
So it feels like some kind of defeat
To comply with rules drawn up by strangers
And measure in metres not feet.

(Bragg 2017)

As the EU referendum inched ever closer, a number of insightful novels not only diagnosed the national pathology by focusing on the politics of race and the debasement of white superiority but also express a clear affinity with a sense of regional *place*, drawing attention to the ties between the English and their natural landscape. Ben Myers' *The Gallows Pole* (2017) speaks directly to the contemporary moment in spite of its historical setting. Myers sets his narrative in an eighteenth-century Yorkshire Moors, retelling the brutal lives of the Cragg Vale Coiners, a band of forgers led by David 'King' Hartley. Running a successful protection racket, Hartley holds court as a nativist 'king that doesn't need no fucking foreign tongue from across no foreign waters', nursing an intimate nostalgia for a time when 'you defended and you fought for your corner of England under the great green canopy' (Myers 2017: 40; 56–7). Hartley's realm is, of course, not threatened by the threat of the post-war European project but the impending industrial revolution which will irrevocably alter the landscape of his beloved England. Yet the same social schisms and sense of national declension which characterize present-day England erupt in Myers' fragile society as left-behind itinerant labourers look to the safety of walls and borders as protective shields against both foreign influence and the incursion of modernity.

As Kumar explains, England (and Britain more broadly) has defined itself against Europe since the Reformation, and the desire to preserve national identity against foreign influence bleeds into Britain's resistance towards the bureaucratic machinations of Brussels. Although entry into Europe offered 'a heaven-sent opportunity for the British to renegotiate their identities, both among themselves and in relation to other peoples [. . .] dissolving hardened and outdated national identities', Britain obstinately rejected alternate configurations of nationhood in recent years and assumed a vituperative stance (Kumar 2003a: 241). Many commentators gesture to the Reformation and Henry VIII's split from Rome's sphere of influence – which Spiering terms 'the first "Brexit"' – as relevant analogous events to Britain's act of political withdrawal, neglecting that the Reformation was a European-wide, German-led movement (2020: 163). For Stephen Wall, 'the Reformation in England was as much a rejection of Continental encroachment as of Roman Catholicism' (2008: 204). Siobhan O'Connor argues Philippa Gregory's historical novels *The King's Curse* (2014) and *The Taming of the Queen* (2015) can be read in the relation to the Brexit vote, 'aligning contemporary figures with their historical counterparts' and offering 'narratives of national grievance, permeated by yearning for a long hegemony and a desire to return to a bygone age' (O'Connor 2020: 232; 235). Gregory's narratorial concentration on the defence of national borders from foreign forces, the ongoing struggle to uphold national sovereignty, and the devious nature of Tudor plots which threaten the native Plantagenet sphere of influence, certainly speaks to the post-Brexit moment and illustrates how contemporary markers of English consciousness have their historical antecedents, developing clear continuities between our national past and present.

For author Paul Kingsnorth, a spirited advocate for environmental reform, to dismiss nostalgia as 'backward-looking' is not 'progressive: is it ahistorical, and culturally naïve': 'what is characterised as "nostalgia" is often, in fact, a recognition that something valuable that once existed is in danger of being lost' (2009: 274). Kingsnorth, a Leave supporter labelled the 'Bard of the Brexiteers', suggests the EU fulfils a rather otiose purpose and holds the polity responsible for contributing to the corrosion of English customs and landscapes. In his essay 'Brexit & the Culture of Progress', Kingsnorth forms direct links between the destructive modernizing tendencies of the EU and the erosion of traditional British landscapes and ways of life. Small spasms of populist revolt are evident under the guise of agrarian reform. Drawing on John Berger's initial criticisms of the EEC, he singles out the EU's lamentable Common Agricultural Policy, claiming that its destructive programmes and practices have had a little detrimental effect on the English rural landscape than 'any other single instrument' in the last 500 years (Kingsnorth 2016). Kingsnorth also launches an attack on Green Party politicians more intent on positioning the EU as a 'benevolent sugar daddy' – claiming the progressive cosmopolitical polity is not a superstate but a 'superdefender' – than tackling environmental destruction or advancing a 'benevolent green nationalism' to ensure the radical re-localization of British regions (Kingsnorth 2017). In his 2015 essay, 'Rescuing the English', Kingsnorth also bemoans the framing of English history within the school system – which often begins with the Battle of Hastings in 1066, 'the date at which England was colonised' – for instilling a sense of victimhood into our national imaginary (2015b). He even attempts to reclaim the term 'Little Englander', suggesting it implies a more ethical nationhood which arrests England's influence at its borders and avoids more 'imperial designs' in favour of a 'radical parochialism', tied intimately to local and regional politics of place (Kingsnorth 2017).

Kingsnorth's novel *The Wake* (2014) builds upon his state-of-the-nation critiques by digging deep into the roots of English history. Set during the Norman conquest, *The Wake* develops clear parallels between the struggles of Edward Buckmaster, a Lincolnshire farmer, against Norman incursions, and British resistance towards the bureaucratic incursions of the EU. The novel's concentration on this turbulent period, in which Buckmaster witnesses his social orders and political institutions overturned by continental invaders, captures a specifically English sense of cultural disenfranchisement evident in the contemporary climate. For fellow author Adam Thorpe *The Wake* serves as 'a modern parallel with our own dispossessed times' (Thorpe 2014). The novel's ethnogeographic focus is almost a eulogy to a lost, innate Englishness which has opened itself up to a malevolent foreignness: 'my folc was in the fenns before the crist cum to angland this ground is in our bodigs deop' (2015a: 18). Kingsnorth's characters suffer the loss of place-identity and experience the fading of locality in landscapes layered with personal meaning, reduced to lowly Calibans dispossessed of territory and honour by manipulative Prosperos. In emphasizing how a magical sense of *memorial* English place and a positive cultural narrative can act as an antidote to the bureaucratic encroachment of a spiritless globalization, Kingsnorth reminds us that a nation 'may be a story, but it is not a fiction' (2015b).

In a 2009 interview, Kazuo Ishiguro admitted he remained 'fascinated with memory', expressing a desire to move away from personal recollections towards national remembrance: 'communities and countries remember and forget their own history. There are perhaps times when a nation *should* forget and when you *can* cover things up and leave things unresolved because it would stir things up' (Matthews 2009: 118 – emphasis in original). Ishiguro's melancholic *The Buried Giant* (2015) marks the point at which we witness a purposeful turn from individual to collective memory in his work, with Ishiguro himself acknowledging this subtle shift in authorial focus: 'I knew that I wanted to talk about societal memory: how a nation remembers and forgets' (qtd. in Rukeyser 2015). Ishiguro is not often considered a particularly political writer (his novels rarely providing overt state-of-the-nation critiques in the style of Jonathan Coe or Philip Hensher), but his body of work does betray a sustained engagement with national identity, memory and loss. *The Remains of the Day* (1989), published over thirty years ago, not only explored the danger of imperial nostalgic regression which often whitewashes the national past and prevents a mature reconsideration of English culture, but accentuated the need for political responsibility and the related dangers of simplifying populist rhetoric. Lord Darlington's denunciation of the claim that 'the will of the people is the wisest arbitrator', for example, rings particularly true given the nature of recent political events (1999: 197). More importantly, Ishiguro has been uncharacteristically vocal on post-Brexit negotiations; in an article for the *Financial Times* he bemoaned that the transformation 'of Europe from a slaughterhouse of total war and totalitarian regimes to a much-envied region of liberal democracies living in near-borderless friendship – should now be so profoundly undermined by such a myopic process' (Ishiguro 2016).

Although *The Buried Giant* is not a post-Brexit novel – it was not written as a response to the political events of 2016 and preceded the fateful vote – Ishiguro has proven himself to be a rather prescient author. The novel was initially greeted with confusion by critics in 2015, unconvinced of Ishiguro's foray into the fantasy genre, but has since been re-evaluated in the post-Brexit period as a haunting reminder of nationalist violence and the mythical construction of Englishness in particular. In spite of its fantastical basis, set in a land populated by ogres, plagues and dragons, the novel speaks to the contemporary moment, unearthing and deconstructing Britain's foundational myths to further detail how contemporaneous events continue to expose the ongoing fallacious nature of our national origins. Further, the timing of Ishiguro's Nobel Prize win (during subsequent Brexit negotiations) is rather telling, as is the committee's curious comment on his body of work, citing his ability to 'uncover the abyss beneath our illusory sense of connection with the world' (Nobel Prize 2017). By questioning the construction of nationhood and the unreliability of cultural and historical memory, *The Buried Giant* serves as an urgent parable for Brexit Britain: a country hung up on the hauntology and spectral nature of its national past, whose own sense of connection with the world is now up for debate.

The opening lines of the novel speak directly to the contemporary reader, immediately confronting us with the constructedness of our island nation. Ishiguro avoids painting a peaceful portrait of an idyllic and pure Albion in which a slumbering Englishness is born, but rather strikes an almost apologetic tone:

> You would have searched a long time for the sort of winding lane or tranquil meadow for which England later became celebrated. There were instead miles of desolate, uncultivated land [. . .] I am sorry to paint such a picture of our country at that time, but there you are. (2015: 3)

Set in approximately 450 AD, in a post-Arthurian Britain, the narrative traces the personal journey of an elderly couple named Axl and Beatrice whose entire village appears to be suffering from some form of cultural amnesia. Though the elderly couple initially set off to find their son's village, their journey swiftly becomes a quest to dispel the mist of forgetfulness, joined on their way by Wistan, a Saxon warrior, Sir Gawain, the ageing knight of King Arthur's famous tales, and Edwin, a young Saxon boy. It is soon revealed that the mist is the product of the dragon Querig – the result of a spell cast by Merlin to make the nation's inhabitants forget the mass genocide on colonizing Saxons during Arthur's rule. Appropriately, in his Nobel Prize speech, Ishiguro debated the merits of a wilful cultural amnesia in order to prevent a recurrent pattern of national bloodshed, questioning 'Are there times when forgetting is the only way to stop cycles of violence, or to stop a society disintegrating into chaos and war? On the other hand, can stable, free nations really be built on foundations of wilful amnesia?' (2017: 11). By aiming to kill Querig, the group hope that this mist will dissipate, enabling the restoration of personal and communal memories; however, in dispelling the mist, the festering, underlying animosity between Britons and Saxons – predicated on the uneasy tension between those considered to be truly British and those marked as foreigners – will once again rear its head with destructive consequences.

According to Carmen Borbely, Querig assumes a unique interpretative function in the narrative, condensing 'threats of aggressive dissolution levelled at the body politic and at its collective memory', and emerging as a 'beneficent figure of containment that protects, preserves and endlessly defers the assignation of sense to this collective memory' (2016: 23). In dampening and almost erasing the memories of the populace, she in turn protects the eruption of further bloodshed between the Britons and the Saxons: an obscure and questionable form of national defence. Under such a reading, it is easy to state the obvious cosmopolitical parallels. The EU, with its roots in the 1951 Treaty of Paris and the 1957 Treaty of Rome, was originally established to stabilize a war-torn Europe, produce diplomatic stability, and prevent further eruptions of nationalist violence. The proposed extermination of the dragon Querig, much like the dismantling of supranational agreements, holds the potential to generate cultural divergence as opposed to the maintenance of an uneasy convergence. The Brexit vote was sold to the electorate as a similar form of national awakening, described as 'a swordthrust in the dragon's heart that would end the suffering of all good people', without a subsequent consideration of 'its unexamined effect on the intricate, fragile fabric of peace, regulation and exchange the British live in' (Meek 2019: 9).

Axl and Beatrice's desire for Wistan to succeed in his battle with Gawain, the protector of Querig, even if it means awakening the metaphorical buried giant, is the ethical fulcrum upon which the narrative uneasily rests. While Querig is a plague upon the land, the removal of Gawain as defender of the English myth will disinter buried memories of past wars, restarting a vicious cycle of ethnic and sectarian vengeance. But this tentative peace is predicated on a lie, buttressed by an historical amnesia which merely exposes the post-Arthurian nation to be an imagined community held together by tenuous bonds and reinforced by historical error and concealment. And yet as Gawain points out, British history is built on this very practice of historical obscuration and erasure, with national imaginaries reliant upon the elision of the very truths which threaten the body politic. Ishiguro has Gawain employ Blakean rhetoric to force his companions to consider the dark underbelly of England's 'pleasant green carpet': 'I dare say, sir, our whole country is this way. A fine green valley [But] Dig its soil, and not far beneath the daises and buttercups [. . .] lie the remains of old slaughter' (2015: 171). The nubilous British terrain of *The Buried Giant* is marked by historical signatures and scarred by material traces of the past.

Ishiguro's resurrection of the figure of Gawain for this narrative function, a mythological figure whose fame and prestige lies at the heart of the mythological English sublime, is rather appropriate. As James Meek reminds us, myth is, after all:

> a story that can be retold by anyone, with infinite variation, and still be recognisable as itself [. . .] It's an instrument by which people simplify, rationalise and retell social complexities. It's a means to haul the abstract, the global and the relative into the realm of the concrete, the local and the absolute. It's a way to lay claim to faith in certain values. (2019: 8)

Once a formidable figure in the court of Arthur, an institution of national vigour and strength, Ishiguro now paints Gawain as a backward-looking old man, a haunting reminder of times past now unable to face emergent geopolitical realities: 'His armour was frayed and rusted, though no doubt he had done all he could to preserve it. His tunic, once white, showed repeated mending [. . .] a sorry sight' (2015: 119). His tattered appearance aligns with what can be interpreted as Ishiguro's active attempt to disrupt the English sublime, peeling away the purity of national mythology, signified by Gawain's 'once white' tunic. The character of Gawain is, like Stevens in *The Remains of the Day*, deeply invested in the false, essentialist constructedness of his position: the belief that he is part of a great tradition. His readiness to comply with Arthur and Merlin's national designs, comforting himself in the mythology of the English sublime, merely alludes to the extent to which nations can remain in stubborn denial about their historical pasts and refuse to face the reality of the present.[14]

Ishiguro has spoken at length on the mythical construction of Englishness and the complicity of the English people in knowingly and willingly sustaining 'that myth of what England is like' (Moore and Sontheimer 2005). Brexiteers during and after the referendum relied on such political tactics and rhetoric, evoking English traditions that awakened a confused and misplaced sense of national pride in voters, and attaching a vague Euroscepticism to historic moments of national defence. Further, Ishiguro's narrative is set in a post-Arthurian Britain, 'the mythological root of British sovereignty'; the 'fulcrum point' at which a 'restive minority population' are considered to be threatening the well-being of the nation's people (Vernon and Miller 2018: 70). In narrating Wistan's victory over the fabled knight – effectively a victory for remembrance over the elision or manipulation of the past – Ishiguro effectively disinters and disturbs the mythical sanctity of the English sublime. After all, although the Britons were, as Ishiguro explains, 'an indigenous people' fighting 'against the migrants who were in increasing numbers taking over parts of the island', the Saxons 'later became the English; they basically took over the whole country' (qtd. in Rukeyser 2015). In turn, defeating the dragon is not merely a form of chivalric victory but an unravelling of an intangible Englishness that has survived and mutated throughout history.

Clear parallels can be established, then, between this fictional post-Arthurian landscape and the increasingly fractured national terrain of the twenty-first century. Returning to Acheson's famous declaration that 'Britain has lost an Empire and is yet to find a role', in the present moment Britain appears to have lost a role and still be missing an Empire, struggling to remember or retain its identity following its geopolitical transition from a global power to a diminished ex-EU member state. This sense of anxiety and confusion lies at the heart of the novel and of contemporary English culture. It is the foreign invader – the Saxon – who threatens the elusive and intangible nature of post-Arthurian Britain, just as it is the contemporary foreigner who so threatens the sacred purity of our national mythology and its obscuration of our ethnopolitical past. What is threatening to re-emerge in the novel is a divided kingdom: a rudderless island vulnerable to further external influence and fresh mythologizing. It remains to be seen whether the defenestration of Querig will prove to be an act of national self-harm; indeed, the closing scenes of the novel are rather revealing. Wistan alludes to the coming attacks by the Saxon people once the mist has dissipated, warning how 'the giant, once well buried, now stirs' (Ishiguro 2015: 340). As Ivan Stacy notes, however, Wistan makes this speech while standing at the 'site of a

---

[14] James Lovegrove's *Age of Legends* (2019) is a fascinating take on the English sublime, depicting a post-Brexit Britain stripped of its elite status within the G7 and forced to cast about for alliances with dubious nations with questionable human rights records. Prime Minister and leader of the Resurrection Party, Derek Drake, full of Johnsonian bluster and powered by Trumpian rhetoric, aims to make Britain great again by defending British soil from immigrants: 'The time for a multicultural nation was over. That experiment had failed' (105). In response to such dangerous levels of populism, victims of Drake's regime are resurrected as iconic figures of national folklore to counteract the wounding of the national psyche, 'the country's sick and we're the symptoms', creating a fantastical form of cultural recuperation which gestures to the mythic origins of nationhood (2019: 185).

cairn [...] a cultural marker of memory' to signify the giant's passing, as opposed to the site of the giant's body itself, insinuating that unless there is a 'respect for the content of memory', any potential reconciliation will be circumvented by the continuation of fabricated histories or cultural misconceptions by splintered factions (2019: 14; 18).

At the close of the novel, Axl ponders, 'Who knows what will come when quick-tongued men make ancient grievances rhyme with fresh desire for land and conquest' (2015: 323). Through Axl, Ishiguro reiterates his own anxieties for a future in which destructive 'ideologies and tribal nationalisms proliferate', even utilizing his Nobel Prize speech to comment on the peace and stability of late-twentieth-century Europe in comparison to the contemporary moment in which a Little Englander racism 'is once again on the rise, stirring beneath our civilised streets like a buried monster awakening' (2017: 14–15). His comments recall Tim Parks' assessment that if the EU has hardly been 'inspiring, it has not yet bred any monsters' (Parks 2016). While it is therefore tempting to agree with James Wood when he claims *The Buried Giant*'s allegory 'manages somehow to be at once too literal and too vague', Ishiguro's fantastical novel carries stark political implications and speaks to our uncertain moment by articulating emergent divisions within English society more narrowly (Wood 2015). Through the guise of fantasy literature, Ishiguro has unintentionally produced perhaps the most prescient and hauntological Brexlit novel, dramatizing how the interdependent ties of community can be threatened or undone by the myopic violence of nation states and the yearning temptation to recover the past. In reading *The Buried Giant* against recent cultural and cosmopolitical developments, the narrative engages with contemporary manifestations of post-conflict resolution and suggests ways by which England – a country disrupted by the hauntology of its past within the British constellation – can come to terms with its historical legacy. Ishiguro gestures to the folly in assuming a backward-looking national perspective, or sustaining an illusion of grandeur to protect us from our diminished position, and insinuates the need to tear down a fabricated national mythology in seeking reconciliation and restitution for the transgressions of the past. As Axl and Beatrice discover at the close of the novel, however, in attempting to transcend our troubled present to achieve a shared future, and attend to the wounds dividing our fragile and disunited kingdom, the distance between us may be too great.

To emphasize the pivotal role of ethnonationalism in the English revolt debate and critique the ways by which Englishness was primarily racially coded in political discourse, this chapter has naturally concentrated primarily on the glorification of English origins and symbolic defences of the realm in resistance to contemporary expressions of multicultural community. As Kevin Davey warned at the turn of the millennium, 'We must urgently attend to the archaic and anachronistic narratives, articulations, alterities and abjections, the many conscious and unconscious horizons of the imaginary Englands that deny our new social reality'; only then can we 'break down the inflexible and exclusive identities and narratives of the Anglo-British, destroying forms of racialised cultural protectionism and pre-empting the revival of an English fundamentalism' (1999: 4). The focus on *white* working-class culture in post-Brexit debates, however, neglects that ethnic-minority groups 'remain disproportionately worse off across a range of indicators in the areas of employment, housing, health and poverty'; this 'play to class as being the preserve of white people is, therefore, at best naïve, at worst, an incendiary racial nativism' (Valluvan 2019: 10). The non-profit organization Operation Black Vote (OBV) ran a campaign from 2015 onwards encouraging Black British citizens to vote, in an attempt to counter low turnout and prevent white cultural fragility from defining debates surrounding the racialization of contemporary Englishness. Black British authors such as Caryl Phillips, Andrea Levy and David Dabydeen have responded to England's ongoing identity crisis and signalled the unprecedented diversification of the national landscape by challenging monocultural conceptions of English identity. According to Mike Phillips, major changes to the culture were 'rapidly rendering archaic the old view of Englishness as an ethnic club' with authors left to 'reinterpret exactly what Englishness and Britishness mean' (2004: 2016). That being said, Black British writing during this period does not contain a strong evaluation of Britain's place in the European constellation. As Aarthi Vadde explains, Black British writers 'attended more to the enigmas and dissatisfactions of long-term residence in a nation that never quite treated members of minority groups as full citizens', going some way to explaining the paucity of Black British literary engagement with the EU (2015: 70). The tendency for BME groups to self-identify as 'more British than English', avoiding the politicization of Englishness which accompanied Euroscepticism, reinforces such an assessment (Wyn Jones et al. 2012). Afua Hirsch has recently suggested non-white citizens were even denied this marker of inclusivity, relegated to a position of 'Brit(ish)', while John Curtice and Anthony Heath conclude that 'Englishness is not something with which many of those from an ethnic minority background feel much empathy' (2018, 2009: 58).

Nonetheless, several novels do confront anxieties which would be integral to the Brexit debate. Monica Ali's *Brick Lane* provides a situated assessment of the struggles surrounding the banal cosmopolitanization of English culture, 'in which everyday nationalism is circumvented and undermined and we experience ourselves integrated into global processes and phenomena' (Beck 2002: 28). The Lionhearts, a far-right wing organization redolent of the English Defence League, represent a small minority of the aggrieved and socioeconomically disenfranchised white underclass who heavily supported nationalist parties in the years leading to the referendum and influenced the Brexit vote. Their local turf war with the Bengal Tigers, a group intent on protecting Muslim rights and culture, identifies the encroaching clash between competing visions of England, anticipates the importance of Islamophobia to the Brexit debate, and reveals the extent to which Englishness continues to be racially coded. The struggle to revive dormant forms of imperial ideology can therefore also be interpreted as a reaction to celebratory multiculturalism and demographic change: normative threats which unsettle not only the security of English culture but the integrity of the British cultural formations. By focusing primarily on the Bengal Tigers and its active members, Ali disturbs the supremacy of the patriotic Lionhearts, who haunt the fringes of the narrative, and unintentionally diagnoses the feeling of displacement reported by white citizens and the hysterical claim that the colonizers have become the colonized.

Dabydeen's *Disappearance* (1993) carves a purposeful distinction between England and Britain, exposing how new conceptions of Englishness and anglicized privilege are complicit with, and influenced by, the colonial coordinates of Empire. In questioning, 'Was it not always thus in England [. . .] the drift into deliberate unconsciousness;

any awakening being a jolt of patriotic sentiment?', Dabydeen's narrator anticipates the victimhood nationalism which was to emerge around the millennium following Maastricht and devolution settlements (1993: 178). Andrea Levy's *Small Island* (2004) contains a similar strain of cultural disaffection, lamenting the erasure of colonial contributions during the Second World War from the national cultural imaginary (and the victimization of Windrush citizens decades after their arrival to British shores). The title itself alludes both to the dawning realization of white English citizens that their nation had become visibly diminished in the wake of decolonization and the dissolution of Empire, coupled with the acknowledgement by the Windrush generation that they must reconcile the idealized conception of the English sublime memorialized in novels and textbooks with the brutal reality of post-war English life. Forecasting the cultural conflicts which will emerge from the spread of multi-racial communities, Levy identifies the maintenance of ethnonationalist paradigms within post-war society (exemplified by characters in the selected novels of Barnes, Hawes and King) which resist any mongrelization of the English character. Bernardine Evaristo has emerged as a crucial voice in Black British literature, with her body of work containing a clear effort to redefine and update the national imaginary, challenging the misconception that Black British citizens lacked any substantive historical or cultural connections to their fellow citizens, engendering a sense of national illegitimacy. While *Lara* (1997) introduces her criticism of Britain as an 'island, the "Great" Tippexed out of it/tiny amid massive floating continents', *Soul Tourists* (2005) advances a re-evaluation of Black British identity within both Britain and Europe, remapping 'Europe's past by recounting the lives of important black men and women who have been marginalised or effaced from official histories' (1997: 140; Gui 2015: 233). Evaristo's *Girl, Woman, Other* (2019) has recently delivered a forceful anti-Brexit corrective to claims of ethnonationalism; her polyphonic novel claims Britain's recent symbolic departure from Europe forces the country 'down the reactionary road' and makes 'fascism fashionable again' (42). Similar concerns are raised in Xiaolu Guo's *A Lover's Discourse* (2020), in which a Chinese woman moves to London hoping to find a new home but struggles to decipher this new 'non-European world' (15). The referendum result dominates the media and citizens are 'Brexhausted' from agonizing over the potential fallout (2020: 251).

Caryl Phillips, an integral member of the movement Writers Against Brexit, wades more directly into the Euro-debate, arguing that the memory of Empire – an 'ugly word that no one in Parliament will say today' – played a significant role in the EU referendum (Denny 2019). In his 1987 travelogue *The European Tribe*, Phillips lambasted the bigotry within post-war Europe, critiquing the ongoing disenfranchisement of Black citizens within prevailing Eurocentric frames of thought. His 2003 novel *A Distant Shore* (2003) narrativized this bigotry within England specifically. Phillips' protagonist Dorothy recounts her father bemoaning 'the fact that we were giving up our English birthright and getting lost in a United States of Europe', accentuating the debilitating monoculturalism of rural locales and the Euroscepticism of older citizens who resent the intrusion of the transnational into the national frame (2003: 27). In his essay 'The Pioneers: Fifty Years of Caribbean Migration to Britain', Phillips engages with his West Indian heritage, suggesting that the blank canvas of the white cliffs of Dover possess a dual symbolic function: a reminder of the narrow and insular qualities of the English, concretizing the racially exclusive political plea to 'Keep Britain White', but also a more inclusive and hopeful territorial marker for those escaping persecution or seeking a new home (2002: 280). Coastlines, after all, operate as both a 'border and a porous point of entry [...] so the cliffs remind us that we are a nation of immigrants' (Baggini 2012). Rather appropriately, during the referendum campaign the cliffs were utilized by opposed factions to champion competing narratives. Vote Leave projected 'Let's Take Back Control' onto the chalk cliffs provoking the organization Global Justice Now to project '#RefugeesWelcome' in response, challenging the media's overwhelming concentration on immigration during the campaign and offering an alternate national vision founded on cosmopolitan hospitality and common humanity. Dover, however, has often been a prime site for rampant Euroscepticism, and went on to vote Leave by 62 per cent. The white cliffs of Dover, then, serve as both Britain's outward-facing window to Europe and a visually arresting bulwark against foreign invasion. The admission of Dominic Raab, former Brexit minister, that he had never appreciated the integral role Dover plays in generating cross-channel trade, testifies to the disarray within the post-Brexit Conservative government, with its lazy appointment of inexperienced cabinet ministers ignorant of glaring geopolitical realities.

As this chapter has argued, the nostalgic historicization of Englishness in public, media and political discourses was a significant factor in understanding attitudes towards the EU and the fear of encroaching external forces on a dominant Anglocentric culture. Colin Wright correctly argues that 'reactions to the very word "Europe" serve as a reliable litmus test' for the 'defensiveness and paranoia' surrounding the perceived erosion of an idealized England in the traditionalist Conservative psyche (2007: 171). The politicized narratives in this chapter suggest Englishness and Europeanness to be incompatible rather than mutually reinforcing cultural identities, gesturing to the ways by which certain political factions draw from past scenes of English glory to buttress the maintenance of traditional national ideologies and provide a comfort blanket to those threatened by rapid cultural transformations. These aforementioned discourses relating to an endangered or vanishing Englishness were widely apparent both during and after the EU referendum. English nationalism, as Gardiner explains, is 'a very diffuse phenomenon, stretching from a simple understanding of the term as state citizenship at one end to a powerful localism at the other, a diffuseness that makes it peculiarly resistant to organisational taxonomies and management' (2018: 107). In analysing the English revolt, we can diagnose the various motivating factors and historical forces precipitating the Leave vote, resulting in distinct and potent strains of post-imperial and post-industrial melancholia being mistakenly directed towards EU bodies. The reactionary response to a perceived deterritorialization is a symbolic *reterritorialization* of the national imaginary but, as Scruton notes, 'To describe something as dead is not to call for its resurrection' (2000: 244).

There is, of course, nothing wrong with national introspection; but when that very introspection develops into an insular and xenophobic mindset it is right to question the formative and foundational myths of our cultural imaginary. This chapter has followed Marr in asserting that any ideological change will first be 'novelistic, rather than legislative', advancing 'the re-imagining of a progressive, open England' (2000:

231). The shape English nationalism will take in a post-Brexit climate is unclear, yet O'Toole predicts that the most likely political entity to emerge from Brexit will be an isolated and independent England, not a 'Britain with its greatness restored or a sweetly reunited kingdom' (2020: 5). After all, as Kenny and Pearce warn, calls for a rejuvenated Anglosphere or Empire 2.0 carry grave 'implications for the internal organisation of the UK itself', setting English nationalist designs on a 'collision course' with Northern Ireland and Scotland in particular, which returned clear majorities for Remain (2018: 165; 166). Talk of an Anglosphere divides, rather than unites, an already tenuous union. With this in mind, it is important to consider the context of devolutionary debates and British cultural formations in preparing the ground for Brexit, shifting the focus to the other, often politically marginalized, territories within our unitary sovereign state: Wales, Scotland and Northern Ireland.

3

The disunited kingdom

Politics of devolution

> *The Brexit vote was a singular event that is one symptom of a continuing organic crisis of the British state and society and a stimulus for further struggles over the future of the United Kingdom and its place in Europe and the wider world.*
> (Jessop 2017: 35 – emphasis in original)

Speaking at the Conservative Party Conference in October 2016, Theresa May accentuated the need to preserve the integrity of the UK following the incredibly combative campaign:

> [b]ecause we voted in the referendum as one United Kingdom, we will negotiate as one United Kingdom, and we will leave the European Union as one United Kingdom. There is no opt-out from Brexit. I will never allow divisive nationalists to undermine the precious union between the four nations of the United Kingdom.
> (May 2016b)

Even a cursory glance at the breakdown of the Brexit vote reveals clear divergences between England, Wales, Scotland and Northern Ireland: divergences symptomatic of the strained attachments between these component territories. As Marr accurately discerns, 'there is no solution to Britain's European problem that does not begin at home, with Britain's British problem' (2000: 206). The EU referendum reopened old wounds and accelerated unresolved grievances, exposing pre-existing intra-UK tensions and fundamentally altering the political landscape. Tom Nairn's seminal text, *The Break-Up of Britain* (1977), identified these fraying ties in the years leading to the first devolution referendums, forecasting the dissolution of the state and forewarning of the potential neo-nationalisms which might emerge in the process. Subsequent post-Brexit negotiations substantiated his warning, revealing the sovereignty and centrality of Westminster, on the one hand, and the more minor role of the Scottish Parliament and Welsh and Northern Irish Assemblies, on the other hand, which lack a substantive voice in EU discussions.[1] For Nicola McEwen, 'the "one nation"

---

[1] The 1998 Scotland Act may have transferred some legislative powers but not jurisdiction over reserved matters such as EU membership.

nationalist rhetoric' of Westminster following the vote, evident in May's Lancaster House speech, 'is at odds with the plurinational character' of the UK, yet the condition of our increasingly disunited kingdom is intimately connected to the stance taken towards the EU (2018: 65). Michael Keating explains, it is precisely because both the UK and the EU are 'plurinational unions without a unitary *demos* or shared *telos*' that their asymmetrical designs complicate the relationship between nations (2018: 40). Devolution may have granted substantial powers and freedoms to Wales, Scotland and Northern Ireland, but the move further undermined the unitary state of the UK, exacerbated the ongoing English identity crisis, and failed to heal existing divisions. Further, devolution dispensations have been 'asymmetrical [. . .] ad hoc and bilateral', and only developed 'in response to specific pressures and demands' as opposed to the encouragement of progressive dialogues and equitable discussions (Wincott 2018: 20). The work of Michael Gardiner (2004) details how devolution was often pursued as a means of restricting regional unrest or delaying plans for national independence, as opposed to a genuine effort at redistributing power away from Westminster, effectively safeguarding the integrity of the British union under the guise of decentralization of Anglo-dominance. Further, the asymmetrical nature of devolution was bound to stimulate a backlash against subsequent devolutionary dispensations, while New Labour's support for devolution – intended to create a more elastic and convivial union – also stimulated the drive for further devolutionary reform as a protective measure. This chapter therefore turns to the internal dimensions of the Brexit debate, namely the plurinational nature of the UK and the tensions between its component territories. It will be argued that diametrically opposed attitudes towards the EU are heavily influenced by historical perspectives on the state-of-the-union and ongoing political tensions following devolutionary reforms and independence referendums.

The Welsh disease

> *In Wales, devolution remains largely a defensive project. Welsh political institutions are seen as providing a degree of protection against the depredations of Westminster rather than an embodiment of an alternative politics.*
> (Wyn Jones 2016)

There was widespread confusion in the aftermath of the Brexit vote as to why Wales, a major beneficiary of EU Structural and Investment Funds, was the only devolved nation to vote Leave in clear defiance of their pro-Remain political class. Welsh devolutionary processes developed in relation to EU membership with devolved power operating under a framework of EU law. The history of Welsh membership of the EU 'is now indivisible from the story of devolution in the UK', with 'Welsh political architecture [. . .] developed within the context of two unions – the UK and the EU' (Hunt, Minto and Jayne Woolford 2016: 826). Accordingly, the first section of this chapter will trace the key factors which stimulated the Leave vote in Wales and the direct intervention of authors in addressing these concerns, including the complex history of Welsh devolution, widespread industrial decline, and re-emergent questions regarding the place of Wales in the union.

In the 1975 referendum, Wales voted 65 per cent in favour of remaining in the Common Market in stark contrast to their Leave vote forty years later. From the 1980s onwards, Plaid Cymru perceived European integration to be a means of securing greater political autonomy, weakening the grip of Westminster and kickstarting the process towards independence in Europe (mirroring the volte-face of the SNP in this period). Yet the second successful referendum on Welsh devolution on 18 September 1997 generated a muted response. The creation of a Welsh Assembly, officially opened in May 1999, was only narrowly approved with a majority of 50.3 per cent based on a low 45.3 per cent turnout, reflecting the persistent divided nature of Welsh society when forced to consider their position within the British union and alternate opportunities for political redefinition.[2] For Scotland, devolution strengthened a viable movement towards independence and nationalism functioned as a unifying force, but in Wales the issue forged deep divisions between the Welsh-speaking north-west regions and the industrial south-east (divisions clearly borne out in the regional breakdown of the EU referendum result). The assertion that Welsh devolution 'remains largely a defensive project', carrying an awareness of internal divisions, seems apt (Wyn Jones 2016).

However, the years leading to the EU referendum saw far stronger public support for Welsh governance and decentralization of Westminster's powers. There was therefore justifiable astonishment when 52.5 per cent of voters, across the vast majority of Welsh council areas, chose to leave the EU. Although the EU referendum produced a noticeably higher turnout than earlier referendums (71.7%), the Welsh Leave vote illustrated the distinctive profile of Wales in comparison to Scotland and Northern Ireland. This profile can be understood by considering the sociopolitical context of pre- and post-devolutionary Wales, crucial failures of communication in the run-up to the EU referendum and disparate levels of socioeconomic inequality in various regions. Wales returned a narrow Leave vote despite being a key net beneficiary of ring-fenced EU Structural and Investment Funds and related regeneration projects, not to mention further EU investment until 2020. Many Welsh voters claimed EU funding failed to protect jobs or provide the economic stability required to overcome pre-existing social divisions produced under Thatcherite rule. Given that the majority vote in Wales did not align with leading Welsh politicians and their parties, all of whom strongly supported the Remain campaign, one can surmise that the vote involved a rejection of the establishment rather than the EU specifically.

A palpable tension clearly exists between England and Wales, yet the Brexit vote revealed that similar underlying anxieties acted as a common political denominator. A similar discontent and alienation which fuelled the English revolt – the electoral success of the far right, the influence of reactionary populist current, disillusionment with established parties and disengagement with politics more generally – was apparent within Wales but assumed a slightly different form. The geographical pattern of voting

---

[2] James Hawes, author of *Speak for England*, points to the Assembly as a progressive forum for Welsh political debate, 'making our representative institutions geographically closer, and demographically more sensitive, to us is absolutely a Good Thing' (2004: 270).

in Wales correlates with trends evident across England: university cities with younger, educated voters such as Cardiff tended to vote Remain while deindustrialized areas of the south Wales valleys such as Port Talbot and Caerphilly returned the highest Leave votes. In total, seventeen of twenty-two Local Authorities returned Leave majorities (including Rhondda, represented by Plaid leader Leanne Wood). However, as 93.2 per cent of the Welsh population was white British at the time of the referendum, the returning vote failed to reflect the feelings of Black British or British Asian voters (groups who predominantly voted Remain within England). With this in mind, it is not accurate to say Wales replicated the English revolt, but there is a clear dialogue between English and Welsh fiction in the years leading to 2016 – the sense of cultural marginalization runs down both sides of Offa's Dyke. Through an analysis of post-devolutionary Welsh fictions, we can identify salient factors which would go on to determine the Welsh Leave vote: fictions which either consider a London-centric Westminster to be responsible for the country's socioeconomic decline or attack the political antipathy of the Welsh people for the country's marginalized position in the union.

The early fictions of Niall Griffiths, often cited as a key figure in the literary devolution process, illustrate the ways in which Welsh literature remains haunted by the failures and successes of the 1979 and 1997 devolution referendums, respectively, as well as the legacies of Thatcherite social policies and the failure of New Labour to correct economic divides. Griffith's second novel, *Sheepshagger* (2001), published soon after the creation of the Welsh Assembly, fictionalizes the social fragmentation and slow disintegration of established communities on the verge of political devolution outside Aberystwyth, dubbed in 2016 'the most Europhile place in Britain' (Lusher 2016). Griffiths, who was born in Liverpool but resides in Aberystwyth, delivers a clear critique of the apathetic 'Can't-be-fuckin-arsed-ness' within Welsh politics, considering the low turnout in the 1979 referendum to be symptomatic of this 'Welsh disease': 'it's a pitiful little nation this. A fuckin boil in-a ocean [. . .] the Irish kill each other, the Scots kill emselves, an us, all we do is kill time' (2001: 74; 75).[3]

The novel's inarticulate and almost feral protagonist, Ianto, is ousted from his impecunious ancestral homestead in the hills outside Aberystwyth by English tourists using the site for their weekend retreats.[4] A victim of childhood sexual abuse and mutilation by an imperious English tourist, Ianto views the territorial disfiguration of his sacred landscape as an egregious act of English colonial occupation. Appropriately, in an article for *New Statesman*, Griffiths labels Wales 'England's oldest colony'; the dismissal of Welsh citizens as *sheepshaggers* by English tourists in the novel, considered incapable of political autonomy and trapped in a state of colonial dependency, denotes the asymmetrical nature of the Anglo-Welsh union (Griffiths 2007).[5] Ianto's very presence in the narrative is diminished once moneyed tourists begin to rip apart the

---

[3] In 2011, a referendum on whether further law-making powers should be increased for the Assembly induced a low turnout of only 35 per cent.
[4] A similar sense of indignation powers Robert Minhinnick's *Nia* (2019).
[5] Simon Thirsk's *Not Quite White* (2010), in which the tellingly named John Bull is directed to leave Westminster and modernise the last remaining Welsh-speaking town, echoes this sense of a colonial relationship existing between England and Wales.

social fabric of his community, indicating how his mountainous areas, which Griffiths dubs 'real Wales', are 'utterly "Other" to the Anglocentric mindset' (Griffiths 2007). Griffiths' use of regional vernacular for Ianto thus 'carries a weight of nonestablishment, marginal knowledge', echoing the fiction of James Kelman and Irvine Welsh in signalling a clear linguistic resistance to Anglocentric conceptions of British national identity (Peddie and Griffiths 2008: 120).

Ianto's day-to-day life is clearly impacted and shaped by geographic and political inequality, along with a sense of loss resulting from the disintegration of communal structures. His disenfranchisement and cultural impotence are evidenced by an ignorance of the TV panel discussion on the impending devolution vote. In this sense, Ianto is reflective of many citizens who feel EU–Westminster decision-making has no personal import on their lives and is determined by faceless bureaucrats 'in some never-to-be-entered office in some marbled and columned building in some never-visited city' (Griffiths 2001: 57).[6] As his friend Danny warns: 'devolution won't change a fuckin thing. Still be answerable to Westminster [. . .] always fuckin will be. If yew got a fuckin big saw an separated the country down Offa's Dyke an let us float out to sea we'd still be in their fuckin power' (2001: 57–8).[7] Danny's resentment towards Westminster could stem from the Welsh Assembly's weak negotiating position and continued lack of devolved juridical powers. Low turnouts in Assembly elections during this period testifies to the lack of public engagement or political awareness in post-devolution Wales, responsible for Ianto's unfamiliarity with current debates. However, the novel fails to advance a cohesive Welsh identity to counteract the imposition of hegemonic models of British governance. Through his inability to fit within existing social systems, combined with his failure to understand the Welsh language, Ianto is alienated from both British society *and* his Welsh heritage, functioning as a distorted caricature of the conflicted national mood within contemporary Wales between pro-Welsh and pro-union factions. *Sheepshagger* thus reflects Daniel John Evans' suggestion that contemporary Wales is in a period of 'interregnum' whereby the country no longer feels attached by the British state but is not quite ready to form a new state (2018: 489). Griffiths himself confirms that 'Brexit has reinforced Cymru's identity as the Other within, as the resistance to hegemony', and strengthened the case for further devolution: 'I actually hope for the disintegration of the UK. It has never been a union of equals. Aberystwyth [has] come to feel [. . .] wilfully separate' from the union to which it only nominally belongs (Personal Correspondence 2020).

Contemporary notions of Welshness, however, much like Englishness, prove to be elusive. In the concluding stages of the novel, Ianto's aggressive and destructive tendencies, induced by his harrowing childhood trauma and compounded by his ongoing sociocultural marginalization and economic precarity, are finally unleashed with devastating ramifications. After brutally murdering two English backpackers in a

---

[6] Roger Scully, who spent a year researching the catalysts of the working-class Brexit vote in the South Wales valleys, discovered voters were sceptical that EU membership benefited their communities (Scully 2017).
[7] An unspoken desire for Welsh independence is echoed by Sioned, the narrator of Griffiths' debut novel *Grits*: 'if Wales ruled itself, the Welsh people would be different – more confident – more laid back – less disposed to self-destruction' (2000: 145).

fit of rage, Ianto is himself murdered by his group of friends, appalled by the discovery of his actions. His visceral and symbolic act of violent resistance serves as an excessive political allegory for the underlying collective discontent brewing within economically depressed regions of Wales, with the general public pronouncing his crimes to be the product of nationalist 'devolution fever' (Griffiths 2001: 226). Accordingly, the narrative moves away from a consideration of Ianto's motivation for the murders towards an evaluation of the cultural, socioeconomic and political inequalities of millennial Wales, which are implied to be motivating factors for the attacks on English tourists: the 'whole bastard system needs revision' (2001: 239). There are therefore several ways to place the character of Ianto within a political dimension: as an emergent marginalized force disrupting Anglocentric privilege; as a violent figure whose own disenfranchisement mirrors the political sovereignty denied to Wales; or as the manifestation of social traumas inflicted under Thatcherite rule. Ianto's displacement from his homestead is itself representative of the sharp rise in home repossessions in Wales during Thatcher's time in office. As Schmitt notes, Ianto's attacks on English-owned homes alludes to the violent actions of the Welsh national movement Meibion Glyndŵr in the 1980s and their opposition to the loss of a distinctive Welsh culture (2018: 97).

Although the 1997 referendum coincided with the end of Conservative rule, and the emergence of the confident Cool Cymru phenomenon in Cardiff, such cultural confidence was evidently not shared in all regions of Wales. Eighteen years of Tory dominance bookended the two referendums during which time industrial decline and structural unemployment dramatically affected the Welsh economy. Economic decline was particularly apparent in the South Wales valleys: regions which voted decisively in favour of devolution in 1997. The valleys, deindustrialized areas with a strong history of pro-Welsh nationalism, are regularly listed as the most deprived regions of Wales and, crucially, all voted Leave. Clear socioeconomic similarities exist between the valleys and left-behind areas of the West Midlands and North East England, reinforcing the argument that the Brexit vote signalled a dissatisfaction with the state of the nation rather than the influence of EU integration. More importantly, the highest Leave votes were returned in Welsh regions which had received the most EU funding in recent years, supporting claims that most voters did not benefit from the implied job creation and still felt vulnerable in a deindustrialized economy. Ebbw Vale, for example, a small former steel town in the valleys, received high levels of EU investment yet 62 per cent of its population voted to leave the EU – the highest Leave vote in Wales. This result is not surprising given that the European Social Fund failed to overturn some of the highest unemployment and educational attainment levels within Wales. Former mining valleys in South Wales were still experiencing the lingering effects of mass unemployment in the 1980s, with employment rates remaining below 70 per cent (thus allowing Wales to qualify for EU structural investment). The chance to vote against the Westminster system in 2016 reignited long-standing resentment in regions which had not yet recovered from the Thatcherite era or the 2008 economic crisis. In a report for the Joseph Rowntree Foundation in 2016, Goodwin and Heath (2016b) identify clear links between levels of socioeconomic poverty, low educational attainment, lack of regional opportunities and the strength of the Leave vote. As Moya Jones succinctly puts it, 'the Welsh vote was predictable' (2017: 1).

A number of related post-devolutionary fictions capture this unstable relationship between economic deprivation, widespread unemployment and social marginalization experienced by citizens in deindustrialized regions of Wales, providing early warning signs of the anger, disillusionment and exclusion felt by many voters in 2016.[8] John Williams' *Cardiff Dead* (2000) and Grahame Davies' *Everything Must Change*, first published as *Rhaid i Bopeth Newid* in 2005, offer pessimistic and prescient evaluations of the 1997 Yes vote. While Williams documents the pre-existing social divisions within Cardiff, Davies critiques the decision to house the Assembly in metropolitan Cardiff and questions the prospective feasibility of EU funding in fostering regeneration or strengthening Wales' political bargaining power. Trezzo Azzopardi's haunting debut novel, *The Hiding Place* (2000), adopts a similar approach, charting the lives of a Maltese immigrant family in both pre- and post-devolutionary Cardiff, detailing the changes to capital following the opening of the Assembly and re-evaluating the evolving parameters of Welshness and Britishness at the millennial turn.

Emma Schofield identifies the increased role of Welsh female authors such as Azzopardi and Trezise in the immediate wake of devolution, whose writing 'marks a period of reconciliation between Wales' complex political, cultural and linguistic past and its aspirations for a future which reflects the new political meaning ascribed to the country' (Schofield 2014). Rachel Trezise's semi-autobiographical *In and Out of the Goldfish Bowl* (2000) follows Rebecca Trigianni, a teenager navigating a 1990s Rhondda valley landscape beset by industrial decline, structural unemployment, low educational attainment levels and a personal homelife fractured by child abuse and drug addiction. Contrary to Anthony Cartwright's fiction, a common industrial heritage fails to establish an oppositional form of cultural identity; instead, the open scars of the insular mining town Hendrefadog, with its decaying buildings of 'rotting green wood' and 'downright poverty', become representative of the festering wounds and traumas suffered by its inhabitants (2000: 9; 78).[9] For Scofield, Rebecca's personal development and 'new-found sense of independence' in the later stages of the novel coincides with the 1997 devolution vote, promising a more hopeful future, connecting her fate to that of her nation. Considering the novel from the post-Brexit moment, the Welsh Leave vote disrupts any supposed reconciliation underway within the country, proving this moment of literary optimism to be short-lived.

The Welsh political class were not alone in their determination to maintain ties with the EU. Various Welsh figures in the arts including Gillian Clarke, National Poet for Wales, were vocal in their backing of the Remain campaign and signed a letter warning of future cuts to the EU Creative Europe fund and its implications for the arts in Wales. Nonetheless, there has been a clear dearth of immediate Welsh literary

---

[8] Roger Granelli's *Dark Edge* (1987) considers the legacy of the 1984 Welsh miners' strike, Christopher Meredith's *Shifts* (1988) and Mike Jenkins' short-story collection *Wanting to Belong* (1997) respond to the trauma of deindustrial decline, and Richard John Evans' *Entertainment* (2000) documents the structural unemployment within the South Wales Valleys during the push for devolution.

[9] Alys Conran's *Pigeon* (2016), which paints a bleak picture of deindustrial life in North Wales, indicates how this undercurrent of disaffection and marginalization is still present in contemporary Wales while Charlotte Williams' *Sugar and Slate* (2002) reappraises the meaning of Britishness and the racial marginalization of mixed-race communities in northern Wales in the context of devolution.

and cultural responses to the post-Brexit moment as Wales considers a future outside the EU. This muted and delayed response can be explained by appreciating the artistic concentration on a string of devolutionary processes leading up to the Brexit vote – referendums which have loomed large in the Welsh creative imagination and which political commentators believed influenced the Welsh Leave vote.

The most significant Welsh post-Brexit text to engage with the legacy of devolution and the political condition of contemporary Wales is John Osmond's *Ten Million Stars Are Burning* (2018). Osmond, a former director of the Institute of Welsh Affairs, provides an exhaustive and meticulously detailed semi-autobiographical account of the build-up to the failed 1979 Welsh devolution referendum (which returned a pitiful Yes vote of just over 12%) and the ongoing national identity crisis.[10] Building on ideas first established in *Welsh Europeans* (1995), a critical examination of potential European futures for Wales, Osmond includes fictional representations of key British politicians such as Enoch Powell, who ardently opposed Welsh devolution, Neil Kinnock, who critiqued the devolutionary policies advocated by the Labour Party, as well as Welsh cultural thinkers such as Raymond Williams. Although the novel is set in the 1970s, the first part of a planned trilogy leading to Welsh devolution in 1997, Osmond creates a number of parallels between the two fateful votes, alluding to their impact on the EU referendum and their foreshadowing of the Welsh Leave vote. In so doing, he captures the national divisions between those citizens wanting devolution and those desiring the maintenance of the British union (namechecking crucial economically deprived areas such as Ebbw Vale which would go on to vote Leave), evaluating the role of the Common Market in securing and influencing national change. Moreover, Osmond dismisses referendums as 'immensely divisive' processes responsible for the destabilization of 'social and political harmony', creating perspicuous links between European integration and devolutionary debates: 'It destroys the so-called sovereignty of Parliament. That's what the referendum on the Common Market did last year. This one on devolution will do the same' (2018: 376; 383). The two movements are positioned as twin complementary processes, 'putting pressure on the system from opposite ends [. . .] the national movements in Wales and Scotland, and the international movement towards an integrated Europe' (2018: 306).

The opening stages of the novel communicate the diverse perspectives of voters in both English-speaking and Welsh-speaking areas of Wales on European integration. Protagonist Owen James, a political journalist for the Western Mail, for whom Osmond was a political correspondent during the 1970s, monitors the approaching devolution referendum and the eventual crushing defeat for supporters of a proposed Welsh Assembly. On the one hand, stronger relations with the European community is suggested to be a viable means of preventing anglicization and 'could be made to fit Welsh aspirations' (an argument which would be rekindled following the Brexit vote and subsequent loss of EU Structural Funds), improving Welsh representation and allowing the country to acquire full national status (2018: 16). On the other hand, Osmond voices fears that devolution or secession would create the conditions for a

---

[10] Fflur Dafydd's *Twenty Thousand Saints* (2008) ruminates on the legacy of the failed referendum from a post-devolutionary perspective.

form of inward-looking nationalism (with any political realignments occurring in the wake of a Welsh Assembly simply creating a novel form of bureaucracy to rival the EU and Westminster), deepen existing internal divisions within Wales, incite related devolutionary movements in the north of England and cede power to a capitalist club: 'All this Common Market business is doing is changing one set of dictators for another [. . .] It'll mean the end of Britain' (2018: 16). As a fictional Enoch Powell warns later in the novel, devolution would lead to a disunited kingdom and 'a parting of the ways [. . .] a declaration that one nation no longer existed' with severe consequences for the future of the British union (2018: 447).

Osmond depicts Phil Williams, the former Welsh Plaid politician, arguing that the European dimension outwrites more archaic notions of Britishness and allows for the reconstruction of a residual Welsh identity – an attachment and belonging to *y filltir sgwar* coupled with an outward-facing cultural commonality. The notion of a Britannic Federation is even floated, which introduces reforms to create greater regional devolution of powers (yet retains a Eurosceptic reticence towards any form of federalism). Unlike the English, who believe the EEC 'is eroding British sovereignty and reducing the power of Westminster', Plaid only disapproves of its capitalist and centrist tendencies, still perceiving its potential role in ameliorating sociopolitical imbalances (Osmond 2018: 283). Despite the suggestion that the nationalist politics of Plaid Cymru reflect the sentimentality of the English revolt, representing a 'gloomy longing for an imagined Wales of the past. It doesn't exist, never has, and never will', there are clear differences between the ways in which England and Wales envisage European integration (2018: 72). In contrast to English Eurosceptic fictions, Osmond repeatedly suggests it is 'not the Common Market that has spoiled things for Wales [. . .] but the inadequate, outdated procedures of the House [of Commons]' which continues to function as a centralist impediment: 'London is the great enemy of Wales, not Europe' (2018: 285; 475). Crucially, the narrative highlights the inferiority of Welsh media during the devolution referendum and an inherent reliance on London-based news, reinforcing the perception that Wales merely functions as a 'small, insignificant province of England' (2018: 335). Similar criticisms would be levelled at the Welsh Remain campaign in 2016. According to Ellie May O'Hagan, the Welsh Brexit vote is the product of Westminster neglect and an unrepresentative London-based media pushing the immigration debate, partly explaining why 'the turkeys had voted for Christmas' (O'Hagan 2016). As Osmond details, Wales has fewer EU migrants than most British regions, 'just 2.6% of the population, or 79,100 out of three million'; nevertheless, he points to startling feedback from the British Social Attitudes Survey which found '71% of Welsh respondents thought EU migrants brought more costs than benefits' (Osmond 2017). The referendum, positioned as an ideological battle, offered the potential to 'Take Back Control' in a slightly different way to the English vote, drawing attention to a lack of Welsh political agency.

Ten Million Stars Are Burning concludes rather ominously with the beginning of Thatcher's reign: a period which would fundamentally reinforce a feeling of Welsh disenfranchisement in subsequent decades given the Conservatives' electoral success rested predominantly on English votes. Although Osmond concentrates on the decline of the welfare state and widening socioeconomic gap between Wales and South East

England as confirmation that Westminster 'actively or consciously exploit[s] the periphery', the novel also accedes that the same under-development applies to the north of England (2018: 536). An area of common sentiment and experience is suggested to exist between Welsh and English working-class citizens in areas such as Durham, Dudley and Dowlais – an interpretation substantiated forty years later by the territorial breakdown of the Brexit vote. In focusing so intently on the vituperative nature and public confusion surrounding Welsh administrative devolution, Osmond indicates potential reasons for the poor turnout and conflicted public response of the Welsh Brexit vote, recognizing how nations 'tend to project on to Europe the experience of our own national systems' (2018: 292). Osmond has been vocal in his coverage of the post-Brexit fallout, asserting that the Welsh public are gradually reversing their support as the financial implications become clear, yet underscores how Welsh political devolution has been overshadowed by greater currents flowing in Scotland. Whereas Scotland is capable of threatening Westminster with another independence referendum, and Northern Ireland can point to the Irish border problem as a significant post-Brexit concern, by voting against its economic interest ('67% of Welsh exports go to the EU compared with 48% for the rest of the UK') Wales is left vulnerable and exposed to the power plays of Westminster (Osmond 2017).

Plaid Cymru proclaimed the Brexit result 'a hammer blow to Wales economically', predicting 'the poorest will pay the price' if power was transferred from Brussels to a dispassionate Westminster (Chaney 2017). Leanne Wood emphasized that 'the UK cannot continue in its current form' and the party emphasized its commitment to operating as an independent Wales within Europe (Chaney 2017). Brexit thus places renewed pressure on nationalist parties to strive for political independence, resist further centralization of governmental powers, and formulate their own arrangements with the EU. While Scotland has assumed a more combative approach by envisioning a future outside the UK and suggesting new potential agreements with the EU, Wales has sought to secure 'a Welsh Brexit as part of a "one UK Brexit"' and participate in 'multilateral partnerships and collaborative ventures' with the EU post-Brexit (Hunt and Minto 2017: 659). As a result, the country occupies a 'lone position among the devolved administrations', positioned as both a 'Good Unionist' and a 'Good European' (Hunt and Minto 2017: 659). The 2019 EU elections captured ongoing sociopolitical divisions within Wales: the Brexit Party won 32.5 per cent of the vote, while parties supporting a second EU referendum garnered 42.4 per cent. Plaid Cymru, finishing in second place with 19.6 per cent, declared Wales to now be a progressive and internationalist 'Remain nation' – a self-image with noticeable flaws. The post-Brexit moment has seen a recent resurgence in calls for further devolution and independence in Scotland and appeals for a reunited Ireland, yet in Wales the economic and political implications are likely to be quite different. Brexit may simply lead to greater devolved powers for a nation likely to be the hardest hit by a retreat from Europe, leaving Wales and England as the only remaining survivors of a dissolved UK. The Welsh Leave vote undoubtedly complicates any desire for independence in Europe, and yet the emphasis on this decision to exit the EU – by a majority of only 82,000 votes – should not be exaggerated. A breakdown of the Brexit vote clearly reveals that Wales returned the lowest Leave vote outside south-east England while Cardiff returned a higher Remain vote than London. Further, the referendum campaign not only immediately followed a long National Assembly elections process but the London-directed Remain campaign focused heavily on English regions and was barely visible within Wales.

Unless Welsh voters in deindustrialized regions feel the benefits of political devolution, the sense of disenfranchisement that powered the Leave vote will remain. For Welsh poet, novelist and playwright Owen Sheers, 'Brexit is not only about our future relationship with the EU but also about the nature of our future relationship with Westminster', arguing the referendum was a vote on 'not being heard, five years of austerity, desperation, unemployment' (Sheers 2019). In April 2018, the *Wales Arts Review* in partnership with Scottish online publication Bella Caledonia published an open letter to Theresa May, signed by notable Welsh writers such as Alys Conran, John Osmond, Niall Griffiths and Rachel Trezise, calling for the protection of existing devolved powers against potential Westminster power grabs (Bella Caledonia 2018). Just as Thatcherism is considered to be the 'midwife' of Welsh devolution, responsible for summoning a staunch resistance to Westminster politicking, Brexit may be the catalyst for a renewed devolved nationalism, triggering a re-evaluation of how exactly Wales balances their commitment to the union with their appetite for independence in Europe (Evans 2018). The chapter will now address how Brexit exacerbates the political divergence between Scotland and England and strengthens support for enhanced devolution or even future independence movements. Indeed, an under-reported context of Brexit is the extent to which Scotland was waging its own battle over sovereignty within the British union and how this was intimately connected to a desire for independence in Europe.[11] The chapter will then demonstrate how Scottish literature has responded to the post-devolutionary landscape and the ways in which Brexit is theorized and represented in the Scottish cultural imagination.

Scotland and the two unions

In Scotland the European question was crowded out or subsumed within the Scottish Question: that is, the relationship between Scotland and the British Union.

(McHarg and Mitchell 2017: 513)

In the 1975 referendum on continued membership of the EEC, Scotland and Northern Ireland returned lower Yes votes than England (58.4% and 52.1%, respectively). The SNP was initially sceptical of European integration – criticizing and challenging the EU over agriculture, fisheries and taxation – perceiving the EEC as an elitist organization which would lead to greater centralization of powers, prove incapable of protecting Scottish interests and dilute the potency of Scottish nationalist movements. In the intervening forty years between the two votes on European membership,

---

[11] Deacon and Sandry (2007) suggest the SNP and Plaid have paid close attention to Ireland's growth since joining the EEC in 1974 and appreciated how EU Structural Funds have transformed their economy.

the EU facilitated and supported deepening devolution, injecting huge sums into both countries via regional development and cohesion funds. During the 1980s, the SNP performed a volte-face and sought independence in Europe, committing itself 'to making membership of the EU the cornerstone of its self-government policy': a move also stimulated by resistance to Thatcherite policy and the centralist nature of Westminster (Dardanelli 2003). Thatcher inadvertently forced the Scottish to question their national identity and reformulate their resistance to the union. The SNP began to perceive the revamped EU as a socially progressive and forward-thinking arena – a broader canvas on which to paint a redefined Scottish political future – which could support their drive for national independence and increase their decision-making power in Europe. It is therefore important to consider the reasons for the territorial divergence in the period between the two votes on EU membership, as well as the influence of European integration on the devolution referendums of 1979 and 1997, and the 2014 indyref.

Although 51.6 per cent of Scottish voters supported the proposal for a devolved deliberative assembly in 1979, the turnout was so low (falling well short of the pre-agreed 40% marker) that amendments prevented the decision being upheld. Scott Hames points to 1979 as an inaugural moment in Scottish cultural politics when 'efforts to re-construct *national political space* were symbiotic with efforts to reconjure *national literary space*' (2019: 11). The drive for cultural devolution – which Hames labels 'the Dream' – bumps up uncomfortably against 'the Grind': namely, the wider British 'machine politics' at work during the devolutionary process (2019: 41).[12] In the shadow of the first failed referendum, Scottish literature immediately responded with defiant creativity and, in stark comparison to Welsh cultural activity, exuded a far more confident sense of national autonomy. As Liam McIlvanney asserts, 'Without waiting for the politicians, Scottish novelists had written themselves out of despair' by engaging in artistic acts of self-determination (2002: 183). For Gardiner, culture and literature in the period between the two referendums of 1979 and 1997 closely responded to ongoing processes of devolution, operating as 'sites of contest for the very possibility of politics' (Gardiner 2009: 182). Scotland consequently became 'a testing-ground for civic nationalism' generated by 'a post-imperial wave of constitutional scepticism which swept throughout the UK' (Gardiner 2012: 12). The 1990s in particular saw 'a substantial subsequent drop' in citizens selecting British 'as their best identity and a symmetrical rise in the proportion choosing Scottish' (Rosie and Bond 2008: 56). The rejuvenated Scottish literary project in this period was a radically creative solution to the political disenfranchisement experienced by certain communities under Tory rule, attempting to symbolically reverse Scotland's position as the weaker or potentially impotent partner in the union, evident in Iain Banks' *The Bridge* (1986) and Andrew Greig's *Electric Brae* (1992). The highly politicized fictions of Allan Massie and Alasdair Gray took up the task of narrating Scotland, ensuring debates concerning the state of the union remained in the forefront of the

---

[12] Hames' *The Literary Politics of Cultural Devolution* (2019) traces the literary and political developments of the 1970s and 1980s to indicate their importance in shaping current debates surrounding Scottish independence and further devolutionary reform under Holyrood.

Scottish literary imagination. While Massie's *One Night in Winter* (1984) envisages a future successful Scottish independence movement, Gray's seminal novel *Lanark* (1981), published in the depressive aftermath of 1979, and his follow-up *1982, Janine* (1984) evaluate a society still haunted by the referendum and register a bitterness at the hegemonic control of Westminster: 'If we ran that race again we would win by a head and a neck so we won't be allowed to run it again' (1984: 66). Gray's subsequent non-fiction polemic on the merits of independence *Why Scots Should Rule Scotland* (1992) amplifies what he perceived as the ongoing political subordination of Scotland in the face of English political dominance. Irvine Welsh's *Trainspotting* (1993), which admittedly also retains a disdain for contemporary Scottish society, goes further in suggesting a process of English colonization was still underway (later echoed from a Welsh perspective in Griffiths' *Sheepshagger*).

When the devolution referendum on the creation of the Scottish Parliament passed in 1997, with 74.3 per cent in favour, political commentators pointed to the actions of Scotland's literary players as key cultural figures in the ideological battle. Cultural devolution arguably *preceded* political devolution and influenced the outcome of the successful 1997 referendum. As Duncan McLean puts it, 'there's been a parliament of novels for years', a sentiment echoed by Robert Crawford in his 1982 study *Devolving English Literature* (1999: 74). The opening of the Scottish Parliament on 1 July 1999 celebrated the clear contributions made by Scottish writers in formulating new expressions of national identity, featuring quotations from poets Hugh McDiarmid, Robert Burns and Iain Crichton Smith. For Scottish writer James Robertson, the inauguration produced an atmosphere 'tenuous with possibility':

in the end a Parliament is not
a building, but a voyage of intent,
a journey to whatever we might be. (2005: 24)

The immediate post-devolutionary moment also saw works by Black Scottish and Scottish Asian writers critiquing narrow and reductive constructions of national identification, instead proposing alternate modes of Scottishness which were convivial, hospitable and constantly evolving, including *Jelly Roll* (1998) by Luke Sutherland, *Trumpet* by Jackie Kay (1998) and *Psychoraag* by Suhayl Saadi (2004).[13] That being said, Yasmin Alibhai-Brown repeatedly points to the 'all white' make-up of the Scottish and Welsh assemblies; devolution has unintentionally raised the issue of ethnicity, revealing that 'ancestral rights, rather than other modes of belonging' remains a key factor, problematizing this narrative of progress for ethnic-minority citizens (Alibhai-Brown 2000). While it would be inaccurate to suggest either support for celebratory Scottish multiculturalism or an outward-reaching political stance was overwhelming, the successful 1997 devolution vote stimulated more encompassing notions of nationhood and post-devolutionary Scottish writing undoubtedly advanced a culturalist discourse

---

[13] Anne Donovan's optimistic novel *Being Emily* (2008) also advocates space for diversity in a Scotland not hemmed in by a bounded national imaginary and suggests the cosmopolitan possibilities open to Scottish citizens in the wake of devolution.

which captures the inclusiveness of twenty-first-century Scotland with diversity in voice, gender, sexuality and race.[14]

According to Douglas Gifford:

> With this new confidence, Scottish fiction approached the millennium as a standard bearer for Scottish culture [...] The new complexities in novelistic vision relate dynamically to the changes taking place in Scottish society at large, not only reacting to them, but influencing the framework of thought in which they took place. (2007: 237)

It is therefore tempting to endorse what Gavin Wallace terms the 'critical orthodoxy, subscribed to also by writers, that Scotland's literature played a central role in articulating the pressures towards political change that led to devolution' (2007: 24). Hames, however, argues against the notion that Holyrood was simply 'dreamed into being by artists' and offers a more balanced assessment, pointing towards the political disenfranchisement which motivated artists to bring such desires to the surface (2012: 7).[15] Alex Thomson goes further, asserting that the disproportionate support for independence among writers and members of the creative industries – such as the National Collective organization supported by Alasdair Gray and Liz Lochhead – exposed 'a disjunction between the cultural sector and society at large' (anticipating similar trends identifiable in the EU referendum), attesting 'not to the critical power of the arts but to their subsumption by contemporary politics' (2016: 3). After all, not all post-devolutionary Scottish texts envision such a quixotic future. As Wallace reminds us, despite devolution and the inception of the Scottish Parliament, Scotland remained 'a stateless nation within the anomalous polity of the UK' and was limited to a form of quasi-political autonomy following devolution (2007: 25). In short, the benefits of political devolution failed to compensate for the ongoing democratic deficit and territorial inequalities felt by Scottish citizens.

Matthew Fitt's *But n Ben A-Go-Go* (2000) paints a bleak dystopic vision of a nationalist Scotland in which cosmopolitan hospitality is rejected in favour of an entrenched islander mentality. Despite the nation's more liberal sensibilities, for Schoene the novel suggests that 'a nationalist Scotland might lack the imaginative power to project its future beyond a mere assertion of independent nation-statehood' (2008: 89). Similarly, Denise Mina's *Garnethill* trilogy and Kelman's *Translated Accounts* (2001) go against the trend by considering Scotland's complicity in the global economy, critiquing the ongoing socioeconomic and class inequalities left unaddressed following devolution. The expression of vernacular Scots and linguistic experimentation, evident in Kelman's fictions, serve a subversive purpose, signalling a

---

[14] Berthold Schoene's *Edinburgh Companion to Contemporary Scottish Literature* provides an extensive overview of the condition of post-devolution writing, charting recent reconfigurations and renegotiations of national identity in Scotland.

[15] Hames' edited collection *Unstated: Writers on Scottish Independence* (2012) contains think pieces from a range of authors who cite dissatisfaction with Westminster politicking, Anglo-centrism and anxieties concerning structural and geographical inequalities as reasons for seeking independence, including Janice Galloway, Alasdair Gray, James Kelman, Denise Mina and Suhayl Saadi.

clear challenge to Anglocentric sociopolitical impositions and marking a resistance to hegemonic structures which fail to represent Scotland's polyvalent cultural identity.[16] As James Robertson's state-of-the-nation novel *And the Land Lay Still* (2010) makes clear, these devolutionary debates were deeply embedded into a longer post-war history of Scotland and its troubled place in the union. Weaving a Scottish national narrative over half a century from the late 1940s to 2008, the novel documents the constitutional debates of Conservative MPs, Home Rule activists and members of the public surrounding shifting attitudes towards decentralization of powers. Robertson's remarks on the stimulus for Scottish devolution could equally serve as a portentous commentary on the intra-UK ideological divides evident in the EU referendum:

> Here is a situation: a country that is not fully a country, a nation that does not quite believe itself to be a nation, exists within, and as a small and distant part of, a greater state. The greater state was once a very great state, with its own empire. It is no longer great, but its leaders and many of the people like to believe it is. For the people of the less-than country, the not-quite nation, there are competing, conflicting loyalties. They are confused. (2010: 534)

For Hames, the novel provides 'the most significant literary realisation' of Scottish cultural devolution (2019: 41).[17] More importantly, Robertson's sprawling narrative exemplifies how literary fiction may provide a creative interpretation of political events, denoting the impact of the past on the present, and the role of literature in conceiving potential futures for submerged nations haunted by their stateless histories.

Although the left-behind narrative of Brexit does apply to certain regions of Scotland, the anger and resentment regarding socioeconomic disparities and regional marginalization was instead channelled earlier through a rejection of Anglocentric politics in the 2014 independence referendum. Scottish voters were particularly tired with the paternalistic nature of British constitutional governance, which ensures the process of cultural devolution comes to be defined and manipulated by party political interests in Westminster. Whereas the monocultural parochialism of the English revolt appealed to sentimental historical attachments and reductive nostalgia, the indyref in Scotland adopted a future-oriented perspective. The kindling of a Scottish resistance has resulted in a politically enlightened electorate with an intrinsic desire for new alternatives and a more egalitarian, outward-facing society. Rather than calling for a return to any 'golden age' of Scottish history, the SNP espoused a 'golden tomorrow' for a devolved Scotland, reinforced by cosmopolitan citizenships developed by remaining with the EU (Leith and Soule 2012: 151). The indyref thus offered the opportunity to

---

[16] Whereas Gardiner asserts that Kelman's *How late it was, how late* (1994) functions as a 'direct representation of devolution' (and Jeremy Black proclaims the novel a 'Scottish literary declaration of cultural self-determination'), Hames refutes the novel's centrality to the literary devolutionary project, suggesting it contains a pointed refusal 'to conceive power *as* representation on the devolutionary model' (2007: 49; 2018: 149; Hames 2019: 288).

[17] Robertson's short story 'Republic of the Mind', first published in his 1993 collection *The Ragged Man's Complaint*, anticipates the arguments set out in his later novel, mediating on a character's inward retreat to a 'Scottish republic' of the imagination in light of stagnating political realities following the 1992 UK general election (2012: 133).

override political asymmetries within the union, readdress the complex negotiation of competing loyalties and reconsider Scotland's ambivalent place in the union. In all, 55.3 per cent of Scottish voters went on to reject independence (on a high 85% turnout), but the margin was sufficiently narrow enough to keep alive hopes of future succession from an ailing union. SNP membership, for example, witnessed a dramatic increase from 25,000 in December 2013 to 120,000 in July 2016. For many cultural commentators, however, the No vote arrested the forward movement of Scottish literature and reignited Anglo-Scottish tensions. Scottish author and playwright Alan Bissett claimed the failed indyref would trigger 'a period of introspection', while the novelist Alan Warner even suggested that the No vote would create 'a profound and strange schism between the voters of Scotland and its literature [. . .] the death knell for the whole Scottish literary "project" – a crushing denial of an identity that writers have been meticulously accumulating, trying to maintain and refine' (Bissett 2015; Warner 2014). By 2014, then, 'the critical and creative endeavour called Scottish Literature was [. . .] often difficult to separate from the political project with which it is entwined' (Hames 2019: 302). For Timothy Baker, the No vote was problematic because 'only a Yes vote allows narrative at all: Scotland's identity is almost wholly situated in the future' (2016: 248). Appropriately, a number of speculative fictions emerged in the period, envisioning new political futures for Scotland. Paul Johnston's *Body Politic* (1997), which imagines a Scottish republic following the dissolution of the UK, and the concentration on a European dimension to Scottishness in Andrew Crumey's *Mobius Dick* (2004) and *Sputnik Caledonia* (2008), suggest Scotland to be undergoing a transformational process of becoming, entailing the construction of imaginative spaces which allow for a radical reconfiguration of national identity in post-devolutionary Scotland.

This recent history of Scottish devolution is vital to any understanding of Scotland's subsequent vote on EU membership. Martin Johnes (2019) argues the EU referendum itself was the product of Scottish developments as the failed indyref convinced the Conservatives that voters were fearful of supporting any major constitutional change. Such sociocultural blindness and institutional arrogance regarding both the EU and the position of Scotland in the British union are communicated in Sarah Hall's *The Wolf Border* (2015). In dissecting the troubled union between England and Scotland, Hall taps into the impetus for the independence vote and the underlying tensions which would re-emerge during the post-Brexit fallout once the territorial divergence in voting patterns became clear. Set during the run-up to the indyref, *The Wolf Border* imagines a counter-factual future in which Scotland achieves independence, raising timely debates regarding intra-UK borders and the matter of future constitutional arrangements. According to Hall, who completed the novel before Scotland's fateful No vote in the referendum, the narrative is deeply informed by the political context of the troubled union.

The novel follows Rachel Caine as she relocates from Idaho to the Lake District to assist Thomas Pennington, the Earl of Annerdale, introduce wolves to the grounds of Pennington Hall, the largest private estate in England. Pennington, an eccentric and antiquated figure, is representative of the English superiority defining the political imbalance of the Anglo-Scotland relationship, dismissing the government white paper on Scottish independence as pure fantasy. Forced to endure dinner parties at her employer's home, Rachel is regularly confronted with the 'usual independence scare story', realizing there is widespread ignorance surrounding the subject: 'Facts versus fear, hatred and irrationality' (Hall 2015: 98; 147). Pennington's acquaintances cite 'the cost of setting up new nations' alongside continued EU membership and 'the impoverished state of Scotland, indebted and in need of European bailout' as essential reasons for maintaining the status quo, leading Rachel to question '[i]s it any wonder they want out?' (2015: 98). Such pro-Union rhetoric continues even after the successful Scottish independence vote which cuts 'the north of the island free' and ominously sentences Sebastian Mellor, Britain's fictional PM during the independence vote, to the same fate of David Cameron following the EU referendum: 'doomed [. . .] to be the premier on whose watch the nation dissolved' (2015: 223). In a political climate where Britain 'no longer exists' and Scotland is accused of wreaking havoc with the union by committing 'economic suicide', Hall unintentionally communicates the same criticisms that will be thrown at post-Brexit Britain just two years later: 'They'll be bankrupt in a year [. . .] It'll be cap in hand to Europe' (2015: 224; 227; 228).

Rachel's re-wilding project, however, is not a success as local residents condemn the wolves as an immigrant threat to the stable English ecosystem of Cumbria and repudiate Rachel's information on the benefits of EU collaboration projects, resulting in the wolves' relocation across the Scottish border. As 'refugees seeking asylum in the newest European nation', the wolves furnish the newly independent Scotland with a 'new icon for a new nation', strengthening the first minister's claim that 'Scotland was, is, and will be a beacon of social enlightenment' (2015: 102; 413). The wolves thus play an overtly symbolic role in the narrative; their introduction signifies the perceived *wildness* of the indyref by pro-Union voices and the resultant threat posed to Westminster decision-making. In signalling an escape from the insular mindset of contemporary England with its anti-EU posters to a future-oriented country more welcoming of otherness, the novel contains a modicum of hope for new political developments on Scotland's horizon – developments which have been radically curtailed by the suspension of Scotland's cosmopolitan future in 2016. However, as Rachel reasons while visiting Holyrood in the concluding stages of the novel, 'the fabric of British politics, state definitions' can be changed 'if people want it badly enough, if they are tired, and hopeful' (2015: 423). A sentiment which may prove to be prophetic as Scotland continues to negotiate its troubled position within a fraying union.

Scotland's vote in favour of remaining in the EU in 2016 (by 62% to 38%), supported by every local authority area, was clearly not just a response to the issue of Europe, but a product of the nation's turbulent devolutionary history and its resistance to Anglocentric systems of political control. Curtice (2016) cites a multitude of reasons for Scotland's strong Remain vote (a number of which are reflected in post-Brexit Scottish literature): the smaller age and educational attainment gaps north of the border; the perception among Scottish voters that the EU was not a threat to their British identity; the rapid injection of funding into the country; and the role of the SNP in securing voters' political sympathies and campaigning heavily for Remain. Arguably, the Scottish and Northern Irish have become more secure with accommodating differing political and cultural identities. Whereas Englishness is often touted as an inward-looking form of identification, and Britishness a more outward-facing identity, for the Scottish and Northern Irish the addition of a European tag fails to attract similar levels of anxiety. Similarly, the Scottish have become more accustomed to multilateral levels of government, as opposed to the heavily centralized governance within England. While Scotland has undergone substantial constitutional change in the last twenty years, England has not witnessed similar legislative devolution, leading the English people to believe that both Westminster and Brussels are incapable of change and must be radically altered. For Scotland pooled sovereignty was potentially a stepping stone to independence in Europe. Scotland's pronounced Remain vote is thus symptomatic of the drive for national independence and a desired detachment from Westminster politicking (an argument heavily promoted by the SNP). Research by Leith and Soule (2012) indicates that a significant number of Scottish voters retain an attachment to their British identity, with the relationship between Scottishness and Britishness remaining highly complex. Brexit will have a fundamental impact on this issue of compatibility, forcing voters to question the legitimacy of holding overlapping forms of identification.

While this Anglo-Scottish bond has long been under pressure, Brexit has undoubtedly revived the Scottish Question and exposed devolution as a limited solution in rectifying entrenched cultural, political, demographic and socioeconomic disparities. It is also worth noting that both Scotland and Northern Ireland returned the lowest turnout figures, indicating that the issues dominating the campaign spoke more to English and Welsh disaffection. Europe was simply not a hot-button issue in Scottish politics.[18] UKIP's core Eurosceptic messages failed to resonate with Scottish voters and the Leave campaign was unable to gain traction in Scotland; their related narratives of strident English nationalism failed to connect with a Scottish public which had seen almost two decades of Tory rule forced upon them. The British electoral system was thus a key determining factor in shaping Scottish antipathy to Tory conservatism and creeping anglicization. Further, as Hames points out, the 'weak cultural basis' of post-devolutionary Scotland – 'that is, the minimal extent to which the rationale for political independence is safeguarding and developing distinctly Scottish culture' – permitted Scotland to 'bypass the "traditionalist" quandary by which a narrative of cultural preservation inevitably imposes past-oriented restrictions on the nationalist imagination' (2019: 257).

The Scottish government has certainly been the most vocal opponent of the post-Brexit process, producing a document in December 2016, 'Scotland's Place in Europe', setting out their staunch opposition to the referendum result. First Minister Nicola Sturgeon labelled May's triggering of Article 50 'a democratic outrage', voicing her party's resentment at 'the prospect of being dragged out of Europe against our will by a right-wing Tory government hell-bent on a hard Brexit' (SNP 2017). By July 2016 Sturgeon had already pressed for a differentiated solution and listed the free movement of people and access to the single market and customs union as red lines

---

[18] Research by McEwen demonstrates Scottish voters were more supportive of European integration and more open to the idea of European identities. That being said, seven boroughs within London returned far higher Remain vote shares than Scotland (2018: 67).

for Scotland moving into post-Brexit negotiations. Sturgeon cited Brexit as a central reason why a second indyref must be scheduled, insisting any exit from the EU constitutes 'a significant and material change of the circumstances in which Scotland voted against independence in 2014' (Sturgeon 2016). Martin McGuinness, former deputy first minister of Northern Ireland, echoed her sentiments, suggesting the result provided the rationale for a referendum on Irish reunification. May's repeated calls to preserve a unitary British state complicated support for such moves. As Schoene appreciates, 'from a cosmopolitan perspective' the SNP's 'ongoing demand for full political independence must appear counterproductive' allowing May to disparage what she termed the 'tunnel vision nationalism' of the SNP in driving for constitutional change at a time of political crisis (2008: 71).

As M. K. Thompson observes, the political rhetoric employed by the SNP 'connects Brexit to earlier episodes of Scotland' and places Brexit in a longer historical narrative (2019: 156). The electoral success of the Thatcher government strengthened the notion that the Scottish people were being governed against their will and Brexit merely compounds this political divergence between the two nations. Accordingly, during post-Brexit negotiations, the SNP has striven to position Scotland as a distinct and autonomous nation capable of acting as a major player on the international stage, as opposed to a submerged and subordinate member of a beleaguered British union. It would be inaccurate, however, to suggest that support for 'independence in Europe' was responsible for Scotland returning the highest Remain vote of any nation in the UK. As Keating identifies, following the SNP's ideological shift they failed to convince the public that independence and EU membership could complement one another, with numerous studies failing to demonstrate a conclusive link between support for European integration and support for independence (2018: 41).[19] Calls for a second referendum by Sturgeon in March 2017 were not well received and the SNP were accused of neglecting more domestic issues such as education, health and policing in their drive to secure independence, ignoring the millions of Scots who voted for Brexit. Despite winning fifty-six out of fifty-nine seats in the 2015 UK general election (displacing Labour as the dominant political force within Scotland), the SNP suffered substantial losses in the snap election of 8 June 2017, reshaping the terms of the independence debate.

Further, the EU has confirmed on numerous occasions that the British government is its sole negotiating partner in post-Brexit discussions and EU law cannot be suspended in England but continues to apply in Scotland (such an arrangement would only emerge following a radical deepening of devolutionary dispensations). As French foreign minister Jean-Marc Ayrault underlined, 'Europe should in no case contribute to the dismantling of nations' (qtd. in Simon Johnson 2016). Scotland thus remains in a state of political limbo, pushed into a new arrangement against its wishes and shackled to an ever more fissiparous union, forced to reposition itself against the evolving political matrix of Holyrood, Westminster and Brussels. It is doubtful that Westminster

---

[19] According to Keating, approximately 30 per cent of SNP supporters voted Leave, 'concentrated in the same working-class and post-industrial areas that had voted most strongly for independence in 2014' (2018: 43).

can resist calls for Scottish independence indefinitely without transferring substantial legislative powers to the Scottish government in order to mitigate further post-Brexit instability. At the time of writing, *Scoxit* seems a remote possibility, the notion of a hard border between England and Scotland is unthinkable, and the EU has firmly rejected any fast-track entry process for nations which have previously been member states. However, any *Scoxit* will appear much more appealing once the adverse effects of Brexit begin to affect the economy, prompting many to echo Sturgeon in wondering if Scotland should decide its own future.

Taking Scotland's strong Remain vote and the history of its devolutionary struggle into account, the Scottish literary response to Brexit has certainly been muted, with even outspoken Unionists such as Allan Massie remaining silent on the thorny issue. Given Welsh literature's similar lacklustre response, this is understandable; writers have been too busy grappling with narrativizing devolution for measured responses to yet emerge. English author and journalist Madeline Bunting's autobiographical *Love of Country: A Hebridean Journey* (2016), for example, published between the indyref and EU referendums, encapsulates ongoing attempts to diagnose Scotland's awkward position in the British union, as Bunting plots her travels around the edges of Scotland and struggles to define the boundaries of 'home' in the months 'before we tip off the continental shelf [and] leave Europe' (2016: 2). Arianna Introna (2020) also notes the critical silence surrounding Brexit in Scottish literature, with writers evincing a focused literary engagement with the legacy of the post-indyref moment. For instance, while Craig Smith's *The Mile* (2014), Jenni Daiches' *Borrowed Time* (2016) and James Robertson's *365 Stories* (2014) directly respond to the sense of anticipation and possibility connected to the indyref, more recent post-Brexit texts, such as John Burnside's *Havergey* (2017) and A. L. Kennedy's *The Little Snake* (2018), 'speak not to Brexit but to the political conjuncture from which Brexit has arisen', engaging with Scottish concerns surrounding sovereignty (2020: 2). Thus, rather than marking a seminal moment, Brexit has merely deepened Anglo-Scottish fissures which were already exposed following the 2014 vote.

For Irvine Welsh, Scottish independence is potentially empowering by redefining the future evolving parameters of the union: 'political separation could promote the cultural unity that the UK state [. . .] with its notions of "assumed Englishness" is constantly undermining' (Welsh 2013). Welsh's *Dead Men's Trousers* (2018a), the closing instalment of the Trainspotting series, situates Renton, Sick Boy, Begbie and Spud against the backdrop of the tumultuous political present as they reunite for the 2016 Scottish Cup final. Set after the indyref and during the run-up to the Brexit vote, the novel delivers an overtly political conclusion to the drug-fuelled lives of the four friends. Welsh, a frequent commentator on the post-Brexit process and Scotland's place in the union, avoids meticulously dissecting the referendum or launching an assault on the neoliberalism of the EU in favour of a more general commentary on how disenchantment in Scotland arises from a sense of redundancy following prolonged periods of deindustrialization and socioeconomic deprivation. Noting the inescapable attention given to the referendum, Begbie betrays an ignorance of current events and dismisses the notion that the vote will affect his day-to-day life: 'One thing ye can guarantee is, whatever happens, things'll be shite for maist cunts' (2018a: 363).

Further evidence of public confusion surrounding the aftermath of the vote is apparent in Chris McQueer's short-story collection *HWFG* (2018a). In a short comedic piece entitled 'Brexit', Glaswegian tradesman Boaby reveals his ignorance concerning the exact purpose of the EU, admitting he was unaware that the referendum had even taken place two years beforehand. When he is tasked by his two apprentices to use the term 'Brexit' in a sentence to prove he understands its meaning, he simply replies: 'You've got mah tape measure aye? [. . .] well, don't gie it tae him incase he fuckin Brexit' (2018a: 36).

The pessimism and divisions of Brexit Britain are conspicuous throughout *Dead Men's Trousers*, evident in Renton's commentary on the distinct 'leakage of hope' in British society due to the rise of aggressive nationalism, 'and its replacement by a hollow rage' (2018a: 31). Welsh's own frustrations and anxieties seep into the novel when Spud acquires a passport to complete a job in Europe and questions Scotland's future role in the union: 'wi Britain mibbe headin oot ay Europe and Scotland mibbe headin oot ay Britain, ay'll probably huv tae get a new yin before long!' (2018a: 158). While no fan of the EU as an institution, Welsh has been vocal in his opposition to the disruptive absurdity of Brexit – 'the idea of having a passport that allows you to bounce around one shit country that you have elected to make poorer, instead of being able to travel around 28 of them. It's nonsense, absolute nonsense' – predicting that Britain will become a mean-spirited backwater with even greater gulfs between the political class and the electorate (Welsh 2018b).

The most considered Scottish response to both the indyref and Brexit came from author Andrew O'Hagan whose keynote lecture at the 2017 Edinburgh Literary Festival, 'Scotland, Your Scotland' (an allusion to Orwell's infamous 1941 essay 'England, Your England'), bemoaned the extent to which Scotland is at the behest of Westminster Tory diktat and lacks 'sovereign force':

> Now that the picture is clearing, we are left with an image of a belated Little England posing an existential threat to a Scotland that has seen itself for years as European [. . .] Britain has mismanaged itself out of existence, and Scotland may not be the beneficiary, but it can certainly be the escapee, free to succeed or to fail in its own ways. (O'Hagan 2017)

O'Hagan, who admits he 'had always believed these islands were better united', argues that the No vote in 2014 did not save the union, but rather confirmed it 'was in fact over', with the territorial divergence of the Brexit vote and May's repudiation of Scotland's 'discreet authority' serving as confirmation of this symbolic termination (O'Hagan 2017). Though his lecture is itself guilty of revelling in nationalist nostalgia, and fails to mention the SNP had recently lost a third of its seats despite assuming a markedly Europhile stance, if a Scottish literary project of resistance and renewal is to emerge, its seeds of discontent are manifest in his passionate denunciation of 'small-nation retreatism' and vociferous opposition to being dragged out of Europe (O'Hagan 2017). Commenting on the evolving nationalist movements in Britain following the EU referendum, playwright Peter Arnott echoes O'Hagan's sentiments, singling out what he considers 'the key difference is between the nationalism of Brexit and that of the SNP': 'one is dreaming of restoring a past that never existed. The other is working for a future that doesn't exist yet either' (Arnott 2019).[20] For O'Hagan, whose debut novel *Our Fathers* (1999) lamented the death of left-wing idealism, Scottish writers are striving to formulate 'an open space of fresh possibility' rather than clinging to late-twentieth-century devolutionary rhetoric (O'Hagan 2017). Despite Scottish literature's initial taciturn artistic response, texts are beginning to emerge which allude to the various sociocultural, ethnopolitical and economic explanations for Scotland's unequivocal Remain vote, assuming a forward-looking approach to the momentous events of 2016.

Responding to the fateful events of referendum night, poet Carol Ann Duffy criticized Cameron for dividing the nation – 'torn in two like a bad poem' – echoing J. K. Rowling's sentiment that 'Cameron's legacy will be the breaking of two unions' (Duffy 2016; Elgot 2016). This ideological sociopolitical divide between England and Scotland is markedly apparent in Fiona Shaw's *Outwalkers* (2018), which alludes to the slightly more outward-facing outlook of modern Scotland and its refusal to shy away from its global responsibilities. The novel follows a group of displaced and vulnerable children as they attempt to travel north to Scotland and escape the clutches of an authoritarian English Coalition government. Although *Outwalkers* is widely regarded as one of the first YA post-Brexit texts, according to Shaw the idea for the novel was originally conceived in 2013 following a dream about the impending indyref. The narrative depicts a dystopic post-Brexit England of the near-future which has ostensibly terminated its relations with continental Europe and erected the New Wall. In the months before its construction, Scotland (which remains a part of the EU) sees its citizens relegated to visiting aliens, Wales is co-opted into the Coalition's designs and England reverts to imperial measurements in resistance to European metrics. Despite the professed formation of an Atlantic Alliance, recalling once again the spectre of the Anglosphere, this is not a Global Britain but a fragmented and partitioned disunited kingdom threatened by the actions of an autocratic and protectionist Little England.

The appointment of a minister for borders – whose remit is to prevent net inward immigration to ensure 'Our English shores stand clean and proud' and obstruct citizens from leaving the country – compounds the country's parochial retreat from the globalized world (2018: 24). Indeed, the novel's draconian government is no longer faced with the challenge of illegal immigrants seeking entry to the country following the introduction of a zero tolerance immigration policy; rather, English citizens attempt to obtain exit documents, undertake treacherous sea-crossings or stowaway on Channel Tunnel freight trains – still in operation despite the Coalition's claims to the contrary – in order to escape to a more liberal Europe. To prevent potential uprising or cross-border movements, the English Coalition government fabricates post-truth reports of Scottish terrorist attacks and spreads rumours of a deadly virus sweeping Scotland and Europe – a cover for a simulated immunization process which

---

[20] Arnott's *A Little Rain*, which premiered in 2000, indicates that if Scotland desires independence it must gather its aspirational energies to formulate an inclusive and hospitable nationalism or risk a confrontation with a Scotland 'no longer protected from its own ugliness by the alibi of Westminster' (2000: 43).

implants a non-removable, nano-microchip into citizens to monitor their activities. Shaw admits her depiction of Scotland was heavily influenced by the political rhetoric and scare tactics of right-wing factions in Westminster – an impulse that she claims has hardened and intensified over the last few years (Personal correspondence 2019). Tracey Mathias' *Night of the Party* (2018) develops this fear of an emergent police state following the spread of aggressive nationalism and post-truth politics in 2016. As in Shaw's *Outwalkers*, a cosmopolitan Scotland offers a means of escape from xenophobic English immigration policies limiting the mobility of EU citizens. Britain's recent exit from the EU has failed to incite a backlash against scheming populist politicians; rather, England doubles down on its mistrust of those who 'don't sound English enough' provoking Scotland into breaking the union and claiming independence (2018: 13). The introduction of a British born policy – prescribing that any foreign-born citizen no longer possesses the right to remain and should be repatriated – as a necessary preventive measure in protecting the security and culture of England thus forecasts a bleak post-Brexit future in which the lessons of 2016 have not been learnt and Britain's initial retreat from European supranational arrangements is but a stepping stone towards a more aphotic political isolationism.[21]

As Keating argues, a key difference between Scotland and England in the context of Brexit has been the salience of immigration and free movement: in particular, the ways in which such issues are framed by Scottish political leaders and received by a generally 'more liberal' public (2018: 42). The third instalment of Ali Smith's seasonal quartet, *Spring* (2019a), marks a departure from the Anglocentric focus of *Autumn* (2016) and *Winter* (2017a) to comment on Scotland's troubled and ambivalent place within the British constellation, as well as clear political tensions between the two nations regarding British immigration policy. In a discussion with Nicola Sturgeon at the Edinburgh Book Festival, Smith reiterated how 'fiction is one of our ways of telling the truth', signalling a literary resistance to post-truth politics and the prevailing inhospitable treatment of refugees by the Home Office (Higgins 2018). The opening section of *Spring* follows Richard Lease, a film director, as he travels from London to Scotland on impulse having recently lost his friend and colleague Paddy. His ignorance of Scottish history and geography immediately denotes the marginalized position Scotland holds in the English cultural imagination and the superiority of London-centric mindsets. The backstory of Richard and Paddy, including their production Sea of Troubles which accentuated the pivotal role of the Northern Irish peace movement, serves as a warning to the British government against 'messing with the ancient hatreds' and gives voice to Smith's own anxiety that 'Ireland will reunite' while other British unions crumble (Smith 2019a: 66; Armistead 2019). Smith thus provides a diachronic response to historic fissures remerging due to Brexit and the predictable cyclicality of antiquated hierarchies: 'Brand new union. Brand new border. Brand new ancient Irish civil unrest. Don't tell me this isn't relevant again in its brand new same old way'

---

[21] Playwright Polis Loizou transitioned into literary fiction with his 2018 novel *Disbanded Kingdom*, a coming-of-age tale set in Kensington. Loizou points to the British public's polarized views on Scottish devolution and immigration – internal debates politicized as an encroaching Europeanization – as causal factors in Britain's withdrawal.

(2019a: 42). With this in mind, Richard's desire to read Percy Bysshe Shelley's 'The Cloud' at Paddy's funeral, gestures to a hopeful metamorphosis and reorganization of existing political structures and cultural moods: *I arise and unbuild it again.*

Richard is joined on his journey north of the border by Brittany Hall, a DCO at an Immigration Removal Centre, and Florence Smith, a mysterious and almost supernatural twelve-year old (reminiscent of Amber from Smith's 2005 novel *The Accidental*) who infiltrates the IRC and coerces Brittany to accompany her to Scotland. Whereas Brittany's empathy for the detainees is complicated by her distaste for both '[p]olitical correct metropolitan liberal shit' and the BBC's attempts to paint British citizens as uninformed, Florence functions as the embodiment of Smith's literary resistance (2019a: 158). Freeing detainees and forcing officials to question their role in the implementation of inhumane British immigration policies (a precursor and by-product of the EU referendum), she 'makes people behave like they should, or like they live in a different better world' (2019a: 314). Rumoured to be a migrant who undertook a sea-crossing from Greece, Florence offers a form of living hope to those facing indefinite detention, attempting to locate her own mother with the help of the Auld Alliance, a nationwide-network of anonymous members utilizing the rail system to help detainees escape IRCs (2019a: 314).[22]

At a critical juncture, however, when Florence has finally reunited with her mother at Culloden – the site of the famous 1746 battle intimately associated with Scotland's vanquished status and the subsequent contested Anglo-Scottish union – Brittany alerts IRC officers who arrest and detain the pair. For Introna, Smith's decision 'to engage with issues of sovereignty through the prisms of anti-migrant policing is apt as borders are central to the exercise of sovereignty' (2020: 19). The novel therefore utilizes the journey to Scotland to underscore the evident parallels of intra-UK and European border debates and their nexus with ideological divisions surrounding the act of migration: 'You don't need [a passport] [. . .] Not for this border. Not yet, anyway' (2019a: 195). As Smith comments, 'I love crossing [borders]. I love the magic line they draw between different places, which then becomes a threshold to new places, possibilities, multiplicities' (qtd. in Elkins 2019). Though Florence's fate remains shrouded in mystery, the closing section of *Spring* contains fragments of hope for a Scotland faced with an impending exit from Europe. In a flashforward to April, 'the anarchic, the final month, of spring the great connective', Florence's cosmopolitan empathy has had a profound impact on her acquaintances (Smith 2019a: 336). As a tribute to Paddy, Richard begins a documentary on the activities of the Auld Alliance, gesturing to the alternative possibilities for global belonging which Scotland could afford were powers of immigration and citizenship not determined by the British state. In response to Richard's initial reticence concerning the feasibility of resisting Home Office protocol and saving migrants 'in any real world scenario', an activist simply explains, 'It's human [. . .] There's no scenario more real' (Smith 2019a: 273). *Spring* reveals the extent to which narrative strategy and reality are symbiotic, encapsulating

---

[22] *Spring* engages in dialogue with Shakespeare's *Pericles*, a play of migration, loss and exile. Each novel in Smith's quartet refashions one of Shakespeare's comedies: *The Tempest*, *Cymbeline*, *Pericles* and *The Winter's Tale* (rather tellingly the intertextual referent for *Summer*).

Smith's repeated refrain that literature is how we learn to 'read the world [. . .] most empathetically, most complexly, most humanly' (Smith 2019b). While this first wave of post-Brexit Scottish fiction fails to offer a detailed explanation of how an independent Scotland might integrate itself into future European geopolitical constellations, the aspirational animating energy is there.

Scottish novelists, poets and dramatists energized the devolution debate in the absence of political initiative, yet it remains to be seen whether the next generation will feel compelled to prepare the ground for post-Brexit independence in the same manner. For example, numerous commentators and politicians questioned Scotland's paradoxical desire to gain independence only to then willingly surrender political sovereignty to Brussels. Analysis by Curtice (2018) indicates that support for independence did not markedly increase during post-Brexit negotiations and Scottish voters still did not favour closing trading arrangements with the EU or more open immigration policies; nonetheless, fears remain that the resultant economic consequences of Brexit will trigger a re-evaluation of Scotland's role in the British union and a greater surge for independence arrived during the Covid-19 crisis when Scotland was offered the opportunity to display its political autonomy. At the very least, selected fictions by Smith, Hall and Shaw evoke an ethical commitment to border crossings, communicating a symbolic embrace of alterity and celebration of hybridity in clear defiance of prevailing English political discourses surrounding migration and the cosmopolitanization of British society. In the post-Brexit moment, literature may once again become a vehicle for the development of devolutionary strategies and the envisioning of viable collaborative endeavours, imagining potential constitutional futures for component territories of the UK. What is clear is that these Brexlit responses are 'structurally nationed', shaped by specific sociopolitical, cultural and economic contexts, and it is likely that the unfinished business of political devolution will continue to find traction in British literature as writers underscore their resistance to separation from Europe (Introna 2020: 26).[23]

Northern Ireland

For the British establishment Northern Ireland is not a place but two places: out of sight and out of mind.

(O'Toole 2020: 73)

To say Anglo-Irish relations have been strained by Brexit is a wonderful understatement. Brexiteers wilfully dismissed the significant of the Irish Question during the referendum as well as internal friction within the island of Ireland; a political position with a long historical tradition. For all the talk of being an island nation, Britain shares a land frontier with an EU member state in the form of the Irish border. The academic and

---

[23] As Hames points out, the matter of whether 'there is still a British literary field, and if Scottish writers see themselves as part of it' will require further consideration in the near-future (Personal Correspondence 2018).

media tradition of employing the shorthand term of 'Britain' for the United Kingdom of Great Britain and Northern Ireland (although understandable) omits Northern Ireland from the frame and betrays an imbalance within the seemingly united polity. As Glenn Patterson reminds us, Northern Ireland is 'an administrative region of the UK. Not a country' (2019a: 7). Frustration with the referendum result was not only driven by Northern Ireland's 55.8 per cent Remain vote, but through a recognition that the accession of both Britain and the Republic of Ireland to the EEC in 1973 went some way to reducing Anglo-Irish tensions and animosities through common membership. And yet, in the 1975 referendum on continued membership in the EEC, Northern Ireland returned a slim 52.1 per cent vote in favour of remaining (on a very low turnout of 48.2%): the smallest majority of any of the constituent territories of the UK. For unionists, continued membership represented an ongoing erosion of Britain's sphere of influence and sovereignty, whereas for nationalists the supranational nature of the European community threatened the dilution of Irish culture.

As Mary C. Murphy so meticulously details in *Europe and Northern Ireland's Future* (2018), although Euroscepticism is markedly reduced in Northern Ireland, the early years of EU membership were met with 'small doses of enthusiasm', particularly following the introduction of structural fund assistance, 'but otherwise dominated by patterns of detachment' due to ongoing sectarian violence (Murphy 2018: 10). Whereas political parties in Westminster were responsible for shaping the public's perception of Europe, in the late twentieth century there was a recalibration of this political narrative in Northern Ireland. During the mid-1970s the Troubles dominated proceedings and forced the issue of European integration to the margins. It was from the late 1980s that the multinational bloc moved from being a peripheral political partner to a crucial strategic ally as the organization helped the constituent country moved towards a peaceful agreement. It is for this reason the EU referendum 'cannot be understood in isolation from the wider history of the Troubles' (Saunders 2018: 300). The European arena proved to be a vital forum for the development of cross-border cooperation; the subsequent Anglo-Irish Agreement in 1985 expressed the 'determination of both governments to develop close cooperation as partners in the European Community' (1985). The re-introduction of devolved administration in May 2007 deepened the level of engagement, and this period witnessed the first stirrings of the Northern Ireland-EU Taskforce (NITF).

In 1998, the multiparty Good Friday Agreement between Britain and Ireland was the cornerstone of the peace process. Joint EU membership was a crucial factor in negotiations, allowing for the inclusion of vital guarantees including an open border between Northern Ireland and the Republic of Ireland due to both territories operating within the Single Market and Customs Union. Since 1995, Northern Ireland had benefited from the EU Special Fund for Peace and Reconciliation: a cross-border programme designed to underpin the peace process, secure economic stability, encourage collaborative projects and improve social relations within divided communities. In the years leading to the Agreement a diverse range of Northern Irish fictions engaged with the destructive consequences and conflict trauma of Troubles violence, including Brian Moore's *Lies of Silence* (1990), Glenn Patterson's *Burning Your Own* (1988) and *Fat Lad* (1992), Pat McCabe's *The Butcher Boy* (1992), Seamus Deane's

Reading in the Dark (1996), Deidre Madden's *One by One in the Darkness* (1996), Robert McLiam Wilson's *Ripley Bogle* (1989) and *Eureka Street* (1996), Bernard MacClaverty's *Grace Notes* (1997), Eoin McNamee's *The Ultras* (2004) and Paul McVeigh's *The Good Son* (2015). The Agreement also weakened the rigid boundaries around contested national identities – offering Northern Irish citizens the choice of identifying as UK or Republic of Ireland citizens – creating power-sharing institutions and increasing support for EU membership in the process. This is particularly relevant to Brexit debates as it set in place assertions that the status of Northern Irish citizens should not be altered without their consent. As Donnacha Ó Beacháin observes, EU withdrawal 'jeopardised rights guaranteed' in the Agreement, including legal frameworks involving the European Convention of Human Rights and European Court of Human Rights, 'both of which Britain was determined to leave as part of the Brexit process' (Ó Beacháin 2019: 259). Connelly points to the irony that 'the gestation period for Brexit coincided with a golden age of Anglo-Irish relations' (Connelly 2018b). That being said, the political terrain in Northern Ireland was still far from stable and sectarianism remained; the Assembly suffered intermittent suspensions in the years following the Agreement. Northern Ireland thus held a liminal position as a problematic polity even after the Agreement. Novels such as Glenn Patterson's *That Which Was* (2004) warn of the dangers in perceiving the Troubles as a cultural conflict, eliding the political inequalities inherent in the system and assuming the Troubles can be closed off with a 'post' marker. For Duncan Morrow and Jonny Byrne, peace in the region was arguably already under severe strain before Brexit emerged as a threat; any 'reconciliation remained symbolic' and dependent on EU funding as 'micro-crises replaced the old macro-crisis' and the devolved government 'floundered over policing (2010), flags (2012), the past (2013), parades (2014), paramilitarism (2015)' and 'welfare changes (2015)' (2017: 151).

Nonetheless, Euroscepticism in Northern Ireland 'has been reformist in nature and has not generally translated into advocacy of withdrawal from the EU' (Mycock and Gifford 2015: 62). Many of the issues which powered the referendum campaign, such as immigration, were less salient factors; moreover, neither the Conservative Party nor UKIP (which lacked an electoral base in the area) were major political players in most regions. Northern Ireland was often overlooked during the referendum debate; Vote Leave purposely retained an Anglocentric purview, understanding that any discussion of the Irish border would compromise their plans for political 'independence'. Novelist Colm Tóibín notes it was clearly not a campaign 'run with Northern Ireland in mind. It's another example, in case we need one, of how little Northern Ireland matters to anyone in Britain' (qtd. in McGrath 2017). Focus was instead redirected towards the Irish border question, related matters of free movement, and the unknowable economic and political impact of an exit from Europe on the recent peace process. Connelly cites Cameron's announcement of the referendum as the moment 'when Brexit anxiety first hit': 'This was not an Irish referendum, but it might as well have been' (2018a: 5; 2). However, campaigns in Northern Ireland were low key, insufficiently financed and suffered from poor coordination, especially between Unionist and Nationalist Remain supporters. Only the Eurosceptic DUP, whose slogan 'Leave makes the Union stronger', advanced a coherent narrative by positioning Brexit as a means of retaining and protecting British national sovereignty in light of the Scottish indyref. While the Agreement attempted to reduce the significance of the border in Irish political discourse, the possibility of EU withdrawal placed the issue firmly back on the table, re-politicizing key debates surrounding sovereignty and national identity responsible for polarizing communities during the Troubles.

Abbie Spallen's state-of-the-nation play, *Lally the Scut* (2015), reinforces how the spectre of the Troubles continues to raise its head in the present and threatens the Agreement, particularly given the imminent EU referendum. Spallen explains,

> *Lally* is set around twenty years after the peace process started. People think that after the Agreement was signed, the Troubles suddenly switched off. They didn't [...] It doesn't go away. The reaction here to the Brexit vote shows that the peace process is hanging by a thread. It could start up again. (qtd. in Sherratt-Bado 2018a)

Set in an unidentified border town, the political satire follows the struggles of a young woman named Lally, who runs up against the institutional incompetence of figures within the political establishment, media and church. The lack of specificity regarding the location of the town 'destabilises the viewer's grasp of its locality' and 'engages extensively with the notion that for many people who live outside the region, the Irish border exists in the realm of the hyperreal', with her characters 'prob[ing] the landscape in an effort to confirm its reality' (Sherratt-Bado 2018a). Lally's son has fallen down a bog hole located directly on the border, 'impossible to tell [...] if it's in the North or the South', adding to the complexities in establishing any form of cross-border initiative (Spallen 2015: 49). Furthermore, efforts to rescue the child raise the risk of disinterring bodies within the field: the tragic missing victims of sectarian violence. If the inability of the establishment to save Lally's son lampoons 'the inadequacy of "post-conflict" political discourse', then the child himself, 'pulled from a dark hole', represents 'the stalled rebirth' of the island of Ireland, its future suspended by the border question (Sherratt-Bado 2018a).[24]

Two days after the referendum result, the front page of the *Belfast Telegraph* summed up the public mood nicely, declaring Britain's exit to be 'A step into the unknown' (Young 2016). Northern Ireland may have returned a Remain vote, but turnout figures were relatively low compared to other regions or recent Assembly elections, indicating a level of political fatigue as evidenced in the Welsh Brexit vote. Edward Mills and Chris Colvin reveal the considerable variation within Northern Ireland, where seven out of eighteen constituencies returned a Leave vote, identifying the 'nationalist vote share' as the single biggest factor in predicting a Remain vote (Mills and Colvin 2016). Although they cite support for Remain among Unionists, the most nationalist constituency, Foyle, returned one of the highest Remain votes, indicating the relevance in analysing potential nationalist/Unionist splits. Religious denomination added an extra element

---

[24] Sherratt-Bado also points to magical realist short-story collections such as *Children's Children* (2016) by Jan Carson, *Sleepwalkers* (2013) by Bernie McGill and *Wild Quiet* (2016) by Roisin O'Donnell as examples of post-Agreement literature which ricochet 'back and forth across the "post-"marker to explore how the past impinges upon the present', bringing to light 'living ghosts' of the Troubles (2018b).

of feverish intensity to the Brexit debate, where Roman Catholic areas such as Foyle voted to remain yet much higher turnouts were reported in Protestant areas such as North Antrim. Further, despite the referendum campaign in England assuming a very different tone, John Garry (2016) identifies some clear parallels in referendum voting behaviour between Northern Ireland and the rest of the UK pertaining to educational attainment levels, immigration and national identity. In total, 63 per cent of those who identify as 'British' voted to leave compared to 13 per cent who identify as 'Irish', while 85 per cent of those who perceive immigration to be a positive force for the economy and society voted to remain compared to 76 per cent of Leave voters who strongly disagreed with the statement. Eva Urban identifies a range of contemporary Northern Irish plays which interrogate the legacy of the Troubles and foreshadow anti-immigrant sentiments which would come to define the referendum campaign. Urban points towards Owen McCafferty's *Quietly* (2009), which captures a specifically anti-Polish mood within Belfast, and Stacey Gregg's *Shibboleth* (2015), which anticipates the redrawing of sectarian markers and refers to a growing disillusionment with the EU. John McCann's *DUPed* (2019), a one-man show exploring the legacy of the Democratic Unionist Party, lambasts the power-sharing agreement and history of social conservatism in Northern Ireland. Lawrence McKeown's *Green and Blue* (2017) adopts a more balanced perspective on the Irish border. Set in the 1980s, *Green and Blue* dramatizes the working relationship between two policemen, on either side of the border, as they come to understand their similar responsibilities to their respective adversarial communities. McKeown gestures to a situation which could once again emerge if the island of Ireland is pulled against its will into the gravitational pull of Anglocentric Westminster politicking.

Just as the protracted peace talks dragged on interminably for years, the post-Brexit negotiation period proved to be just as fractious and drawn-out. In the post-referendum fallout, the Irish Question went from being a neglected factor in Leaver dreaming to the most crucial stumbling block preventing a clean break from EU regulations and thus a successful implementation of the Brexit project. Zadie Smith remarks, 'it was clear that one thing [Brexit] certainly wasn't about, not even slightly, was Northern Ireland, and this focused the mind on what an extraordinary act of solipsism has allowed this long-brutalised little country to become the collateral damage of an internal rift' (Smith 2018). The Anglocentric sentiments of Brexiteer politicians were apparently shared by Leave voters; a 2018 study revealed 87 per cent of such voters viewed 'the collapse of the peace process as an acceptable price for Brexit' (Future of England Study 2018). Brexiteers even began to perceive the Irish problem as an opportunity not a hurdle: the means by which Britain could retain some benefits of membership. For O'Toole, Northern Ireland is 'not the tail wagging the British dog, it is a different kind of beast altogether – the Trojan horse within which all of Brexit is smuggled into the promised land of frictionless access to EU markets without the political obligations of membership' (2020: 189). The concerns of Northern Ireland were certainly not given enough coverage in the English media nor were the consequences understood by Leave factions in Westminster. Karen Bradley, former secretary of state for Northern Ireland, admitted on taking the job in 2018 that she was unaware of the 'deep-seated and deep-rooted issues' at play, seemingly surprised that 'people who are nationalists don't vote for unionist parties and vice versa' (qtd. in Carroll 2018). Donald Tusk, however, warned Westminster 'the key to the UK's future lies – in some ways – in Dublin, at least as long as Brexit negotiations continue' (qtd. in McGee 2017). Where once Northern Ireland was merely 'an afterthought' in the context of Brexit, Murphy concludes, 'the post-referendum landscape places Northern Ireland at the heart of UK politics' (2018: 63).

The crude, binary nature of the referendum undoubtedly threatens to rouse the spectres of Irish sectarianism. An exit from Europe fuels a push for political change and leaves vulnerable communities open to further violence by paramilitary forces, resulting in the calcification of polarized political positions. The 2017 Northern Irish Assembly elections saw a marked increase in support for Sinn Fein, which won its largest ever share of seats, accusing the DUP of refusing to honour key principles of the Agreement. Just as the SNP saw Brexit as an opportunity to renew calls for independence, Sinn Fein made an immediate push for a future referendum on Irish reunification and called for a border poll, escalating fears that Northern Irish voters were moving back towards entrenched positions and deepening the political cleavage. A year after the vote, inflation in Northern Ireland had already increased by 0.47 per cent more than the UK average and unemployment was predicted to rise, with Brexit considered a major contributing factor in both cases (Breinlich et al. 2017: 3). In January 2017, Northern Ireland was hit by a more immediate threat: the collapse of power-sharing in the Stormont Assembly. Brexiteers, including Former Northern Ireland Secretary Owen Paterson, used the crisis to argue the collapse demonstrated the Agreement had 'outlived its use' (qtd. in O'Carroll 2018). For Murphy, the suspension of the devolved institution was a contributing factor in the failure of Northern Ireland to meet the economic and political challenges which Brexit presented and paralysed 'any ability to forge a position on Northern Ireland's Future outside the EU' (2018: 152). The suspension of the consociational Assembly, dependent on a power-sharing arrangement between opposing and antagonistic groups, highlighted the absence of a viable political forum in which to confront post-Brexit realities (not to mention the continued decision by Sinn Fein MPs to refuse to take their seats in Westminster).[25]

As the introduction discussed, the meticulously planned 2017 UK general election, intended to give Theresa May a stronger hand in post-Brexit negotiations, resulted in the Conservatives losing their overall majority and becoming reliant on a confidence-and-supply arrangement with the Eurosceptic DUP to gain a majority. May's arrangement not only lent credence to the view that Westminster was continuing to ignore the perils of being seen to privilege one political group over another, leading to further polarization within Northern Irish communities, but rekindled the dream of Irish unity for nationalists who feared the influence of the DUP in the post-Brexit decision-making process. At the 2018 annual Conservative conference, Theresa May unveiled plans for a Festival of Britain and Northern Ireland in 2022 claiming the proposed festival, ostensibly harking back to the empire exhibitions of pre-war Britain and 1951 national exhibition, would celebrate the close ties between our constituent

---

[25] The tragic murder of journalist Lyra McKee reignited movement to re-initiate talks and the Assembly reopened in January 2020.

nations and strengthen 'our precious union'. Her failure to note that the festival would coincide with the centenary of the foundation of the Irish State in 2022 added further fuel to the complaint that the British government was neglecting the Irish Question in post-Brexit negotiations. Plans for a strict Brexit timetable was immediately derailed by one simple reality: the Northern Irish border. This lack of strategic planning in relation to the border was a defining trait of the Leave campaign. While the Agreement helped to depoliticize the border, ensuring cross-border, post-conflict institutions were established to limit the border's effect on cultural identities and ideological positions, Brexit threatens to unsettle the fragile constitutional settlement. An interdependent economic relationship between Northern Ireland and the Republic of Ireland is heavily dependent on cross-border trade and the Common Travel Area has been integral in allowing border communities to self-identify as British or Irish. The Centre for Cross Border Studies estimates that up to 30,000 people on the island of Ireland are cross-border workers, whose lives will be immediately impacted by any reimposition of border control (Centre 2016: 8). Accordingly, Carr claims 'about 65 percent of voters in the border counties chose to remain': a much higher majority than the national average in favour of maintaining the status quo (2017: 75).

As Dawn Miranda Sherratt-Bado argues, 'contemporary literature of the borderlands can elucidate the fraught context of Brexit and Ireland' (2018b). A number of Northern Irish writers penned psychogeographical responses to the potential effects of Brexit on the borderlands. Garrett Carr's *The Rule of the Land: Walking Ireland's Border* (2017) and Glenn Patterson's *Backstop Land* (2019), drawing inspiration from earlier works such as Colm Tóibín's *Bad Blood: A Walk Along the Irish Border* (1994), engage with the region's troubled past to indicate the psychological effects of reinstalling a border for communities still deeply traumatized by Troubles violence. Author Darran Anderson's memoir *Inventory* (2020) provides a personal account of growing up in the border city of Derry (officially known as Londonderry) during the Troubles, disinterring old ghosts which are now beginning to arise once again due to the Brexit result and subsequent border arrangement disputes. Derry, 'perched on the very edge of Europe, an outland', may have witnessed the 'added sense of European identity' dilute 'the old "us and them" mindset' in intervening years, but for Anderson it is clear 'London is doing all in its power to re-establish the old divisions' (Anderson 2017). Writer Sean O'Brien, who grew up in the borderlands of County Armagh, shares his concerns, arguing the border may once again become a site for paramilitary aggression, while Derry poet Susannah Dickey claims the border gave her identity a fluidity which is often absent from reductive debates on the binary nature of Northern Irish nationhood (Patterson 2019b).

Both the EU and British government repeatedly stressed their commitment to avoiding a hard border; May's letter to Donald Tusk in 2017, triggering Article 50, cited the importance of the peace process, while the UK-Ireland Joint Report affirmed a mutual commitment to the avoidance of a hard border or customs checks. Post-Brexit negotiations, however, revealed a startling lack of consensus between all concerned parties, as the British government negotiated with the European Commission with only occasional input from the Republic of Ireland as an EU member. Any suggestion of a Northern Irish 'backstop' – the maintenance of a seamless land border which keeps

Northern Ireland in the customs union – was flatly rejected by May as it tied Britain to the EU for an indefinite period. Speaking in Dublin in January 2017, May stated her aim for the border to be *frictionless* in order for trade to remain unaffected. This inability of the British government to perceive the Irish border in anything other than economic terms – a liminal territorial zone designed to facilitate the free movement of consumer goods and services – testifies to Westminster's ignorance of the cultural idiosyncrasies and identity politics within Northern Ireland which necessitated the creation of the border in the first place. Further, given that the rapid electoral support for English nationalism was stimulated by intra-UK devolutionary strategies, the British government should have been more attuned to the dangers of neglecting Northern Ireland and instead focused on protecting the Agreement and developing a viable post-Brexit civic culture.

When Johnson took over at the helm, he re-emphasized the return of a hard border 'would be economic and political madness. Everybody understands the social, political and spiritual ramifications', yet his government proved just as inept at confronting or appreciating the ideological and cultural issues underpinning the border debate, which held the potential to reignite political instability in the region (qtd. in Patterson 2019a: 184). Unionists were alarmed further when Enda Kenny warned the EU should 'prepare for a united Ireland' (Offices of the Houses of Oireachas 2017).[26] Such a development remains more probable than an *Irexit* given the staunch pro-EU sentiments held by both Irish political parties and the Irish public. Fears of a hard border arguably *softened* the form of Brexit that emerged, yet doubts remain over whether any border management arrangement can remain frictionless following an agreement that Northern Ireland will continue to abide by EU single market rules. The poem 'Speech' by Northern Irish poet Elaine Gaston voices early doubts on the feasibility of a hard border:

> We don know yet fthere'll be
> a clean Breggsit ra messy Breggsit
> nur a hard Breggsit nur a saft Breggsit
> But mnot going te build a hard boarder.
> It'll be a soft boarder, waitn see. (qtd. in Patterson 2019a: xxi)

A border in the Irish Sea merely pushes the border problem into unchartered waters – presenting a multitude of logistical problems, not to mention debates surrounding economic commitments – and effectuates a re-territorialization of the haunting partition. Bogdanor recognizes 'the most important effect of the re-establishment of border controls would be not economic nor even constitutional, but psychological'; hence the power of literature is heightened in giving voice to border debates (2019: 243). David Wheatley's poem 'Flags and Emblems' (2018) accentuates the difficulty in imposing any new territorial markers on communities still engaging with existing border debates. On handing over a 'Northern Irish fiver [. . .] crinkling the Queen in his palm', a man in a post office ponders whether 'they' are 'part of us', concluding 'but

---

[26] 2016 witnessed a rapid increase in the number of applications for Irish citizenship: an increase of 27 per cent from 2015 (Fenton 2018: 273).

for the flags on / the lampposts you'd hardly / know what country it was' (Wheatley 2018). A number of recent fictions suggest Northern Ireland is trapped in an anxious, backward-looking temporal state; the territorial consequences of EU withdrawal merely complicate the healing process for communities still coming to terms with the past and gesture to the potential for the forces of politicization to reignite age-old feuds. As O'Toole warns, for the island of Ireland 'there can be no "clean breaks" [...] just slow and delicate efforts to disentangle the present and the future from the worst aspects of the past' (2020: xvii).

Sherratt-Bado, whose significant work illuminates the animating energy of Northern Irish literature in anticipating and responding to political developments, identifies contemporary Irish poet Siobhán Campbell as a perceptive voice in debates surrounding the Agreement, the Irish border, Stormont crises and the post-Brexit fallout. While Campbell's fifth collection *Cross-Talk* (2009) considers how the border's historic 'divisive geopolitical structure has a self-replicating effect within sociocultural structures', her sixth collection, *Heat Signature* (2017) responds directly to the EU referendum result and its immediate consequences for the island of Ireland (Sherratt-Bado 2018c). Her poem 'Why Islanders Don't Kiss Hello' vilifies David Cameron as a 'Judas' figure slipping 'out the side door' after his great miscalculation, ripping apart the hard-fought peace process supported by subsequent EU funding initiatives: 'Perhaps we are not fully of the Europe / where the lean-to nature of a kiss can denote / who will be shafted in a vote' (Campbell 2017: 58). Campbell's work demonstrates that poetic discourse serves as 'an ideal medium in which to explore the polysemic nature of Brexit's "internal conflict"', claiming 'a bifocal vision is required to acknowledge how tightly Ireland is enmatrixed within multiple geopolitical networks' (Sherratt-Bado 2018c). The island of Ireland has already 'learned because we must' to assume a bifocal vision 'where the view over one shoulder is as good / from this side as the other' (Campbell 2017: 58). Britain's deep-rooted cultural Euroscepticism might wipe away that tentative 'peck of venture in a shared future', consolidated by the Agreement and gradual embrace of Europe, but Campbell suggests the cultural myopia underpinning Brexit ideology is not shared by those who voted in favour of closer supranational cooperation as a bulwark against the re-emergence of the past (2017).

Set immediately after the IRA ceasefire in 1996, Michael Hughes' *Country* (2018a) looks back to the final days of the border conflict, as an IRA gang refuses to decommission and reignite tensions by storming a British army base.[27] Drawing on the characters and structure of the *Iliad*, Homer's epic poem documenting the dying embers of the Greco-Trojan War, *Country* insinuates that the same territorial conflicts continue to inform the present. While the British in the novel play the role of the Trojan army, the 'scheming gods of Mount Olympus' become the 'politicians on both sides, casually manipulating the fates of those fighting on the ground, mere pawns in their petty power games' (Hughes 2018b). Hughes, whose hometown of

---

[27] Michelle Gallen's *Big Girl, Small Town* (2020), set a decade after the ceasefire, communicates how deeply a family can be moulded by Anglo-Irish politicking. Like her protagonist, Majella O'Neill, Gallen grew up near the Irish border and is well aware of the divisions that would arise should any attempt be made to reinstate a hard border.

Keady, Armagh was affected by sectarian violence, recognizes that his region is once again a site of heightened contestation, complicating any stable sense of belonging: the 'border ran through my national identity, pushing me to stand on one side or the other [. . .] hanging around on the threshold' (Hughes 2018c). The implied continuation of sectarian violence in the closing stages anticipates further parallels between 1990s Anglo-Irish conflict and the EU referendum: two historical periods when allegiances and national loyalties were pushed to their limits. Hughes admits the tense relationship between England and Ireland in the run-up to the vote was on his mind during the writing process, a period in which 'militant ideas of nationalism [were] resurfacing', and accepts *Country* can be read as a 'Brexit novel':

> It's coming out of that moment when a political conflict reaches a stalemate and there's a certain amount of bitterness. That sense of militancy and those ideas of political rivalry bubble up again. That happened during the Troubles, and it's finding its way into the Brexit situation, as well as into the novel. (qtd. in Sherratt-Bado 2019)

A vocal Remainer, he forcefully argues Brexit and the installation of a new border not only runs the risk of destabilizing the fragile equilibrium put in place by the Agreement, but pushes Northern Ireland into the arms of the Republic, thus preparing the ground for future reunification. Indeed, Hughes was concerned the title of the novel 'might sound too romantically nationalistic, like I was taking sides in the book. I wanted to make sure that both sides got to have a voice' (Sherratt-Bado 2019). Yet the 'multivalent' title is rather appropriate to the Brexit debate where the term 'country' is applied and understood differently by warring factions in British politics (Sherratt-Bado 2019).

Jez Butterworth's *The Ferryman* (2017a) reinforces the danger Brexit poses in reigniting old grievances for political purposes. Set in 1981, when hunger strikes were attracting greater attention to the Republican cause, the play retains a microscopic focus on a family who have experienced the violence of the Troubles first-hand. Quinn, the head of the Carney family, learns that the body of his brother Seamus has been discovered preserved in a peat bog, years after his disappearance during the bloody period of the early 1970s. Suspected of being a police informant by the IRA, it is thought Seamus was yet another member of the Disappeared, citizens abducted and murdered as a form of extrajudicial punishment by paramilitary forces. His exhumation brings to the surface long buried animosities within the family, particularly for Quinn whose past links to the IRA return to haunt the political silence of the present. The play's domestic setting within a small farmhouse kitchen heightens the suffocating tension, attending to the ways by which larger national debates, and antagonistic forces of polarization, are played out in claustrophobic familial quarters. *The Ferryman* premiered at the Royal Court Theatre, London in 2017, drawing English attention to the dangers of resurrecting buried battles simply to satisfy national developments (even alluding to Northern Ireland's reluctant initial entry into the EEC). In re-politicizing the Troubles, Butterworth warns old traumas are deeply preserved in cultural memory and will continue to resurface in the contemporary moment despite concerted efforts to silence the past: 'the years roll by, and nothing changes' (2017a: 8). For Butterworth, 'the politics of the play are so buried, and yet it speaks to us so loudly now', reminding us that when it comes to the victims of paramilitary violence, the bodies are far from cold (Butterworth 2017a).

Anna Burns' *Milkman*, winner of the 2018 Man Booker Prize, continues this backward-looking concentration on the trauma of the Troubles and legacy of the Agreement, and their combined relevance to the heightened frictions surrounding Brexit and the Northern Irish border.[28] *Milkman* delivers a tense account of the daily life of a politically detached, nameless young woman, Middle Sister, who attracts the oppressive attention of an older, high-ranking paramilitary in Belfast, the titular character, during the height of the Troubles. The unnamed narrator realizes any attempt to ignore the fraught political conditions – particularly literary escapism – are futile; and yet, 'having awareness [. . .] didn't prevent things from happening or allow for intervention on, or reversal of things that had already happened' (2018a: 65). As Clare Hutton (2019) identifies, Middle Sister may be recounting events during the Troubles, but she is narrating from a vantage point twenty years after the signing of the Agreement, when the decommissioning of paramilitary groups has taken place. Burns never explicitly mentions the narrative is set in Belfast or even Northern Ireland; instead, she employs a series of key phrases to allude to the violent sectarian conflict and internal struggles between the 'renouncers-of-the-state' – the IRA – and 'defenders-of-the-state' – the loyalist UDA – during the 1970s. Burns brings to light the rules of allegiance governing societal relations in the period as Middle Sister is threatened and stalked through her fractured landscape while her maybe boyfriend is powerless to help or enter no-go areas. Indeed, *Milkman* has far more interesting things to say regarding female oppression, public shaming and affect, but the novel does uncover key divides relevant to the Northern Irish response to the Brexit debate. Burns finished the novel before Brexit, which she labels an 'absolutely disastrous and a tragic mistake', but constructed her narrative so it could be perceived as a commentary on any enclosed community and acknowledges its timely narratological focus on 'barriers and boundaries and the dreaded "other"' speaks to the urgent present (Burns 2018b).

Political tension in the narrative, of course, revolves around 'anything that could be construed – even in the slightest, even in the most contorted [. . .] as to do with the border', but it is maybe boyfriend's acquisition of a Blower Bentley which best exposes the fraught 'pyscho-political atmosphere, with its rule of allegiance, of tribal identification' (Burns 2018a: 24; 237).[29] Despite broader issues of territory and political positioning, it is the instinctual 'flags-and-emblems' issue which is immediately 'pathologically, narcissistically emotional' (2018a: 25). The racing car with its 'national self-gratifying connotations', fits too snugly into the 'quintessential British imaginary', inciting fears surrounding the loss of a 'sovereign, national and religious identity' in Northern Ireland. Burns' narrator notes the car's emblematic British flag, containing

---

[28] Nick Laird's *Modern Gods* (2019), set in post-Agreement Ulster, contains a similar fascination with the borders of the past.

[29] The 1999 Patten Report addressed the crucial role played by national symbols in fuelling sectarian conflict, stating the police should 'adopt a new badge and symbols which are entirely free from any association with either the British or Irish states' (Patten 1999).

a 'quintessential, nation-defining, "over the water" patriotism', was also that same flag from 'over the road', with the latter seemingly far more capable of stoking division than the former (2018a: 118). In these 'knife-edge times', the Bentley becomes symbolic of wider discourses concerning collusion and disloyalty, indicating the ways by which a symbol can come to stand for that much more (2018a: 27). Anglo-Irish divisions are also wrapped up in debates surrounding English boys' names from 'over the water', which are socially banned for being politically contentious or connoting a 'taunting, long-memory, backdated, we-shall-not-forget, historical distaste reaction', but happily accepted by those 'over the road' (2018a: 24). It is tempting to establish easy parallels between Burns, born and raised in Belfast, and her unnamed narrator, but the novel communicates a deeper psycho-political mood was prevalent in 1970s Northern Irish society, infused with a 'loss of hope and absence of trust and with a mental incapacitation over which nobody seemed willing or able to prevail' (2018a: 90). In providing a suffocating and acutely personal account of everyday life during the Troubles, *Milkman* contributes to a movement in Northern Irish literature towards the empathetic consideration, and reconciliation, of past divides.

Four years after the referendum, the Irish border remains the most fundamental issue affecting a viable withdrawal agreement and the greatest threat to the stability of the UK. A proposed sea border not only angers Unionists but reinforces an already precarious territorial demarcation between Great Britain *and* Northern Ireland. It is widely assumed that Brexit will actuate a more destructive impact on Northern Ireland, exacerbating strains to its fragile economy by negatively affecting foreign trade and investment, reducing GDP, and ensuring the loss of structural funds. It also redirects attention away from existing challenges, many of which needed to be addressed before the issue of EU membership could be adequately deliberated, including a structural reliance on the public sector, long-term unemployment, the development of devolved politics, and a harmonization of regional policy agendas. Brexit thereby effectuates the disproportionate economic marginalization of those voters most likely to have voted to leave, merely reinforcing the sense of disenfranchisement and disaffection which powered the referendum result. It remains to be seen whether future post-Brexit fictions will depict Northern Ireland as 'a relic of old imperial conflicts or as portent of new kinds of civic community based on newly developed kinds of national identity' (Dix 2013: 190). However, the need for literary voices which can communicate an all-island dialogue, anticipate the development of cross-party alliances, consider the consequences of Brexit on cross-border cooperation and peace building, and provide both critical and imaginative solutions to the struggles facing Northern Ireland, become more urgent and necessary as border negotiations continue to stumble on indefinitely.

Although much post-Brexit media attention has understandably been focused on the Irish border and Scottish independence, the neglect of Gibraltar and its overwhelming rejection of the proposed European withdrawal is just as intractable. Gibraltar entered the EEC alongside Britain in 1973 and its overwhelming vote to remain in 2016 (on a 95.9% majority) testifies to the Gibraltarian's geopolitical awareness of Spain's territorial claim and their inherent desire to remain tied to Britain and the EU for protection rather than suffer the indignity of co-sovereignty. M. G. Sanchez's short-story collection *Crossed Lines* (2019) documents the movement of Gibraltarians and Spaniards as they commute to work across the border on a daily basis. Sanchez, a Gibraltarian author now residing in Britain, indicates how Brexit not only contradicts the wishes of the vast majority of its citizens, but suggests Gibraltar's geo-strategic positioning escalates Spanish claims to the territory and hinders the free-flowing movement of citizens and services across the Gibraltar-Spain border. *Crossed Lines* reveals the extent to which the triggering of Article 50 will directly impact Gibraltar, which now serves as a spectral reminder of imperial Britain's global reach and its complicated historical relationship with Continental Europe. In the fallout of Brexit, Gibraltar emerged as Britain's forgotten partner, with their concerns either dismissed or ignored in strategic phases. In drawing attention to the continued relevance of borders and bordering processes to Gibraltarian identities, Sanchez's fiction thus delivers an urgent reminder of the ties that bind.

English devolution

England is a nation; Britain is a political convenience.

(Kingsnorth 2009: 12)

But we must return to England for, as Gardiner reminds us, devolution deeply affects a 'nation crippled by the idea of its own majority', and finding it more difficult than Scotland, Wales or Northern Ireland in 'identifying a specific national culture' (2005: ix; 4). O'Toole seemingly concurs, arguing 'To throw one's hands up in exasperation at the old familiar eruption of the Irish Question is to miss the whole point of the moment [. . .] the English Question' (2020: 220). Kenny identifies that much political and media commentary on the English identity crisis takes devolution 'as both a chronological and causal point of origin' but follows Wellings (2014) in recognizing the complex relationship European integration played in establishing a 'seedbed for a new nationalist orientation' among the English public (2014: 27; 29). The axiomatic assumption that England constituted 'the stable and secure heartland' of the UK no longer seemed to hold (2014: 232). Whereas Scotland has learnt that 'union does not mean that national identity disappears', a post-Maastricht England is riven with fears that a federal Europe will erase its distinct cultural identity: 'her history has given her no experience of the loss of sovereignty, or of the possibility of survival of identity' (Smout 1994: 112). In 1962, Scottish writer John Douglas Pringle predicted England's fate in the evolving European Union would be similar to the loss of Scottish culture within the United Kingdom in the eighteenth century. Pringle goes on to explain the lack of Scottish resistance to EU membership compared to the palpable anxiety of the English: 'having lost our national identity once already, it matters less if we lost it again. Indeed, Scotland may even recover her sense of distinction if Britain is merged in a larger European union. But will England preserve hers?' (Pringle 1962). Beneath all the devolutionary fervour, then, ran an inherent fear that any splintering of the union would allow Brussels to escalate the drive for the integrationist project. After all, a federal Europe is a far more threatening proposition to England than to Scotland, Wales or Northern Ireland, who can only stand to gain from greater political centrality.

Haseler argues the 'English tribe' was incensed by the feeling that the EU were playing a pivotal role in 'breaking asunder' Britain's 'unitary character' in order to create a 'Europe of the regions', provoking a renewed Eurosceptic stance towards any political or monetary union (1996: 7).[30]

Paul Kingsnorth, in *The Search for Real England* (2009), claimed the post-1997 devolutionary scene 'created a situation in which the English [were] now ill-suited by British democracy', suggesting that while Scotland and Wales have reclaimed some measure of political nationhood, England has been subsumed within the political entity of Britain and remains 'in limbo' (279). He poses the valid question: If England is without devolved legislature, how does the country locate its sense of self in the multinational state? In calling for England 'to be re-democraticised, from the top down', Kingsnorth anticipated the feelings of many Leave supporters, for whom the Brexit vote provided outlet for renewed demands for greater political autonomy (2009: 279). For Bogdanor, Brexit is thus the closest the English have come to a 'constitutional moment' (2019: 276). Years before the EU referendum appeared on the horizon support for an English Parliament was already gaining traction. Over half of Leave voters backed calls for an English Parliament compared to only 34 per cent of Remainers.[31] Gardiner recognizes, just as with the Brexit vote, the drive for an English Parliament over the years 'has trodden a thin line between reaction ("grievance") and a wishful search for a working-class reconnection with Englishness' (2012: 160). Similarly, the West Lothian Question – an acute concern over whether Scottish and Northern Irish MPs should have the right to vote on English matters given the same rights were not afforded to English MPs in the devolved assemblies – had long troubled various traditionalist factions in the House of Commons. As Conservative MP William Hague warned, a festering resentment would develop in the electorate which had the potential to erupt in as yet unknown ways, discerning the 'first stirrings of the sleeping dragon of English nationalism' in the wake of devolution and accusing the Labour government of 'constitutional vandalism' (Hague 1999). Immediately following the indyref, after the much greater threat of Scottish independence had been quashed, Cameron turned away from the idea of an English Parliament and tabled a vote on English Votes for English Laws. The symbolic importance of EVEL, passed on 22 October 2015 due to strong support from Conservative and UKIP MPs, cannot be understated, even in spite of the vehement opposition to the legislation. EVEL contributed to the strengthening of nationalist sentiments in the lead-up to the EU referendum and revealed a heightened national awareness of the support for regional devolution in regions outside of London.

The progressive civic nationalism associated with parties such as the SNP, Plaid Cymru and Sinn Fein has failed to materialize as a viable force in England; instead, the familiar tremors of English nationalism developed as an unintended consequence

---

[30] A. L. Kennedy's *Looking for the Possible Dance* (1993) acknowledges how, even from a Scottish perspective, 'England seemed more and more like a foreign country, even to itself' (2005: 38).

[31] Rather than pursue an English Parliament, Blair experimented with the possibility of devolved assemblies, but the idea was rejected in the 2004 north-east devolution referendum. Cummings, later campaign director of Vote Leave, first deployed his post-truth tactics and populist advertising in this referendum, many of which would reappear in 2016, including the mendacious claim that voting against regional devolution would save millions of pounds for the NHS.

of devolution. As the post-Brexit political landscape has shown us, exiting the EU has failed to satisfy the demands of disillusioned English Leave voters – particularly in the North – who felt George Osborne and James Wharton's shameful Northern Powerhouse proposals presented no viable strategies for overcoming the widening North-South divide. It also may have fuelled re-emergent calls for regional devolution in England, including support for the media-driven Power Up The North campaign which aims to redirect investment north of the M25, but the introduction of elected metro-mayors in England during 2017 failed to correct any representational imbalances (in Tees Valley there was so little interest in the role that an inexperienced lightweight was able to be elected). If even Brexit, one of the most fundamental constitutional crises of recent times, is incapable of satiating nationalist forces and generating more control to left-behind communities, then England (and, in turn, its literature), may start looking inward to correct radical intra-English imbalances of power.

The potential break-up of Britain is fictionalized in Rupert Thomson's dystopic novel *Divided Kingdom* (2005). Set in a near-future in which Britain has recently undergone a political and territorial 'Rearrangement' – the forcible dissection of the territory into four zones, each with its own flag – the novel speaks to fears surrounding turn-of-the-century devolutionary reforms from an English perspective, questioning the preservation of 'a kingdom united in name only' (2006: 335). With the populace resettled into separate and bordered autonomous republics, new national distinctions become exaggerated to the point of parody. The divided kingdom becomes a self-perpetuating and 'self-fulfilling prophecy' as a psychological 'border sickness' quickly sweeps the kingdom as a consequence of territorial segregation, with watchtowers, barbed wire, minefields, search lights and detention centres erected along borders to prevent contamination by citizens traversing borders illegally from adjoining zones (2006: 23; 114). Thomson's critique of corrosive border politics is clear, warning that the construction of intra-UK psychological and territorial borders not only fosters a form of exclusive ethnonationalism but creates an island fortress mentality which destabilizes European communication channels. Although various characters attempt to map out alternate geographies to challenge the arbitrary enforcement of internal divisions, the novel still leaves us with a debilitating post-devolution vision of a dissolved and enfeebled disunited kingdom which has 'thrown off all pretence to be anything other than what it was [. . .] inward-looking' (2006: 8).

The UK is at a critical juncture where the devolved nations are undergoing pivotal transitions which may destabilize an already fragile union. Understandably, the complex motivating factors (and eventual potential impact) of Brexit differ between and within England, Wales, Scotland and Northern Ireland. British Euroscepticism is clearly 'realized across the four nations of the UK in plural and diverse forms that reflect differing interactions between state and sub-state national sovereignty and the overarching supra-state framework' (Mycock and Gifford 2015: 67). Internal relationships and tensions between component territories – concerning conflicting layers of identification and belonging which complicate a sense of political enfranchisement – will be as vital to managing the post-Brexit transition as relations with other European member states. As Gardiner recognizes, the conditions of pre-Brexit Britain had already created 'a vacuum in which new national cultures must be negotiated' and we may begin to see the emergence of further *devolved nationalisms* in response to the territorial differentiation of the Brexit vote (2005: 4). If Scotland chooses to rerun a second Indy Ref, Wales seeks further devolutionary dispensations, or Northern Ireland confronts the possibility of a united Ireland, Brexit will have acted as the primary catalyst on a radical alteration of the political allegiances (and dissolution of the territorial boundaries) of the UK. Even if one, or all, of these political shifts occurs, the English Question remains unresolved.

Devolution has radically modified the British union and it remains to be seen whether a post-Brexit Britain will be flexible enough to house and contain such competing alternate identities and strident nationalisms. Any refusal to acknowledge the disparate political wills of constituent territories will be costly. The history of devolution has been an inherently British process and devolved nations must play more central roles in intra-UK discussions even after post-Brexit negotiations have concluded. On a special edition of Front Row on Radio 4, discussing how Britain's literary and creative communities should respond to Brexit, Scottish writer Val McDermid suggests that literature has failed to give voice to certain factions within society and has a responsibility to become more representative of Leave-voting communities. If the UK is to re-evaluate its position on the world stage, then it may be the role of literature to begin with the British problem first.

4

Fortress Britain

The great immigration debate

> *A world in which communities are neatly hived off from one another seems no longer a serious option, if it ever was.*
>
> (Appiah 2006: 10)

This chapter will examine the key cultural issue that defined the EU referendum: immigration. As the introduction theorized, immigration was widely heralded as the most critical factor for undecided voters – even those gravitating towards a vote for Remain – and exposed the resounding symbolic sensitivity to politico-cultural borders.[1] Accordingly, both Leave and Remain camps purposefully avoided promoting the merits and benefits of immigration either in their political rhetoric or respective manifestos and the *politicization* of intra-EU immigration became integral to the debate. Once the political conversation during the campaign shifted to freedom of movement and national border policies, Remain's lead in the polls rapidly diminished. The publication of immigration figures on 26 May 2016 – revealing that net migration had risen from 177,000 in 2012 to 330,000 in 2015 (with EU countries contributing to approximately half that number) – gave greater momentum to the Leave campaigns (Goodwin and Milazzo 2017: 463). The figures torpedoed David Cameron's empty pledge to reduce immigration 'back to the levels of the 1990s – tens of thousands a year, not hundreds of thousands' and guaranteed future quotas were easily dismissed as meaningless rhetoric (Conservative Party 2010).[2] Following the Maastricht Treaty in 1992, free movement had been reinforced as a central principle of the single market and non-negotiable factor in membership. During the referendum campaign, EU

---

[1] As Dennison and Goodwin demonstrate, utilizing data from BSE and BSA surveys, the British public 'is not divided on immigration. A large majority of the population wants levels of immigration reduced' (2015: 175). In the British Election Study (BES) of March 2014, 78 per cent of respondents viewed immigration as bad for the British economy. Areas that had become more ethnically diverse (or experienced a higher influx of EU nationals between 2005 and 2015) were more likely to support leaving the EU (Goodwin and Heath 2016a). These findings are consistent with earlier research identifying reasons behind the rise of UKIP and other nationalist parties (Goodwin and Milazzo 2015).

[2] L. M. McLaren (2012) has identified clear links between the erosion of public trust in political parties and the refusal to resolve immigration concerns.

membership was denounced as a direct catalyst for rising immigration and its erosion of parliamentary sovereignty, while free movement continued to be perceived as a direct threat to Britain's ability to protect its borders and regulate immigration levels. Borders were utilized as polysemic political resources and instruments of control: from London's 'ring of steel', to the territorial boundaries of the nation state, to the (expanding) perimeter of the EU and the Schengen immigration zone. The Leave campaign insinuated that borders should operate asymmetrically, permitting the flow of transnational mobilities and goods and services required for global trade, while blocking the passage of demonized 'others'. Unfortunately for the Remain camp, these geopolitical tensions, fears surrounding securitization, and a resilient politics of self-determination, ensured that a noxious brand of atavistic nationalism, rather than a genuine debate concerning the merits of institutional cosmopolitanism, came to define the referendum.

The issue of immigration has long coloured British electoral debates and resulted in a continual re-evaluation of the nation's social and legal obligations to the EU and the European continent more generally. Whereas in the late twentieth century the discussion of British immigration policy focused heavily on the Caribbean and Asian diaspora, with the attendant stereotypes of racial otherness, in the twenty-first century the EU migrant has assumed new relevance. A vote to leave became a solution in tackling the great immigration debate that has plagued British politics for decades. Ashcroft polls indicated that over 80 per cent of voters who held negative opinions towards immigration were likely to vote Leave, particularly in lower-income areas outside of London (Ashcroft Poll 2016). This pronounced cultural insularity was not simply motivated by a historical hostility to the EU as a bureaucratic and intrusive entity but a determined action to 'Take Back Control' of national borders and delineate which citizens had a right to belong in the nation: a move designed to cement and jealously protect Britain's geographical insulation. The omnipresence of this prominent Vote Leave slogan during the referendum campaign attests to the claim that immigration and border politics were the pivotal issues swaying an electorate who feared refugees would struggle to assimilate in a new culture, place a significant strain on host economies and public services and increase competition for jobs thus reducing national wages.

On 1 May 2004, the EU expanded to include ten Central and Eastern European (CEE) states – the largest enlargement in its history – increasing existing British tensions regarding EU membership.[3] The influx of Eastern Europeans was initially considered a boost to the national economy and provided a cheap source of labour. As T. H. Eriksen notes, the relationship of immigrants 'to the imagined national community becomes subject to negotiation whenever the culturally hegemonic see fit' (2015: 3). Yet EU expansion exacerbated existing fears regarding further integration and sparked a fresh media debate concerning cultural compatibility, unprecedented immigration levels and the economic impact to working-class citizens. Marlene

---

[3] In 2003, the year before enlargement, the European Commission reported there was 'often exasperation' within Britain 'at the phenomenon of immigration and the scale it has reached' (European Commission 2003).

Herrschaft-Iden (2020) argues that between 1997 and 2010 the Conservative Party was initially positive about the prospect of EU enlargement, predicting the policy would generate prosperity due to free trade and remove Eastern European countries away from Russia's insidious influence. The Conservatives only began to criticize New Labour's more flexible position on free movement and intra-EU migration following an influx of support for UKIP from 2011 onwards. The expansion (which had its roots in the 1990s when the Maastricht Treaty introduced European citizenship and the Schengen Area afforded EU citizens the opportunity to live and work across member states) was interpreted as a neoliberal move designed to improve the economies of Western European member states, with the British labour market opened up to a high number of migrants looking to take advantage of free movement. Over the next decade, there was a dramatic increase in intra-European migration; by 2013, half of all (intra-EU) migrants came from those new member states that joined in 2004 (Castro-Martin and Cortina 2015). The enlargement was of particular relevance to Polish migrant workers as it occurred during a prolonged employment crisis while Poland (the largest of the accession states and now the sixth largest member state within the EU) negotiated a tentative post-communist transition to a capitalist economy.

During the referendum campaign, Polish citizens were categorized as Eastern, rather than Central, Europeans; a discursive strategy reproduced by the media in order to reinforce the negative imagery of 'benefit migrants'. The 2004 expansion naturally provoked a substantial rise in electoral support for far-right and nationalist political parties, including the British National Party, English Democrats and UKIP, that all placed opposition to both the EU and immigration at the forefront of their respective manifestos.[4] The 2005 BNP manifesto pledged to deport immigrants and refugees already residing within Britain, positioning white Britons as members of an indigenous culture whose homeland was becoming overrun by foreign migrants threatening British democratic values. Their provocative rhetoric struck a chord with economically insecure working-class voters and the squeezed middle class, and the BNP saw their influence increase from one council seat in the late 1990s to forty-six seats in 2006.

Immigration was certainly the defining *emotive* electoral issue in the years leading to the referendum. In 2013, Theresa May (then home secretary) employed billboard vans for her controversial advertising campaign Operation Vaken. The pilot programme, operating with six London boroughs, warned illegal migrants to either leave the country willingly or face arrest, but was swiftly abandoned following a public outcry at the creation of the Conservative's 'hostile environment'. At the 2015 Conservative Party

---

[4] Far-right populist parties were also enjoying widespread support in Continental Europe: the Five Star Movement and Northern League in Italy, France's Front National, Greece's Golden Dawn, Austria's Freedom Party, Denmark's People's Party, Poland's Law and Justice and the Netherlands' Party for Freedom all drew on the same nationalist identities and traditions. Resistance to immigration is widely considered to be a defining feature of Euroscepticism across Western Europe (De Vries 2018). The populist backlash was not limited to Europe, with the Minuteman and Tea Party movements in the United States and One Nation Party in Australia contributing to this global reaction to rising immigration levels.

Conference, May claimed immigration was to blame for the ongoing economic malaise following the financial crash of 2008:

> When immigration is too high, when the pace of change is too fast, it's impossible to build a cohesive society. It's difficult for schools and hospitals and core infrastructure like housing and transport to cope [...] for people in low-paid jobs, wages are forced down even further while some people are forced out of work altogether. (May 2015)

Labour reinforced this view in its 2015 manifesto by attacking levels of low-skilled migration. The negative stance taken towards immigration by both major parties paved the way for the rise of far-right nationalist forces and their discursive dehumanization of migrants as an invasive and unwelcome species during the referendum. As O'Toole so insightfully notes, the threat of 'invasion' operates as 'a structure of feeling' which unites divergent grievances, fusing 'the war, the end of Empire, immigration and the EU into a single image' against which anger must be directed (2018a: 90). Author and journalist Lionel Shriver pre-empted the rhetoric of Brexiteers in this regard, claiming 'the arrival of foreign populations can begin to duplicate the experience of military occupation – your nation is no longer your home' (Mishra 2017). Xenophobia consequently developed into a politico-institutional and sociocultural phenomenon whereas immigration became the key predictor in determining who would vote for Brexit (Goodwin and Milazzo 2017). For example, areas which experienced the highest rate of increase of immigration, such as Lincolnshire, were the most likely to vote Leave (Goodhart 2017: 121). Unable to direct their anger towards those responsible for their cultural and financial disaffection, voters transposed their discontent towards EU immigrants and their assumed drain on national resources and services. The referendum also witnessed a widespread denunciation of refugees – lambasted as the root cause of housing shortages and responsible for the 'necessary' introduction of Tory austerity measures. Vote Leave was consistently guilty of manipulating anxieties regarding free movement, linking EU immigration to criminal activity. The fear of *crimmigration* has its roots in Thatcher's infamous 1988 Bruges speech to the College of Europe whereby she insinuated the weakening of European border controls would result in greater levels of terrorism, trafficking and crime. The urgent relevance of contemporary border politics associated with Brexit is thus intimately entangled with a longer cultural disaffection relating to multiculturalism, the cosmopolitanization of society, and a resistance to both legal and illegal forms of immigration.

This chapter will not conflate immigration and asylum but consider how the two were falsely tied to a nationalist rhetoric that emerged during the referendum campaign, with the Leave camp glossing over the differences between EU migrants and wider forms of transnational migration to further their own ends. As Robert Miles and Paula Cleary (1993) identify, there also exists a historical legacy within popular and political discourse to conflate refugees and multiculturalism as a conjoined threat to British culture. The act of immigration is a contributing factor in the growing defamiliarization of the national imaginary discussed in the previous chapter. For Giorgio Agamben, if 'the refugee represents such a disquieting element in the order of the nation state, this is so primarily because, by breaking the identity between the human and the citizen and that between nativity and nationality, it brings the originary fiction of sovereignty to crisis' (2000: 20). To this we can add a conflation of British immigration policy with the perceived imposition of EU bureaucracy. Such national insularity is exacerbated by Britain's long legacy of evading EU commitments relating to free movement. The Schengen Agreement – signed in 1985 but not effected until a decade later – aimed to gradually abolish internal border checks within the EU while the Amsterdam Treaty (which entered into force in 1999) attempted to harmonize immigration and asylum policies by devolving powers from the national government to the European Parliament. Britain opted out of the proposed Schengen Area (only committing to policies relating to criminal law and policing), citing its unique status as an island nation with *natural* borders as a justification for this fresh spell of British exceptionalism and Euroscepticism. Indeed, the Channel remains the most potent geographical obstacle for refugees and exemplifies Britain's special position within the EU constellation. By opting into Dublin Regulation directives – requiring asylum applications to be made in the first country an individual enters (or has their biometric data stored) within the EU – the British created further barriers to entry, guaranteeing border controls were conducted on the French side of the Channel.

The 2015 Syrian refugee crisis intensified the already fraught issue of immigration and its potent capacity as an emotive political resource. The crisis reinforced the perceived desideratum to defend the borders and sovereignty of the nation state, undermining what Shakespeare termed England's 'Moate defensive', designed to protect the fortress nation 'Against infection'. A viral media image of a dead three-year-old Syrian refugee, Alan Kurdi, face down on a Turkish beach, precipitated some public support for the crisis but failed to result in significant governmental intervention. The absence of national empathy was evident in the media representation of the refugee crisis as a *British* emergency: a besieged kingdom under attack from foreign infiltration. The widespread denunciation of minorities, migrants and refugees by the media enabled the public to frame their racist inclinations as a more *sanitized* argument regarding cultural protectionism and economic precarity without fear of reprisal. As I have argued elsewhere (Shaw 2019), any discussion of contemporary border politics and immigration in the context of the EU referendum must address the various challenges to member states in confronting an unprecedented surge in migratory movement. According to the IOM (International Organisation for Migration), the EU received approximately 1.2 million first-time asylum claims (up from 563,000 registered claims in 2014), primarily due to an increase in claims by Syrian refugees fleeing civil war, economic instability and militant organizations such as ISIS (2015). The humanitarian crisis was part of a wider global intensification in forced displacement that was higher than at any point since the Second World War and revealed the British tendency to adopt a nonproximate approach of externalization in dealing with unwanted forms of immigration or asylum, often detaining or restricting the movement of individuals beyond its territorial borders. In 2015, Theresa May diverted £15 million of funds to strengthen control checks around rail and ferry terminals, including the intensification of police presence within Calais (a move reinforced by Cameron the following year). Political discussions relating to the need for humanitarian support in tackling the refugee crisis were immediately hijacked and framed as attacks on the sanctity of British sovereignty and political autonomy.

For many voters, terrorist attacks in Berlin, Brussels and Paris during the months leading to the referendum reinforced the links between EU membership and global risk, validated the pursual of right-wing ethnonationalist policies, and impelled major parties to impose more restrictive asylum and immigration policies over the following decade. UKIP enjoyed far greater public support than the BNP by fusing hostility to immigration and EU membership in the minds of the electorate, conflating wider cultural grievances within a negative cultural frame. Farage advocated a points-based system for immigration (which had been phased in from 2008 onwards) in which migrants would be judged on their educational attainment levels, wealth and language proficiency. As William Davies argues, a points-based system is demeaning and neoliberal, calculating 'different human capabilities according to the economic metaphor of human capital', evident in complaints by Brexiteers that Britain was suffering from high numbers of low-skilled EU migrants (Davies 2017). In the 2015 UK general election, UKIP secured ownership of immigration as an electoral issue and won 12.9 per cent of the national vote (nearly 4 million votes), supplanting the Liberal Democrats as the third largest party. UKIP heightened their ethnonationalist rhetoric in the run-up to the EU referendum, releasing their provocative 'Breaking Point' poster, depicting refugees appearing to enter Britain (the photograph actually captured migrants crossing the Croatian-Slovenian border). The poster, reminiscent of fascist wartime propaganda, was widely denounced for scaremongering and inciting racial hatred, but nevertheless effectively demonstrated the cross-fertilization of crimmigration and anti-EU rhetoric in the public imagination.

Subsequent calls by Farage for the British electorate to 'Take Back Control' in 2016 – with the emphasis very much on the word 'back' – were rightly perceived by ethnic-minority voters as a resistance towards any act of cultural divergence against which the national imaginary stands guard, not least an imperial nostalgia for a monocultural landscape. Journalist Afua Hirsch, for example, suggested her erasure from the national narrative was due to her mixed cultural heritage, stating 'It is only because of my ethnicity [. . .] that I am associated with immigration' (2018: 283). For Evaristo, the 'idea that black and British was an oxymoron' has lingered in the public imagination and BAME groups are often considered to be somehow associated with the immigration debate by far-right forces (2018). In his meticulous deconstruction of the Brexit vote, Derek Sayer reports 'the great majority of the 102 districts in England and Wales where 60% or more voted Leave are among the most ethnically homogenous', concluding that 'far from the presence of immigrants inclining people to vote Leave, the more ethnically diverse the area, the more likely it was to vote Remain' (2017: 99). That being said, the British public's attitude towards immigration cannot be explained by a traditionalist ethnonationalism alone. Although the majority of Black British and British Asian voters were pro-Remain, it would be inaccurate and offensive to state (as several commentators did in the aftermath of the vote), that the BAME community voted as one voice. The success of Muslims for Britain, an anti-EU campaign group dedicated to winning support for withdrawal among ethnic-minority voters, indicates the Brexit vote cannot be explained by simple nativism. Further, Neema Begum (2018) reports older Indian voters were 'almost twice as likely to support Leave as other minority groups', perturbed by the freedom of movement afforded to Eastern European immigrants in comparison to their own hazardous points of entry (drawing attention to an attendant 'colourism' by which Polish workers were rewarded economically for their aesthetic proximity to white British citizens). Hirsch considers the Leave support among older immigrants a 'betrayal of the tolerance towards immigration that facilitated their *own* ability to come to the UK and improve their lot' (2018: 273). Unfortunately, the established fault lines of class, age and educational attainment continued to rear their heads and divide communities.

Opening the door?

God separated Britain from mainland Europe, and it was for a purpose.
(Thatcher 1999)

Literature, as a medium of empathetic identification, translation and relational understanding, is a key site for the discussion and evaluation of immigration, cultural difference and ethnonationalism. The literature of migration, after all, 'reflects a shift from nation-based paradigms to new ways of understanding community and belonging and to transnational models emphasizing a global space of ongoing travel and interconnection' (Walkowitz 2007: 533). Rose Tremain's *The Road Home* (2007) encapsulates how migrant narratives challenge and subvert the secure and established borders (both geographical and psychological) of the nation state, charting the migration of Central and Eastern Europeans as they head to Britain following accession. The novel's protagonist, Lev, a former lumberyard worker but now an unemployed widower, travels to London on a Trans-Euro coach in search of better economic prospects: 'England is my hope' (2007: 5). The narrative's opening sentence, placing him on the *coach*, immediately concentrates on the westward movement of these migrants and recalls *Europa*'s allusion to the ongoing development of the EU as a future-oriented journey with forward momentum. Lev's forthright assertion of his legal right to work substantiates claims that Polish migrant workers have become 'excellent market actors', adapting 'to the new culture as mobile, flexible workers', and demanding 'full rights as European Union citizens' (Jordan 2013; Datta and Brickell 2009: 443).[5] However, rather than promoting the merits of border-crossing and cross-cultural exchange, Tremain dismantles her character's initial perception of his host nation as a symbolic space of economic and cultural progression. Lev is immediately confronted with hostility and prejudice by certain sections of the British public and finds himself cast into a series of social situations where his lack of familiarity with national customs and the English language result in his socioeconomic marginalization. His confusion of the phrase 'May I help you?' with 'May you help me?' provides brief comedic relief, but also alludes to the systems of economic exchange and cultural hospitality

---

[5] It is worth noting that Poland's own ambivalence and often outright hostility towards the EU is reflected in the recent electoral success of the populist Law and Justice Party.

which govern intra-European immigration and accentuates how casual employment contracts diminish the transactional value of migrants and indicate their tentative footing within the labour hierarchy (2007: 4).[6]

Initially mistaken for an asylum seeker, he is physically harassed and searched by a policeman until he can prove his legal status, exacerbating his disillusionment with British life and demonstrating the extent to which the migrant body is subject to constant surveillance and scrutiny. His decision to take a bath is a symbolic act of self-renewal, demonstrating a sensitivity to the acts of cultural assimilation and processes of integration that will govern his acceptance: 'This is the mud of my country, the mud of all Europe, and I must find some rags and wipe it away' (2007: 18). Significantly it is Lev's fellow immigrants, such as Lydia, a fellow passenger on the Trans-Euro coach, who offer empathy and assistance following a period of sleeping rough on the streets of the capital. Focalized through the protagonist's third-person perspective, London is depicted as a site of intense economic inequality and cultural imbalance, with manual labour throughout the narrative conducted by Eastern European and other immigrant workers stranded at the margins of public life. Lev conveys a transparent revulsion towards the consumerist agenda of certain London residents in comparison to the bleak economic realities faced by poorer members of the city's populace. Following his physical assault by two youths, who label him a terrorist and asylum seeker, he even expresses sympathy for the plight of working-class British citizens. Dismissing Ahmed's lament that 'no matter what country you from, these days, they just look at you and think, Shitty Arab, suicide-bomber, Muslim scum', Lev concludes that the attack simply encapsulates a transference of economic disenfranchisement by deprived children 'from poor homes, silted up with prejudice and misery' and suffering under the same economic precarity as himself (2007: 311). Such anti-immigrant rhetoric is not limited to the capital; abandoning his life in London in favour of arduous agricultural manual labour in Suffolk, Lev encounters melancholy rural communities facing economic decline and farmers harbouring a deep resentment towards the influx of EU nationals. The widespread opposition to further EU enlargement in the narrative, in spite of the dependency of British agricultural and service sectors on migrant labour, anticipates the xenophobic sentiments towards EU migration which would re-emerge with a vengeance a decade later. As the Brexit fallout demonstrates, the Polish community remains intensely vulnerable to xenophobic attacks and attitudes, despite being one of the largest foreign-born groups within Britain.

With Lydia's help, Lev becomes a kitchen porter in the kitchen of G. K. Ashe, a famous chef, before budgeting for his own kitchen when he eventually returns to Eastern Europe.[7] Tremain's depiction of Lev as an active agent capable of shaping his own future conceals the extent to which migrant workers are often passive subjects manipulated by neoliberal and exclusionary logics. The closing section of the novel, abandoning its stark state-of-the-nation critique in favour of the evolution of Lev's

---

[6] *Everything I Found on the Beach* (2011) by Cynan Jones reinforces the hardships faced by Polish economic migrants.
[7] Monica Ali's *In the Kitchen* (2009) also concentrates on the EU immigrant's role in sustaining the British culinary sector.

own restaurant, is certainly less plausible in its starry-eyed optimism. Rather than suggesting an auspicious future for EU migrants, the development of Lev's enterprising restaurant business compounds Tremain's simplistic dichotomy between Western and Eastern European politico-economic structures: 'the seductive, light-filled void of the liberal market' and the lingering 'dark rockface of Communism' (2007: 337). However, while the novel paints a rather simplistic picture of Eastern European migration post-enlargement and often affirms rather than subverts national stereotypes, Tremain captures the sense of economic precarity and social marginalization faced by migrants attempting to reside in London's more affluent boroughs. The novel's title not only references the sense of temporariness and economic necessity associated with Eastern European migration, but Lev's clear intent to force his country 'to leave behind their dirt roads, their spirit rags, and join the twenty-first century world' (2007: 344). This individual need to move 'forward, not back' corresponds with Eastern Europe's ideological restructuring as it enters a 'new era of openness' within the EU (2007: 163). Crucially, although Tremain reveals how interviews with Polish field workers informed her narrative, Lev himself is never specifically identified as Polish. His function as an unknown quantity, a proto-typical Central or Eastern European, enables *The Road Home* to capture the British public's homogenous treatment of post-enlargement workers – 'Bela-whatsit, Kazak-wherever' – and deliver a wider commentary on the experiences of all migrants from new member states who attempt to make this country their home (2007: 196).[8]

Marina Lewycka's *Two Caravans* (2007) offers a more pessimistic depiction of the superficial interactions between EU migrant workers and the British public, exposing the dark underbelly of neoliberal market dynamics and suggesting that Eastern European criminal structures are also accountable for widespread economic exploitation (including the sexual exploitation of female migrants and Britain's culpability in perpetuating this system). While Lewycka's debut novel, *A Short History of Tractors in the Ukraine* (2005), concentrates on settled British citizens who possess Eastern European heritage, *Two Caravans* deals specifically with the experiences of economic migrants following EU expansion. The narrative follows the daily lives of Ukrainian and Polish agricultural labourers, alongside illegal non-EU migrants, working as strawberry pickers in the Kent countryside, estranged from their family or social structures of belonging. Ukrainian Irina possesses idealized notions of her new country before her personal lived experiences gradually deconstruct this vision of the English sublime: 'This air – so sweet, so English [. . .] all the cultured, brave, warm-hearted people that I'd read about in Chaucer, Shakespeare, Dickens [. . .] I was

---

[8] In 2015, to counter prevailing media and political assaults on Eastern Europeans, BBC Radio 4 invited Polish authors residing in London to contribute radio plays which depicted the experiences of Polish migrants living in Britain. Agnieszka Dale's 'Fox Season', and A. M. Bakalar's 'Woman of Your Dreams', aired in 2015, provided an immigrant perspective of post-millennial life in the capital, communicating the struggles faced in assimilating and integrating within British society. Following a surge in anti-Polish rhetoric during the referendum campaign, Dale was invited to pen another story, 'A Happy Nation', that directly engaged with the Brexit immigration debate. Marek Kazmierski's *Damn the Source* (2013) also examines scattered Polish immigration, anticipating the growing xenophobia towards Eastern European migrants and fears surrounding freedom of movement within the EU.

ready to meet them' (2012: 26). While the young and educated Irina looks towards the EU as a future protector of Ukraine's interests, her countryman Andriy is cautious of its business-oriented agenda and warns it is only interested in eastern integration to further its neoliberal interests and provide migrant labour.

Two Caravans depicts a British society devoid of the 'hospitality, conviviality, tolerance, justice, and mutual care' associated with Gilroy's diverse model of convivial national culture (2004: 108). Isolated in their cold, damp caravans in a rural area, the workers inhabit dilapidated dwelling places that emphasize their socioeconomic precarity and expose sites of inclusion and exclusion operating within Britain's borders. As Joshua Hoops et al. note, immigrants are 'framed in terms of their "foreignness", which translates into the literal and discursive ghettoization of the immigrant experience' (2016: 729). When the strawberry pickers move to the Majestic Hotel they discover it to be infested with cockroaches and populated by fellow migrant workers and asylum seekers as well as homeless British families. The hotel's ironic name, alluding to Britain's former imperial grandeur, merely accentuates the nation's diminished stature and operates as a slum for marginalized figures. Rather than empathize with non-EU migrants and refugees, the workers blame the poor economic conditions on the presence of other foreigners within Britain, indicating the extent to which anti-immigrant rhetoric bleeds into the public consciousness. Lewycka thus suggests that new modes of immigration associated with the EU migrant do not necessitate novel forms of cultural hospitality or cosmopolitan empathy. When Polish migrant Tomasz gains employment at a poultry farm, he learns illegal Brazilian workers are now preferred because entry into the EU made Eastern Europeans begin to ask for minimum wage: 'What's the point of having foreigners if you got to pay 'em same as English, eh?' (2012: 117). Lewycka accentuates the dehumanization of her characters – involving the conflation of migrant and animals – to encapsulate the degradation and oppression suffered by field workers. The fate of the chickens corresponds to the workers' precarious social situation: exploited for profit in the global marketplace, forced to live in impoverished and cramped conditions and cast aside once they have fulfilled their economic function.

A negative discourse surrounds the process of EU immigration even when the migrant is not tied to the brutal history of colonial oppression. Lewycka's novel oscillates between Gilroy's 'convivial' version of British culture – 'the processes of cohabitation and interaction that have made multiculture an ordinary feature of social life' – and a 'melancholic' phobia 'about the prospect of exposure to either strangers or otherness' (2004: xi; 108). There is a notable lack of meaningful contact between EU migrants and the British public in the novel; when brief interactions occur, nativist exclusionary impulses are immediately evident. While in London, Andriy accidentally bumps into a woman and detects both the national hostility to migrants and the hauntological spectrality of his presence in Britain, noting the 'look in her eyes – it was worse than contempt. She looked straight through him. He didn't register in her eyes at all' (2012: 144). In documenting fictional accounts of EU workers (based on personal interviews with migrant workers), the narrative forces the reader to examine their own prejudices concerning recent British immigration and points towards the role of literature in challenging assumptions surrounding economic migration.

Lewycka's personal ironic responses to anti-immigrant rhetoric and claims of EU bureaucracy acknowledge the prevailing inimical perception of migrants in the British media. Her fiction provides a counter discourse to social anxieties associated with immigration and challenges right-wing media reactions to cultural diversity – reactions that would intensify in the years leading to the Brexit vote. Speaking after the EU referendum, Lewycka, who was born in a refugee camp in Germany to Ukrainian parents before relocating to Britain when she was a child, concedes she is 'left with the feeling that this country, which I [for] so long thought of as home, isn't really my country at all' (Lewycka 2018). Accordingly, her fictional migrant workers quietly return to their own respective Central and Eastern European countries, having failed to create a new future for themselves or their families, and abandon their struggle for integration within an inflexible British community unreceptive to cultural change and resistant to redefinition. *Two Caravans* thus attains a new relevance in the post-Brexit moment, containing an anticipatory logic which indicates the potency of public and media responses in fomenting anxieties and deepening divides within British society.

John Lanchester's *Capital*, set before, during and after the 2008 financial crisis, focuses on a single south London street, contrasting the day-to-day lives of privileged citizens with the struggles of industrious immigrants attempting to negotiate their position in the British capital. The residents of Pepys Road are the beneficiaries of the pre-crash property boom as their once ordinary residences are transformed into multi-million-pound assets – symbols of London's financial wealth and global reach. Lanchester responds to the financial crash by depicting the pre-crunch conditions of the British economy when the divide between the 'haves' and 'have nots' in London was achingly apparent: 'Britain had become a country of winners and losers, and all the people in the street, just by living there, had won' (2013: 7). His novel diagnoses national anxieties and anti-immigrant sentiments that were to be exploited during the 2016 referendum campaign, with his fictional account of 'winners and losers' in London an apt and more general 'slogan for British life in the last three decades' (Lanchester 2012b). A lack of community between the multi-ethnic inhabitants of Pepys Road is immediately evident. When anonymous cards are pushed through residents' doors, stating 'We Want What You Have', the police interrogate Kosovans, Ghanaians and Nigerians in the wider area before eventually realizing 'the fact that these people were so cut off from the area they worked in was part of the problem, rather than the key to the mystery' (2013: 414).

In his 2016 article 'Brexit Blues', Lanchester points to the economic precarity and cultural insularity of the white working-class as the motivating factor for the Leave vote – 'a real darkness in this country, a xenophobic, racist sickness of heart that is closer to the surface today than it has been for decades' – but *Capital* specifically exposes the pre-existing subtle prejudices of privileged British citizens whose guaranteed wealth is often improved, not diminished, by Eastern European migrant labour (Lanchester 2016). Pepys Road is populated by residents who resent 'immigrants from god knew where' and yet employ the services of Polish builders, indicative of the ideological ambivalence surrounding EU migration: 'I'm all in favour of buying British [. . .] but a third cheaper is a third cheaper' (2013: 79; 362). Appropriately, *Capital* retains a close focus on Polish builder Zbigniew, revealing the difficulties EU migrants face in integrating themselves into British society and constructing a sense of home. Replicating the actions of Lev in *The Road Home*, Zbigniew evinces an economic pragmatism by moving to London and recognizing the opportunities EU expansion offers: 'the British had lots of money. He was there to earn it from them' (2013: 72). The character positions himself relationally to English builders – considering them to have a bad reputation for being inefficient, lazy and expensive – to emphasize his versatility, superiority and work ethic in a competitive trade and move up the ladder in a global city dependent on migrant labour.

The infiltration of the Polish worker into the building site, a traditional safe space for the British working-class male, demonstrates the opportunities offered to Eastern European workers by post-EU enlargement, but also alludes to the fear that the working-class remain passive victims of globalizing processes, their incomes and identities directly affected by EU membership. In the years following EU enlargement, Hoops et al. (2016) recognize how the *Daily Mail* and *Daily Mirror* would vacillate between blaming Polish workers for the loss of British jobs and sovereignty, and framing Polish workers as flexible, temporary migrants who would contribute to the British economy before returning home to their country. By positioning Poles as 'solely economic actors', the paper sporadically overcame their ideological ambivalence towards immigration, 'reconciling the seeming contradiction between neoliberalism and nationalism, reifying migrant workers' one-way benefit to the nation-state' (Hoops et al. 2016: 735). Polish workers such as Zbigniew are thus more integrated into British economy and society on account of their economic skill-sets and the perception that they will not function as a strain on public services or burden on the welfare state (anticipating the mobilization of such claims during the referendum campaign). Referred to as Bogdan the builder by British clients, Zbigniew's erroneous moniker serves as a reminder that 'he did not really live in London, that his life here was a temporary interlude: he was there to work and make money' (Tremain 2007: 71). As Lanchester (2016) himself notes, EU immigrants are significant net contributors to Britain's economy, being less likely to claim benefits than native-born citizens.

In positioning themselves as hard-working and well-integrated, the novel's Polish characters demonstrate an early consciousness of cultural stereotypes and racial hierarchies of migrants within British society. Zbigniew in particular demonstrates a sensitivity to the biological construction of race and the privileges associated with European 'whiteness', practising inclusionary strategies such as linguistic mimicry, conforming to middle-class cultural norms and embracing meritocratic values in his attempt to become a model migrant. Indeed, John Eade, Drinkwater and Garapich (2006) find that, even though Polish migrant workers suffer xenophobic abuse, they consider their whiteness to be a source of protection, isolating them from the fate suffered by Asian workers and providing the cultural capital necessary to gain sufficient employment in the British labour market. Zbigniew discovers, in spite of his own socioeconomic precarity, some British citizens are 'just grateful you aren't Pakis' (2013: 73). This construction of whiteness enables the workers to avoid being cast as the racialized other, and can therefore more easily assimilate into society due to the superficial and aesthetic association of whiteness with Englishness. In the context of Brexit, Magdalena Nowicka considers the Leave campaign to have heightened this 'relevance of economic value and labour market fit of Eastern Europeans in Britain and their racial and cultural proximity to the British white middle class', as EU workers acknowledge and attend to 'neoliberal and culturalist logics of belonging' (2018: 538; 536).

Capital identifies a lingering civilizationalist approach to EU immigration, which suggests a parasitic infiltration of ethnic 'others' to be a contamination of the purity of European heritage and cultural values. The underlying anti-immigrant atmosphere of Pepys Road forces Zbigniew to re-evaluate his perception of Britain as 'a moderate, restrained nation. It was funny to think of that now. It wasn't true at all' (2013: 289). Speaking in 2012, Lanchester admits that he shares his character's oscillation 'between thinking that something fundamental has changed in Britain, in the direction of abandoning previous restraints, and conversely that what's happened is really just the reversion to a historical character that is largely intact' (2012a). Lanchester's London thus emerges as a fraught and contested ideological site in which EU immigration and the wider processes of globalization come into close and unavoidable conflict with individual desires for greater financial security and national insularity. As a diagnosis of British society in the years leading to the referendum, then, *Capital* not only responds to the legacy of the 2008 financial crash but possesses clear predictive power in forecasting the cultural and socioeconomic terrain on which the Brexit immigration battle would be fought.

Closing the door?

Not all Englishmen can live in a castle. But they all want their moats and drawbridges.

(Paxman 1999: 170)

From 2008 onwards, in response to public calls for tighter controls on immigration, the British government merged various departments to form the UK Border Agency and devoted its effort towards 'exporting the border' by introducing further detention controls in France to prevent immigrants crossing the Channel: 'a step change in the management of immigration controls' (Cabinet Office 2007: 7). This decision to externalize the border can be interpreted as an ongoing symbolic effort by a Eurosceptic Britain to reinforce their separateness from Continental Europe. The sudden onset of the Syrian refugee crisis in 2015 undoubtedly intensified the potent capacity of immigration as an emotive issue. British political discourses and media commentary during the electoral campaign safeguarded the assessment that border politics was not the result of lingering racial categorization, but rather a respectable attempt to preserve national sovereignty. The very purpose of the media concentration on immigration control, of course, was to render visible the spectacle of otherness and reinforce the perception of a beleaguered nation struggling to defend its borders. In deepening the externalization of border controls in order to distance itself from the worst excesses of the humanitarian crisis, Britain sought to 'Take Back Control' of its borders and safeguard the sanctity of the nation – an act of cultural nostalgia masquerading as international security. May's call for a more definitive qualification between refugees and economic migrants minimized the commitment required in tackling the crisis and delegitimized the trauma and suffering of refugees requiring asylum and hospitality. In responding to the geopolitical crisis, Britain seemed satisfied to reject those EU immigration policies which did not work in their favour, while permitting Frontex (the European Border and Coast Guard Agency) to police the Mediterranean and coordinate European responses, far from its own national borders. The refugee crisis found an immediate literary response in Olumide Popoola and Annie Holmes' co-authored short story collection *Breach* (2016). The collection was specifically commissioned by Peirene Press to respond to public concerns regarding immigration during the EU referendum campaign, detailing the lives of displaced peoples as they attempt to navigate European border controls and negotiate the Calais camp in order to cross the Channel. The short stories resist a teleological narrative following a single individual and instead provide a series of heterogeneous perspectives that neither generalize nor homogenize the experiences of the various migrants. By sharing their idiosyncratic histories and memories with one another the migrants begin to recognize their shared predicament and the need for a more interdependent global community which overrides the divides of national affiliation or ethnic origin. The collection situates individual disparate stories in the same quarantined space, forging a commonality of experience, while simultaneously exposing the circular and repetitive motions of migration that prevent a hopeful resolution.

Popoola and Holmes offer a harsh critique of the externalization of British border controls and their application in curtailing migration with their intense concentration on the Calais refugee camp across the collection. The camp – nicknamed the Jungle – gained notoriety during 2015 due to the sudden expansion of makeshift camps as thousands of refugees were denied access across the Channel by restrictive Anglo-French border controls. As a result, the population of the Jungle reached over 9,000 people in August 2016 (the surge coinciding with the aftermath of the Brexit vote). For Oli Mould, the Jungle should be regarded as 'a slum of London's making' due to a combination of the externalization of border controls and prejudicial immigration policies (2017: 388). The crisis was consequently produced by the interlinked processes of: 'dispersal', following the exacerbation of conflict in the Middle East; 'securitization', concerning the physical and political attempts by Britain and the EU to intensify border controls in order to preserve Fortress Europe; and 'precarity', as a natural result of insufficient living conditions and Britain's opt out from the Schengen Agreement (2017: 391).

An acute disclination by the British and French to immediately address the crisis is apparent when considering the unofficial nature of the camp – neither nation granted legal approval to its construction enabling authorities to engage in acts of domicide. Thom Davies, Arshad Isakjee and Surindar Dhesi interpret such negligence as 'violent inaction', a passive form of border control which merely serves to emphasize existing institutional systems of inclusion and exclusion (2017: 1). Although the crisis emerged on Britain's doorstep, ostensibly necessitating an expeditious policy response, by externalizing border controls across the Channel and refusing to officially recognize its construction, British immigration policies sent a strong message as to the nation's future stance towards global refugee crises. A failure to allocate sufficient housing or coordinate resources was also a sign of negligence on the part of the EU, who were sensitive to the populist movements emerging in European member states and appeared more concerned with prioritizing the fortification of European borders than protecting human life. For William Walters, Calais consequently emerges as the 'signifier for Europe's "crisis" of immigration' (2008: 196). Several nations obligated to abide by the Schengen Agreement, such as Austria and Hungary, erected fences and refused to contribute to resettlement strategies to combat public fears that the refugee exodus contained criminals or even terrorists who posted a direct threat to Western culture. As Ivan Krastev argues, the refugee crisis was arguably a 'turning point' for the EU, with the use of exclusionary policies creating 'a dynamic in which the European project is seen no longer as an expression of liberal universalism but as a sour expression of its defensive parochialism' (2017: 59). Such widespread nationalist sentiments demonstrate how the Brexit immigration debate was certainly not a British issue and merely representative of a broader populist movement affecting Western societies. The EU's response to the migrant crisis was lamentable with a lack of coordination between member states proving the decisive factor, allowing Eurosceptic forces to claim that Europe remained a divided terrain of competing financial and cultural interests rather than a coordinated network of cosmopolitan connectivities.

Popoola and Holmes situate their short stories from within the temporary Calais camp, a contested site of conflict and instability, giving materiality and substance to the makeshift shelters and precarious lives of their inhabitants. The site operates as a palimpsest, crystallizing the various layers of racial discrimination and brutal intolerance suffered by the refugees into a deeper commentary on global inequalities and the violence of borders. Popoola depicts Calais as an unstable border zone in which a variety of cultures come into close and unavoidable contact through forced circumstance. Their narratives follow refugees forced to either exchange sexual favours for small amounts of money ('Extending a Hand'); working for traffickers within the Jungle ('Ghosts'); or concealing themselves inside refrigerator trucks heading Dover ('Oranges in the River'). In functioning as both an entry point and a liminal space – a threshold upon which the refugees nervously tread in a transitional state – the camp becomes a lived space of resistance in which anti-nationalist hospitalities are at work. The collection is representative of a humanitarian struggle which aims to draw attention to the plight of refugees, reduced to provisional and contingent lives, while simultaneously hinting at new forms of belonging which transcend the violence of national border policies. In 'The Terrier' and 'Paradise', the camp becomes a cosmopolitan assemblage of differing subjectivities where 'young Sudanese men', 'Eritrean women', 'Kurdish families' and 'Afghan men' converge in dynamic interplay with non-governmental actors such as volunteers, charity workers and border authorities (2016: 66; 67). In 'Paradise', a young British student named Julie arrives at the Jungle to volunteer with her auntie Marjorie in clear defiance of her right-wing father (representative of the division Brexit created within families), who disapproves of both the Jungle and Britain's decision to supply refugees with housing: 'Not our fault, not our responsibility' (2016: 79).

The volunteer activism of citizens in Britain and Continental Europe engendered organic forms of cultural connectivity and expressions of solidarity that existed outside the purview of government-initiated aid. As opposed to established activist networks such as No Borders, these volunteers did not seek to delegitimize immigration controls or propose open-border policies; instead, "Paradise" illustrates how public volunteers created spaces of affectivity, representing sections of the British public outraged by Cameron's denunciation of the 'swarm' of refugees coming across the Mediterranean, and the *Daily Mail*'s xenophobic concentration on the 'flood' of specifically young male migrants in the run-up to the EU referendum (Cameron 2015; Afzal 2016). Popoola and Holmes directly respond to such Orientalist thought and dehumanizing rhetoric, indicating how contemporary border politics and immigration policies continue to be underpinned by racial othering in the cultural imagination. European nation states thus continue to be positioned as racialized projects in the collection, maintaining imperial logics that resist any external threats which destabilize their foundation. In comparison, the Jungle becomes a sociopolitical space for the contestation of human rights more generally, challenging the exclusionary hierarchical systems of control and surveillance that continue to govern national border politics in the twenty-first century. The designation of the camp as the 'Jungle', however, illuminates the perception of refugees as uncivilized by sections of the British populace and reveals how racial hierarchies are sustained and reproduced, continuing to be intimately linked to the brutal enforcement of border politics.

In 'The Terrier', French citizen Eloise permits two young refugees, Omid and Nalin, to leave the camp and stay in her grandparents' farmhouse, accepting city council money in compensation. The Kurdish siblings recount their border-crossing odyssey from Syria to Calais, disclosing how they managed to avoid providing biometric data in any of the EU member states they passed through in order to enter Britain under a new law to reunite with their mother. 'The Terrier' therefore alludes to the Dubs Amendment (the Dublin III regulation): a reluctant piece of legislation permitting unaccompanied minors to enter Britain even if they cannot verify existing family links within the nation. As a subsequent analysis of Herd and Pincus' *Refugee Tales* volumes will demonstrate, stringent British immigration policies resisted the obligations of the Amendment to ensure that refugees were prevented safe passage and remained in a spatial limbo for several months. The Amendment merely reproduces a post-war British legacy of seeking to 'delegitimise refugees, enact tighter barriers to entry, and cast them as economic "migrants" and as suspect figures', evident in Britain's delayed decision to accept minors from Calais (Ibrahim and Howarth 2018: 348). Popoola and Holmes' concentration on how the crisis directly affected children addresses the IOM statistic that of the 870,000 refugees and migrants reaching Europe's shores in 2015 more than 1 in 5 was a (often unaccompanied) minor (IOM 2015). However, even landlord Eloise begins to question her altruism, doubting her refugee tenants' given identities and their real purpose in Europe, giving voice to the widespread European aversion to cultural infiltration during the 2015 crisis: 'Perhaps she wasn't even his sister. Perhaps they weren't refugees at all, but criminals, or even terrorists' (2016: 41). The story thus offers a pragmatic evaluation of the limitations of conditional hospitality and an insight into the mindset of those European citizens who fear letting 'others' beyond the threshold of their home.

David Herd and Anna Pincus' edited volumes *Refugee Tales I* (2016), *Refugee Tales II* (2017) and *Refugee Tales III* (2019) draw attention back to British shores, inviting contributions from authors, poets, political activists and academics to formulate a politics of dissensus and confront the nation's hostile approach to immigration and the practice of indefinite detention. Recent British immigration policy has worked in agreement with border controls, tightening the loopholes for asylum applications to ensure unsuccessful applicants could be quickly detained and deported. Political enforcement of physical national borders is complemented by the psychological bordering of Britain espoused by (both pre- and post-Brexit) media narratives, often accurately reflecting the widespread xenophobic rhetoric of public opinion. Governmental plans for a new Immigration Bill in 2016 coincided with the refugee crisis, deepening May's pledge in 2012 to create 'a really hostile environment for illegal migration' – insular sentiments recently reinforced by proposed post-Brexit policies (Kirkup and Winnett 2012). The subsequent introduction of the 2016 Immigration Act reinforced the existing policy of 'deport first appeal later' and introduced new provisions which make it more difficult for asylum seekers to obtain accommodation once they have been released from detention. As Kim Rygiel observes, detention should not only refer 'to enclosed spaces of detention but also to a diversity of administrative procedures ranging from incarceration, containment, expulsion, and deportation', evident in both the institutional practices of the British government and the EU (2011: 5). The polemical and provocative content of the narratives is a direct assault on the insular zeitgeist of British national culture, calling instead for more symbiotic cosmopolitan connections based on empathy, openness and global belonging. The *Refugee Tales* volumes therefore contain urgent and uncompromising politically charged narratives that confront the prejudice and racism faced by refugees to paint a bleak picture of British immigration policies.

Inspired by the work of the Gatwick Detainees Welfare Group, *Refugee Tales* grew out of a physical crossing of 'a deeply national space', 'A Walk in Solidarity with Refugees, Asylum Seekers and Detainees' from Dover to Canterbury, in the name of those whom the nation attempts to deny hospitality or asylum (Herd and Pincus 2016: 138). Utilizing these 'ancient pathways' of southern England to begin a literary conversation on detention (Britain is currently the only nation state in Europe where non-citizens can be detained indefinitely), the volumes reconstruct the prevailing 'inhuman discourse' surrounding immigration and issue a challenge to the language of national identity which functions 'to hold the migrant out of view' (Herd and Pincus 2016: x; 138). Chronicling the stories of these persons, for whom 'every day is a negotiation', in a range of quintessential British literary forms from the Middle English tale to modernist stream-of-consciousness, and a heterogeneous repertoire of styles, from news reports to political commentary, the *Refugee Tales* volumes write the refugee into the national consciousness by employing the 'oldest action' of oral narratives 'to make a language / That opens politics / Establishes belonging' (Herd and Pincus 2016: 83).

Hubert Moore's 'The Visitor's Tale' and Ali Smith's 'The Detainee's Tale' register the harrowing waiting process for those refugees who are granted indefinite 'leave to remain' and the dehumanizing aesthetic of detention centres. The room set aside for visiting detainees in 'The Visitor's Tale' is anything but 'neutral ground of course. It's detention centre ground [. . .] arrangements which help an essentially inhumane set-up to seem caring and respectable' (Herd and Pincus 2016: 43). As Moore claims, if an individual is indefinitely detained 'they have no date to live for' and are denied the sense of an ending to their trauma (Herd and Pincus 2016: 47). Smith (whose 2011 novel *There But For The* also tackles the institutional processes of granting asylum) narrates her tale 'all in the present tense [. . .] because it is all still happening', detailing the traumatic experiences of a Ghanaian who escapes slave labour in his home country only to become subject to human trafficking and detained for two years after writing to the Home Office for assistance (Herd and Pincus 2016: 50). The confusingly labyrinthine London university building, where the interview with the detainee is conducted, captures to the inaccessible nature of asylum applications: 'We go through a lot of corridors, then some more corridors, then down more stairs and along more identical corridors [. . .] We go through some swing doors, round some corners to some dead ends. We double back on ourselves' (Herd and Pincus 2016: 49). In giving voice to the refugee (who appropriately remains nameless throughout the narrative), Smith evokes Hannah Arendt's infamous assertion that '[a] life without speech and without action [. . .] is literally dead to the world; it has ceased to be human life because it is no longer lived among men' (1958: 176). The process of detention, then, in isolating refugees from family and friends and denying them the opportunity to form social relations, symbolically removes the refugee's claims to citizenship or to the city in which they currently reside.

Drawing on and reworking Chaucer's iconic tales, both structurally and geographically, enables the volumes to reconstitute the discourses of nationhood and bear witness to the unseen detainees and refugees excluded by British immigration legislation.[9] In so doing, the contributors critique the ethnonationalist sentiment that Britain is a racially, culturally and religiously homogenous polity. Chris Cleave's short story 'The Lorry Driver's Tale' directly responds to the political moment, registering the public antipathy towards immigration during the run-up to the EU referendum. Cleave initially appears to present a contradictory stance on the humanitarian crisis to other contributors in the volume. The story, told in the first person, follows the journey of a lorry driver, who acknowledges how his age and occupation position him as the stereotypical UKIP voter, in his vehicle which contains 'space for 40 tonnes of cargo but no room for basic humanity' (Herd and Pincus 2016: 31). He is joined in his cabin by an Italian colleague, Mr Hyde, who seemingly harbours a hatred of refugees, and a British journalist sympathetically reporting on the crisis. Despite his narrator's vocal dismissal of the plight of refugees – 'If immigration is a horror film then Calais is the scene where the zombies are massing' – during the border-crossing to Dover, Cleave's story reveals (the appropriately titled) Mr Hyde to be a Syrian refugee posing as an Italian (2016: 26). The ostensibly xenophobic driver has concealed the identity of his passenger to ensure their safe passage, challenging the perception that anti-immigration rhetoric can be easily associated with particular groups within British society.

---

[9] Patience Agbabi's *Telling Tales* (2014) provides a similar reworking of Chaucer to comment on contemporary migration.

Herd and Pincus' second and third volumes, *Refugee Tales II* (2017) and *Refugee Tales III* (2019), maintain this struggle for recognition, emphasizing the psychological borders that continue to restrict the post-detention existence. Monica Ali's 'The Son's Tale', David Constantine's 'The Orphan's Tale' and Bernardine Evaristo's 'The Social Worker's Tale' intimately capture the effects of detainment on the mental health of refugees. As Josh Cohen states in 'The Support Workers' Tale', 'it goes beyond the material deprivation, down to the destitution of the whole self. It means being *in* but not *of* the world' (2017: 74). Constantine's 'The Orphan's Tale' details the trauma of a former refugee from Sierra Leone, M, who is later adopted and moves in England. The threads of M's seemingly stable existence are unravelled by opaque systemic racism until he is reduced to his former state of precarity. Caroline Bergvall's 'The Voluntary Returner's Tale', Rachel Holmes 'The Barrister's Tale' and Alex Preston's 'The Witness' Tale' document the obscure bureaucracy faced by refugees on entering Britain, which continues to deny a sense of belonging and imposes new structural borders: 'having arrived / might never arrive' (Herd and Pincus 2017: 66). Unlike the brutal territorial reality of national borders encountered by refugees in *Breach*, the characters in the *Refugee Tales* series are confronted with a more insidious aspect of border imperialism, the 'slow violence' of immigration policies, 'a pervasive yet elusive form of bureaucratic abuse' (Herd and Pincus 2017: 69). The narrator of 'The Barrister's Tale' insinuates these legal ambiguities and technicalities are purposeful acts by a hostile state, highlighting that British society has witnessed eight immigration bills in the last eight years and '45,000 changes to immigration rules since 2010' (Herd and Pincus 2017: 58).

In a statement on the European Council in October 2016, May unveiled Britain's 'new global approach to migration' and declared 'all countries have the right to control their borders' (May 2016a). She went on to emphasize that a clear distinction must exist between refugees and economic migrants, arguing that the latter may not qualify for certain protections. In framing refugees as opportunistic economic migrants, Britain justified its insular global outlook and reluctant acknowledgement of its obligations under the Dubs Agreement (the UNHCR recently included poverty as a legitimate factor in determining who qualifies as a refugee, weakening Britain's denunciation of economic migrancy). Yasmin Ibrahim and Anita Howarth argue these 'interchangeable terminologies between migrant and refugee in political discourses locate them through opportunism rather than highlighting the risks and trauma they should be protected from' (2018: 378). May's speech merely confirmed Britain's reluctance to resettle more refugees within its borders (citing vague and unfounded concerns about economic security and crimmigration), as well as its continuing reluctance to engage in a coordinated global approach to the crisis.

Just as *Breach* intimates how the Calais Jungle unintentionally engenders a creative space for cosmopolitan exchange, Herd suggests the short stories in his volumes – collaborations between writers and detained refugees – open up 'a space of recognition' which allows 'new forms of language and solidarity' to emerge in response to opaque administrative legalese employed by British, French and EU institutions (2017: 115). In Jackie Kay's 'The Smuggled Person's Tale', refugee G struggles to accept his eventual welcome into J's home in Chorlton, Manchester: 'She opened the front door. It was a simple enough thing for her [. . .]. But to him it was quite something' (2017: 105).

Kay's short story reflects Bhabha's poignant comment that 'The globe shrinks for those who own it; [but] for the displaced or the dispossessed, the migrant or refugee, no distance is more awesome than the few feet across borders of frontiers' (1992: 88), with subsequent mental and sociocultural borders emerging through acts of cultural integration. Having left Afghanistan, negotiated the Mediterranean and traversed Italy, Austria and France over the course of seven years, it is accepting hospitality that proves the real psychological border: 'You could measure the distance in the look that crossed his face as he crossed the threshold into her house' (1992: 88). These discourses of cosmopolitan hospitality that run through the volume work in opposition to the xenophobic rhetoric of the Leave campaign and prevalent vocal anxieties that an admission of refugees would destabilize core British values.

While attempts to transgress borders in the narratives often end in failure and further detention or deportation, the effort symbolizes a potent rejection of Western exclusionary systems of control and the inherent racial implications of its enforcement. As Angela Mitropoulos and Brett Neilson argue, 'the attempt to violate or evade the border [. . .] is thus a politically significant act. Involving complex relations between heterogeneous agents [. . .] it signals a politics of potentiality or of *what might be* in the face of, and despite, existing geopolitical divisions and territoralisations' (2006). The border-crossing mobilities of refugees challenge the alleged security of Fortress Europe and throw into question fixed institutional notions of citizenship and belonging, ensuring the texts operate in formal opposition to acts of political isolationism and xenophobic legislative agendas. Alongside other recent edited collections, such as Lucy Popescu's *A Country of Refuge* (2016) and *A Country to Call Home* (2018), these works serve as transformative resources of social resistance, place pressure on a post-Brexit government to revise immigration policy and reveal the power of the short story as an appropriate form in capturing the liminality of those individuals excluded from the national frame. The short stories thus contain a humanizing impulse and serve as containers for traumatic remembrance, articulating the cultural connectivities that can continue to emanate from sites of exception and exclusion. It is this mobilization of empathy and compassion, indicating literature's potential as a vehicle for empathetic engagement in a post-Brexit Britain, which these collections of short stories bring so arrestingly to light.

Hari Kunzru's *Transmission* (2004) provides a related critique of sovereignty and national citizenship, anticipating the racial discourses that were to emerge in Western, anti-globalist, populist movements a decade later. Kunzru's satirical depiction of the EU, reimagined as a Pan European Border Authority (PEBA), reveals a Europe still stained by white hegemony and cultural prejudice, calling into question existing immigration policies and the preservation of racial hierarchies. Despite the EU's best attempts to build a self-congratulatory grand narrative of cohesive integration and cultural unity through the introduction of the 1986 Single European Act (heralding a 'Europe without Frontiers'), the continued erection of territorial defences around the borders of Europe in the 1990s revealed an inherent ethnocentric bias and a hostility to external global flows threatening the economic stability of the Eurozone. The problem with a proposed European community is that for some it naturally implies a hard, external border that excludes non-European others. A continued commitment to austere fiscal policies in the twenty-first century has ensured that the EU is rarely associated with the protection of human rights, and instead appears as an authoritative, neoliberalist institution more interested in economic expansion than true egalitarian isonomy. Kunzru's portrayal of the organization is no less flattering, drawing attention to the divisive and exclusionary role borders continue to play in European institutional policies, as well the failure of the Schengen Agreement to prevent racially motivated cultural immobilities. In attempting to develop a common border policy based on biometric data for the purposes of securitization, PEBA merely improves relations between Western member states while reinforcing Europe's perimeters from perceived 'Eastern' cultural contagion, forging spurious connections between immigration and acts of terrorism. The organization seeks the advice of Guy Swift, an English CEO of a global advertising firm, to rebrand Europe as an elite cultural space, harmonizing 'the immigration and customs regimes of all the member states' (2005: 130). Guy's design for a Fortress Europe with a gated community and an imperial outlook – an elitist space that operates on systems of inclusion and exclusion – exposes how non-white immigrants still exist on the periphery of globalized life and how their very presence provokes a surge in belligerent nationalism. Further, planned designs for this Fortress Europe mark the re-emergence of wartime analogies, in this case alluding not to German occupation of the Continent but rather the defence of European spaces from the threat of illegal immigration via a system of detention centres, digital surveillance and detention centres.

The concluding stages of the narrative provide a form of poetic justice. A digital virus disrupts global information systems and PEBA's own centralized databases – deleting immigration records – resulting in Guy being mistakenly classified as an asylum seeker. The rapid dissemination of the virus, a hyperbolic manifestation of 'what is lurking outside our perimeter', functions as an overt authorial criticism of the hysterical anxieties of British society towards the act of immigration and the influence of external cultural forces (2005: 271). Forced to suffer the indignity of deportation, the narrative places Guy in the role of marginalized 'other', experiencing first-hand the physical corporeality of nation state borders in a supposedly borderless Fortress Europe: the very perimeter he aimed to manipulate and police to enforce forms of racial exclusion. *Transmission* thus provides a potent critique of the role nation states play in exploiting fears surrounding immigration and the failure of Western nations to acknowledge the ways by which non-elite migrant workers are integral to the globalized system.[10] Kunzru's *Red Pill* (2020) draws on recent European populist movements to continue this examination of white Europeanness and the threat of intrusion. The nameless narrator interprets the political slogans scrawled on walls in Paris as 'signs of the new dispensation': '*Europe en danger*' (2020: 201 – emphasis in original). Following the publication of *Transmission*, the 2007 UK Borders Act extended the government's use of biometric data to detain asylum seekers and introduced further powers of detention, indicating how easily borders are operationalized to establish clearly defined spatial parameters between European citizens and non-European others and

---

[10] Sunjeev Sahota's *Year of the Runaways* (2015) charts the experiences of Asian migrant workers faced with a political climate of atavistic nationalism from within Britain's borders.

how ethno-exclusionist policies could be framed as matters of national security. As the post-Brexit fallout has demonstrated, a revival of territorial borders fails to provide a reclamation of national sovereignty, but rather encapsulates an inward-looking desire to purposefully disregard the emergent risks of the twenty-first-century life.

China Miéville's *The City and the City* (2009) also attains a new relevance in light of recent events. The novel's twin, Eastern European palimpsest states of Beszel and Ul Qoma occupy the same geographical space but citizens in each are policed to 'unsee' any events taking place in the other. Any potential re-unification, linked to the existence of a potential third site, Orciny, situated in-between the two cities, is left unresolved. Miéville's novel points both to the dangers of imposing a cleavage between previously united territories and the effects of symbolic borders on those existing outside their remit (a charge often levelled at the European Union and the Schengen zone). As Kamila Shamsie writes, while 'Britain is re-negotiating the meaning of its borders without seeming to know the purpose of these re-negotiations, and EU citizens in Britain live day after day in the cusp of "stay" and "go", and the Irish border seems to need to be both a hard and a soft border', the 'absurdo-logic of boundaries' intrinsic to Ul Qoma and Beszel suddenly appear 'plausible' (Shamsie 2020).

Mohsin Hamid's geopolitical novel *Exit West* (2017) fictionalizes the Syrian refugee crisis and engages with the broader ethnopolitical issues which influenced the referendum campaign. The narrative follows a young Muslim couple, Saaed and Nadia, in an unnamed Middle Eastern country suffering under Islamic insurgency and civil war. Fleeing their city – 'swollen with refugees' – they join the wave of displaced migrants attempting to enter European nation states, initially running up against the implacability of border controls (2017: 1). The intimidating presence of coast guard agencies in the novel provide an authorial response to the practices of Frontex, the EU's border management agency, which patrols the Mediterranean and prevents asylum seekers and refugees from infiltrating or even reaching the secure borders of EU member states. Hamid – whose earlier works include *The Reluctant Fundamentalist* (2007), a timely novel that responds to Western anxieties surrounding Islamic fundamentalism in the wake of 9/11 – positions contemporary asylum to be yet another inevitable consequence of globalization's capacity for deterritorialization. However, the sudden appearance of magical black doors, permitting free movement across national borders, allows the couple to first arrive at a migrant camp on the Greek island of Mykonos, before eventually gaining passage to London. The post-Brexit 'dark London' Saaed and Nadia encounter is peopled by anxious migrants scrutinized by surveillance and securitization measures and angry nativist mobs aiming to 'reclaim Britain for Britain' in order to reverse rising levels of immigration (Hamid 2017: 132; 142).

The black door portals utilized by the migrants are a useful stylistic device in gesturing towards the need for new forms of connectivity to transform existing cultural relations: 'they had grasped that the doors could not be closed, and new doors would continue to open' (ibid: 164). The doorways – potent counter-spaces detached from secure bounded space – advance a *fantastical* cosmopolitanism, overriding the fixity of geopolitical barriers. As sites of exchange they not only offer passage between disparate cultures but draw attention to the commonality of transnational lived experiences and encourage the need for global coordination. Hamid thus utilizes magical realism to administer a critique of European border policies that prevent free movement and merely ensure exclusionary practices continue to isolate and ostracize non-Western others. If nationalistic resistance to immigration reveals a rejection of cultural multiplicity, then the doorways signify an affirmative defence of the spatial politics of multiculturalism and a nomadic politics of redemption for victims of border policy. On the one hand, while the doorways can be perceived as an elimination of bounded space, allowing migrants to pass through national borders unseen, they also represent a recuperation of space, a symbolic desire to welcome migrants into the space of the nation. Their magical realist construction, however, exposes the idealistic and hopeful sentiments (as opposed to analytical value) of cosmopolitan paradigms in formulating a borderless world, a position Hamid purposely assumes: 'having a sense of hope for me is a direct political response to [. . .] Brexit' (Hamid 2017). Hamid's direct engagement with the Syrian refugee crisis underscores that many EU citizens desired the maintenance of Fortress Europe to guard against undesirable cultural influence. Though *Exit West* gestures to the need for more cosmopolitan hospitality in our interdependent global community, the brute force of EU policy merely continues to reinforce Europe's external borders while weakening internal ones, ensuring an embrace of alterity remains ultimately deferred.

In his work *Archipelagic Modernism* (2014), John Brannigan explains how the archipelagos of the British Isles have at times been imagined as a fortress, an enclave and a retreat, but, while the sea has been what cut Britain off, it is also what has connected it to a larger world.[11] For Eurosceptics, the encircling sea of the British Isles operates as a vital *cordon sanitaire* against infection. Cameron's invocation of cultural exceptionalism in his Bloomberg speech, asserting 'the British have the character of an island nation', was admittedly tempered by the concession 'that ours is not just an island story – it is also a Continental story' (Cameron 2013).[12] Spiering recognizes that Britain's 'Grand Island Narrative' is, at heart, not a matter of geography but 'a story', a 'cultural construct' designed to reinforce British exceptionalism (2015: 42). Island analogies continue to resound in twenty-first-century British fiction. John Lanchester's 2019 novel *The Wall* illustrates just how much geography has shaped the psychology of the British populace, affording them a separate status from their Continental partners. The novel imagines a dystopic near-future where the British Isles are now entirely surrounded and protected by what is simply called the Wall, a ten-thousand kilometre National Coastal Defence Structure ostensibly designed to keep out the water, but its true purpose is to discourage and restrict those seeking sanctuary and hospitality. The Wall is manned by civilians called Defenders who act as exclusionary gatekeepers within the Border Defence Force, preventing immigrants from entering the heavily barricaded island nation. Defenders in turn are aided by Flight, a fictional organization mirroring the actions of Frontex, the EU border patrol agency, whose job

---

[11] Appropriately, Margaret Atwood (1972) claims that if English literature were to be represented by one unifying and informing visual symbol it would be an island: an insular and contained structure reflective of the national mindset.

[12] Cameron cited the Edwardian children's book *Our Island Story: A History of England for Boys and Girls* (1905) by H. E. Marshall as his favourite childhood book.

is to scan the seas for refugees and sink their boats. Refugees are occasionally allowed to reside within the island fortress, but only if they serve as the Help: effectively slaves employed to satisfy the running of the regime, raise satisfaction levels and thus prevent any bottom-up resistance movements.

In spite of Lanchester's explicit commentary on exclusionary processes and enforced immobilities affecting the contemporary moment, the novel provides further support for the contention that post-Brexit fiction demonstrates a movement away from pre-Brexit Eurosceptic fiction via a more focused and purposeful critique of cultural insularity.[13] As David Reynolds argues, we must move away from 'a tightly "islanded" sense of identity' and recognize 'the intricately "storied" character of Britain' (2019: 249). Lanchester's Defenders themselves resent their presence on the Wall and dream of 'a new way of living, more communal [. . .] where we would live together and look after each other and maybe other like-minded people would join us' (Lanchester 2019: 119). Lanchester's political outlook clearly aligns with that of an underground network in the novel which strives to dismantle the political regime responsible for the protectionist barrier and interprets the Wall as symbolic of the nation's 'selfish, self-interested turning away from the world. A refusal of our responsibilities' (2019: 112). The novel's liberal ideology becomes apparent when a group of Defenders are cast out for failing to prevent the infiltration of a flotilla of refugees and are forced to become members of a floating community themselves. Denied both citizenship and political sovereignty, they are left adrift, reduced to the wretched of the dystopian world (mirroring the fate of Guy Swift in Kunzru's *Transmission*). The pedagogical demonization, denaturalization and dehumanization of the expelled citizens stokes this fear of external influence and reinforces the mandatory maintenance of the island fortress; yet the sudden reversal of power engenders an ideological paradigm shift in the Defenders, symbolizing a movement from national and bounded to more cosmopolitan and fluid forms of belonging: 'we were Others now', but 'If I was an Other and they were Others perhaps none of us were Others but instead we were a new Us' (2019: 203; 246). The novel's cosmopolitan vision disrupts established neo-colonial systems of representation and communicates the need for a discursive transformation of the refugee crisis. Beck and Grande suggest cosmopolitanism, with its 'both/and' logic, empowers cultures to move beyond restrictive nationalist ideologies and logics that often suffer from an exclusive 'us/them' dichotomy (2007: 18). Further, this interplay between racial politics and ethical relationality allows Lanchester to comment on the 'small human margins' still existing in British society, resisting cultural isolationism and allowing 'space for forgiveness or acceptance' – an empathetic identification with otherness which resists geopolitical provincialism and gestures towards the need for global cooperation (2019: 48). *The Wall* ultimately draws on the age-old experience of exile and statelessness to respond to the political displacement affecting contemporary global citizens and accentuates how the reality of rightlessness for refugees is often overlooked or distorted by related debates on national legitimacy. For the authors

---

[13] German author Christoph Hein's *Willenbrock* (2000) reveals that similar protectionist sentiments are shared within his own nation: 'They should build walls. Walls everywhere. It's impossible to stop all these people. A wall round Germany, around every country' (2003: 157).

discussed in this chapter, writing about immigration and displacement is clearly a viable means of critiquing immigration policy at a time of geopolitical upheaval, but also a way of questioning the nature of national and European belonging as Britain considers its political future.

Reflecting on Brexit and the refugee crises in Europe in his last interview before his death in 2016, sociologist Zygmunt Bauman warned, 'Hospitality possibilities are not limitless', but 'the human ability to ensure suffering and rejection is not limitless either. So we have to exercise what is called empathy [. . .] Dialogue is a long, long process' (Bauman 2016). In the immediate fallout of the EU referendum the racist vitriol directed at migrants did not abate; xenophobic graffiti was scrawled across the Polish Social and Cultural Association in west London while refugees continued to be subject to verbal and physical abuse. The death of Polish migrant Arkadiusz Jozwik in Harlow, Essex, on 27 August 2016, viciously beaten to death for speaking Polish, was dubbed the 'Brexit murder' by the media and marked a particularly low point in British race relations (Harlow had returned the national average of a 52% Leave vote). As Freedland reports, there has been a '500% increase in the number of hate crimes reported' within British society following the vote, 'as if 23 June were a permission slip to every racist and bigot in the country' (Freedland 2016b). The Brexit vote reinforced what had been apparent for a number of years: a substantial political divide was emerging between those voters who favoured open societies and those who wished to shut down and deny cultural interdependence. Immigration became the terrain upon which these ideological battles could be fought. Contested zones of inclusion and exclusion ranged from the local and regional to the national and global and such zones are configured differently in the minds of the populace. A vote to leave became a solution in tackling the immigration debate that has plagued British politics for decades. The EU served as an appropriate scapegoat for those dissatisfied with the multicultural face of Britain while the ongoing conflation of illegal immigration with multiculturalism in public and political discourses was evident in the hostility directed towards descendants of the Windrush in 2018. May's government, in an attempt to create a 'hostile environment' by making it difficult for those migrants without 'leave to remain', subjected Commonwealth citizens to pernicious immigration policies and threatened them with deportation. As Ashuman Mondal rightly comments, the 'Commonwealth' remains 'about as abject a misnomer for an entity so deeply scarred by Britain's former colonial rapacity as can be imagined' (2018: 89). Attempts by the government to use EU nationals as bargaining chips to extract further concessions in post-Brexit negotiations cemented the view that brutal British immigration policies would outlive the immediate repercussions of the referendum.[14] As Mireille Rosello and Stephen Wolfe recognize, borders (particularly *cultural* conceptualizations of borders) often 'continue to have effects after the symbolic differences that caused them have disappeared or lessened' (2017: 2). An exit from the EU thus failed to quell fears surrounding immigration; Leave-supporting voters continue to believe the government

---

[14] Data from the Office for National Statistics (2018) indicates how Brexit may have resulted in an instant decline in EU immigration, but non-EU immigration remains unaffected and continues to increase.

has failed to 'Take Back Control', while supporters of a 'hard Brexit' consider the loss of Single Market access a small price to pay for reduced EU immigration and tighter border controls.

This fourth chapter has demonstrated how the combination of post-EU enlargement, historically unprecedented net migration levels and the Syrian refugee crisis contributed to widespread hostility to both EU membership and further cultural integration. The selected fictions examined in the chapter present Britain as a racially and culturally divided nation as it entered the twenty-first century, revealing how the threat of EU (and non-EU) immigration spoke to broader national anxieties concerning fragile economic conditions, reinforcing the loss of cultural identity and national sovereignty discussed in Chapter 2. In responding to the post-2004 enlargement, Lanchester, Tremain and Lewycka communicate the socioeconomic vulnerability of EU migrants and anticipate the numerous reasons why the Remain camp could not alter the widespread public belief that immigration placed a strain on public services and the welfare state. More importantly, *Breach*, *Refugee Tales* and *Exit West* demonstrate how the critical timing of the Syrian refugee crisis enabled the Leave campaign to link anti-immigrant rhetoric to the need for greater national security. Documenting a resistance to that which threatens the purity and inviolability of European space, these fictions indicate why immigration is likely to remain the most deeply contested issue in British politics long after Brexit is resolved. And yet, by offering clear authorial critiques of British immigration policies, the fictions also position literature as an emancipatory vehicle to counteract myths surrounding the act of migration, mark an attempt to destabilize institutional optics of power, and serve as a cultural impetus for political change.

5

L'espirit de L'escalier

Post-Brexit fictions

In novel, perhaps in redemptive, forms, new kinds of art and thought [could] contribute to a revised and properly cosmopolitan definition of what Europe was and what its values would need to be in the future. Culture could reacquaint Europe with the humanity from which it had been comprehensively estranged.

(Gilroy 2013: 123)

Brexit did not divide the nation, it simply gave voice to existing social, cultural, political and economic grievances within society. The forces of politicization ramped up public dissatisfaction with the EU, often with regards to pre-existing issues affecting the body politic. For Michael Zürn, politicization involves this transportation of 'an issue or an institution into the field or sphere of politics – making previously unpolitical matters political' (2016: 167). The referendum result was the manifestation of over three decades of Euroscepticism, resistance to mass migration from Eastern Europe and the Middle East, impotent rage regarding the Eurozone crisis, and the corresponding failures of the left to either wholeheartedly endorse European integration or acknowledge the values of modern patriotism.[1] As Darren McGarvey writes, on the morning after the referendum result, 'multiple crises were announced simultaneously by middle class liberals, progressives and radicals, who were suddenly confronted with the vulgar and divided country the rest of us had been living in for decades' (2017: 148). Goodwin is correct in asserting that 'most people never really had an interest in exploring what underpinned Brexit', with much analysis focusing solely on post-truth tactics employed by the Leave campaign rather than the historical roots of the result; however, this criticism cannot be directed at Remain-supporting academics alone (Goodwin 2018). Leave support did not solely consist of working-class voters opposed to an elitist system; the campaign itself was run by Westminster elites implicated in the very systems responsible for ingrained economic inequalities to which Leave voters were so opposed.

---

[1] Nonetheless, the campaign did play a vital role in shaping the narrative. In the run-up to the 2015 UK general election, the market research organization Ipsos MORI found that fewer than 10 per cent of British voters named the EU as a 'top three' issue affecting their decision (Ipsos MORI 2015).

For political commentator Robert Peston, the vote gave a voice to millions of disenfranchised voters 'who quite liked the idea of giving a bloody nose to the posh boys' (Peston 2017). In this light, Brexit emerges self-flagellating pleasure or revenge fantasy fuelled by the Conservatives' increasingly austerity-driven political programme. Moreover, members of the left shared UKIP's fears of an 'ever closer union' but for differing reasons, perceiving the organization not as a progressive forum for cosmopolitical debate but an exclusive, injurious and undemocratic capitalist club. The EU has, nonetheless, been championed as a valid attempt to reconcile existing tensions between national and cosmopolitan forms of belonging and identification. Daniele Archibugi goes so far as to hail the EU as 'the first international model which begins to resemble the cosmopolitan model' (1998: 219). The supranational polity arguably translates cosmopolitanism's universal abstractions into pragmatic practices, evident in the legislative frameworks, transnational projects and trade agreements established between nations. However, as Chris Rumford has persuasively argued, EU policy-makers 'almost never refer to cosmopolitanism', its politicians 'tend not to allude to Europeans as cosmopolitans', and its reports in general 'eschew the language of cosmopolitanism' (2007: 4). The top-down bureaucratic mechanisms of the EU lead Beck and Grande to suggest that a 'deformed cosmopolitanism' emerges, produced by 'egoism of the member states, economic self-interest and the asymmetries in influence on political decisions' (2007: 20).

At the core of the Brexit debate was the question of national borders: How should they be controlled? In a globalized world of transnational mobilities are porous borders an inevitability? Or is the maintenance of existing borders a form of defence from acts of global terrorism and undocumented immigration? For many British citizens the ongoing Syrian refugee crisis encapsulated these concerns and fuelled nationalist rhetoric. Angela Merkel described the crisis as one critical element of 'our rendezvous with globalisation' and acknowledged the importance of this battle (reflected in her subsequent forthright refusal for a post-Brexit Britain to opt out of freedom of movement): 'we will have to take on more responsibility in an open world for what happens outside our European borders' (Merkel 2016). Brexiteers maintained that the nation state could become a so-called Global Britain without relying on restrictive regulatory obligations to the EU or suffering further cultural influence detrimental to British ways of life. Theresa May's blueprints for a Global Britain, predicated on these suggested trading ties outside Europe's domain, intimated an inherent opposition to cosmopolitan ideology: 'If you believe you're a citizen of the world, you're a citizen of nowhere' (May 2016b).

The Brexit vote became a convenient catch-all for a range of internal struggles hindering the political functionality of an increasingly, inappropriately titled *United Kingdom* – a belated expression of a well-established structure of feeling. Building on the issues discussed in previous chapters, including the inheritance of a deeply entrenched cultural Euroscepticism, ongoing struggles to define contemporary modes of Englishness, anxieties over the failing integrity of the Union, and the backlash against EU and non-EU migration, this final chapter will examine the ways by which the *first wave* of post-Brexit fiction provides an immediate response to the referendum result. The chapter will also demonstrate how writers are confronting associated developments which impacted and led to the Brexit vote, including legitimate grievances relating to radical inequalities of access and socioeconomic imbalance, fears surrounding authoritarian populism and simplified notions of British national identity. As the introduced explained, these selected works could be more accurately termed *post-referendum fictions*, given that withdrawal did not occur on 31 December 2020; however, Brexit has come to be associated with that fateful date of 23 June 2016, when Britain finally gave voice to the Euroscepticism which had haunted its post-war identity.

Established literary figures such as Ian McEwan, Hilary Mantel and Zadie Smith all immediately engaged with the charged political events of 2016, speaking out on Britain's apparently troubling act of national self-harm. J. K. Rowling labelled the rhetoric deployed during the referendum campaign 'uglier than I can remember in my lifetime', while Scottish poet Jackie Kay described the news of the result as 'a bereavement [. . .] It's a trauma. A body blow to the country' (Elgot 2016; Kay 2016). Numerous authors and poets also contributed to *A Love Letter to Europe* (2019), a collection of pro-European think-pieces on Britain's political withdrawal, including Alan Hollinghurst, Sebastian Faulks, Margaret Drabble, A. L. Kennedy and Alan Moore.[2] In comparison to the post-war literary scene, many writers and artists believed Europe should be embraced not rejected and further debate was required before any withdrawal agreement could be ratified. Former Labour Party MP Denis MacShane, who arguably coined the term 'Brexit', expresses the feelings of many writers when he points out Leave voters did not truly constitute the majority: 'Of the 44.56 million British voters, 27.1 million did not vote for Brexit – they either voted Remain or did not vote at all; 17.4 million voted for Brexit and 16.1 million voted against' (MacShane 2019: 36). While he is undoubtedly correct in questioning the legitimacy of an advisory referendum in a parliamentary democracy, decisions are made by those who show up, and it is difficult to argue that an overall turnout of over 72 per cent is unrepresentative of the 'will of the people'. Nevertheless, the majority of post-Brexit literary works indicate a pronounced disgust with the national turmoil continuing to embroil British politics and betray an authorial resistance to the outcome of the referendum.

---

[2] Literary responses to Brexit were, of course, not limited to the novel form. Yet David Wheatley, a contributor to the anthology *Wretched Strangers* (2018), suggests poetic responses have been more muted and queries the lack of an immediate response from 'pro-Brexit bards'; he concludes that, given the enmity of the campaign, 'Brexit is a place where language goes to die' (Wheatley 2018). Nonetheless, figures such as Jackie Kay, Gillian Clarke, Imtiaz Dharker, Benjamin Zephaniah and John Agard have all produced work engaging with the referendum. The most significant Brexlit poetry collections are Jane Commane's *Assembly Lines* (2018), Charly Bishop's *The Ballad of Brexit and Other Brexit Poems* (2018), Hugh Dunkerley's *Kin* (2018), Vidyan Ravinthiran's *The Million-Petalled Flower of Being Here* (2019) and David Clarke's *The Europeans* (2019). By articulating a nuanced consideration of Brexit's stimulants and provocations, and inhabiting the lives of diverse others, these collections demonstrate the capacity of language to stem (if not heal) bleeding wounds. Similarly, although the study does not have the space to delve into the realm of theatre, much can be said about key works including *My Country* by Carol Ann Duffy and Rufus Norris; *Jamais Vu* (2017) by James Ellis; *People Like Us* (2018) by Julie Burchill and Jane Robins; *Brexit: A Play* (2018) by Robert Khan and Tom Salinsky; *A Strong Exit* by James Graham (2016); *Lear in Brexitland* by Tim Prentki (2017).

Post-truth, populism and the culture war

In this era of post-truth politics, an unhesitating liar can be king.
(Freedland 2016a)

A number of caustic autofictions responded directly to the consequences of the referendum and their impact on a shell-shocked Britain. Rachel Cusk's *Kudos* (2018) is inhabited by various characters who dismiss Leave voters as uninformed nationalists while Olivia Laing's semi-autobiographical *Crudo* (2018a) concentrates on the tumultuous summer of 2017 following 'the car-crash of Brexit': an environment in which events 'still happened, but not in any sensible order [...] and anyway the space between them was full of misleading data, nonsense and lies' (2018a: 62; 240). Laing adopts the unusual approach of combining elements of her personal life with that of American post-punk writer Kathy Acker to condemn the deployment of post-truth political rhetoric in a feverish, incessant news cycle. The wonderfully understated remark, 'A lot had changed this year', positions Brexit as merely one development in a radically changing and increasingly absurd political landscape: 'Twin victories for Trump and Brexit had inaugurated a season of chaos, cartoonish, frightening and increasingly violent' (2018a: 63, 2018b).[3] While it seems counter-intuitive for a cultural critic to turn to fiction in order to analyse the post-Brexit chaos, Laing explains that while non-fiction does indeed instil 'order and perspective, clarity and objectivity', the 'only way to capture the feeling of chaos, confusion and paranoia was by way of inhabiting an invented character's consciousness' (Laing 2018b). Literary fiction's power thus lies in its capacity to create 'room to reflect and regroup', provide 'therapy or catharsis' and snatch 'back the truth' in a post-truth era (Laing 2018b). As Laing succinctly puts it (quoting American modernist painter Philip Guston), 'That's the only reason to be an artist: to escape, to bear witness to this' (2018a: 87).

Both the run-up to (and immediate aftermath of) the Brexit vote also witnessed the first forays into fiction by numerous mainstream political commentators. Andrew Marr and Stanley Johnson (father of Boris) penned overwrought political thrillers occupied with the fallout of the referendum result. Marr's *Head of State* (2015) offers satirical glimpses of the inner workings of pre-Brexit dealings while Johnson's *Kompromat* (2017) and James Silvester's *Blood, White and Blue* (2018) vilify the EU as a Janus-faced and treacherous organization. Chris Mullin's *The Friends of Harry Perkins* (2019), a sequel to his 1982 semi-comic political thriller *A Very British Coup*, continues the trend of political figures delving into the sphere of literary fiction. Mullin, a former Labour MP for Sunderland South, projects a gloomy vision of a post-Brexit future where withdrawal from the EU has failed to alleviate internal ailments affecting the body politic. Whereas *A Very British Coup* chronicled the trials and tribulations of Harry Perkins, a socialist Labour prime minister in the 1980s (now considered to be a fictional forerunner for the unlikely rise of Jeremy Corbyn), the sequel imagines a Britain that has finally completed its negotiation period and exited the EU but without

---

[3] Laing's passing reference to Lauren Berlant's *Cruel Optimism* suggests an authorial critique towards those citizens who allegedly voted against their interests.

reaching any significant trade agreements. Mullin paints a depressing but predictable picture of a post-Brexit British economy striving to react to its recent political retreat:

> The symptoms were unmistakable. Long queues of lorries at custom posts [. . .] A succession of announcements by British business that they would be relocating to the Continent. Regular crises on the border between Northern Ireland and the Republic when the new technology that was supposed to have resolved the customs problem failed to work. The triumphalism that had once surrounded Brexit had long since faded. (2019a: 135)

Mullin's political stasis of 2025 looks frighteningly similar to the stagnation characterizing post-Brexit negotiations. If the 'great Armageddon' prophesized by passionate Remainers has not quite emerged, then neither has the 'economic miracle promised by the Brexiteers', and the 'long, steady decline into insularity and irrelevance' proves to be just as painful and debilitating (Mullin 2019b). Like the prescient political analysis within *A Very British Coup*, Mullin's post-Brexit sequel offers a pragmatic prognostication of the deadening bureaucratic process which Britain must endure before a new national chapter can begin.

Such sensitive narratorial balance is certainly not evident in Ian McEwan's *Cockroach* (2019) which clearly speaks to a much smaller literary audience to expound a decidedly pro-European political commentary. The novella subscribes to the Swiftian political tradition, with Pynchonian comedic elements thrown in for good measure, providing a searing slice of anti-Brexit satire written for Remain-supporting voters unable to locate any sense or reason in Britain's act of political isolationism. McEwan, a prominent critic of the post-Brexit process who has been vociferously opposed to Eurosceptic meddling for decades, admits to being in denial about the referendum result, labelling Brexit 'the most pointless, masochistic ambition ever dreamed of in the history of these islands' (McEwan 2019b). Rather than attempting to seek answers for the nation's slide into populism, he makes plain his views on the political farce that has engulfed British politics, suggesting any EU withdrawal on the basis of an advisory referendum is tantamount to an abnegation of political responsibility.[4] Set in the present day following the events of the Brexit vote, Jim Sams, a grotesque parody of Boris Johnson, finds himself tasked with delivering the referendum result. From the opening line, the novella's political take on Kafka's *The Metamorphosis* is clear; however, McEwan inverses the process and Sams awakens to find himself in 10 Downing Street. McEwan's utilization of a cockroach inhabiting human form proffers an oblique commentary on the ways by which those that thrive on squalid societal conditions exploit the insalubrious political landscape for personal gain. By operating as one body, Sams and his metamorphosed far-right cabinet operate reinforce McEwan's disparaging critique of the hive-mind mentality buttressing populism.

---

[4] In *Machines Like Me* (2019), McEwan reinforces his distaste for governments which decide 'policy by plebiscites', imagining a counter-factual history of the 1980s in which Prime Minister Tony Benn masterminds Britain's exit from Europe.

As leader of the Reversalist Party, Sams champions the bizarre economic theory of Reversalism – by which consumers are paid to purchase goods and in turn have to pay employers to work – in order to somehow generate national renewal. This inversion of the financial system clearly gestures to (what McEwan perceives as) the economic illiteracy of Brexiteers in perceiving a brighter financial future outside of EU control. Brexit and Reversalism are one and the same beast. The Clockwise Conservative Party, in a direct mirroring of the pre-Brexit political landscape, finds itself dragged to the right in order to counter the insurgence of Reversalists, eventually promising a referendum on the reverse of money flow in order to placate wavering factions in their ranks. In place of 'Take Back Control', the Reversalist slogan 'Turn the Money Around' becomes an omnipresent slogan, uniting disparate sections of the nation in a tenuous alliance:

> The old, by way of cognitive dimming, were nostalgically drawn to what they understand to be a proposal to turn back the clock. Both groups, poor and old, were animated to varying degrees by nationalist zeal. In a brilliant coup, the Reversalist press managed to present their cause as a patriotic duty and a promise of national revival and purification. (McEwan 2019a: 29)

By running on a populist platform, Sams successfully stirs up enough nationalist fervour that Archie Tupper, a poorly veiled Donald Trump, threatens to reverse the US economy in turn. However, the eventual reluctance of other nations to follow Britain's lead and adopt the policy leaves the nation once again isolated and adrift, promising trade deals which will never be implemented and practising a humiliating form of 'Reversalism in One Country' (2019a: 31).

Curiously, despite the novella forging multiple parallels with the post-Brexit moment, from a creeping anxiety and weariness over EU negotiations, to vague threats regarding prorogation, to multiple nationalist attacks on serving politicians, McEwan fails to provide an originating impetus for this pursuit of Hard Reversalism. Sams simply feels impelled 'to embrace a mystical sense of nation' and free the British from their 'elective captivity' to the EU: an organization guided by a dangerous 'arid rationality' (2019a: 21; 22). When the wearied and exasperated German chancellor asks Sams: 'Why are you doing this? Why, to what end, are you tearing your nation apart?', McEwan simply furnishes his metamorphosed protagonist with a hollow and meaningless explanation: 'Because. Because that's what we're doing. Because that's what we believe in. Because that's what we said we'd do. Because that's what people said they wanted [. . .] That, ultimately, was the only answer: because' (2019a: 86–7). The cockroaches only leave their human hosts once the Reversalism Bill is passed into law and Britain completes its act of political isolationism, leaving the reader with more questions than answers as to their purpose. For McEwan, the efficacy of his novel is clear: 'As the nation tears itself apart, constitutional norms are set aside, parliament is closed down so that the government cannot be challenged [. . .] a writer is bound to ask what he or she can do. There's only one answer: write.' (McEwan 2019c).

In McEwan's defence, he concedes his novel avoids delivering a 'balanced view' and prefers post-Brexit novels which attempt to locate the intersection between 'despair and laughter' rather than delve into the minds of Eurosceptics: 'I'd much rather read a savage satire on Remainers from a Brexiter' (qtd. in Lynskey 2019). It may be, however, that Brexit is beyond satire – the absurdities of the contemporary political moment proving to be poor ingredients for satirists – and McEwan, often referred to as Britain's *national* novelist, seems more bewildered than ever by recent events. His implication that the Brexit vote was a moment of political *akrasia*, with the British people voting against their best interests, reinforces the criticism that liberal authors perceive the populace to be gullible and unwitting pawns manipulated by their base instincts. Unlike his earlier works, *The Cockroach* lacks McEwan's acerbic acuity and his bitterness regarding the referendum seeps into the novel; by savagely mocking proponents of Leave, the novel does little to bridge the fracture within our post-Brexit society, nor does it make any attempt to understand Leave voters.

The global political landscape of 2016 created unique conditions for populist leaders to tap into public disenchantment and mobilize widespread electoral support, evident in the electoral success of several European political parties, including the Danish People's Party, the Sweden Democrats and the Austrian Freedom Party. Norris and Inglehart position the Leave campaign as a populist movement stimulated by a combination of 'economic grievances', evidenced in the widening gap between London and more economically depressed regions in Britain, and a 'cultural backlash' by older generations threatened by the rapid changes in contemporary culture and the loss of established traditions (2019: 459). The two factors reinforce one another in deepening this national cleavage. *Time of Lies* (2017) by Douglas Board and *Perfidious Albion* (2018) by Sam Byers envision worlds in which Brexiteer-minded populist movements have maintained their political momentum and an inherent breakdown in Britain's cosmopolitan optic continues to run unchecked. Both novels engage with the emergence of authoritarian reflexes as a reaction to the gradual shift towards more socially liberal values, as well as the sinister tactics authoritarian leaders employ to suppress dissent and strengthen their political footing.

Board, a former civil servant, started work on *Time of Lies* in 2013, identifying early a 'big gulf of ignorance contempt between the ruling class and ruled [. . .] long before Brexit', yet he defines the work as a post-truth novel which also responds to the shocking political events of 2016 (Board 2017b).[5] Set in a post-Brexit Britain, the darkly comic novel charts the rise of the Britain's Great party, projected to achieve a landslide victory in the 2020 UK general election. Running on a populist platform geared around controlled immigration, tighter border policies, the reclamation of British sovereignty, and the abolition of the House of Lords, Britain's Great takes advantage of the power vacuum created by the erosion of support for UKIP following Brexit and the evaporation of Labour's red wall due to Corbyn's divisive leadership. The party is spearheaded by Bob Grant, an ex-football hooligan who holds his political rallies in his beloved Millwall FC stadium; the party's adoption of Millwall's football chant 'no one lies us, we don't care' echoes Conservative peer Chris Patten's comments that Theresa May's dogmatic approach to EU negotiations had created a 'Millwall Britain' (Chakelian 2017). Stirring up a vitriolic anger directed at neoliberal bankers, the sickly influence

---

[5] The novel is dedicated to the memory of Jo Cox MP.

of generic foreigners and the shadowy machinations of Europhilic organizations – effectively 'saying boo to the IMF' – Grant rides the populist tide to become swiftly installed as PM, testifying to the lingering discontent and disenfranchisement long after the Brexit vote (2017a: 98).

The widespread support for populist parties reflected the sentiment that the political class should be held answerable to the democratic will of the people. After all, 'democratic politics is politics in the vernacular', as Will Kymlicka stresses, suggesting 'that the more political debate is conducted in the vernacular, the more participatory it will be' (2010: 441). Yet Grant's rapid rise and electoral support is dependent on questionable assertions and a loose association with the truth. His fusion of neoliberal ideology with the brute force of authoritarian populism recalls the much-quoted dictum that bringing facts to a culture war is like bringing a knife to a gun fight. For Sarah Helm, Boris Johnson's 'half-truths' during his time as a Brussels correspondent in the 1990s served a similar function, creating 'a new reality [...] shaping the narrative that morphed into our present-day populist Euroscepticism' (qtd. in Freedland 2016a). Grant's socially conservative and ethnocentric values (which share empirical links with authoritarian populism) serve as a counter to the perceived dominance of liberal lifestyles which threaten British cultural traditions, and symbolize a resistance to the supranational pluralism of the EU which undermines the legitimacy of the nation's democratic institutions. In depicting himself as a political outsider, disillusioned with the mainstream parties and willing to offer radical solutions in alleviating national grievances, Grant draws on populist rhetoric to align himself with working-class people staging an ideological battle against elitist, Eurocentric vested interests. Donald Trump, and Nigel Farage to a lesser (and less successful) extent, ran on similar platforms and relied on complementary narratives, leading an insurgency against bureaucrats, intellectuals, fake media and political correctness. As Donald Trump Jr wrote in 2019, 'you could say that Brexit and my father's election are one and the same' (Dallison 2019). Gove's declaration that 'Britain has had enough of experts' stems from the same populist impulse, implicating the Conservatives in this tactic of manipulating democratic energies to destabilize established democratic orders (qtd. in Mance 2016).

Although the Leave campaign's success robbed UKIP of its raison d'etre, the delay in implementing Brexit led Farage to establish the Brexit Party, applying further pressure on a gridlocked parliament unwilling to enact the will of the people. Support for authoritarian-populist parties clearly remains strong even after the cathartic release of the Brexit vote. Parallels can be drawn between the transformation of the Brexit Party and the populist language and authoritarian rhetoric of Britain's Great, which occupies the political space UKIP once held. As Mondal argues, Farage's declaration that 23 June 2016 was Britain's 'independence day' evokes 'ideas of colonial dependency' but 'also enacts a reversal', projecting a Britain 'for so long held to account by the forces of "political correctness"' (2018: 82). For Norris and Inglehart, populist sentiments can exert a positive influence, helping to 'reduce corruption, strengthen responsive governance, expand the issue agenda [...] and reengage participation among groups alienated by mainstream party politics'; however, by exploiting fears relating to national loyalty and security, authoritarian populism generates 'a combustible mix' which leaves a power vacuum and opens the door 'for rule by strongmen leaders, social intolerance, and illiberal governance' (2019: 461). An inward-looking nativism or protectionism emerges that fails to rebuild trust in either the media or the political system and simply leads to entrenched dogmatic attitudes, the curtailing of democratic freedoms and the silencing of the press (as evidenced in the political policies of Marine le Pen in France, Recep Tayyip Erdogan in Turkey and Viktor Orban's 'illiberal' democracy in Hungary).

Accordingly, while Grant's social policies initially speak to the material realities affecting British society – such as a plan to protect economically depressed areas of the country by offering priority housing to British citizens – his strong-man leadership soon assumes an autocratic Putinesque edge, and he threatens to nuke Brussels for its disclination to support British interests. A bottom-up populist protest vote directed against the establishment is thus transformed into a top-down authoritarian populism which exploits socioeconomic grievances and fails to alleviate national divisions. In retaliation, the fictional president of the European Commission promises that the EU will be 'as creative as the UK is insolent' and plans are put in motion to avert a subsequent *Frexit* by positioning Britain as the problem-child of Europe: 'It is as if Europe has had a miscarriage. But now we can move on. We have cut the umbilical cord' (2017a: 138; 230). Grant's chokehold over Britain slowly loosens (much to the delight of his Guardian-reading, left-leaning brother Zack) in spite of LKGB's (Labour for the Kinder, Gentler Britain) policies failing to resonate with voters. A coup masterminded by the Civil Service ensures Britain's Great is eventually supplanted by a national coalition of established parties which promises a second Indy Ref, indicating once again that Scottish devolution is the most likely legacy of this slide into populism. It is significant that the eventual reclamation of the centre ground is only achieved via a coup, rather than a paradigm shift in the political consciousness of the electorate, potentially deepening a resentment of the bureaucratic meddling of a London-centric elite and disregarding the motivating factors which led to the Brexit vote.

Sam Byers' *Perfidious Albion* reinforces this attack on a post-truth political culture, directing his ire at those political factions 'waxing lyrical about a "lost" England comprised entirely of hedgerows and loam' (2018: 6).[6] The cover of Byers' novel references the Pieter Bruegel the Elder's The Tower of Babel, yet bastardizes the infamous painting by depicting a stagnating post-Brexit Britain still-under-construction, littering the edifice with empty political slogans and corporate waffle, appropriate for an increasingly post-truth culture. Set in a near-future following Britain's recent departure from the EU, the dystopic yet disturbingly plausible narrative centres on a dilapidated East Anglian housing estate, Larchwood, in the sleepy fictional town of Edmundsbury. The estate is under threat of redevelopment and gentrification by a global tech company, Downton, while a multinational tech giant Green (its name sardonically evoking popular visions of an idyllic, rural England) is slowly insinuating its way into the lives of Edmundsbury's inhabitants, harvesting personal information in a manner redolent of Cambridge Analytica.

---

[6] The archaic, pejorative phrase perfidious Albion (its current usage first associated with British acts of perfidy during the French Revolution) re-emerged during post-Brexit negotiations, pointing to acts of diplomatic disloyalty among the Westminster elite.

Darkin, an elderly, white working-class male, refuses to vacate the estate yet is manipulated by far-right media commentators, such as journalist Hugo Bennington, into perceiving immigrants as the root cause of his plight as opposed to the austerity programmes and public sector cuts instigated by a progressively conservative, corporate political culture.[7] Bennington utilizes his newspaper columns in a popular tabloid to launch incendiary attacks on Muslims, strains to the NHS and politically correct liberal dogma. In peddling simplicity to his readers, Bennington contrasts the perceived horrors of contemporary England with 'another historical England, which had once made him proud and secure': 'Through nostalgia, he was selling the politically equivalent of escapism. And through reductive blame-mongering, he was, he knew, selling a potent combination of the two' (2018: 103). Bennington soon translates his public support into electoral success via the creation of a nativist, Eurosceptic political party, the UKIP-lite England Always, which derides Westminster elites and draws on Brute Force – a civilian vigilante militia parodying the English Defence League – to enforce control and intimidate voters. As a pint-drinking, chain-smoking everyman, Bennington is a clear caricature of Nigel Farage, running his party on an anti-immigration platform which proves enticing to Edmundsbury's threatened inhabitants. England Always aims to reignite the pre-Brexit revolutionary mood that has been dampened by endless negotiations and media prattle, ensuring the concerns of disenfranchised voters are not forgotten:

> chests puffed with post-exit pride, had begun their transformation from a party concerned with redefining England's place in the world to a party preoccupied with people's place in England, and had moved from shaping England's post-Europe future to recapturing its pre-contemporary pomp. Brexit was over, but the energy it had accumulated had to be retained. Fears needed to be redirected. Hatred needed to pivot. (Byers 2018: 119)

Disillusioned communities such as Edmundsbury naturally become a prime location for the targeted tactics of populist England Always: the small town 'was home to fewer immigrants than almost anywhere else in the country, yet anti-immigration sentiment had never been higher' (2018: 106). Byers demonstrates just how easily cultural *wounding* develops into white rage and thoughts of white supremacy, exposing the questionable values of his nominally inclusive nation. Appropriately, negative attitudes towards immigration were a significant predictor of populist values in relation to both the Leave vote and the success of UKIP in the 2015 and 2017 general elections, often focused in areas which had seen the lowest rates of immigration. The unnuanced rhetoric of populism is also well suited to online social media; unsophisticated populist soundbites draw together heterogeneous groups motivated by related grievances under the same broad (if amorphous) umbrella. As Timothy Snyder points out, this

---

[7] For Brian M. Hughes, Brexit is 'psychological, not political', affected by personal and collective social attitudes towards events, revealing the dangers of groupthink, confirmation bias and casual attribution bias, and a reliance on an availability heuristic which simplified complex perceptions of the EU (2019: 151).

sociopolitical movement can be more accurately defined as 'sadopopulism', whereby voters 'can believe that he or she has chosen who administers their pain, and can fantasise that this leader will hurt enemies still more', converting 'pain to meaning, and then meaning back into more pain' (2018: 273). Voters such as Darkin direct their displaced rage at immigrants or pro-EU quislings and miss the real target. When Thomas Mair, the murderer of MP Jo Cox, announced to the courtroom that his name was 'Death to Traitors, Freedom for Britain', he was responding to this same deluded fear of invasion and the misguided perception that Britain had been reduced to a vassal state. *The Sun* headline during post-Brexit negotiations, 'PUT EU HANDS UP, claiming German officials desired Britain's unconditional surrender in Brexit talks', testifies to the role of media figures such as Bennington in stoking these anxieties (Hawkes 2017).

Trina, a black British tech worker and fellow resident of the Larchwood estate, resists what she perceives as 'the tsunami of whitewashed nostalgia and chocolate-box history' espoused by England Always, tweeting '#whitemalegenocide. Lol' in response to Bennington's claim that white men are being culturally and politically marginalized by recent multicultural and gendered developments in British society (Byers 2018: 134). However, her tweet is weaponized by Bennington as evidence for the exact ultra-liberal prejudice he considers responsible for diminishing his beloved England and he marshals his bigoted forces to expel Trina from the estate. Yet Bennington is not simply inciting racial hatred or asseverating post-truth rhetoric in order to win electoral seats, he genuinely experiences a cruel nostalgia for a culture he longer recognizes. Faced with expulsion from his own party, Bennington gradually realizes that for:

> all the years he'd spent banging on about how much he loved England [. . .] he hated England: its hordes of immigrants; its filthy street markets of foreign tat [. . .] its prancing, marrying queers; its blaring, feral, feminist bitches [. . .] that was the platform on which he should have stood: not England Always but England Eroded, England Besmeared. (2018: 316)

Perfidious Albion thus demonstrates how quickly and conveniently in-group dynamics between 'Us' and 'Them' come into play when tribal securities are placed under threat by elected representatives or foreign influence. As Byers notes, 'Both remain and leave became surprisingly inflexible identities for people [. . .] which helped them make more straightforward sense of what up to that point might have been quite complex political positions' (Personal Correspondence 2020). In predicting potential national developments as a result of recent illegal data harvesting, corporate privatization, online misogyny, the gig economy and post-truth politics (the consequences of which are already germinating in British society), Byers' panoramic novel treads a fine line between reality and fiction, leaving the reader to wonder whether his visions tend towards the portentous or the absurd.

The referendum also contributed to a resurgence in speculative political-dystopia novels, continuing a Eurosceptic trend established in post-war British fictions such as Edwina Currie's *The Ambassador* (1999), which imagine potential futures for a culturally isolated Britain ruled by a European superstate. In such fictions the referendum is now a passing everyday reference, illustrating the extent to which the fateful vote has already reshaped the landscape of present-day Britain and been immortalized in the social history of our isles. William Gibson's *Agency* (2020) projects an alternative 2017 in which Brexit (positioned as the darkest timeline) did not occur, while Jeanette Winterson's science-fiction novel *Frankissstein* (2019), a speculative reimagining of Mary Shelley's seminal work, suggests the overpowering and omnipresent staccato-like syntax of post-truth media threatens to overshadow genuine developments in AI technology. Narrated by Ry Shelley, a transgender doctor, the novel alludes to a 'Small-minded, smug, self-righteous, unjust' England that 'hates the stranger' (2019: 247). In G. L. Kaufmann's *A Hard Fall* (2018) the Britain of 2025 is a splintered nation in social and economic decline; any citizen Verified Not British is cast out of the country while a cosmopolitan resistance movement is reduced to operating under the gaze of an authoritarian Home Security network. For Kaufmann, the referendum was 'a failed conversation' which exposed the corrosive effects of post-truth politics; in its place, stories 'can captivate, convince, and coax in a way that political rhetoric and expert discussion cannot', providing an alternative vision to a bleak prospective future (Kaufmann 2018b). Heinz Helle's *Euphoria* (2017) is an early effort at depicting what a post-apocalyptic, post-Europe future may resemble, while Mark Billingham's crime novel *Love Like Blood* (2017) envisions a disproportionate rise in racial attacks and xenophobic hate crimes as a wave of nationalist triumphalism follows the referendum vote.[8]

John le Carré's *A Legacy of Spies* (2017a) and *Agent Running in the Field* (2019) mark a return to the Cold War themes of his earlier work, re-evaluating England's turbulent relationship with Europe during the twentieth century, but purposely speak to the contemporary moment and the rise of post-truth rhetoric.[9] Le Carré makes no qualms about revealing his own political outlook, gesturing to the deceitful application of affect memories by the Leave campaign in securing an exit from the EU:

> I'm not just a remainer. I'm a European through and through [. . .] If Johnson and his Brexiteers had their way, it would be declared St Brexit's Day. Church bells across the land would peal out the gladsome tidings from every tower. And good men of England would pause their stride and doff their caps in memory of Dunkirk, the Battle of Britain, Trafalgar, and mourn the loss of our great British empire. Empires don't die just because they're dead. (le Carré 2020)

---

[8] A similar strain of dystopic Brexit fiction has emerged in Germany. Tom Hillenbrand's sci-fi-inflected *Drone State* (2014), published two years before the referendum, offers a chilling Orwellian vision of a European superstate forty years in the future which monitors the movements of citizens in thirty-six member states. While his fictional British withdrawal is a smooth operation, Hillenbrand jokes the chaos of post-Brexit negotiations ensures 'the real Brexit is actually much more dystopian' (qtd. in Oltermann 2019). His subsequent post-Brexit novel *Hologrammatica* (2018), set in 2088, continues the efforts of Britain to position itself post-Europe, renaming itself New Albion and resorting to radical privatization in order to retain some semblance of national wealth in a future threatened by the heightened effects of climate change. Sibylle Berg's *GRM Brainfuck* (2019) adopts a related stance, mapping the rise of the far-right in deindustrialized regions of a post-Brexit Britain.

[9] Brexit has inspired a number of spy thrillers including *London Rules* by Mick Herron (2018), *Curtain Call* (2019) by Graham Hurley and *Accidental Agent* (2019) by Alan Judd.

In *A Legacy of Spies*, George Smiley, le Carré's customary protagonist, alludes to May's infamous Conservative Party conference speech in 2016 contemplating exactly whom he was serving in the intelligence service and which nation state held his loyalty: '*whose England? Which England? England all alone, a citizen of nowhere?* [. . .] *If I had an unattainable ideal, it was of leading Europe out of her darkness towards a new age of reason. I have it still*' (2017a: 303). Speaking in 2017, le Carré explains how Smiley, who 'has spent his life defending the flag in one way or another' and is now exiled in Freiburg, 'feels a stranger in his own country, and that's why we find him and indeed leave him in a foreign place' (le Carré 2017b). Like his author, Smiley detests the rise of populist orators like Farage and Trump, and watches helplessly as his dream of a unified Europe and legacy of his Cold War espionage is undone by far worse post-truth treacheries. Le Carré joined a long list of writers, including Neil Gaiman, Max Porter, Marina Lewycka and Philip Pullman, in signing an open letter to *The Guardian* pleading voters to support the EU in the 2019 European parliamentary elections. The letter points to the fact that 60 per cent of UK publishing revenues are generated from book exports (with 36% of physical book exports heading to European markets) and ridicules the post-Brexit negotiation process: 'We are the people who spend our lives making things that are not true seem believable, and we don't think Brexit is even a good effort' (Flood 2019).

Mind the gap: London and the rest

As a center of steady economic productivity and conduit to the world's economic, London has often been compared to the goose that laid the golden egg. It has simply been too valuable to kill. Until June 2016, when the majority of UK voters decided to strangle the goose.

(Toly 2017: 46)

The fact that most London boroughs voted to remain in the referendum – with eight London boroughs among the highest ten Remain rates – raises urgent questions about the capital's troubled relationship with the rest of the UK.[10] Tim Shipman immediately characterized the result as a 'victory for outsiders over insiders' and a violent repudiation of both the political class and liberal, metropolitan London (2017: 583). Zadie Smith's 'Fences: A Brexit Diary', first published in *The New York Review of Books* in August 2016, offers a levelled and vigorous response to Britain's sudden and unexpected political isolationism, denouncing the referendum as 'a very ineffective hammer for a thousand crooked nails' (Smith 2018: 25). The article acknowledges the capital's unique role as a model for cross-cultural conviviality – an 'outward-looking city [. . .] so different from these narrow xenophobic places up north' – and its increasingly awkward position in the national constellation: 'around here change is the rule. The old grammar school up the hill became one of the largest Muslim schools

---

[10] Only Barking and Dagenham, Bexley, Havering, Hillingdon and Sutton – council areas on the fringes of London – returned Leave votes.

in Europe [. . .] Waves of immigration and gentrification pass through these streets like buses' (Smith 2018: 22; 27). Smith concedes that for too long an affluent London-centric elite has chosen to 'lecture the rest of the country on its narrow-mindedness while simultaneously fencing off its own discreet advantages', engendering a 'London vs. the rest' attitude which merely serves to deepen existing class divisions; and yet, the referendum revealed the 'painful truth [. . .] that fences are [also] being raised everywhere in London', exposing the existing inequalities *within* the capital (Smith 2018: 27; 31). Although Smith slightly misinterprets voting data (positioning Brexit as a 'working-class populist revolution' and neglecting the integral role played by affluent middle-class liberals in southern counties), her core argument, echoing the claim reiterated throughout this study that Brexit reveals 'a deep fracture in British society that has been thirty years in the making', is certainly valid (Smith 2018: 25; 27). A. L. Kennedy's *Serious Sweet* (2016) and Jonathan Coe's *Number 11* (2015), both published in the run-up to the referendum, echo the work of Smith in diagnosing the pre-existing ailments of contemporary London, interrogating Tory spending cuts and prevailing fiscal attitudes within the capital.

The political shift in the nation following Brexit reflects the socioeconomic and racial tensions evident in Smith's *Swing Time* (2016), as well as her earlier works such as *NW* (2012) and *The Embassy of Cambodia* (2013), and influences subsequent readings of these pre-Brexit novels. *The Embassy of Cambodia* in particular captures Smith's fascination with the localized ethics of British cultural engagement. The novella follows Fatou, a domestic servant from the Ivory Coast, in her day-to-day duties for an affluent London family. To escape the drudgery and isolation of her restricted domesticity, Fatou regularly visits a swimming pool and becomes intrigued by the embassy of Cambodia she passes on her route. The embassy comes to represent the reflexive and interconnected relationship between local and global spheres within London, once again emphasizing how the prosaic and pedestrian often operate in tension with sweeping globalism and transnational fragility in Smith's fiction. For Barbara Korte, the story 'registers the social rifts in Britain that preceded the Brexit vote', capturing an emergent 'structure of feeling' which was to define the events of 2016, namely a rising public dissatisfaction with perceived increases in immigration levels and a simmering anger towards refugees (2020: 25).[11] By employing the first-person plural 'we' throughout the narrative – 'We are from Willesden. Our minds tend toward the prosaic' – the story emphasizes Smith's continued efforts to impose a cosmopolitan empathy upon the capital and its residents, establishing a counter-narrative that works in opposition to the prevailing political climate and enduring racial divisions.

Smith's subsequent post-Brexit offering 'The Lazy River' provides a less covert metaphor for the ongoing stagnation and political follies tearing apart an increasingly absurdist Brexit Britain. The short story follows a group of Leave-voting British tourists

---

[11] Smith's 2013 short story 'Meet the President' in *Grand Union* adopts a dystopic angle on potential near-futures for our bordered island nation, envisioning a post-Brexit Britain in which Felixstowe is no longer an important hub for European connectivity but a radically reduced rural settlement unable to maintain its ties with the Continent. The 'sad little town had retreated three miles inland and up a hill' while Britain itself has been left behind by an ever-adapting globalized world: 'The only people left in England were the ones who couldn't leave' (2019: 160).

on a package holiday in Southern Spain, critiquing the short-sighted, insular mindset that gave succour to Eurosceptic political factions in Westminster: 'most of us voted for Brexit and therefore cannot be sure if we will need a complicated visa to enter the Lazy River come next summer' (Smith 2019: 28). Though the contingent contains 'a few souls from London, university educated and fond of things like metaphors and remaining in Europe and swimming against the current', Smith bemoans the fact that Europhilic factions of British society were beginning to resign themselves to defeat or refuse to accept the brute political implications of Brexit in 2017, even while they are swept away in the same currents of populism and atavistic nationalism: 'It's a pose: it can't last long' (Smith 2019: 26). Smith's characters ultimately remain floating in an uneasy state of suspension, forced to contemplate the absurdity of our current political turmoil while the reader is left to lament the questionable ethical legitimacy of our current fortress mentality.

A YouGov poll released on 11 July 2016 found public backing for the idea of London splitting off to form its own country (Cecil 2016). Support was particularly strong among Remain supporters; 29 per cent of respondents also favoured a devolved London Parliament with similar decision-making powers to the Scottish Parliament. A number of post-Brexit London fictions gesture to the cultural divide opening up between the capital and its troublesome *outer* regions. Linda Grant's panoramic account of life in contemporary London, *A Stranger City* (2019), captures a capital darkened by growing nationalist sentiments – sentiments out of step with the cosmopolitan optic of its populace. Although it is only explicitly addressed once in the novel, the spectre of Brexit looms large and haunts narrative events, affecting the lives of London's inhabitants who encounter 'old triumphalist signs embedded in all the fields and hedgerows. Leave leave leave leave leave' when they dare to escape the confines of the capital (2019: 129). *A Stranger City* gives shape to Grant's own concern about Britain's ideological retreat and the related rise in xenophobic abuse: 'my anxiety about Brexit has spilled into absolutely everything' (Hughes 2019). Grant's novel opens by detailing the tragic death of an unnamed woman who commits suicide by jumping off London Bridge, her body later dredged from the Thames attached to the chains of HMS Belfast. The woman is later revealed to be Valentina Popov, originally from the border between Romania and Moldova; born a few metres away from the borders of the EU, Valentina is thus an illegal immigrant deprived of free movement and the right to work in Britain. The mournful incident sets the tone for a wide-ranging novel which articulates fears relating to the Syrian refugee crisis and the Windrush scandal to systematically expose the emergent fault lines across a city which, for some British citizens, has seen its 'essential Englishness [. . .] permanently breached' by ethnic diversity (2019: 24).

Brexit places an indirect strain on the marriage of native Londoners, retired policeman Pete and his wife Marie, due to their contrasting views on Brexit. Marie wishes to escape the overwhelming multiculturalism of the London bubble in favour of the predominantly white Lake District and its absence of ethnic minorities, her anxieties correlating with shifting racial demographics in the capital. Goodhart points out that 'as recently as 1971 the white British made up 86 per cent of the London population [. . .] In 2011 it had fallen to 45 per cent' (2017: 136). Pete, on the other hand, recognizes that depriving London of its transnational associations would simply leave 'some lily-white National Trust mock-up' predicated on a disconcerting ethnonationalism (Grant 2019: 302). Weaving together multiple strands to locate London's voice in Brexit times, Grant suggests a burgeoning Euroscepticism is mutating into a rejection of multicultural paradigms more broadly: 'Europeans were only the start. The rest would follow on later' (2019: 167). This fictional London is not an inclusive cosmopolis of cultural hospitality and empathetic receptivity; London may indeed be a city of strangers, but strangers loosely connected by increasingly frayed bonds which fail to override national configurations of space. As the nation withdraws back into itself 'like a mollusc to its shell', repudiating the multicultural liberalism associated with contemporary London, *A Stranger City* gestures towards a grim future in which the growing ideological divide between London and the rest of the country is exacerbated, cultivating the conditions for 'a united Ireland' while England is left isolated in a 'little whites-only rump state' (2019: 242; 319).

The evident socioeconomic disparity between 'London and the rest' also inspires Amanda Craig's timely novel *The Lie of the Land* (2017). The narrative concentrates on a failing marriage of a seemingly privileged middle-aged couple, Lottie and Quentin Bretin, who decide to relocate from metropolitan London to a cheap cottage in Devon after losing their jobs due to the credit crunch. Published on the one-year anniversary of the referendum, *The Lie of the Land* swiftly turns its attention away from the infidelities of marriage to the regional inequalities of Brexit Britain. The Bretin family experience an instantaneous culture shock when they arrive in the fictional village of Trelorn, missing the cosmopolitan buzz of the capital and dismissing Devon as a 'foreign' country, 'poorer than Romania' (2017: 30; 99). When Lottie's daughter Stella melodramatically demands to know if they will ever return to England, Lottie can only offer the inadequate reply, 'London isn't England [. . .] This is England, too' (2017: 50). Given that Craig began work on the novel almost seven years before the referendum, she is well-positioned to cast a critical eye over the palpable social signs of a burgeoning sociocultural and economic divide between London and the rest of Britain's regions. Paraphrasing Cecil Rhodes' famous dictum, Quentin recognizes the beneficiaries of English life to be progressively confined to the south-east: 'if you're English, you have won first prize in the lottery of life [. . .] Well, it's even more true if you're a Londoner' (2017: 313).

Lottie's mixed-race teenage son, Xan, the product of a previous failed relationship, takes a temporary job in the local pie factory, the appropriately named Humbles (a figurative reminder of his previous entitlement), being immediately mistaken for a non-European illegal immigrant on account of his skin colour in an overwhelmingly white region. Working alongside Eastern European migrants on zero-hours contracts such as Polish Katya, who emphasizes her desire to work rather than claim benefits, Xan gradually learns to cast off his perceived misconceptions towards England-outside-London. A strident Remainer, Craig wrote the novel to challenge the predominant assumption that Leavers were 'stupid, jingoistic, racist fools': 'They are brave people who work and labour the land. I don't agree with the way they voted but I respect their views' (McGlone 2017). Her novel consequently empathizes with a plethora of reasons why the Leave vote gained such traction in Devon: local farmers bemoan the mountains of EU paperwork required for subsidies; precarious workers threatened by the spectre of post-2004 EU immigration 'vote UKIP, because nobody else cares'; young couples whose futures are impeded by the housing crisis and middle-class squeeze; and frustrated parents struggle to find school places for their children, despite having resided in the area for generations: 'You want to know why we want to leave Europe? That's why' (2017: 151; 202). Craig's novel is more than simply a hand-wringing state-of-the-nation affair, espousing a narrative hospitality for those vulnerable individuals who have attempted to make Britain their home, and suggesting how the tentative microcosmic adjustment of the Bretin family's perspective to Devonshire life hints at the potential for national reconciliation.

Martyn Waites' folk-horror-infused crime novel *The Old Religion* (2018) marks a similar sociocultural tension between London and the south-west, specifically. Set in a bleak, rural Cornish village named St Petroc, whose inhabitants feel economically disenfranchised and left behind by the pace of contemporary Britain, the novel employs a distinct Brexit analogy to indicate how a community can abandon rational thought and become swept up in a collective delusion, implementing drastic measures to counter prevalent threats to local traditions and values. Waites, who defines his novel as 'Brexit Noir', purposely situates the narrative in Cornwall, which he claims is 'the area of the country most heavily reliant on EU subsidies' (Waites 2018). The influence of folk horror, involving the dislocation of characters in rural environments, is thus a 'perfect metaphor' for the 'collective Brexit-inspired economic and social death wish' of the south-west (Waites 2018). By utilizing St Petroc as a microcosm for the battles being waged internationally, Waites forces a reconsideration of the ways by which an imagined community can redraw the boundaries of their territory.

Anthony Cartwright's *The Cut* (2017) is a unique post-Brexit novel in that it was specifically commissioned by European publisher Peirene Press to provide a direct response to the vote and construct 'a fictional bridge between the two Britains that have opposed each other since the referendum day' (2017: n.p.). Cartwright dramatizes the media-reinforced divide between nationalist and cosmopolitan forms of identification within his native Black Country landscape, picking through the industrial strata to indicate how class inequality continues to run deep and informs the public mood towards European integration. Cairo Jukes, a labourer on a precarious zero-hours contract in Dudley, and Grace Trevithick, a documentary film maker (and personification of an elite British media) from Hampstead in London, give voice to the two competing discourses of this fractured post-Brexit nation. *The Cut* encapsulates how geographical inequality emerged as a crucial factor in the referendum result, echoing John Lanchester's insightful remark in his article 'Brexit Blues' that 'the primary reality of modern Britain is not so much class as geography. Geography is destiny. And for much of the country, not a happy destiny' (Lanchester 2016). Those left out of the national narrative have little reason or motivation to continue its story. After all, it was England-outside-London which tipped the balance in favour of a Leave vote, indicating the evident disconnect between the capital and the rest of Britain. O'Toole (2018a) notes that in the Midlands the percentage of constituencies with Leave majorities was the highest in the UK at 87.6 per cent. The Leave campaign secured its strongest regional support in the West Midlands in particular, the setting for Cartwright's novel, gaining 53.9 per cent of the vote. Whereas the south-east of England has enjoyed the benefits of global economic interdependence, in post-industrial edgelands of the north, Midlands and Wales – areas which had failed to recover from Thatcherite policies – a sense of powerlessness and impotent rage fuelled unexpectedly high turnouts.[12] As John Harris comments, it 'may have been easy to miss in the London-centred haze of the "knowledge economy" and the birth of the digital future, but this is where millions of lives have been heading since the early 1980s' (Harris 2016).

Support for Leave was partly mobilized by the financial marginalization and social deprivation of an underclass confronted by a 'lack of educational qualifications, low incomes and bleak economic prospects', resulting in a backlash against EU membership which had failed to improve their daily lives (Goodwin and Milazzo 2017: 457). Research by Goodwin and Heath (2016b) clearly indicates that the Leave vote was substantially higher in economically deprived areas; also, 75 per cent of those without educational qualifications voted Leave compared to 27 per cent of those with the highest qualifications. It is worth reiterating, however, that the overall 'proportion of Leave voters who were of the two lowest social classes was just 24%', providing a sobering corrective to overly simplistic media claims that the 'left behind' and anti-establishment working class were primarily to blame for the Brexit vote (Virdee and McGeever 2018: 1803). Cartwright's realist narrative renders the lived experiences of those citizens left behind by globalization, 'Tired of change, tired of the world passing by', conveying just how easily a destructive nostalgia can stimulate a belligerent national autarchism as a psychological defiance to socioeconomic disparities (2017: 100–1). For Craig Calhoun, nationalism is often 'denigrated by proponents of transnational society who see the national and many other local solidarities as backward or outmoded, impositions of the past on the present' (2007: 170). But nationalism itself operates as a source of social integration 'insofar as it structures collective identities and solidarities' and should not be treated as 'a sort of error smart people will readily move beyond – or an evil good people must reject' (2007: 7; 152). For many undecided and floating voters in 2016 it was difficult to perceive the benefits of a vague supranational identity when their regional and national identity was much more tangible and intrinsically tied to their cultural memory and day-to-day lives.

Although the nation is often conceived of as an imagined community (following Anderson), Cartwright's novel captures the attachments and affection individuals continue to hold for their local communities and national customs in place of more rootless forms of citizenship, which seem to be the purview of privileged elites alone. The narrative articulates this resistance to visions of a Global Britain advanced by Westminster, signalling a defiant challenge to London-centric discourses and media reports of Leave-supporting areas. Victor Seidler argues traditional areas in the North and Midlands viewed London as 'another country', a 'city-state that somehow thrived in ignorance of what was going on in the rest of the country', and such communities were 'ill at ease with the urban cosmopolitan multiculturalism that had been celebrated in

---

[12] According to Goodhart, 'eight out of the top ten high-wage low-welfare cities are located in the South East, while nine of the bottom ten low-wage cities are in the North or the Midlands' (2017: 151).

response to the terrorist attack of 7 July 2005' (2018: 23). Individuals who attracted the attention of the media for voting Leave, such as Cartwright's fictional community, found they had become 'the objects of the research process': 'research came to speak in the same language as the political elites; and it was a language often regarded with suspicion, if not disdain' (2018: 25; 26). In reinforcing the need for a heightened consciousness of the regional inequalities and political peripheralities still existing within our divided kingdom following a prolonged period of economic decline, Cartwright accentuates how any contemporary analysis of the Black Country and its inhabitants can only be achieved via an appreciation of its socioeconomic and political past in comparison to the concentration of wealth within London. For Toly, global cities 'have in some ways become the elegant façades of their national contexts, accompanied by deeply shadowed regional backstages. This regional dynamic can lead to resentment of and alienation from global cities and the open global economic system that has fuelled their rise' (2017: 144). Uneven regional development lends itself to the perception of an incommensurate democratic deficit, particularly in England following the policy failures of the Northern Powerhouse and the Midlands Engine. Successive generations of communities in deindustrialized areas experience an inheritance of loss as their local material practices now enjoy a diminished value, with professional opportunities relocated to larger cities.

The Cut reminds us that 'the England of frivolous Etonians, the swollen House of Lords and the London-based elite is not the only England' (Marquand 2018). Working on a 'wasteland' amid the canals of Dudley – open scars of a battered post-industrial landscape – Cairo is unable to relate to either metropolitan Grace or a wider world that has ignored and forgotten the presence of his community (Cartwright 2017: 37). Facing the slow cancellation of his future, and locked out of the British success story, Cairo almost exists in a separate, economically poorer country. His quiet desperation and resentment capture how bitter social and political histories worked to radicalize the people's revolt and stoked the desire for structural change away from failed economic models. Cartwright utilizes his narrative to engage in a dialogue with his earlier Black Country fiction, reiterating the ways by which the spectral past infringes on the present and assumes a hauntological edge.[13] Lingering social memories and scattered spatial memoranda of a region which 'used to be somewhere' hinder any forward momentum, trapping Dudley in a backward-looking inertia and reducing its inhabitants to a liminal presence in the narrative: 'here were the ruins, and here were the ghost people among them, lost tribes' (2017: 44; 100). As Linkon reminds us, 'People and communities are shaped by their histories – by experience, by memory, and by the way the economic and social practices of the past frame the structures, ideas, and values that influence our lives long after those practices have ceased to be productive' (2018: 1). Engaging in a mournful flanuerism through the forgotten architecture of the industrial past, Cairo

---

[13] The hauntological presence of the past is particularly evident in Cartwright's debut novel *The Afterglow*, which concentrates on the closure of Midlands' steelworks. Collective social memories of industrial communities linger on in the narrative as spectral remnants of industrial heritage while the physical structures themselves – 'disused factory buildings [...] the corpses of outlandish beats decomposing, rotting into the black ground' – are dismantled and erased (2004: 155).

assumes a spectral presence, curating the decline of his region and grappling with the legacies of austerity that have exenterated his community.

The desolate landscape itself becomes a monument to the democratic deficit existing between English regions, while also serving as a reminder of the Black Country's former industrial glory. By giving Grace a tour of these post-industrial sites – remnants of his cultural heritage – Cairo is forcing her (and thus the implied media) to bear witness to the deindustrialization that continues to destabilize working-class communities outside the London bubble. Yet as Baucom writes, if a 'nation's memory resides in its architecture' then 'memory must be understood as both the recuperation of the past in the present and the redemption of the present in the future' (1999: 73). To interpret Cairo's flaneurism in a more positive sense, he is seeking a form of psychological protection from the landscape, reinscribing the identity-defining sites as evidence that the working-class continue to possess some latent power in affecting political events, fortifying a spatial understanding of collective identity and securing his own identity in the process. Cartwright acknowledges that his accentuation of the psychogeographical 'aspect[s] of the landscape, concentrating on the decline and the ruin, is an aesthetic decision, but it is also a political one, and you can't really separate them' (qtd. in O'Brien 2015: 402). Accordingly, Cairo's lament for the decline of regional industry recalls Gilroy's diagnosis of a resurgent 'postimperial melancholia' ingrained in the national psyche and its influence in shaping a political narrative: 'A lot of it is gone, erased. The industrial past [. . .] Now you act – we act – like there's some sort of shame to it all. The rest of the country is ashamed of us. You want us gone' (2004: 109; Cartwright 2017: 111). His involvement in Grace's documentary, and assertion that the approaching EU referendum signifies 'the weight of the past on the present, a sense of betrayal [. . .] of retribution on some grand, futile scale', is a desperate attempt to justify both his own life choices and a passionate defence of his abandoned community: 'He wanted to say something, about the sense of his world being made invisible, mute' (2017: 24; 30).

As the third chapter discussed, Cartwright's previous novels help us to understand the key sources of voter frustration and the surge in electoral support for UKIP and rising memberships for other nationalist political parties: integral components in the decision to leave the EU. According to Ford and Goodwin, UKIP's radical right revolt was 'a working-class phenomenon', 'anchored in a clear social base: older, blue-collar voters, citizens with few qualifications, whites and men' (2014: 175; 270). A strong argument can be made for the impact of Cameron's severe austerity programme from 2010 onwards. As Mary O'Hara bluntly puts it, 'Austerity was a choice made by the British government' rather than an external body (2015: 5). Thiemo Fetzer also finds austerity and the dismantling of the welfare system under Cameron to be key drivers in the Brexit vote, going so far as to claim that the referendum 'either may not have taken place, or [. . .] could have resulted in a victory for Remain, had it not been for austerity' (Fetzer 2018). *The Afterglow*, *Heartland* and *Iron Towns* allude to the re-emergence of English nationalism in working-class industrial areas worn down by austerity and deindustrialization brought about by globalizing forces. According to Cartwright, *The Cut* marks the 'end of this sequence, which runs 1979-2016 (although not chronologically)', documenting the 'ongoing political catastrophe that has been playing itself out in this country for 40 years or so [...] but in itself with much longer roots (in industry, empire, the class system)' (Personal Correspondence 2020).

Socioeconomic deprivation fuelled anti-immigration rhetoric and the EU referendum provided disempowered and disenfranchised voters with the opportunity to direct their anger towards an external organization that could become a scapegoat for their various ills. UKIP (emerging from the ruins of the BNP) exploited this animosity and positioned themselves as a more respectable anti-immigration party in comparison to the far-right movements of the English Defence League and Britain First. While Grace's intentions are seemingly genuine, Phil McDuff has identified what he terms a 'prole whisperer' industry, in which right-wing journalists exploit the socioeconomic concerns of specifically white working-class voters outside London to suggest immigration or cultural diversity is at the heart of their floundering narrative, rather than the internal neglect of successive governments (McDuff 2017). Goodwin and Milazzo (2017) correctly argue that a deeper anxiety lies behind this surface fear of immigration and EU membership: namely the erosion of national identity and traditional values rooted in the cultural imaginary. Characters across Cartwright's body of fiction offer variations on the optimistic and stubborn refrain: 'we're still here', voicing relevant concerns regarding corporate neoliberal policies and existing socioeconomic inequalities rather than immigration specifically. Crucially, Cairo is not a supporter of UKIP and feels no connection to either the Leave-supporting newspapers or perceived elites who treat the debates surrounding cultural loss as merely a game. He simply warns Grace, 'people here will vote against whatever they think the perceived elite will vote', even if the consequences may be disastrous (2017: 43). In this light, the resultant Leave vote again alludes to Snyder's notion of sadopopulism and the desperate conversion of socioeconomic pain into meaning.

Grace's initial implied repudiation of his concerns symbolizes the Remain camp's dismissal of nationalist rhetoric as simple bigotry or evidence of Little Englander syndrome, ignoring the fears of many undecided voters and appearing out of touch to those outside the London bubble. As Cairo stresses in his interview, 'all you people want to say is that it's about immigration. That we'm all racist [...] You doh wanna hear that its more complicated than that', insisting instead that disenfranchised citizens have identified a bogeyman in the shape of the EU at which to direct their impotent anger following the 2008 financial crisis and prolonged periods of austerity (2017: 24). Brexit became the most salient means for these characters to 'take back control' of their culture, their neighbourhoods, and their identities, voting for outsider parties who most accurately voiced their valid concerns. In his Orwell Prize-winning analysis of British austerity, *Poverty Safari* (2017), Darren McGarvey emphasizes this rarely discussed deficit in how class experience is reported and represented, leaving working-class individuals adversarial towards political parties, misrepresented by the media, and excluded from cultural debates, creating 'a fertile bed of resentment from which anger and apathy have grown' (95). When Cairo's interview is broadcast on news cycles they place subtitles on the screen, 'translated into his own language', alluding to the media's failure to understand or respond to the genuine fears of English voters (2017: 21). Cartwright appropriately deploys what O'Brien (2018) terms a 'Dudley demotic' to capture the regional dialect of his Black Country characters, juxtaposed by the received pronunciation of metropolitan Grace: linguistic markers of a dialectal divide which gesture to the complications in bridging the political and geographic disconnect facing a post-Brexit Britain, as well as an obstinate regional resistance to dominant structures.

In his study on the rise of populism in a divided Brexit Britain, *The Road to Somewhere* (2017), David Goodhart separates the nation into two main groups: Anywheres and Somewheres. Anywheres are effectively young, wealthy and rootless 'global villagers' or insouciant members of the political class, holding little affection for their nationhood or heritage. Predominately based in British cities (particularly London), Anywheres adhere to their 'achieved' identity, often determined by their job, elevated status or university education. Somewheres, in comparison, are socially conservative, place-bound authoritarians who have an 'ascribed' identity determined by their local communal ties and family structures. Goodhart maps his suggested Somewhere-Anywhere distinction directly to the Brexit vote, indicating that the Somewhere/Leave and Anywhere/Remain camps possess opposing views on immigration, the economy, national identity and even corporal punishment. While Somewheres suffer from rapid changes to the global marketplace, Anywheres benefit from greater cosmopolitanization and support multinational structures such as the EU. For Goodhart, working-class white citizens are most affected by the effects of globalization, being dispossessed of any 'encouraging narrative of advance', often due to widespread processes of deindustrialization: 'skilled industrial employment which once provided a kind of social and economic ballast to our society has been largely swept away' (2017: 177; 209). Goodhart's premise is slightly unrefined: he treats the categories white and working class as co-equal, neglecting the complex and often contradictory role played by ethnic minorities in relation to these categories. Nevertheless, his argument captures the media's binary typecasting of various groups based on their age, geographic location or social class in the fallout of the Brexit vote. Moreover, Goodhart's distinction maps quite neatly onto Cartwright's novel, exposing the ways in which opinions on Brexit are acutely divided between metropolitan London and provincial West Midlands towns, between university graduates and non-graduates, and between the cosmopolitan young and older, more conservative members of society.

Recounted in alternating chapters, 'Before' and 'After', the structure of *The Cut* pivots around the momentous Brexit vote. The novel's title not only alludes to the post-Brexit divide but echoes the sentiments of Zadie Smith, A. L. Kennedy and Jonathan Coe in blaming Tory austerity for both the abandonment of the industrial order (the open 'cuts' of the canals signifying that 'this place used to be somewhere') and the subsequent neglect of the working-class in the north and the Midlands (Cartwright 2017: 44). But rather than play to established stereotypes, wallowing in an empty nostalgia or longing for the restoration of Britain's industrial past, the novel challenges expectations surrounding class-based politics and place-bound identities by the British media in the wake of the Brexit vote. Cartwright's focused engagement with the Brexit vote gestures towards the need for regional devolution and a revision of the political process in order to address geographic inequalities and the democratic deficit within Britain. After spending time with Cairo and his community, Grace begins to question her own preconceived perceptions of the Black Country, recognizing how the referendum exacerbated pre-existing regional divides: 'She felt like there was some kind of invisible veil between her and these people. *These people* [. . .] prejudice on the scale of a whole country' (2017: 19 – emphasis in original). By forcing his characters to re-evaluate their sociocultural prejudices, Cartwright opens a space for dialogue and offers a modicum of hope for cultural recuperation and regeneration.

The Cut thus reinforces this study's claim that the historic referendum on the *fate* of the nation was, in fact, a referendum on the *state* of the nation, reviving socioeconomic, cultural and political grievances that had lain dormant for decades. Despite Cairo and Grace's burgeoning relationship during the novel, the reconciliation between the two opposing sides (Cartwright intimates that – while it is not explicitly stated – Grace supports Remain while Cairo votes Leave) is ultimately deferred by a rather melodramatic denouement (Personal Correspondence 2020). Cairo's self-immolation in the final scene – following Grace's revelation that she is pregnant with his child – is replete with political intent, reinforcing the psychogeographical ties between his community and their landscape: '[t]hey voted to re-light the fire. He will be the furnace and the flames' (2017: 127). On the one hand, his desperate act is the result of a miscommunication, reinforcing the breakdown in dialogue between Dudley and a distant London; on the other hand, through Grace's pregnancy, the seeds of communication are (potentially) sown. Nevertheless, Cairo's suicide, a symbolic act of frustration and disenfranchisement, arguably forecloses the potential for democratic revision, encapsulating the burning anger and resentment of those who have been cut out of the national narrative. As Goodhart warns us, 'if people feel the game is stacked against them, they often just refuse to play' (2017: 153).

Glen James Brown's multi-layered, intergenerational *Ironopolis* (2018) transposes these same social anxieties onto a dilapidated north-east landscape, mapping the dark history and gradual decline of the Burn council estate in post-industrial Middlesbrough following the recent closure of local iron and steel industries. Early returns on referendum night revealed the Leave campaigns enjoyed extremely high levels of support in areas of the north-east such as Hartlepool and Sunderland. Middlesbrough, once a solid Labour heartland, returned a strong 65.5 per cent Leave vote: the natural consequence of a region ravaged by Thatcherite social policy and subsequent failures to rectify structural unemployment. Brown's fictional estate is haunted by an ageless Peg Powler, a grotesque witch-like figure of folklore who drowns her victims in the River Tees: a metaphor for the spectre of class struggle which continues to pervade the post-industrial landscape and the powerlessness of working-class communities to her siren call. Surrounded by tower blocks satirically named after past prime ministers whose systemic failures progressively weakened the region, Peg's power begins to wane, testifying to her symbolic resonance as a fading emblem of working-class culture: 'without a stable community to pass down her name, she is about to vanish forever' (Brown, Personal Correspondence 2020).

Middlesbrough, once nicknamed Ironopolis in its industrial prime, has continued to suffer from international competition, with the British chemical company ICI recently dismembered and sold off to foreign competition in the years leading to the referendum. Brown's novel therefore attests to the fact that pre-Brexit 'disaffection was already there, prior to the crash, in many parts of the country – especially the former industrial Labour strongholds that never recovered from 1980s de-industrialisation'

(Goodhart 2017: 168). Commenting on Brexit and its relation to the novel, Brown hopes his compassionate portrait of a post-industrial community not only changes perceptions of working-class culture, but communicates the multiplicity of working-class experience. Alluding to the widespread unemployment, zero-hours contracts and brutal welfare cuts which have gutted Teesside since Thatcher's time in office, Brown argues that the novel's engagement with socioeconomic decline and the 'bubbling grievances' surrounding the referendum 'are two sides of the same coin' (Personal Correspondence 2020). By employing multiple, interlocking narratives, delivering myriad perspectives on the slow depredation of the region, *Ironopolis* demonstrates how working-class culture cannot be reduced to a single story.

In the immediate aftermath of the vote, much media attention concentrated on the northern working-class resentment, an apparent nativist response to immigration, and a general rejection of the post-war liberal consensus, as the major drivers for a strong Leave vote. Yet this narrative was swiftly challenged and widespread evidence shows it was not the left behind or a disaffected working class alone who delivered victory to the Leave campaign. Drawing on data concerning deprivation levels by parliamentary constituency in England, Dorling and Tomlinson (2017) report that the greatest support for Leave came from middle-class voters in leafy Tory shires; within Middle England, roughly 80 per cent of constituencies returned a Leave majority, indicating it was the squeezed middle which secured Britain's exit from the European arena. Evans and Menon concur, pointing to the privileged bleating of the 'highly educated middle classes' in particular in providing 'the major source – some 59% in total – of the Brexit vote' (2017: 84).[14] The very notion of a 'middle England' is defined by its embodiment of an essentialized Englishness, operating in opposition to recent demographic changes, political correctness, multiculturalism and obstructionist EU bureaucracy. The institutional architects of Brexit were not from working-class backgrounds, but those located closest to the spheres of socioeconomic power, such as Nigel Farage, whose class posturing garnered the support of a heterogeneous People's Army, fuelled by disparate grievances but united under the same banner.

As an immediate reaction to the post-Brexit moment, British authors have revived the state-of-the-nation novel, examining the motivations for the Leave vote, as well as the extent to which modes of remembrance and a deferential treatment of the national past transfigured the discourses and issues surrounding the referendum.[15] Jonathan Coe's *Middle England* (2018) is the most direct attempt to capture the zeitgeist of our turbulent times and the psychopathology that drives Brexit, deconstructing a febrile national landscape in which the political conscription of the past becomes amplified. Coe's novel revives characters first seen in *The Rotters' Club* (2001) and *The Closed Circle* (2004) and re-establishes the sense of a *roman fleuve* in his body of work. Documenting sociopolitical developments in British society between 2010 and

---

[14] That being said, as Goodwin and Heath (2016b) outline in their study 'Brexit vote explained: poverty, low skills and lack of opportunities', it was undoubtedly voters who were struggling financially that were *most likely* to vote Leave.
[15] A similar response emerged following the 2008 financial crash in works such as Amanda Craig's *Hearts and Minds* (2011), John Lanchester's *Capital* (2012), Sebastian Faulks' *A Week in December* (2009), as well as Coe's earlier novel *Number 11* (2015).

2018, the social satire offers a wide-ranging diagnosis of the rancorous condition of pre- and post-Brexit England, referencing a plethora of baffling yet much-cited tangential reasons for the evident decline in Britain's tempestuous relationship with the Continent and explanations for the subsequent volatile Leave vote, including the interference of Vladimir Putin, the MP's expenses scandal, the London riots, the first-past-the-post parliamentary system, the ban on fox hunting, an ongoing austerity programme, politicians trotting out the old adage that 'we can never have a serious debate about immigration in this country' and 'the contentious result of the Eurovision song contest in 1968' (2018: 5; 416). Coe's Middle England landscape emerges as a site of quiet disaffection with national discontent often intimately tied to unforgotten local grievances surrounding immigration. By positioning the vote as a suburban revolt directed at cosmopolitan London, the novel suggests Brexit offers a form of salvation for those citizens desiring a return to the sacred past and a retreat from the rapid changes of contemporary Britain. Indeed, in an article for *New Statesman*, Coe jokes that the subtitle for Middle England could have been 'Britain: where did it all go wrong?' as his novel maps the 'trigger points' which enabled the radicalization of England-without-London (Coe 2019).

The novel directs its attention on Benjamin Trotter, a major player in Coe's early novels, who sells up in London and retreats to a converted mill house near Shrewsbury – an area populated by National Trust houses and English Heritage sites – in order to complete a novel narrativizing unrest in European history following Britain's accession to the Common Market. Benjamin's house is situated by the River Severn, which assumes an almost anticipatory psychogeographical power. The river's murmur turns progressively more turbulent as political tensions begin to rise during the referendum campaign: 'supposing the river were to abandon its quiescent and reasonable habits [...] What form might that anger take?' (2018: 22). Coe's decision to utilize the Severn for this purpose becomes more telling when considering the river's meandering route across the Anglo-Welsh border – the two nations which returned a defiant Leave vote – charting the directions in which anger can be channelled and spill over. Having retreated from the fast pace of London, Benjamin encounters a Middle England landscape determinedly attempting to hold on to outdated national symbols and ways of life.

Woodlands Garden Centre near Benjamin's house becomes a sanctuary for those seeking a quintessential Englishness, encapsulating the cultural conservatism at the heart of Middle England and exposing the fear that external cultural influences are diluting the nation's sacred, if intangible, essence (an English version of *la France profonde*). Serving traditional English fare, and trading in nostalgic items such as jigsaw puzzles of Spitfires, British war films and local history books, the centre is frequented by troubled conspiracy theorists who claim the EU is part of pan-European plot to eradicate the white race. By naming the middle section of the novel 'Deep England', Coe subscribes to Wright's contention that the national past is defined 'not just in relation to the general disappointment of earlier historical expectation [. . .] but the leading tensions of the contemporary political situation' (1985: 2). Safe spaces such as the centre, with what Wright would term their 'past-present alignment', do not exist to stabilize an accurate representation of the national past; instead, they 'mobilise a legitimising but abstract sense of "pastness" around present social and political events or issues' (1985: 147). In the process, they refuse the encroachment of cultural change and sustain a monocultural representation of the national body. What emerges is a *deformed invocation* of a nation's cultural history which ceases to cohere with the disorienting realities of twenty-first-century British society – replacing contemporary uncertainties with comforting simplicities where 'the grey torpor of everyday life in contemporary Britain lifts and the simpler, more radiant measures of Albion declare themselves again' – validating Wright's claim that 'a simplifying nostalgia can replace any principled democratic consideration' (1985: 76; 244).

Yet Coe structures his novel by charting the lives of three generations of the Trotter family and a Dickensian cast of friends and relations around the Midlands, evincing the most crucial Brexit divides relating to age, geography and educational attainment. Benjamin's ageing father Colin ensures his last act is to vote Leave in defiance of an increasingly liberal society; he considers the decline of the British Leyland car plant at Longbridge a chilling reminder of the decline of post-war working-class communities in the Midlands. For Charlie, working as a children's entertainer at Woodlands garden centre, Britain's fate was sealed following Thatcher's rise to power in 1979, which established insurmountable fault lines within communities and unravelled any prospect of a consensual, cohesive society emerging from the ruins of deindustrialization. Doug Anderton, another of Benjamin's old school friends and now an accomplished left-leaning political journalist, recognizes his impotent position as a metropolitan spectator. Cut off from 'the common man' in his multi-million-pound Chelsea pad and restricted by his narrow London-centric perspective on British society, Doug's naïve think-pieces on the London riots fail to gain traction and he laments the ways in which Leave voters have been manipulated by post-truth politics and anti-immigration scare tactics: 'There can't be more than about twelve people in the country who understand how the EU works [. . .] This campaign is going to be won on slogans and soundbites, and instincts and emotions' (2018: 269).

Immigration again emerges as the 'subject that divided people more than any other', with Coe charting its galvanizing, substantial effects on the final stretch of the referendum campaign, giving voice to the pre-existing unspoken resentment characterized by 'those most English of all qualities, shame and embarrassment' (2018: 90). Benjamin's niece Sophie, an art history lecturer and staunch Remainer, laments the racism and prejudice espoused by older voters, yet is suspended from the university after a false accusation of transphobia is levelled at her by Doug's daughter Coriander, a spoilt and arrogant student union representative. Sophie's partner Ian, on the other hand, lets his bitterness at being passed over for promotion in favour of a junior Asian female colleague lead to the breakdown of his marriage and he throws his weight behind the Leave campaign. Helena, Ian's mother, reinforces his sense of disillusionment and impotent rage, quoting Enoch Powell's 'rivers of blood' speech in response to the subsequent influx of Eastern European workers into her quiet Middle England suburbs following the 2004 EU enlargement. Even Sophie's liberal-minded university friend Sohan concedes that London no longer feels like a British city, citing foreign affluence as a casual factor in the sense of decline pervading society. Coe also parodies various players and groups implicated in the Brexit debate, including Ronald Culpepper, a withering caricature of Jacob Rees-Mogg. Coe's overt critique of Culpepper's pro-Brexit Imperium Foundation takes a swipe at the practices of the European Research Group, detailing how Brexit was not sustained by the will of the people, but stoked by 'a disparate, amorphous coalition of vested interests', harnessing and sustaining the vitriolic energy and hysteria gripping the nation (2018: 357).

During the course of the novel, the EU becomes the most viable threat to national heritage itself (and, more specifically, the English autostereotype), predicated on 'ceremonies of remembrance and recollection' (Wright 1985: 85). Coe's lengthy deconstruction of the London 2012 Olympics Games opening ceremony in the Deep England section, however, merely highlights the extent to which the backward-looking tendencies of English nationalism were pre-existing conditions bolstered by a resistance to the heterogeneity of the present (serving as anathema to the right). In his welcoming remarks, Boris Johnson, then Mayor of London, boldly proclaimed, 'London enjoys a diversity unrivalled anywhere in the world. This diversity [. . .] is now thoroughly twined into London's DNA, both cause and effect of its phenomenal success and much-envied reputation' (London Media Guide 2012: 7). As Michael Silk notes, the Games, designed for global consumption, functioned as 'a highly affective, and extremely public, political, pedagogic, corporate and powerful media spectacle though which to define the parameters of *the* "sanctioned" nation', and demonstrated how histories of 'corporeal recollection and embodiment become ingrained with the discourses of nation, subjectivity, fear, regulation and consumption' (2014: 69; 78). The ubiquitous coverage of athletes, draped in the treasured Union flag, marked an attempt to safeguard Britain's structural integrity and thus mask the frailties of the trembling union. London's ceremony, directed by Danny Boyle, juxtaposed rural, nostalgic visions of a fabled monoethnic Albion with contemporary visions of a multicultural, globalized Britain. Symbolizing an effort to incorporate progressive visions of the multicultural present into the treasured national fantasy of Britain's hegemonic past, the Games were designed to confront: 'where have we come from [. . .] what are we now and where are we going' (Boyle 2012). Utilizing communal memories alongside mythical and discursive histories, Boyle's ceremony not only constructed a microcosm of the national heritage (in the vein of Nora's *lieux de memoire*) but narrated and negotiated complex and differing conceptions of Britishness, providing an inclusive spectacle which challenged essentialist forms of cultural identification and redefined who belongs in the national imaginary.

The broadcast of the opening ceremony in the novel provides the last moment of perceived national unity before the descent into the referendum, yet even this patriotic celebration of Britishness reveals the early warning signs of intergenerational factions emerging within Middle England. The opening chronological prologue, reminiscent of the 1951 Festival of Britain, depicted a bucolic, prelapsarian Britain, the widespread industrialization of the nineteenth century and a remembrance of the First World War: visual sources of identification for a beleaguered populace unsure of their position in the world. The self-referencing national indulgence of the ceremony also revealed a sense of cultural superiority, opening the national sensory pathways to more traditional times. Scenes of idyllic British village life, a Blakean 'Green and Pleasant Land', featured icons of cultural conservatism which could have been taken directly from *England, England*'s 50 Quintessences of Englishness. Conceding that the utopian rural scenes in this tableau were influenced by Kenneth Grahame's *The Wind in the Willows* (1908), a 'countryside we all believed existed once', Boyle acknowledges how British nostalgia is dependent on a quasi-mythical popular imaginary as opposed to lived experience (London 2012 Media Guide).[16]

This 'Green and Pleasant Land' section of the ceremony with its adherence to the English sublime, drawing on images of Morris dancers and cricket to enforce a decidedly monocultural depiction of an archaic Albion, is immediately juxtaposed with the following 'Frankie and June' section, which follows a young mixed-race couple in contemporary Britain and seemingly celebrates tolerance towards diversity alongside a reinscription of British identity based on civic multiculturalism. While Sohan and Sophie revel in Boyle's use of intertextual references to deconstruct youthful versions of Britishness, these later scenes within the ceremony sparks a strong defensive reaction from Coe's older characters, who believe multi-ethnic citizens should be forced to adopt core British essentialist values and resent the destabilization of England's mythical foundations. For Colin and Helena the inclusion of contemporary events such as the HMS Windrush (not just an historical moment but an ongoing ethnopolitical crisis affecting the nation) into the sacred national imaginary or celebration of athletes such as Mohamed Farah ruptures the belief in an 'essentially incommunicable deep nation' and is lambasted as the intrusion of left-wing bias and political correctness into the BBC (2018: 85). Coe is tapping into Wright's contention that the 'nation' is not perceived as a 'heterogeneous society' which moves forward into the future, but 'an already *achieved* and timeless historical entity which demands only appropriate reverence and protection in the present' (qtd. in Hewison 1987: 141). The ceremony thus operates as a performative theatrical space for antagonistic, opposing versions of Englishness which would divide the nation only a few years later: a globalized Great Britain versus an endangered Little England.

This oscillation between nostalgic visions of quintessential Englishness and a progressive re-evaluation of contemporary England aligns with Littler and Naidoo's notion of a 'white past, multicultural present': a formation which occurs 'simultaneously as a lament and a celebration – a celebration of our nation being modern, young, hip and in tune with the globalised economy as well as harbouring a nostalgia and lament for a bygone contained, safe and monocultural world' (2004: 338). The conjuring of these idyllic, pastoral English scenes in the opening segment of the ceremony – an attempt to stitch these quintessential templates of nationhood once again to the popular cultural imaginary – leads Sohan to divert his literary research in order to examine this elusive concept of 'Deep England': 'a psychogeographical phenomenon' as much 'to do with village greens, the thatched roof of the local pub, the red telephone box' as questions of cultural identity or citizenship (2018: 202). This retention and reconstruction of a stable and monocultural national narrative, which continues to linger in twenty-first-century Britain, allows Colin and Helena to defend their sacred sources of communal memory and resist more recent forms of multicultural heritage. Coe's deconstruction of the Olympic Games thus recalls the pervasive presence of 'post-imperial melancholia' which continues to underscore contemporary debates surrounding national identity

---

[16] The ceremony also utilized literary narratives to negotiate tensions surrounding citizenship, community and identification with the nation, featuring characters from works by authors such as J. K. Rowling, J. M. Barrie and Lewis Carroll, reinforcing the fictional basis of our national heritage.

(Gilroy 2004: 109). *Middle England*'s lengthy concentration on the Games is not surprising; a re-examination of the ceremony provides fertile ground for discussions which would come to define the EU referendum. As Alan Tomlinson and Christopher Young state, a global sports spectacle 'foregrounds the sculptured and commodified body and orchestrates a physical display of the body politic' (2006: 3). The glossing over of regional differences, particularly between constituent nations, signalled an attempt to narrate the nation: the affirmation of a false coherence which elided the socioeconomic and cultural contestations affecting a disunited kingdom. When it came to Brexit, the ceremony's vision of a monocultural, pastoral Little England won out over the vibrant multiculturalism of a modern Great Britain.

With post-Brexit hindsight, Sophie becomes nostalgic for 'that week in the summer of 2012 and the missed opportunity' that it represented, as the optimistic vision of a cosmopolitan Britain rendered in the ceremony is unable to maintain its energy following the Games (2018: 411). The various reactions of Coe's characters to the Olympic opening ceremony anticipate emergent fissures in the imagined national community between generations and signal an underlying resistance to a more inclusive Britishness accepting of multiple forms of identification. Yet we should also heed Scruton's warning that 'when people discard, ignore or mock the ideals which formed their national character – then they no longer exist as a people, but only as a crowd' (2000: 67). It is Coe's rendering of the referendum and its aftermath which consolidates these deep divisions in British society. After all, Brexit negotiations became 'one long closing ceremony for games that refuse to end' (O'Toole 2020: 356). The final section of the novel, the appropriately titled 'Old England', documents the post-Brexit condition of the nation in which a polarized atmosphere of backward-looking impulses continues to divide England long after the vote. Whereas for older characters such as Colin the vote symbolized an attempt to return to an earlier historical period before globalization and multiculturalism irrevocably altered the country they remember – an aggressive mourning for an accomplished national past in the face of the inferior present – members of the younger generation such as Sophie feel an integral part of their 'modern, layered, multiple identity' has been stolen (2018: 326). Sitting on a bench by the pier in Hartlepool, a strong Leave-voting constituency, Sophie acknowledges her 'anywhere' cosmopolitan identity and sense of estrangement from large swathes of her fellow countrymen: 'She considered herself a Londoner, now, and from London she could not only travel by train to Paris or Brussels more quickly than she could come here, but she would probably feel far more at home on the Boulevard Saint-Michel or Grand-Place' (2018: 369). After resorting to 'Post-Brexit counselling' with her estranged ex-husband Ian, recognizing their contradictory opinions on the vote 'weren't about Europe at all [. . .] something much more fundamental and personal was going on', Sophie begins to understand her unconscious complicity in perpetuating social divides while Ian recognizes his internalization of Helena's racial stance (2018: 325; 327). Coe's novel therefore attests to the strain Brexit placed on familial relations and social circles, creating poisonous rifts that have yet to fully heal.[17]

---

[17] Following the referendum, the relationship support Charity Relate reported 20 per cent of their 300 employees had offered counselling to couples divided over Brexit (Worley 2016).

On the one hand, Ian and Sophie's eventual reconciliation and creation of their 'beautiful Brexit baby' intimates a 'tentative gesture of faith' by Coe that British society may overcome the painful fault lines disfiguring the face of the nation; on the other, Benjamin's eventual decision to sell his property in England and relocate to France to open a creative writing school can be interpreted as a form of defeat (2018: 421). Brexit, after all, was not a swift and clean delivery, but a painful childbirth which traumatized the body politic. The closing scene of the novel, in which Benjamin shares an evening meal with Lithuanian, French and Italian friends, may appear an overwrought example of 'European harmonization', but it also represents a retreat from a Britain that has failed to reconcile its divided self (2018: 415). Further, while Benjamin acknowledges the democratic deficit in European political institutions in a think-piece on the referendum for a newspaper, he neglects to mention how such perceived deficits serve as a convenient proxy for pre-existing democratic structural imbalances within Britain. His stream of consciousness rant on the state-of-the-nation – debating 'whether writers should attempt to be engagés' or retreat from reality as 'a means of responding to it, creating an alternative reality, something solid, something consoling' – is a direct commentary on the role of the writer in the age of Brexit and it is tempting to view Benjamin as Coe's fictional mouthpiece (2018: 337). Given that the novel was partly written during Coe's residency in Marseille, funded by a French literary organization, Benjamin's comments further allude to the need for writers to recognize their own political leanings and established assumptions when commenting on our moment of political rupture. *Middle England* thus serves as 'a story of loss, of loss of privilege', capturing the simmering resentment and 'quiet rage of a middle class which had grown used to comfort and prosperity and now saw those things slipping out of their reach' (2018: 19–20).

With this in mind, Brexit becomes a rather apt portmanteau, capturing the English electorate's nostalgic longing for a return to the wartime spirit and their desire to exit a contemporary landscape marred by deindustrialization, structural inequality and widespread multiculturalism. Marina Lewycka's *The Good, the Bad and the Little Bit Stupid* (2019) continues this concentration on the irreconcilable differences and toxic familial relationships arising from Brexit fatigue. Sid recognizes that the referendum has exposed a fissure, similarly evident in his parent's marriage, which no amount of politicking can ever truly heal. Sid's partner, Jacquie, hopes their 'Referendum Baby' will be a British citizen, but her sense of purpose to the NHS overrides any desire to leave 'this grey foreigner-fearing island' (Lewycka 2020: 82; 261). Lewycka notes that the novel marks an attempt to avoid the deadening political process and instead understand the reasoning behind the vote; literature, after all, 'lets you walk in the shoes of the Other' (Personal Correspondence 2020).

A poll conducted by the Creative Industries Federation in 2016 found 96 per cent of its members supported remaining within the EU (Creative Industries Federation 2016). It is unsurprising the British literary community in particular are so staunchly pro-Remain; organizations under Arts Council England have been the recipients of major funding from the EU for decades. In an article on Brexit and the decline of the English novel, David Martin Jones lambasts the Brexlit trend for its 'contempt for the working classes' on the one hand and 'unqualified respect for Labour politicians, liberal journalists, the progressive European establishment or Remainer civil servants' on the other hand, attacking the emergent genre for lacking real insight (Jones 2020). Commenting on the work of numerous authors covered in this chapter, including Coe, Ali Smith, Sam Byers, Olivia Laing and Douglas Board, Jones concludes:

> No Brexlit character pauses to consider that the conduct of the European Commission might explain Brexit's popular appeal. Instead, Brexlit saves its self-righteous indignation for the old, the white and the working class who spoilt their cosmopolitan dream. In Brexitland all Europeans and migrants receive bouquets, the brickbats are reserved for the dull, racist, nostalgia-obsessed, provincial Brits. (Jones 2020)

Jones also levels an attack on academic responses to Brexit (singling out Robert Eaglestone's *Brexit and Literature* collection), claiming the Brexlit genre merely 'reinforces the smug, self-referential worldview found in English literature departments, literary reviews and progressive publishing houses', ensuring the 'viewpoint of a cosmopolitan Remainer elite is thus Brexlit's default mode' (Jones 2020).[18] Alice O'Keeffe adopts a related line of questioning, pointing to the difficulties faced by the 'lefty metropolitan types [. . .] the arbiters of culture' within the publishing industry in responding to pro-Brexit voters: 'How can an industry so fervently remainer in spirit engage with the arguments in favour of leave?' (O'Keeffe 2019).

Brocken spectres of the past

> *[C]atastrophe itself is its own anchor, a ruination self-willed is just a holed boat when everything is sinking anyway.*
>
> (Griffiths 2019)

Author Adam Thorpe, a staunchly pro-European voice in the literary field, has been extremely vocal during the post-Brexit transition period, critiquing several motivating factors for the Leave vote, from the British government's removal of support for heavy industry and material production in favour of the London-based service sector, to the media-driven xenophobia saturating the minds of the British electorate. For Thorpe, the referendum result was frustrating in that its consequences will impact those most in need of EU funding:

> If I imagine myself as a rural conservative, or as a Welsh villager, or as a factory worker in a northern city left stranded by industrial decline, then logically I would see the EU as being a subsidy-providing benefactor with an ambient noise of social democratic goodwill, protecting my basic rights as a citizen to a minimum wage [. . .] But no, these very same people voted to leave the EU. They voted against their own interests. (Thorpe 2016)

---

[18] Jones lambasts the comments of several contributors within Eaglestone's collection but curiously fails to cite my own chapter on Brexlit despite engaging with the same texts.

Thorpe's 2017 novel *Missing Fay* documents the distressing home life and eventual disappearance of a schoolgirl on a Lincoln council estate. The narrative ties her disappearance to several interconnected, ideologically opposed characters whose lives are (directly or indirectly) impacted by the event: *Daily Mail*-reading Sheena, the coquettish manager of a children's boutique, considers 'Missing Lincs' to be 'at least two decades behind the rest' of Britain; David, an environmentalist, becomes obsessed with Fay's disappearance during a frustrating family holiday; Mike, a snobbish bookshop owner, blames the EU for destroying the 'sleepy, grassy little places' of England yet dismisses local working-class council estates as undesirable no-go zones; Cosmina, a Romanian working in a Lincolnshire care home following her home nation's accession to the EU; and Howard, a retired steel worker who lambasts the 'European mollycoddling' of EU healthy and safety regulation and laments the '[f]loods of immigrants' into Lincolnshire, ensuring what he perceives as the 'demise of the indigenous. Bye bye, England' (Thorpe 2017: 53; 56; 163). While *Missing Fay* avoids painting simple caricatures or stereotyping communities, the novel communicates a glaring pro-European message and an authorial opposition to a prevailing Little Englander mentality is evident.

In the autobiographical *Notes from the Cévennes* (2018), Thorpe writes at length on his pastoralist way of life (protected by EU funding and the Rural Development Programme) in southern France, his home for over twenty-five years since emigrating.[19] Forging explicit parallels between the two countries, he cites economic precarity and racial tensions as key factors in the development of 'a feeding ground for the extreme right' and expresses the fear that, without a stable EU, Europe will return to the habits of the past (2018: 208). For Thorpe, our British Isles are simply 'splinters off a massive core to which we also belong' and he has spoken passionately on the struggle to inhabit 'these Brexited minds' for whom the EU is 'primarily a foreign force': 'To put myself in their shoes, I have to allow an algal growth of emotional anger and blatant prejudice, mixed with wilful blindness, to cover the clear waters of thought' (Thorpe 2016). The setting of Lincolnshire is, therefore, rather appropriate: not only did the region return exceptionally high Leave votes, but, like the Cévennes, contains 'the essence of the neglected provinces [...] hollowed out by factory closures and agricultural change [...] prowled by the far right' (Thorpe 2018b).[20] Fay embodies both the frustrated spirit of a Lincolnshire people, overlooked and ultimately abandoned by a Westminster bubble, and an emblem of the unrepresented white working-class more broadly, relegated to the margins of British politics for decades. Despite its tangible response to Brexit, the novel takes place in 2012 at a point when any exit from the EU was wrongly perceived as a dubious fantasy. By exposing these pre-existing class divisions in Lincolnshire, *Missing Fay* suggests regional squabbles were as much of a motivating factor in the EU referendum as Euroscepticism or xenophobia, complicating the argument that Brexit was a singular animating force in the creation of a broken Britain. Although Thorpe

---

[19] In this sense, he follows in the footsteps of John Berger who claimed that, with regards to Brexit, he 'voted with his feet long ago' by relocating to the French Alps in the 1970s (qtd. in Kellaway 2016).

[20] Boston in Lincolnshire returned the highest Leave vote in the country (75.6%) and experienced an extremely high rate of demographic change in the years leading to the referendum. Its non-British population rose from 1,000 in 2005 to 16,000 in 2015 (Goodwin and Milazzo 2017: 455).

admits any pro-European hopes have 'long drained away in the seemingly endless, smooth curve of decline', it is quite possible that such a decline contains the seeds of a vigorous, unanticipated renewal; cultural and political responses must offer 'a fresh language to combat despair, to defeat the cynical, to wash us free of that deadliest of acids' (Personal Correspondence 2020).

Jon McGregor's *Reservoir 13* (2017) unintentionally echoes the plot of *Missing Fay* (published earlier the same year) and assumes a similar narratorial approach. The novel chronicles the disappearance of a thirteen-year-old girl, Rebecca Shaw, on New Year's Eve in an unnamed Derbyshire village and its subsequent longitudinal effects on the local community. Whereas Thorpe establishes a distancing strategy in directing narrative attention away from Fay or her potential demise, traces of Rebecca remain in the community's social memory and her absence continues to inform the unfolding present. The rural landscape itself becomes a spectral site as recurrent sightings of Rebecca continue years after her disappearance. Given McGregor's oft-repeated 'allergic [reaction] to trying to make points in fiction', avoiding 'great state-of-the-nation' pronouncements, it seems erroneous to classify *Reservoir 13* as Brexlit; and yet, the referendum and the social issues relating to that historic vote haunt the margins of the narrative – ghostly reminders of the turbulent world outside of this carefully nurtured rural locale (McGregor 2017b). McGregor admits that the prevailing political atmosphere began to seep into his writing process, debating whether his characters would be Remainers or Leavers: 'I started looking at them while I was editing [. . .] and realised that yes, I probably could tell' (McGregor 2017b). Further, although the bleak fate of Syrian refugees attempting to reach British shores is relegated to background media noise and fails to take precedence over the minutiae of everyday life, the interruptive power of the outside world is evident in the lingering economic crisis affecting the farming community; the secluded valley is subject to the same precarious market logistics as the rest of the country. The agricultural rural rhythms of the village are not only broken by Rebecca's disappearance, but by an insidious form of austerity-driven, imperceptible violence gradually eating away at the fabric of the community. In this sense, valid political and ethical parallels can be drawn between a troubled nation's attempt to introduce an inward-looking protectionism, and a vulnerable local community which is 'not, despite appearances, closed in on itself, sovereign and autonomous, but dependent on the wider world' (Ganteau 2018). Both Thorpe and McGregor's novels seem incapacitated from providing a sense of closure – communities trapped in a state of suspension until the root causes of their loss becomes clear.

Melissa Harrison's *All Among the Barley* (2018), the winner of the European Union Prize for Literature in 2019, offers a situated perspective on what she terms 'the dangerous allure of nativism, nostalgia and xenophobia' in 'politically unstable times' (Harrison 2019). The novel's hauntingly atmospheric and deeply evocative portrait of 1930's rural life in East Anglia – a love letter to a time gone by – is offset by the impending threat of fascism. Harrison's narrator Edith Mather, a quiet and awkward adolescent living on Wych Farm, 'a world of ancient and immovable rhythms and beliefs', casts an eye back on the village of Elmbourne in the summer of 1933: a community still reeling from the economic and personal impact of the First World War (Harrison 2018: 96). *All Among the Barley* reinforces how cultural responses to Brexit so often engage with the legacy of the world wars; in the post-millennial national imaginary the wartime period remains the most significant point at which a united England resisted the external threat of Continental dominance. The spectral sound of the 'gone away' haunts the footsteps and livelihoods of the farm's inhabitants and a yearning to retreat 'back in time to the olden days [. . .] to be granted a temporary reprieve from all the anxieties of the modern age, the sense of things speeding up and going wrong', speaks equally to our globalized present (2018: 2; 61). It is therefore tempting to read Wych farm, 'entire unto itself', as an explicit metaphor for a bounded and backward-looking English nation in the age of Brexit (2018: 225). Harrison, however, refrains from espousing the traditional discourses espoused by Little Englanders, choosing not to position Wych Farm as an idyllic site of English fortitude and cultural heritage; instead, the introduction of mechanization in farming offers a welcome respite to a community depleted by wartime loss and highlights the necessity for even rural communities to reject cultural stasis and embrace national developments.

The parochial tenor of the farm is ruptured by the appearance of Constance FitzAllen, a young woman from London hoping to document and thereby preserve fading rural practices. Despite her metropolitan upbringing, Constance echoes Stanley Baldwin in bemoaning the erosion of 'the old ways' in the countryside and the estrangement of the English from their 'birth-right', preaching of the necessity to preserve 'our ancient way of life [. . .] England is the country, and the country is England' (2018: 91). In a series of related articles for a London journal, Sketches from English Rural Life, Constance valorizes the farming community as a potent repository of self-sufficiency and source of national pride, supplementing her aim of constructing a 'perfect English Arcadia' (2018: 243). Positing a preference for archaic traditions rather than a reliance on intellectual elites in the cities, she echoes the rhetoric of Brexiteers aiming to move away from international systems of regulation and control. Crucially, rather than bowing to Constance's assumptions and rendering a halcyon vision of a self-sufficient, contained English community governed by the rituals of rural life, the novel documents the economic precarity faced by farmers in inter-war Britain and intimates the distant yet influential role played by international politics in shaping regional dialogues. Following Constance's arrival, Edith begins to note the encroachment of European politics into family discussions and how it serves as a proxy for various pre-existing ills affecting the health of her farm community. Her father and brothers debate the intrusion of Westminster politicking into the lives of rural citizens, what they term 'Farming from Whitehall', instead advancing a narrative of national self-sufficiency; Harrison thereby establishes clear parallels between the need for 'proper import controls to protect our native English farmers' from international financiers and the current protection of farmers from EU law (2018: 44; 113).

But Constance's alien presence on the farm administers a stark and timely warning as to how easily fascism can emerge from the familiar stirrings of national protectionism and cultural conservatism. Her claim that she is not simply propagandizing backward-looking elegies for a mythical Englishness, and instead aims to remake the country in a new image, again mirrors the rhetoric of Brexiteers whose plans for a future-oriented Global Britain was predicated on isolationist economic policies and nostalgic reveries of imperial grandeur. During a public meeting in the village, she advocates the actions of the Order of British Yeomanry, a group of 'honourable patriots' protecting 'the health and purity of our English soil' by preventing international financiers or European markets from encroaching into national systems (2018: 299). In a historical note to the novel, Harrison explicates how the Order of British Yeomanry may operate as a fictional society within the novel, but similar unnamed groups and movements existed in socioeconomically deprived areas of 1930s Britain. Capitalizing on a widespread sense of disenfranchisement and cultural paralysis, such disparate groups 'drew from a murky broth of [. . .] nativism, protectionism, anti-immigration sentiment, economic autarky, secessionism, militarism, [and] anti-Europeanism', attracting members from all sides of the political spectrum (2018: 329).

Constance also begins to operate as a mouthpiece for the British Union of Fascists, who championed a prelapsarian return to an agrarian utopia free of the corrupting cultural influence of immigration, and her arrival marks an insidious rise in xenophobia within the sleepy English village. When an indigent Jewish family settle at the abandoned neighbouring property of Hullets they are immediately subject to suspicion and vilification, becoming the scapegoats for socioeconomic anxieties. As Harrison comments, 'When people feel they have no voice and no agency at all, they will find a way to take some', intimating how virulent strains of English nationalism are manipulated and sustained by disaffected factions within society (qtd. in Ferguson 2019). Constance's unsubstantiated claim that hordes of outsiders are now arriving in the countryside responds directly to right-wing media rhetoric in the build-up to the referendum and exposes the exclusionary forces at work surrounding issues of English heritage. By denying the Jewish family a voice in the novel, Harrison cements their role as spectral figures, existing in a liminal space on both the margins of both the farm and the narrative: a symbolic bordering of the cultural other that speaks, albeit indirectly, to the Calais refugee crisis. In casting the undesirable Jewish family from the village, Harrison reveals how human rights are often suspended for outsiders, who serve as a floating signifier which encapsulates the potential threat of external cultural influence more generally: 'they're not *from* here, and if we're not careful they'll mar the character of England forever' (Ferguson 2019: 199 – emphasis in original). For farmers faced with the threat of bankruptcy and poor returns in the inter-war years, such rhetoric sowed the seed of nativism and national protectionism. The novel's swift and brutal denouement, detailing the outbreak of a devastating fire on Wych Farm and Edith's incarceration in later life for mental health problems, points to the vulnerabilities of victims caught up in struggles over national ideologies, and the futility of preserving outdated practices or pursuing isolationist policies. Looking back on the period from within 1980s Thatcherite Britain, Edith continues to dream of the 'lost Eden' of her childhood, yet recognizes the danger in Constance's backward-looking fantasies: 'you can never go back, and to make an idol of the past only disfigures the present' (Ferguson 2019: 324). Harrison's microcosmic examination of the rhythms and rituals of English rural life ensures Edith's personal and localized tragedy supplies a broader commentary on the historical roots of post-Brexit Britain's ongoing national trauma, substantiating the epigraph's assertion that the past continues to inform and shape our contemporary moment.

Sarah Moss' *Ghost Wall* supplies a related commentary on the historical impulses of political events such as Brexit, untangling the traumatic roots of the national past to decipher the turbulent present. Set in the 1990s, following the fall of the Berlin Wall, the novel evokes a world recovering from the removal of borders, and the immediate desire to raise new ones in their place. The novel follows Silvie, a seventeen-year-old from Burnley, forced by her abusive father Bill to join an experiential university archaeology course researching the prevalence of Iron Age ritual sacrifice in rural Northumberland. Moss' intense concentration on, and deconstruction of, outdated historical practices and belief systems, preserved in the British mindset like Bronze Age relics in the bog and peat, delivers an indirect rebuke of the danger in celebrating an idealized past or resurrecting old rites to face contemporary concerns. Unlike Professor Slade leading the course, with his detailed academic knowledge of the Iron Age, Bill relies on an instinctual perception of the era, twisted by his own psychological distrust of immigrants, a staunch belief in the purity of hereditary nationality, and a distaste for feminist ideology. For Moss, who grew up in northern areas which returned strong Leave votes, the desire to satirize these widespread 'national myths of origin and racial purity' is necessary given the rise of increasingly nationalistic political discourses in the wake of the referendum (Moss 2019). Nursing a predilection for 'dead things', Bill prizes himself on the stubborn use of offensive racial terms and drags his daughter to the memorial sites of abandoned imperial English landmarks in order to mark their decay: 'Look at this [. . .] Used to send ships all over the world from here. Look at it now' (Moss 2018a: 25; 44). As a result of her father's misplaced fetishization of an idyllic and isolationist British past, Silvie is denied ownership of a passport and confused by the other students' talk of inter-railing across Europe.

It is revealed that Bill named his daughter after Sulevia, an ancient British goddess, as he wanted her to have 'a proper native British name', neglecting the fact that Sulevia is itself corrupted from the Latin (2018a: 19). In an argument with Professor Slade, Bill obsesses over inter-tribal battles which ensured darker skinned peoples were prevented from inhabiting Britain for millennia, in his mind drawing clear parallels between Bronze Age struggles and the threat of contemporary immigration. He even bristles at the suggestion that Hadrian's wall was more of a physical symbol to mark the edge of Europe than a national defensive barrier built by foreign slaves (before current nation state formations were even developed) and rejects any attempt to vilify or deconstruct Britain's fabled borders, failing to acknowledge that the Ancient Britons themselves were Celts originating from Ireland and France:

> Foreigners coming over here, telling us what to think. He wanted his own ancestry, wanted a lineage, a claim on something. Not people from Ireland or Rome [. . .] but some tribe sprung from English soil likes mushrooms in the night. (2018a: 45)

His veneration of ancient Britain as an island nation not only contradicts England's blurred, fragile margins and the brute geographic reality of Doggerland, which once formed a Neolithic European bridge from Denmark to Northumbria, but misguidedly attempts to lock Englishness in stasis.

Moss has been vocal in her acknowledgement of how the novel resonates with contemporary meaning and channels a damning indictment of isolationist practices and bordered discourses deployed by Western governments. The notion of tracing or locating an 'original British identity' in order to escape foreign influence is a wasted endeavour, exposing the evident critique underlying the novel: 'When, I wonder, was that? Before the Windrush? Before the Empire brought people from India and Ireland and parts of Africa to live and work in Britain in the nineteenth century? Before the transatlantic slave trade?' (Moss 2018b). On the one hand, Bill functions as a mouthpiece for the nativism animating British politics, fruitlessly striving to scrape together the foundational myths of our nation and honour the still-beating heart of a lost heritage. Such a reading is supported by the novel's psychogeographic mapping of the Brexit divide; Bill's mood improves as he leaves Remain-voting urban areas and instead draws strength from Hadrian's wall, 'a physical manifestation of Ancient British resistance still marked on the land' (Moss 2018a: 26). However, although the novel's ideological divide provides a clear parable for the split between nationalist belonging and more cosmopolitan forms of cultural identification encapsulated by the Brexit vote, the novel speaks to older historical divisions, including the cyclical nature of historical violence and the preservation of national imaginaries. Moss' underlying critique of Brexit rhetoric, encapsulated by Bill's anti-cosmopolitan outlook, thus alludes to the public's more general rejection of post-war social progress.

Bill's resurrection of patriarchal structures and abusive tendencies take a darker turn towards the end of the novel; under the Professor's guidance he directs the students to re-enact a series of historical practices performed in Iron Age Britain. Their initial reconstruction of a ghost wall – a palisade of ancestral human skulls designed to deter foreign invaders – merely serves to highlight the impotence of the island mentality in resisting either contemporary globalization or supranational structures which challenge Britain's proposed isolation. Further, the ineffectual construction of the simulated wall not only attests to the danger in placing trust in nativistic forms of cruel nostalgia, but the falsity in erecting a bulwark to preserve cultural tradition and reinforces a critique of the wider global desire to erect symbolic defences to resist change. Such historical reconstruction (echoing the narrative events of *England, England* and *Speak for England*) ensures English heritage itself ultimately settles as a spectral presence in the novel, haunting the actions and mindsets of the nation's older inhabitants: 'that was the whole point of the re-enactment, that we ourselves became the ghosts' (2018a: 34). By collapsing history in such a manner, recalling the willed preservation of a mythical Englishness evident in Kingsnorth's *The Wake*, Moss' novel delivers an anachronistic treatment of the ways by which the past bleeds menacingly into the present.

However, it is when Professor Slade and Bill subsequently decide to re-enact an Iron Age ritual sacrifice, roping and cutting Silvie on the moor, that Moss delivers her most potent critique of the destructive psychological impulses powering the Brexit agenda. The willing participation of two students in the performative sacrifice attests to the collective power of a mob mentality, in this case literally energized by the drumbeat and war cries of atavistic nationalism, satirizing the almost ceremonial reverence with which shadowy aspects of British history are treated. The sinister re-enactment symbolizes more than a selfish desire to destroy that which is soon to be lost – sacrifice as a means of ownership and preservation – it creates a historical parallel between the Iron Age bog victims sacrificed for unknown reasons and the scapegoating of ethnic minorities or EU citizens in order to protect and preserve the English *tribe*. Silvie simply becomes another victim of nationalistic violence (her fate all the more feasible following the brutal murder of Jo Cox). The arrival of the police, alerted to the disturbing re-enactment by a female student, prevents the reconstruction from reaching a darker conclusion and leaves open the question of how far a toxic nationalist ideology may proceed if left unchecked.

Ghost Wall thus delivers a stark warning as to how cultural misconceptions and veneration of British history can lead to the re-emergence of archaic practices in the present, resulting in dangerous abuses of power and its mutilatory effects on the younger generation. Moss' concentration on experiential archaeology establishes how closely a modern society can effectively recreate the mistakes of the past: an attempt to restore authenticity resulting in a radically inauthentic re-enactment of the era. Tellingly, both Moss and Harrison employ young female narrators who forensically excavate our ancestral heritage to uncover truths relevant to the current state of the nation, providing a youthful glance at the curious belief systems of older generations and exposing the intergenerational divide at the heart of Brexit debates. Although it is difficult to wrest some optimism from Moss' bleak tale of regressive patriarchal control and self-destructive nativism, Silvie's eventual emancipation from her father's clutches gestures (however tenuously) at the possibility of escaping the backward-looking cultural imaginaries dominating public and political discourses and moving beyond 'the crossroad of our sacred ways' (2018a: 81).[21]

Sarah Moss' subsequent polyphonic novel, *Summerwater* (2020), retains this concentration the weight of British history on contemporary paradigms of national identity. Set over a 24-hour period, *Summerwater* captures the boredom and anxiety of several characters each confined to their separate cabins in a holiday park near Loch Lomond as they wait for the incessant rain to stop. The park, of course, serves as a microcosm for the wider nation, scaling down the class-based, racial, political and generational divisions scarring British society. The spatial and social detachment between the cabins gestures to the lack of dialogue between disparate factions in post-Brexit Britain as well as Anglo-Scottish tensions regarding the vote. As an elderly Scottish GP asks driving along a 'fine EU-funded miracle': 'How could the English be so stupid [. . .] how could they not see the ring of yellow stars on every new road and hospital and upgraded railway and city centre regeneration of the last thirty years?' In capturing the sense of isolation and paranoia experienced by the families trapped in their separate cabins, Moss forms explicit parallels between the referendum and the Covid-19 pandemic: 'Brexit is a form of lockdown [. . .] the narratives overwrite each other, but actually encode a lot of the same anxieties about foreignness and invasion'. She continues, 'After all, a virus is an invader, which is a foreign toxin coming into the

---

[21] Fiona Mozley's *Elmet* (2017), offering an empathetic insight into the plight of rural citizens attempting to protect their forest grid from wealthy external influences, speaks to these same urgent nativist urges.

body [...] the Brexit narrative sets out a canvas on which we paint COVID', borne out of the same fears of infiltration and cultural infection. Moss has questioned whether a national 'society' still exists given recent events, but suggests a pandemic may 'show us what "fabric" remains' (Moss 2020; Personal Correspondence 2020).

Broken Ghost (2019) by Niall Griffiths offers the most haunting rendering of the troubled post-Brexit period, documenting the malaise of those left behind on the margins of contemporary Welsh society. Griffiths projects a seething authorial anger towards 'tax-dodging Bullingdon Club restaurant-smashing fucking stinking' hypocrites responsible for vicious public service and welfare cuts: 'fuckin Farage and fat Boris . . . all these cunts that do their best to defer blame, to fuckin weasel out of everything bad that they've done' (2019: 55; 65). Given that Griffiths began work on the novel in 2014, it is clear that, as this study has repeatedly stated, the animating energies that engender such bitterness long precede the events of 2016. In ironically celebrating the vision of a 'bright new Brexit Britain' which fails to inject new hope into the fragile socioeconomic environment of Wales, Griffiths makes clear his denunciation of those who merely exploit the fractious political landscape to further their causes and exacerbate the lives of his protagonists (2019: 215).

Returning once again to the regions surrounding Aberystwyth (the favoured locale of his early fiction), Griffiths provides a convincing case in suggesting that the Welsh Brexit vote was motivated by a long legacy of broken social contracts. The narrative opens in the wake of an overnight rave in the mountains, as three stragglers, Emma, Adam and Cowley, stumble home at dawn and unexpectedly witness a radiant vision of a floating, glowing woman suspended in the air. The ghostly apparition speaks a series of seemingly unconnected words including *bridge* before dissipating. As Emma reasons, the symbolic resonance of a bridge rings false at a moment when 'we're building mostly walls', later interpreting the word to be a signal for a rejuvenated sociopolitical resistance: '*bridge* is not a noun. It is an instruction' (2019: 97; 171). For Emma, a single parent and part-time carer struggling to survive on benefits, the spectral encounter equips her with a new sense of spiritual resolve and her subsequent online blog posts detailing the experience begin to trend on social media, with her followers attaching an almost religious fervour to her faith in the vision. If we attend to Griffiths' comment that the 'voices online are just the sounds of people searching for meaning' then the novel's subtle critique of Brexit swiftly becomes clear (2019: 150). The sudden intrusion of aggressive online message board conversations into the narrative indicate the increasingly disconnected national conversation taking shape around the vision and the means by which mediatized digital platforms often reduce citizens to shallow stereotypical caricatures.

The ghostly encounter initially has a reduced effect on the two male characters, who return to their separate lives and dismiss the apparition as the effects of their late-night exploits. Adam, a recovering addict sporadically volunteering at a rehab centre, relapses into his old social patterns and returns to a shadowy life of using and dealing narcotics. Yet it is through Adam that Griffiths voices his most direct attacks on the Brexit vision, holding the Conservative government accountable for the vulnerable socioeconomic conditions in which his protagonists find themselves: 'The politicians blether on about the great new opportunities for Britain outside of the EU [. . .] Endless shite.

And in all the fuckin job centres up and down the land not one thing changes' (2019: 137–8). Travelling through England, with its quiet suburban greens and St George's flags 'hanging limp in the gardens', Adam recognizes how a slumbering populace were manipulated and enervated by the referendum, the 'dull and diffuse docility' of Middle England easily swayed by 'state-approved mass distraction and intoxication' (2019: 224). Adam's concluding assessment that Britain is 'dead and it doesn't realise [. . .] Brexit is just fucking digging up the corpse' speaks volumes about the attempt to read an epiphanic vision into a political event which instead merely reveals the disturbing shadows of our national past (2019: 225). In comparison, Cowley, a labourer with a violent streak, obsesses over his increasing marginalization in the building trade, his work slowly being undercut by Eastern European immigrants. His dwindling fortunes and xenophobic stance towards 'cabbage suckers [. . .] thousands of-a cunts all swarmin' in' motivate him to evince some Leaver sentiments but he remains largely indifferent to the fact that Britain has 'said tara to fuckin Ewrop' (2019: 86). When Cowley hears an expert on TV dismiss his ghostly apparition as a brocken spectre, an atmospheric phenomenon projecting the observer's shadow onto a patch of cloud, his only comment is that the expert should have just spoken the words 'broken ghost' in place of the foreign-sounding words, articulating the underlying Goveian resistance to expert analysis during the referendum campaign.

By suggesting that the ghostly brocken spectre satiates 'the contemporary need for something transcendent [. . .] To offer meaning in uncertain and turbulent times', Griffiths is clearly insinuating the ways in which Brexit operates not as a national epiphany but a conduit for a misplaced confrontation with personal grievances and blighted socioeconomic pasts (2019: 264). It may be that the apparition is simply a broken ghost for a broken Britain – an ignoble vision that falls well short of the sublime – enabling citizens to buy into a spectacle that ultimately offers nothing and leaves an absence of catharsis. Griffiths concurs that the 'tawdry, empty, salvationist ideology' of Brexit and the Brocken Spectre 'appeal to very similar urges' relating to:

> some legitimation of existence [. . .] I see that quest as being fundamentally undermined years before the Brexit vote with the constant proclamations from the Cameron government of what, in effect, constitutes a meaningful life: the colourless tyranny of work in 'alarm clock Britain', 'strivers v skivers', Gove's hollow praise of those who 'get on in life'. (Personal Correspondence 2020)

He goes on to confirm that the three protagonists of *Broken Ghost* symbolize various aspects of the atomized society that emerges, and under such conditions 'we flounder for something to touch' (Griffiths 2020). The hauntological intrusion, however, serves a deeper purpose, kindling a spiritual regeneration in some while simultaneously igniting a passionate defence of nationalist self-determination in others. The fact that the vision is later revealed to be the product of heroin affecting the protagonists' opioid receptors, mixed with sounds playing on a nearby iPod, is almost immaterial; Griffiths' symbolically rich brocken spectre (very much like the figurative significance of Brexit) projects the profound with the absurd, provoking both a healthy scepticism and near-revelatory zeal. As Sebastian Mitchell explains, the brocken spectre as a literary device has a long heritage of 'encapsulating a global political threat' and 'of contrasting the nature of optical deceit with inspired revelation' (2007: 169). Given that the shadow cast by its effects often appears 'inflated' and occurs in conditions 'where it is difficult to judge distance and perspective', we can perceive Griffiths' brocken spectre to possess a crucial interpretative function, once again illustrating how Britain's national past continues to cast long shadows over the tumultuous political present (2007: 168).

In the final section Cysllt, meaning *contact*, Griffiths reunites his scattered protagonists at the site of the ghostly apparition. A spontaneous and organic counter-cultural commune which crosses political and ideological lines begins to take shape on the mountain, created by heterogeneous groups who trust in the veracity of Emma's experience, with attendees suddenly find themselves filled with a curious empathy for their fellow man. Holding 'flags aloft of crosses and dragons and the EU stars' (2019: 262), the gathering effects a revolt against societal atomization via a neoromantic attachment to the landscape and sociocultural regeneration strategies. The Conservative government immediately try to discredit the commune and limit its viral influence by falsely suggesting illegal immigrants are utilizing the site to escape the authorities, reporting that the gatherers should instead support the government during EU negotiations. Nor is the British public fully supportive of the commune, with several nationalist factions fundamentally opposed to its development voicing their disapproval online, dismissing the notion that public or common land should be occupied for this purpose: 'Bunch of whingers/hypocrites/parasites/libtards. Bet theyll be Remoaners. Get them down NOW [...] Traitors must lose all rights!!!' (2019: 293). While the commune is far from utopian, Emma, Adam and Cowley experience a series of cathartic encounters with figures from their past and present, gaining some semblance of psychological release from past traumas and their precarious positions at the edges of Britain's eroding social fabric. Just as the gathering reaches a frenzied peak, however, the authorities launch a brutal attack on the commune in an effort to clear the site, shattering an unlikely post-Brexit mood of tolerance and inclusiveness. Referencing the Battle of the Beanfield, Orgreave, the London riots and pre-referendum Brexit skirmishes, Griffiths situates the violent confrontation within a chequered history of governmental abuses of power, signalling how the first victims of cosmopolitical power plays are those in the most vulnerable circumstances.

Despite the violent and disturbing denouement, *Broken Ghost* contains a genuine literary spirit of ethico-political possibility and serves as the most uplifting post-Brexit fiction published thus far. Looking beyond the 'void, a spread of black nothingness' that accompanies the destruction of the commune, Griffiths imbues his narrative with a small modicum of hope for the eventual resuscitation of progressive dialogue in our splintered national community, healing divisions across established generational, racial and class divides (2019: 345). On the one hand, through the commune Griffiths gestures towards a possible redemptive future for Britain, where 'a sun burns brightly and waits to rise again' once the nation has learned to overcome its long legacy of regional and cultural disunities (2019: 356). On the other hand, the subtle deconstruction of the brocken spectre articulates the danger in blindly following someone's else's vision (particularly when that vision is later revealed to be predicated on misinformation). At the very least, Griffiths resists the temptation to accept, passively and obediently, the continuation of regional inequalities or post-austerity measures diminishing an already ailing Welsh economy. In yearning for new forms of community to overcome our bordered moment, *Broken Ghost* hints at something on the sociopolitical horizon though we may not yet be able to perceive its true form.

The need for connective values in overcoming the construction of borders (both physical and psychological) is central to Ali Smith's seasonal quartet: *Autumn* (2016), *Winter* (2017), *Spring* (2019) and *Summer* (2020). Smith's quartet is both timely and timeless: embedded in the tradition of English literature but intimately tied to the urgent present due to its dynamic temporal and palimpsestic play.[22] The first instalment, *Autumn* (arguably the first significant post-Brexit novel), offers a sustained mediation on the anus mirabilis that changed the political and cultural landscape of twenty-first-century society, embedding the divisive events of the EU referendum within a wider cyclical process of British history and natural decline. Smith acknowledges her novel 'had to (and I had to, too) square up to what was happening if the notions of contemporaneousness in it were to mean anything at all' (qtd. in Anderson 2016). In directly referencing a range of recent events from the murder of Jo Cox to the refugee crisis (with tourists 'holidaying up the shore from the dead'), Smith immediately places the reader in a post-Brexit landscape where 'a new kind of detachment' dictates social interactions (2016: 12; 54). As in Coe's *Middle England*, the celebratory memory of the London 2012 Olympics has been eroded and betrays the inward-looking melancholia behind the outward-facing façade: 'now you couldn't tell that any of these summer things had ever happened. There was just empty field. The sports track had faded and gone' (2016: 115). Smith's own festering authorial anger at the political elite is evident throughout *Autumn* as she looks ahead to a forthcoming winter of discontent: 'I'm tired of having to wonder whether they did it out of stupidity or did it on purpose' (2016: 57). *Autumn* may also claim the title of the first British 'post-truth' novel, alluding to the conscious manipulation of national newspapers like the *Daily Mail* with their simplistic Beaverbrookian rhetoric pitting British citizens against homogenous foreign 'others'. Smith's characters are aware that 'Facts don't work', identifying right-wing nationalistic propaganda as a contributing factor in the demise of democracy as a pragmatic form of political governance (yet could equally serve as a rebuke of the left's failure to foster a dialogic and collaborative tone during the campaign): 'It has become a time of people saying stuff to each other and none of it actually ever becoming dialogue. It is the end of dialogue' (2016: 112; 137). This is a Britain in less splendid isolation.

The narrative begins with the fallout of the Brexit vote – the opening lines serving as a riff on Charles Dickens' *A Tale of Two Cities* ('It was the worst of times, it was the worst of times') – following the lives of Elisabeth Demand, an art history lecturer in London, and Daniel Gluck, an older neighbour from her childhood (2016: 3).[23] The divisive consequences of the referendum are complemented by the collage-like, disjointed temporality of the narrative structure, with brief, fragmentary chapters

---

[22] Smith admits she had planned to write a seasonal quartet for decades (qtd. in Elkins 2019).
[23] Elisabeth's surname comes from the French – *de* and *monde* – alluding to the notion of being a cosmopolitan citizen 'of the world' (2016: 50).

shifting from Daniel's youth in 1930s Europe to Elisabeth's childhood in 1990s England, emphasizing that their relationship '[is] about history, and being neighbours' (2016: 45). These memoryscapes enforce a backward-looking focus on the narrative, interrogating the national pathology that resulted in the referendum campaign and subsequent fracturing of the populace:

> All across the country, there was misery and rejoicing [. . .] All across the country, people felt it was the wrong thing. All across the country, people felt it was the right thing. All across the country, people felt they'd really lost. All across the country, people felt they'd really won [. . .] All across the country, people looked up Google: *what is EU?*' [. . .] All across the country, people said it wasn't that they didn't like immigrants. All across the country, people said it was about control. (2016: 60–1)

The tense parochial interactions of Elisabeth's village serve as a microcosm for Britain's deteriorating relationship with the EU, revealing a community split between hospitality and hostility. The words 'GO' and 'HOME' are daubed over a cottage in the village, under which someone later adds 'in varying bright colours' representative of a resistant multiculture: 'WE ARE ALREADY HOME THANK YOU' (2016: 53; 138). While the 'wild joyful brightness painted on the front of that house in a dire time' suggest a resistance to such nationalistic fervour and the possibility of communal empathy in the aftermath of such a divisive political campaign, moments of cultural conviviality are punctuated by the frenzied imperial invective of angry nativists long after the referendum has passed: 'Rule Britannia [. . .] Britannia rules the waves. First we'll get the Poles. And then we'll get the Muslims. Then we'll get the gyppos, then the gays' (2016: 197).

The erection of an electrified chainlink fence on common land near the village, topped by razorwire and security cameras, operates both as a territorial reminder of a nation divided and an allusion to the enforcement of toxic anti-immigration policies on the horizon. Enclosing 'a piece of land that's got nothing in it', the fence soon doubles in size and is patrolled by a security agency named S4FA who are unable to adequately explain the fence's purpose (2016: 55). The decision by Elisabeth's mother, Wendy, to defy its presence by throwing a stockpile of antiques at the fence in the closing scenes, 'bombarding that fence with people's histories and with the artefacts of less cruel and more philanthropic times', symbolizes a resistance to borders both figurative and corporeal, both internal and external to the nation (2016: 255). Smith has spoken at length elsewhere of the writer's responsibility to practice a form of narrative hospitality, reiterating this outlook through Daniel's neighbourly guidance of Elisabeth: 'always try to welcome people into the home of your story' (2016: 119). As Smith's polemical stance makes clear, if good fences make good neighbours, then the need for cosmopolitan hospitality becomes an urgent necessity in a post-Brexit world.

Winter marks the point in the quartet where Smith begins to probe the deep-rooted historical divisions within British society and the motivating impulses of the referendum. Referencing the 'ordinary everyday terribleness' of the ongoing refugee crisis, the Grenfell Tower fire, the rise of Donald Trump and the proliferation of fake news, *Winter* plays out the antagonistic binaries that persist long after the vote has been decided (2017a: 30). The events of Grenfell in July 2017 testified to the ongoing devaluation of the most vulnerable in British society, particularly within Kensington and Chelsea, the country's richest borough, exposing the empty sentiment behind George Osborne's claim 'we are all in it together'. The tragedy forced a renewed concentration on the pain of everyday austerity, yet even this ethical turn was short-lived; the revanchist nationalism associated with Brexit continued to dominate political proceedings and an official re-evaluation of lacklustre social welfare within London failed to materialize.

Smith's narrative details a tense and fractious Christmas in Cornwall, as retired businesswoman Sophia Cleves welcomes her estranged sister Iris, her son Art, and his mysterious friend Lux (whom he has hired to masquerade as his girlfriend Charlotte) into her home.[24] The family surname immediately gestures to the state of cleavage and political mourning in which the nation finds itself. Smith's characters are representative of various polarized groups and factions at the heart of the Brexit debate: Sophia, a defiant Leave voter, relies on the questionable media narratives of *Daily Mail* journalists; Art, a nature writer, is politically uninformed about current events; Iris, a rebellious eco-activist and equal rights campaigner, detests her sister's lack of cosmopolitan empathy; and Croatian-Canadian Lux questions the British tendency to slip into protectionist rhetoric when confronted with global flows of immigration, dismissing the 'empty gestural' goodwill advocated during the Christmas period (but denied to global masses abandoned on Europe's shores) (2017a: 195).[25] Fragments of Brexit discourse are riven deep into the national conversation – particularly a clear linguaphobia which has only intensified since the vote – as the characters see their Christmas disturbed by Dickensian visitations and reminders of the irreducible ideological gap separating the British electorate. It is rather fitting that Smith pays homage to Dickens' *A Christmas Carol*; after all, Brexit is as much a confrontation with the ghosts of our national past as it is with our troubled present.

Sophia desperately tries to resist facing the fractious state of the nation by clinging to the cultural imaginary of the English Sublime, willing it to assume a new relevance: 'That red postbox on the front of the Radio Times: why does it mean so much and at the same time so little? She wants it to mean again like meaning used to mean' (2017a: 125). For Iris, however, Brexit and Trump operate as the twin forces of atavistic nationalism, hovering like a spectre over 'England's green unpleasant land' with the core Leave aesthetic of insularity threatening her more utopian dreams of ethical communal living (2017a: 208). The chronological narrative is persistently interrupted by memories, visions and hallucinations, including a disembodied head which both forces Sophia to reflect on the reverberations of historical causality and alludes to the inability of the British public to perceive objective reality. Art's real girlfriend Charlotte also experiences troubling visions, describing a recurring dream where she cuts herself open until she represents 'a quartered kingdom', disfigured beyond repair, and

---

[24] In 2016, 56.5 per cent of voters in Cornwall supported Leave despite the region's evident history of EU funding assistance.
[25] Lux's name derives from the Latin referring to a unit of illuminance: it is a foreign-born citizen who brings Britain's cultural myopia so arrestingly to light.

laments the ways in which 'pre-planned theatre is replacing politics' (2017a: 56; 57). Indeed, Smith points the reader towards the overt structural allusions between Britain's moment of crisis and Shakespeare's *Cymbeline*, 'a play about a kingdom subsumed in chaos, lies, powermongering, division and a great deal of poisoning and self-poisoning' (2017a: 200). Employing Lux as her fictional mouthpiece, Smith suggests Shakespeare's 'tangled-up messed-up farce' is writ large in post-Brexit Britain:

> it's like the people in the play are living in the same world but separately from each other [...] But if they could just step out of themselves, or just hear and see what's happening right next to their ears and eyes, they'd see it's the same play they're all in, the same world, that they're all part of the same story. (2017a: 201)

The allusion to *Cymbeline* does, however, allow a modicum of hope to seep into the national narrative; as Art recalls, Shakespeare's tragedy may revolve on treachery and deceit, but it gestures towards 'the balance coming back. The lies revealed. The losses compensated' (2017a: 315). For Smith, the novel form plays a minor role in restoring this tentative equilibrium, altering the reader 'to the workings of the people who make fictions of our world and call what they're doing truth' (Smith 2017b).

Lux draws attention to this recent devolution of language into political soundbites and empty rhetoric until it is devoid of signification, singling out Boris Johnson as a man not 'interested in the meaning of words' but 'one whose interests leave words meaningless' (2017a: 285). The disruptive presence of social media is threaded throughout the novel as Smith carefully attends to the role of digital platforms such as Twitter – a fertile playground for alt-right or extreme nationalist commentators – in spreading fake news, amplifying public discontent, and giving voice to alienated citizens. Art's girlfriend Charlotte criticizes his decidedly apolitical nature writing blog; her subsequent development of the blog demonstrates how such platforms also enable counter-narratives of grassroots resistance to emerge, transforming hatred into a progressive impetus for positive change. Over the course of the novel, however, Art (read *art*) develops an awareness of the consequences of the referendum. As Smith writes, 'I think all art is political [...] and that anyone not responding in their aesthetics to a time of immense political ferment and speed-of-sound change and regression like this one we're living through is acting every bit as politically as anyone who is' (Elkins 2019). For Smith, literature functions as an antidote to the political fictions masquerading as truth. During a family argument on the post-truths of the referendum campaign, Art seems to perceive 'a slab of landscape' above their heads, crumbling onto the dining table below. His fantastical vision, serving as a moment of revelation for a character seemingly oblivious of the societal implications of Brexit, captures the precarious fate of a nation left hanging in the balance, 'suspended by nothing' (2017a: 217).

In the third chapter, the study argued that the third instalment of the quartet, *Spring*, captures the divergence of Anglo-Scottish ideological stances towards emergent crises of the twenty-first century. Though the maintenance of a unitary order will prove a challenge for an increasingly disunited kingdom, Smith utilizes her familiar trope of a spectral Other, evident in *There But For The* (2011), to infiltrate inward-looking institutions and point towards new possibilities for affective narrativization and engagement across staunchly defended political lines during Britain's moment of constitutional and cosmopolitical crisis. Like Lux, the character of Florence in *Spring* inhabits the narrative as a mysterious presence, moving through policed checkpoints and established barriers in ways which defy the fortified present. The arrival of the stranger, however ghostly or spectral, necessitates a level of hospitality, and operates in radical opposition to the cosmopolitan notion of being at home in the world.

Summer (2020) completes the quartet, set just as the Covid-19 pandemic begins to take hold and exposes 'borders and passports' to be as 'meaningless as nature knows they are' (345). Commenting on the Black Lives Matter movement, the Windrush scandal and the inexorable rise of Dominic Cummings, *Summer* follows the Greenlaw household in Brighton, continuing the literary trend of capturing how Brexit exacerbated underlying familial divisions and created domestic sites of conflict. Mother Grace, a Leave voter, is abandoned by her Remain-voting husband Jeff; teenage Sacha questions and abhors Britain's hostile environment; while her younger brother Robert emerges as a Johnson-acolyte, dismissive of the hardships faced by the populace. For Peter Boxall, the novel form possesses a 'uniquely powerful capacity to critique the cultures from which it emerges and within which it is read' (2015: 10). Smith has previously emphasized the necessity to recognize a 'conflict in almost everything' in order to develop the narratorial debate; states of conflict, then, also produce 'a conflict of possibilities' (Smith qtd. in Beer 2013: 138). While summer resists a 'kinder finale', Smith accentuates that the word derives 'from the Old English *sumor*, from the proto-indo-european root *sam*, meaning both *one* and *together*', reflected in the reconciliation of several characters as her quartet draws to a close (2020a: 263; 289 – emphasis in original). With this in mind, Smith goes some way to explaining the socioemotional arrangement of her seasonal cycle: 'start with *Autumn*, so we could end on the open leaf, the long light days of summer [. . .] Leaves. Bare branches. Frost. Buds. Leaves again' (Smith 2020b). For Smith's tetralogy, the whole is greater than the sum of its parts.

In crystallizing our traumatic political present, her works of political allegory are powered by contemporary pressures and indicate the ways by which novels can be socially and politically transformative: 'if you can read the world as a construct, you can ask questions of the construct and you can suggest ways to change the construct. You understand that things aren't fixed' (qtd. in Laing 2016). As Daniel explains to Elisabeth in *Autumn*, 'whoever makes up the story makes up the world' (Smith 2016: 119). Smith's quartet, however, contains dreams of Remaining. The sentiments within the quartet appear to be out of step with the majority of the electorate; cosmopolitan values may never be needed more, but never wanted less. Smith appears to project the first two stages of grief: denial and anger; acceptance is far from her mind. Though the quartet has been charged with advancing its author's own political bias, as opposed to reaching out across both sides of our polarized society, there are flashes of redemption and mutuality amid the disorder and decay. As the quartet unfolds Smiths slowly develops an intricate collage-like web of textual interconnections. For example, in *Winter* Art works for SA4A, the shadowy conglomerate which first surfaced in *Autumn*; sections from Florence's notebook arguably emerge in earlier instalments of the quartet; and *Summer* sees the return of Iris, who houses homeless asylum seekers impacted by the Covid-19 pandemic and Britain's hostile environment. The collage-like construction of Smith's quartet contains elements of what can be termed a *transglossic* framework, involving the alignment of aesthetics and ethico-political imperatives, a productive optimism of renewal and a deep *simultaneity* committed to the contemporaneous occupation of multiple positions (Shaw and Upstone 2021). By forging bonds of connectivity and establishing forms of dialogue between characters on both sides of our divided Brexit Britain, Smith communicates the potential for emergent modes of political recuperation and captures a more radiant vision of the power of literature.

The study of contemporary fiction, rather like the immediate analysis of a political climate, is inevitably vulnerable to hindsight. If Brexit has effectively eroded the meta-narratives of European cooperation, centralization and supranationalism, what forms of new narrative will emerge to legitimize the relevance of cultural interdependence? The EU referendum, after all, forced the electorate to choose between a more cosmopolitan allegiance to a remote European family and a more tangible attachment to the nation. Author Sunjeev Sahota perceives Brexit to be 'a stain on our national identity, our sense of ourselves and our place in the world', but gestures towards literature's capacity to interrogate how we relate to one another across national and cultural boundaries, offering an imaginative space for the envisioning of political futures: 'I think writers will continue to write globally and won't be hemmed in by these boundaries that politicians try to impose on our minds. I think writers will write truth to power' (Shaw 2017). It is not altogether surprising that the longlist for the Man Booker Prize 2017 contained several novels which immediately engaged with a post-Brexit world. One would expect that planetary challenges requiring the mobilization of a global citizenry (or at least a re-embrace of a European demos), such as climatological risk or viral pandemics, will undoubtedly stimulate this form of literary response, as well as the inevitable emergence of Scottish, Northern Irish and Welsh devolutionary fictions that forge new dialogues with the question of British cultural identity. And yet, the risk remains that the literary discussion of such critical national and global concerns will simply create another leftist echo chamber that neither heals nor speaks to an already fractious nation. Several post-Brexit fictions appear overly schematic in their attempt to give voice to various groups within society yet "are" merely depicting, rather than interrogating, the very divides which gave rise to the referendum.

As the previous chapters have argued, Britain (and British literature) employed a *jamais vu* mindset towards the EU; familiar and repeated attempts at European fraternity were viewed as novel developments threatening national sovereignty. Rather than engaging with the larger realities of European life, the first wave of *post*-Brexit fiction largely seems to be detailing the specific frailties and parochial trivialities of an insular and diminished small island – updated forms of state-of-the-nation novels that retain a narrow focus on British society and its isolation from the continent. The British public have witnessed what happens 'when the subtle checks and balances of representative democracy are subordinated to the crude majoritarianism of referendums' (Dorling and Tomlinson 2017: 240). Brexit is arguably a self-inflicted wound which withdrawing from the EU will not heal. However, as opposed to late-twentieth-century works of British Euroscepticism, this chapter has suggested that certain post-Brexit fictions betray a further purpose, gesturing towards more inclusive and diverse forms of public culture, identifying the social divisions affecting the nation, and engaging in a struggle with our prevailing political climate. The first wave of post-Brexit fiction seems to find itself in the predicament of *l'espirit de l'escalier*, espousing an outward-looking cosmopolitan engagement as a *belated* form of resistance to an increasingly nationalistic and inward-looking cultural landscape.

Conclusion

Life after Europe

'Let's go' [They don't move].

(Beckett 1952)

The Brexit vote can be interpreted as the end-result of Britain's post-war legacy as an awkward partner in the European project. However, as this study has demonstrated, Europe was not the key issue affecting the referendum result: it was the trigger which focused the electorate's minds onto a number of underlying, tangential issues affecting the body politic. To quote Charles Bukowski, 'it is not the large things that send a man to the madhouse', but 'the continuing series of small tragedies', that 'swarm of trivialities'; it is 'a shoelace that snaps with no time left' (1972: 114–15). The process of leaving the EU has become painfully protracted and British politics remains trapped in a tiresome and adversarial struggle. Most political commentators and academics agree that Britain will be forced to accept its reduced remit as a medium-sized political player whose power and influence will diminish further in the coming years. It will continue to navigate and negotiate between its various commitments but from a greatly weakened position. Britain now exists in a liminal cosmopolitical zone, stagnating in political stasis and suffering from a form of national post-traumatic stress, with each passing month providing a parodic replay of the cyclical Brexit psychodrama. Waiting for Brexit has been a Beckettian experience – a constitutional drama with no evident final act. On 14 February 2019, senior British ambassadors released an open letter decrying the 'Brexeternity' of endless negotiations and uncertainty.

If May's proposed 'Global Britain' was simply a cheap reworking of imperial Britain and a redevelopment of our ties with the Commonwealth, then post-Brexit negotiations under a Johnsonian government have certainly appeared a tragedy masquerading as farce. For O'Toole, Johnson 'is a figment of the English imagination, a necessary invention', with his 'comic anecdotes of crazed bureaucracy' not only redolent of Churchillian resilience but a more quintessential vision of John Bull beset 'by dastardly foreign maniacs trying to bind him in red tape' (2018a: 138). As this study has shown, Eurosceptic political speeches of the immediate post-war years and post-Brexit period are virtually interchangeable, except for the fact that Johnson often adds a level of knowing irony to his Europhobic rambling. The task for Britain is to maintain a viable working relationship with the EU while establishing a strategic economic and political relationship with the rest of the world. Yet Johnson is doomed to fail as he embodies 'a fatal flaw in the Brexit project'; namely, that the referendum was not a noble struggle against oppression but rather responded to a range of 'self-pitying grievances': 'there were no EU dungeons to be thrown open. There were only trivial fictions' (2018a: 134). As a result, Brexit is 'a strange kind of resurrection: the tomb is empty but the vanished body has not been seen alive' (2018a: 190). In reducing legitimate concerns to absurdity – hyper-exaggerating over bendy bananas and metric systems – the Leave campaign broke Eurosceptic concerns down into 'microcosmic minutiae and then blew them up again into a macrocosmic tale of oppression' (2018a: 135). Political uncertainty is not the fault of Leave-supporting politicians alone; the liberal left remains in denial over the result of the referendum. Talk of a second referendum, a corrective to the surprising result, dominated the media during 2017. A month before the EU referendum, Cameron confirmed another referendum would be off the cards even in the event of a Leave victory, stating: 'You cannot have neverendums' (Parker 2016). Referendums, as Thatcher once proclaimed (quoting Clement Attlee), are 'a device of dictators and demagogues', framing issues in isolation without considering the wider historical or cultural factors and their influence on the proposed question (Thatcher 1975). The EU referendum was a blunt instrument for what should have been a delicate and nuanced operation, removing the nuances in the various ideological positions towards Europe traced in this study, bludgeoning British citizens into binary thought-patterns, and creating a crude dichotomy in the process. For certain factions within Westminster, a referendum was a politically irresistible solution which redirected attention away from pre-existing internal ailments impairing the body politic. As O'Toole writes, England's 'sore tooth problem' was undoubtedly 'disturbing the whole body politic', yet Brexit proved to be a 'radically invasive surgery' which left the sore tooth intact (2018a: 191).

Pro-Leave factions, of course, have seen their grievances manipulated by elitist forces and will count among the first casualties of Brexit as underlying inequalities continue unaddressed, ironically leaving Britain more politically volatile than it was before the referendum and its poorest citizens more economically vulnerable. As Lanchester laconically notes, 'They should be used to that by now' (Lanchester 2016). Leaving the EU fails to protect those 'left behind' by globalization, nor stall the rapacious demands of market fundamentalism; Britain already suffers from one of the worst rates of income equality in Europe. If anything, the backlash towards the referendum result has contributed to the British public's belief that they are ruled by faceless and unaccountable Westminster elites, who merely promote the EU's benefits in order to maintain the status quo. Armingeon and Ceka argue that 'the most significant determinant of trust and support for the EU remains the level of trust in national governments', explaining the decline in support for the EU following the financial crisis of 2008 among citizens for whom neither national nor supranational governmental systems are deserving of trust (2014: 83). Support for the EU, then, 'is a proxy for trust in national governments' (2014: 86).

Evans and Menon suggest Brexit represents a form of 'punctuated equilibrium', adapting the term from evolutionary biology, whereby social systems which have existed in stasis for many years may be disrupted by sudden shifts or sharp shocks; yet such systems can also produce radical change when they are subject to new conditions, particularly given the absence of alternatives for Britain's political future (2017: 120).

As the third chapter suggested, Britain must first conduct a long overdue reappraisal of the relationships between its constituent nations and reinstitutionalize identities within the constitutional order to confront the internal inequalities dividing the nation. Implementing any common framework between the British government and devolved bodies will be fraught with difficulties but engaging with the concerns of national identity and representation prevents cultural and ideological issues being appropriated and corrupted by far-right reactionaries. Radical constitutional and socioeconomic change are therefore required if Britain is ever to confront its unequal and disunited kingdom. As Freedland acknowledges, there 'can be no moving on until we have reckoned with what exactly was done to the people of these islands – and by whom' (Freedland 2016b).

While Brexit continues to loom large in the British psyche, new fault lines scar the face of contemporary Britain. In March 2020 the Brexit timetable was overshadowed by a much more important and epoch-defining event: the Covid-19 pandemic. The EU was accused of being structurally impotent in addressing the political and economic fallout (echoing charges thrown at the supranational polity during the Eurozone crisis) and neglecting to act with the immediacy, focus and empathy of independent nation-states.[1] The subsequent economic shutdown and delayed trade talks among the EU-27 following the Covid-19-crisis increased the chances of a no-deal Brexit. With regards to Westminster and the devolved governments, the absence of a four-nation approach or exit strategy to the crisis does not bode well for the future of the union. Other recent post-Brexit developments, including a heightened awareness and mobilization of the global Black Lives Matter movement, have accelerated calls for an institutional recognition of the critical intersectionality of race and class. A multi-ethnic class politics of recuperation and solidarity must arise from the groundwork of such groups and social movements, inspiring emergent modes of identification and association through which individuals conceive of their place in the nation. The unlikely political debates and radical discourses thrown up by the EU referendum has ensured Britain's Overton Window is becoming more open; this shifting political landscape should be the impetus for progressive economic policies and accommodating cultural narratives considered unthinkable only years before. New modes of Britishness – outward-facing, tolerant, inclusive and willing to relinquish its outdated imperial identity – both attuned to the globalized condition and comfortable with more equitable and transparent devolutionary developments, will effectuate the progressive regeneration of an insecure English identity and galvanize a post-Brexit Britain. Speculating on future political recalibrations is always a questionable endeavour, particularly when our current political system rests on such shaky foundations; however, it is likely the cultural, ethnopolitical and socioeconomic impact of Brexit will be felt for decades to come. Whether that impact inspires a redrawing of Britain's political map is a debate that will stretch long into the twenty-first century.

---

[1] There is, strangely enough, a body of fiction which anticipates the dual crisis of viral infection and European disintegration. Dave Hutchinson's crime novel *Europe in Autumn* (2014) is a stunningly astute vision of a post-Brexit world in which Europe is in the grip of a flu pandemic; an economic collapse exposes the fault lines between seemingly united continental nations and suggests the progressive EU rhetoric of ever closer union – codified in the 1957 Treaty – to be nothing more than an empty gesture.

In his 1922 inaugural lecture as professor at Merton College, Oxford, George Gordon declared 'England is sick, and [. . .] English Literature must save it', citing literature's unique ability to 'delight and instruct us, but also, and above all, to heal our souls and save the State' (qtd. in Eagleton 1983: 20). Given the vital application of other digital and cultural forms during the referendum campaign, it is unlikely post-Brexit fictions will perform this emancipatory, animating function in healing fractious divides. TV and media in particular have displaced the primacy of literature as a pedagogical tool with regards to cultural understanding and awareness and we are already witnessing the wider emergence of Brex-art – a catch-all for creative engagements with Brexit across all mediums, from film and TV to art and music. While literature may not be able to redirect political outcomes, it remains fundamental to ways of thinking about identity, community and otherness. As Bhabha writes, narration forces the reader to consider 'the cultural construction of nationness as a form of social and textual affiliation' (1990: 292). It may also be that the fallout of Brexit contributes to the ongoing ethical turn in literature towards a deeper consideration of the role of the writer. However, literature which celebrates a potential Eurotopia is unlikely to emerge – the shortcomings of the EU are too widespread for such an unnuanced vision. That being said, the development of the EU has always been a mutable, if refractory, process: it is likely the union will transform itself once again to meet the demands of a changing geopolitical landscape. It is impossible to know the exact effects Brexit will have on the literary community, but it is undeniable that the loss of EU funding and an ideological retreat from European relations will hardly nurture a sector which is already hanging by a gossamer thread. The EU referendum mobilized fears and prejudices as opposed to hopes and visions for a restructured and independent Britain, yet there has been an efflorescence of literary works which offer flashes of redemption for Britain's future in refusing to be seduced by simplistic binaries. Texts of loss, separation and decline exist alongside works which espouse an ethics of social responsibility and radical action, demonstrating the redemptive and recuperative capacity of literature in offering revisionary possibilities for twenty-first-century society. A literary politics of *hope* not fear.

A study of Brexit through the medium of literature is somewhat appropriate given the extent to which the referendum was based on mendacious fictions. Britain's postwar struggle to achieve some semblance of cosmopolitical balance in its European relations has certainly proven to be stranger than fiction. British literature is not a cultural field that has been sympathetic towards European integration, nor has it championed the EU as a progressive organization worthy of fictional representation. Rather, writers have remained (like their political representatives) largely reluctant to engage with Europe, employing a variety of textual strategies to deliver endless variations on the theme of Euroscepticism. Sceptical of the potential merits of an 'ever closer union', certain writers appear wilfully dismissive of the EU's purpose, or, as Tim Parks puts it: 'genuinely unaware that such an entity existed' (1997: 5). What the literary works in this study expose is that the national narratives fabricated by politicians to envision Britain's future involved a return to the past, ensuring Brexit emerges as 'the afterlife of dead fantasies' (O'Toole 2018a: 213). Brexit did not create a new national narrative: it symbolized a retreat to comforting fantasies out of step with the cosmopolitical realities of the twenty-first century. The EU referendum has raised more questions than answers and the struggle to confront these urgent, innumerable issues is only beginning.

Britain's withdrawal will undoubtedly continue to encourage the emergence of fictions which contain a longing for a lost moment in British politics and society. *Brexlit* has concentrated on British literature's reluctant post-war stance and resultant exit from Europe, but further work remains to be done on *European* perspectives of migratory processes and Britain's act of political isolation. Speaking immediately after the referendum result, Jeanette Winterson asserted her faith in the power of literature to respond to our moment of national schism, 'If we're living in a post-facts world – let's have better stories [. . .] We can find a narrative that unites us, not one that divides us', as every 'political movement begins as a counter-narrative to an existing narrative' (Winterson 2016). Literature must be tasked with imagining alternate futures and new relationships not just with Europe, but between the constituent territories of the UK. A novel form of global thinking is required that remains sensitive to the significance of national traditions, identities and attachments, which are often too easily transcended and elided by cosmopolitan imaginaries and transnational associations. The role of literature is not to negate or downplay the relevance of nationhood, but present new perspectives which affirm and reinvigorate the national imaginary as a space of tolerance and openness to the globalized world. Although the act of reading stimulates an empathetic identification with otherness, it does not remove established 'thick' ties relating to national identity, tradition, culture and class. Concerns surrounding heritage and nostalgia are often attached to the diagnosis of a diminished culture unable to compete in the contemporary environment, but fictions may yet emerge which gesture at ways of overcoming the inherent tensions between cultural decline and rapid social change, and establish new national narratives sensitive to historical legacies. Just as postcolonial literary studies forced an acknowledgement of the Empire's role in sustaining the British state, and Scottish devolutionary fictions sought to find a creative solution to disenfranchisement within the British constitutional order, so too must post-Brexit fiction attempt to influence, rather than simply react to, the framework of thought governing global interdependence. Literature is the space in which such alternate imaginaries can be envisaged, articulated and pursued.

In moments of national crisis, it is understandable to question literature's ability to impact or shape the direction of future political decision-making. Parodic deconstructions of our national icons and originating myths are necessary strategies in confronting the spread of ethnonationalism. Cole Morton warns, 'if we don't rethink and reimagine the emblems of our nationhood, and celebrate what they say about us, then the far right will' (qtd. in Gardiner 2012: 152). Literature remains a useful instrument in overcoming the British tendency towards national autopoiesis and a backward-looking cultural imaginary; the creation of more outward-facing and future-oriented narratives will allow British society to advance beyond a destructive and unhealthy preoccupation with the nation's past glories towards new political arrangements for a shared European future.

Universities also have a crucial pedagogical role to play in shaping forthcoming narratives regarding life 'after' Europe (despite Michael Gove's remarks that British society has had enough of 'experts'). As Pippa Norris identifies, 'Western universities are generally cosmopolitan institutions that thrive on the international movement of researchers and students, and on the flow of ideas that movement can bring', thus the rise in nationalist populism (as well as recent developments such as Covid-19) and its effect on migration and international student numbers poses 'a direct threat to the university culture' (Norris 2016). British universities must hope for the continuation, or redevelopment of, programmes such as Erasmus and Horizon 2020 following the transition period, designed to support higher education institutions and European transnational partnerships. It is also worth remembering that the recent increase in tuition fees contributes to increasing class divisions and contradicts claims that universities naturally serve as progressive engines of social mobility. To perceive universities as drivers of cultural openness reinforces the sense that such institutions only speak to a certain section of society. Looking at the map of the electoral result, James Meek notes how university towns have become small 'island[s] of European feeling'; a 'Remainer archipelago' separated by 'open Leaver country' (2019: 111). The referendum result led to charges from certain sections of the media that universities inculcate socially liberal values in their student bodies. Nevertheless, May's Conservative government recognized the inherent threat university culture posed to public opinion. In 2017 Chris Heaton-Harris demanded that all UK Vice-Chancellors supply names of academics working directly or indirectly on Brexit: a form of Eurosceptic McCarthyism which attempted to silence academic freedom of speech. If, as Rumford suggests, cosmopolitanism is 'a political strategy which draws upon resources of the imagination in order to constitute an alternative social connection' between global citizens, then the teaching of literature offers the means to inspire and reinvigorate cultural imaginaries of national and transnational identity (2007: 107). It may be up to the Arts to decipher what Brexit *really* means.

Over four years after the 2016 referendum, British society remains deeply divided over both the vote and the subsequent process of leaving the EU. There remains widespread uncertainty regarding the reasons behind the result as well as anxiety over the consequences. One thing is clear: Brexit marks a profound change in the political landscape of the nation – one that could lead to the eventual dissolution of the UK and a reshaping of our national culture. Whether Brexit will initiate a 'domino-effect' on other EU member states and lead to the break-up of Europe's political organization, or whether such disintegration will result in new forms of European collaboration oriented to global challenges, untethered by the EU's more neoliberal and bureaucratic tendencies, remains to be seen. History, of course, repeats. In 1932, against the backdrop of growing nationalist sentiments, Austrian novelist Stefan Zweig wrote, 'European economies and European politics share a common fate [. . .] no individual country can escape from a common world crisis through such separation' (Zweig 2016). His words remain as felicitous now as they were almost a century ago. As Kymlicka identifies, the boundaries of a political 'community of fate' are not determined by 'the forces people are subjected to, but rather how they respond to those forces, and, in particular, what sorts of collectivities they identify with when responding to those forces' (2010: 437). If Brexit does mark the re-emergence of sociopolitical anti-cosmopolitan ideology that will define international relations in the twenty-first century, then the role of literature as a bastion of cultural cosmopolitanism becomes all the more significant.

Bibliography

Personal interviews/correspondence

Glen James Brown. 5 March 2020.
Sam Byers. 13 March 2020.
Anthony Cartwright. 25 May 2020.
Niall Griffiths. 13 March 2020.
James Hawes. 13 March 2020.
John King. 11 March 2020.
Marina Lewycka. 18 May 2020.
Sarah Moss. 10 March 2020.
Fiona Shaw. 14 August 2019.
Adam Thorpe. 1 November 2018; 4 March 2020.

Primary sources

Amis, Kingsley ([1958] 1968), *I Like It Here*, London: Penguin.
Arnott, Peter (2000), *A Little Rain*, Unpublished Typescript, Scottish Theatre Archive, Glasgow University Library.
Ballard, J. G. ([2006] 2007), *Kingdom Come*, London: Harper Perennial.
Barker, Nicola ([2012] 2013), *The Yips*, London: Fourth Estate.
Barnes, Julian ([1996] 2007), *Cross Channel*, London: Picador.
Barnes, Julian ([1998] 1999), *England, England*, London: Picador.
Board, Douglas (2017a), *Time of Lies: A Political Satire*, Much Wenlock: Lightning Books.
Bradbury, Malcolm (1983), *Rates of Exchange*, London: Secker & Warburg.
Brown, Glen James (2018), *Ironopolis*, Cardigan: Parthian.
Burgess, Anthony, ([1978] 2013), *1985*, London: Hutchinson.
Burns, Anna (2018a), *Milkman*, London: Faber & Faber.
Butterworth, Jez (2009), *Jerusalem*, London: Nick Hern.
Butterworth, Jez (2017a), *The Ferryman*, London: Nick Hern.
Byers, Sam (2018), *Perfidious Albion*, London: Faber & Faber.
Cartwright, Anthony (2004), *The Afterglow*, London: Tindal Street Press.
Cartwright, Anthony ([2009] 2010), *Heartland*, London: Tindal Street Press.
Cartwright, Anthony (2016), *Iron Towns*, London: Serpent's Tail.
Cartwright, Anthony (2017), *The Cut*, London: Peirene Press.
Coe, Jonathan (2018), *Middle England*, London: Viking.
Craig, Amanda (2017), *The Lie of the Land*, London: Little, Brown.
Dabydeen, David (1993), *Disappearance*, London: Secker & Warburg.
Deighton, Len ([1978] 2016), *SS-GB*, London: Harper.
Evaristo, Bernardine (1997), *Lara*, London: Angela Royal.

Evaristo, Bernardine (2005), *Soul Tourists*, London: Penguin.
Evaristo, Bernardine (2019), *Girl, Woman, Other*, London: Hamish Hamilton.
Grant, Linda (2019), *A Stranger City*, London: Virago.
Gray, Alasdair (1984), *1982, Janine*, London: Jonathan Cape.
Griffiths, Niall (2000), *Grits*, London: Jonathan Cape.
Griffiths, Niall (2001), *Sheepshagger*, London: Jonathan Cape.
Griffiths, Niall (2019), *Broken Ghost*, London: Jonathan Cape.
Guo, Xiaolu (2020), *A Lover's Discourse*, London: Chatto & Windus.
Hall, Sarah ([2015] 2016), *The Wolf Border*, London: Faber & Faber.
Hamid, Mohsin (2017), *Exit West*, London: Hamish Hamilton.
Harris, Robert ([1992] 2012), *Fatherland*, London: Arrow Books.
Harrison, Melissa (2018), *All Among the Barley*, London: Bloomsbury.
Hawes, James (2005), *Speak for England*, London: Vintage.
Hein, Christoph ([2000] 2003), *Willenbrock*, New York: Metropolitan Books.
Herd, David and Anna Pincus, eds. (2016), *Refugee Tales I*, Manchester: Comma Press.
Herd, David and Anna Pincus, eds. (2017), *Refugee Tales II*, Manchester: Comma Press.
Herd, David and Anna Pincus, eds. (2019), *Refugee Tales III*, Manchester: Comma Press.
Hughes, Michael (2018a), *Country*, London: John Murray.
Ishiguro, Kazuo ([1989] 1999), *The Remains of the Day*, London: Faber & Faber.
Ishiguro, Kazuo (2015), *The Buried Giant*, London: Faber & Faber.
Kennedy, A. L. ([1993] 2005), *Looking for the Possible Dance*, London: Vintage.
King, John ([1998] 1999), *England Away*, London: Vintage.
King, John (2016a), *The Liberal Politics of Adolf Hitler*, London: London Books.
Kingsnorth, Paul ([2014] 2015a) *The Wake*, Minneapolis, MN: Graywolf. Press.
Kunzru, Hari ([2004] 2005), *Transmission*, London: Penguin.
Kunzru, Hari (2020), *Red Pill*, London: Scribner.
Laing, Olivia (2018a), *Crudo*, London: Picador.
Lanchester, John ([2012] 2013) *Capital*, London: Faber & Faber.
Lanchester, John (2019), *The Wall*, London: Faber & Faber.
Le Carré, John (2017a), *A Legacy of Spies*, London: Viking.
Lewycka, Marina ([2007] 2012), *Two Caravans*, London: Penguin.
Lewycka, Marina (2020), *The Good, the Bad and the Little Bit Stupid*, London: Fig Tree.
Lodge, David ([1970] 1985), *Out of the Shelter*, Harmondsworth: Penguin.
Lovegrove, James (2019), *Age of Legends*, Oxford: Solaris.
Mathias, Tracey (2018), *Night of the Party*, London: Scholastic.
McEwan, Ian ([1990] 2016), *The Innocent*, London: Vintage.
McEwan, Ian (2019a), *Cockroach*, London: Jonathan Cape.
McGregor, Jon (2017), *Reservoir 13*, London: Fourth Estate.
McQueer, Chris (2018), *HWFG: Here We F**king Go*, Edinburgh: 404 Ink.
Menasse, Robert (2019), *The Capital*, London: MacLehose Press.
Mitford, Nancy ([1960] 1963), *Don't Tell Alfred*, London: Penguin.
Moss, Sarah (2018a), *Ghost Wall*, London: Granta.
Moss, Sarah (2020), *Summerwater*, London: Granta.
Mullin, Chris (2019a), *The Friends of Harry Perkins*, London: Scribner.
Myers, Benjamin (2017), *The Gallows Pole*, Hebden Bridge: Bluemoose Books.
Osmond, John (2018), *Ten Million Stars are Burning*, Ceredigion: Gomer Press.
Parks, Tim (1997), *Europa*, London: Secker & Warburg.
Phillips, Caryl (2003), *A Distant Shore*, London: Secker & Warburg.
Popoola, Olumide and Annie Holmes (2016), *Breach*, London: Peirene Press.

Roberts, Andrew (1995), *The Aachen Memorandum*, London: Widenfeld & Nicolson.
Robertson, James (2010), *And the Land Lay Still*, London: Hamish Hamilton.
Sebald, W. G. (2001), *Austerlitz*, London: Penguin.
Shaw, Fiona (2018), *Outwalkers*, Oxford: David Fickling Books.
Smith, Ali (2016), *Autumn*, London: Hamish Hamilton.
Smith, Ali (2017a), *Winter*, London: Hamish Hamilton.
Smith, Ali (2019a), *Spring*, London: Hamish Hamilton.
Smith, Ali (2020a), *Summer*, London: Hamish Hamilton.
Smith, Zadie (2013), *The Embassy of Cambodia*, London: Hamish Hamilton.
Smith, Zadie (2019), *Grand Union*, London: Hamish Hamilton.
Spallen, Abbie (2015), *Lally the Scut*, London: Faber & Faber.
Thomson, Rupert ([2005] 2006), *Divided Kingdom*, London: Bloomsbury.
Thorpe, Adam (2017), *Missing Fay*, London: Jonathan Cape.
Thorpe, Adam (2018a), *Notes from the Cévennes: Half a Lifetime in Provincial France*, London: Bloomsbury.
Tremain, Rose (2007), *The Road Home*, London: Chatto & Windus.
Trezise, Rachel (2000), *In and Out of the Goldfish Bowl*, Cardigan: Parthian.
Welsh, Irvine (2018a), *Dead Men's Trousers*, London: Jonathan Cape.
Wilson, Angus ([1961] 1992), *The Old Men at the Zoo*, London: Penguin.
Wilson, Elizabeth (1993), *The Lost Time Café*, London: Virago.
Winterson, Jeanette (2019), *Frankissstein: A Love Story*, London: Jonathan Cape.

Secondary sources

Acheson, Dean (1963), 'Our Atlantic Alliance: The Political and Economic Strands', *Vital Speeches of the Day* 29 (6): 162–6.
Afzal, Nazir (2016), 'Why Britain Should be Worried by this Flood of Young Male Migrants', *Daily Mail*, 8 January. Available at: https://www.dailymail.co.uk/news/articl e-3389734/ Why-Britain-worried-flood-young-male-migrants-Leader-lawyer-s-son -immigrants-gives-stark-warning.html.
Agamben, Giorgio (1998), *Homo Sacer: Sovereign Power and Bare Life*, Stanford, CA: Stanford University Press.
Agamben, Giorgio (2000), *Means Without End: Notes on Politics*, Minneapolis, MN: Minnesota University Press.
Alibhai-Brown, Yasmin (2000), 'Muddled Leaders and the Future of British National Identity', *Political Quarterly* 71 (1): 26–30.
Amis, Kingsley (1963), 'What's Left for Patriotism?', *Observer*, 20 January.
Amis, Kingsley (1970), *What Became of Jane Austen? And Other Questions*, New York: Harcourt Brace Jovanovich.
Anderson, Benedict (1983), *Imagined Communities: Reflections on the Origin and Spread of Nationalism*, London: Verso.
Anderson, Darran (2017), 'The Kingdom and the Republic: How the Irish Border Could Derail Brexit', *Prospect*, 16 August. Available at: https://www.prospectmagazine.co.uk/ magazine/how-the-irish-border-could-derail-brexit.
Anderson, Eric Karl (2016), 'Ali Smith on *Autumn*, Brexit, and the Shortness of Life', *Penguin*, 12 October. Available at: https://www.penguin.co.uk/articles/2016/ali-smith-o n-autumn/.

Anglo-Irish Agreement (1985), 'Agreement between the British and Irish Governments, Hillsborough', 15 November. Available at: http://cain.ulst.ac.uk/events/aia/aiadoc.htm.
Appiah, Kwame Anthony (1998), 'Cosmopolitan Patriots', in Pheng Cheah and Bruce Robbins (eds), *Cosmopolitics: Thinking and Feeling Beyond the Nation*, 91–114, Minneapolis: University of Minnesota Press.
Appiah, Kwame Anthony (2006), *Cosmopolitanism: Ethics in a World of Strangers*, London: Penguin.
Archibugi, Daniele (1998), 'Principles of Cosmopolitan Democracy', in Daniele Archibugi et al. (eds), *Re-imagining Political Community: Studies in Cosmopolitan Democracy*, 198–228, Cambridge: Polity Press.
Arendt, Hannah (1958), *The Human Condition*, Chicago: University of Chicago Press.
Armingeon, Klaus and Besir Ceka (2014), 'The Loss of Trust in the European Union During the Great Recession Since 2017: The Role of Heuristics from the National Political System', *European Union Politics* 15 (1): 82–107.
Armistead, Claire (2019), 'Ali Smith: This Young Generation Is Showing Us That We Need to Change and We Can Change', *The Guardian*, 23 March. Available at: https://www.theguardian.com/books/2019/mar/23/ali-smith-spring-young-generation-brexit-future.
Arnot, Chris (2009), 'Landscape of Neglect Is Fertile Breeding Ground for Far Right Extremism', *The Guardian*, 4 November. Available at: https://www.theguardian.com/society/2009/nov/04/flagging-spirits-heartland.
Arnott, Peter (2019), Twitter, 7 July.
Ashcroft Poll (2016), 'How the United Kingdom Voted on Thursday . . . and Why', 24 June. Available at: http://lordashcroftpolls.com/2016/06/how-the-united-kingdom-voted-and-why/.
Aslet, Clive (1997), *Anyone for England?: A Search of British Identity*, London: Little, Brown.
Attlee, Clement (1963), '"I Say Halt!" Britain Must Not Become Merely a Part of Europe', *Sunday Express*, 4 February.
Atwood, Margaret (1972), *Survival: A Thematic Guide to Canadian Literature*, Toronto: House of Anansi.
Baggini, Julian (2012), 'Why the White Cliffs of Dover Are So Special', *The Guardian*, 19 August. Available at: https://www.theguardian.com/commentisfree/2012/aug/19/white-cliffs-of-dover.
Bakalar, A. M. (2016), 'Woman of Your Dreams', *BBC Radio 4*, 4 September. Available at: https://www.bbc.co.uk/programmes/b06810q7.
Baker, Timothy C. (2016), 'Writing Scotland's Future: Speculative Fiction and the National Imagination', *Studies in Scottish Literature* 42 (2): 248–66.
Barber, Michael (1975), 'The Art of Fiction LIX: Kingsley Amis', *Paris Review*, 64. Available at: https://www.theparisreview.org/interviews/3772/the-art-of-fiction-no-59-kingsley-amis.
Barnes, Julian (2002), *Something to Declare*, London: Picador.
Barnes, Julian (2017), 'Diary: People Will Hate Us Again', *LRB*, 20 April. Available at: https://www.lrb.co.uk/the-paper/v39/n08/julian-barnes/diary.
Barnett, Anthony (2017), *The Lure of Greatness*, London: Unbound.
Bassnett, Susan (1996), 'The Myth of the English Hero', in Marialuisa Bignami and Caroline Patey (eds), *Moving the Borders*, 337–48, Milan: Unicopli.
Baucom, Ian (1999), *Out of Place: Englishness, Empire, and the Locations of Identity*, Princeton: Princeton University Press.

Bauman, Zygmunt (2016), 'Behind the World's "Crisis of Humanity"', *Aljazeera*, 23 July. Available at: https://www.aljazeera.com/programmes/talktojazeera/2016/07/zygmunt-bauman-world-crisis-humanity-160722085342260.html.
Beaumont, Paul (2016), 'What the Euros 2016 Football Fan Violence Tells Us About Tribalism in Europe – and Anger in the Brexit Debate', *Independent*, 15 June. Available at: https://www.independent.co.uk/voices/football-violence-euro-2016-france-marseille-brexit-tribalism-eu-referendum-a7083171.html.
Beck, Ulrich (2002), 'The Cosmopolitan Society and Its Enemies', *Theory, Culture & Society* 19 (1–2): 17–44.
Beck, Ulrich and Edgar Grande (2007), *Cosmopolitan Europe*, Cambridge: Polity Press.
Beckett, Samuel ([1952] 2006), *Waiting for Godot*, London: Faber & Faber.
Beer, Gillian (2013), 'Gillian Beer Interviews Ali Smith', in Monica Germana and Emily Horton (eds), *Ali Smith: Contemporary Critical Perspectives*, 137–53, London: Bloomsbury.
Begum, Neema (2018), 'Minority Ethnic Attitudes and the 2016 EU Referendum', *The UK in a Changing Europe*, 6 February. Available at: https://ukandeu.ac.uk/minority-ethnic-attitudes-and-the-2016-eu-referendum/.
Bella Caledonia (2018), 'Hands Off Devolution: An Open Letter to Theresa May', *Bella Caledonia*, 6 April. Available at: https://bellacaledonia.org.uk/2018/04/06/hands-off-devolution-an-open-letter-to-theresa-may/.
Benn, Tony (1975), Parliamentary Speech, 18 March.
Bennett, Gill (2013), *Six Moments of Crisis: Inside British Foreign Policy*, Oxford: Oxford University Press.
Bentley, Nick (2007), *Radical Fictions: The English Novel in the 1950s*, Oxford: Peter Lang.
Bentley, Nick (2015), 'Rewriting National Identities in 1990s British Fiction', in Nick Hubble, Philip Tew and Leigh Wilson (eds), *The 1990s: A Decade of Contemporary British Fiction*, 67–94, London: Bloomsbury.
Bergonzi, Bernard (1970), *The Situation of the Novel*, Basingstoke: Macmillan.
Berlant, Lauren (1989), 'America, Post-Utopia: Body, Landscape, and National Fantasy', *Arizona Quarterly* 44 (4): 14–54.
Berlant, Lauren (1991), *The Anatomy of National Fantasy: Hawthorn, Utopia, and Everyday Life*, Chicago: University of Chicago Press.
Berlant, Lauren (2011), *Cruel Optimism*, Durham, NC: Duke University Press.
Bhabha, Homi K. (1990), 'Introduction: Narrating the Nation', in Homi K. Bhabha (ed.), *Nation and Narration*, 1–7, London: Routledge.
Bhabha, Homi K. (1992), 'Double Visions', *Artforum*, January: 82–90.
Bischoff, Lisa (2020), 'The Dystopian Nightmare of a European Superstate: British Fiction and the EU', in Ina Habermann (ed.), *The Road to Brexit: A Cultural Perspective on British Attitudes to Europe*, 143–61, Manchester: Manchester University Press.
Bissett, Alan (2015), 'Scotland's No Vote Has Forced Its Artists to Rediscover Ambiguity', *The Guardian*, 15 October. Available at: https://www.theguardian.com/commentisfree/2015/oct/15/scotland-no-vote-artists.
Black, Jeremy (2018), *English Nationalism: A Short History*, London: Hurst & Company.
Black, Jeremy (2019), *Britain and Europe: A Short History*, London: Hurst & Company.
Blair, Tony (2000), 'Speech to the Polish Stock Exchange', 6 October. Available at: www.number10.gov.uk.
Blair, Tony (2002), 'PM: A Clear Course for Europe, Cardiff', 28 November. Available at: nationalarchives.gov.uk.

Board, Douglas (2017b), 'Rotherhithe-Based Author Pens Political Satire Based in Bermondsey', *Southwark News*, 22 June. Available at: https://www.southwarknews.co.uk/news/rotherhithe-based-author-pens-political-satire-based-bermondsey/.
Bogdanor, Vernon (1997), 'Sceptred Isle – or Isles?', *Times Literary Supplement*, 27 September.
Bogdanor, Vernon (1999), *Devolution in the United Kingdom*, Oxford: Oxford University Press.
Bogdanor, Vernon (2019), *Beyond Brexit: Towards a British Constitution*, London: I. B. Tauris.
Borbely, Carmen-Victoria (2016), 'The Monster as a Placeholder of the Memory/Oblivion Divide in Ishiguro's *The Buried Giant*', in Petronia Petrar and Amelia Precup (eds), *Constructions of Identity VIII*, 23–32, Cluj-Napoca: Presa Universitara Clujeana.
Boxall, Peter (2015), *The Value of the Novel*, New York: Cambridge University Press.
Boyle, Danny (2012), 'Boyle Reveals Opening Ceremony', *The Telegraph*, 12 June. Available at: https://www.telegraph.co.uk/sport/olympics/olympicsvideo/9326706/London-2012-Olympics-Opening-Ceremony-details-revealed.html.
Bradbury, Malcolm (1991a), 'Frontiers of the Imagination', *The Guardian*, 15 December.
Bradbury, Malcolm (1991b), 'All Aboard for the New Europe', *The New York Times*, 3 February. Available at: https://www.nytimes.com/1991/02/03/magazine/all-aboard-for-the-new-europe.html.
Bradbury, Malcolm (1991c), The Gravy Train Goes East. October. Channel 4.
Bradbury, Malcolm (1994), 'New Rates of Exchange: British Fiction and Britain Today', in Ludmilla Kostova et al. (eds), *Britain and Europe*, 21–30, Sofia: Petrikov Publishers.
Bradbury, Malcolm (1995), *Dangerous Pilgrimages: Transatlantic Mythologies and the Novel*, London: Penguin.
Bragg, Billy (2017), [Song] Full English Brexit, Street Level Studios III, London.
Brannigan, John (2014), *Archipelagic Modernism: Literature in the Irish and British Isles, 1890–1970*, Edinburgh: Edinburgh University Press.
Breinlich, Holger, Elsa Leromain, Dennis Novy and Thomas Sampson (2017), 'The Brexit Vote, Inflation and UK Living Standards', *The UK in a Changing Europe*, 1–15.
Brennan, Timothy (1990), 'The National Longing for Form', in Homi K. Bhabha, *Nation and Narration*, 44–70, London: Routledge.
British Future (2013), 'England, My England: A Festival of Englishness', *IPPR*, 11 October. Available at: http://www.britishfuture.org/articles/festival-of-englishness-explores-our-national-identity/.
Brown, Gordon (2007), Green Paper, The Governance of Britain, HMSO, 1–63.
Brown, Gordon (2016), 'Jo Cox's Legacy Should be an End to the Downward Spiral in our Politics', *The Guardian*, 17 June. Available at: https://www.theguardian.com/commentisfree/2016/jun/17/jo-cox-legacy-end-downward-spiral-political-culture-tackling-prejudice-intolerance.
Brown, Gordon (2017), *My Life, Our Times*, London: Bodley Head.
Brown, Wendy (2010), *Waning Sovereignty*, New York: Zone.
Bryant, Arthur ([1940] 2001), *English Saga: 1840–1940*, London: House of Stratus.
Buckledee, Steve (2018), *The Language of Brexit: How Britain Talked Its Way Out of the European Union*, London: Bloomsbury.
Bukowski, Charles (1972), *Mockingbird Wish Me Luck*, Santa Barbara, CA: Black Sparrow Press.
Bunting, Madeleine (2016), *Love of Country: A Hebridean Journey*, London: Granta.
Burgess, Anthony (1966), 'Here Parla Man Marcommunish', *Spectator*, 25 November, 674–5.

Burns, Anna (2018b), '"I've Been Homeless Myself: You Start Thinking, I'm Not Entitled": Novelist Anna Burns on Winning the Booker Prize', *The New Statesman*, 24 October. Available at: https://www.newstatesman.com/culture/books/2018/10/i-ve-been-homeless-myself-you-start-thinking-i-m-not-entitled-novelist-anna.

Bush, Stephen (2019), 'David Cameron's Downfall', *The New Statesman*, 25 September. Available at: https://www.newstatesman.com/culture/books/2019/09/david-cameron-s-downfall

Butterworth, Jez (2011), 'Playwright Jez Butterworth on Jerusalem, England and Englishness', *The Guardian*. Available at: https://www.youtube.com/watch?v=efbHIyk4Nx0.

Butterworth, Jez (2017b), 'Jez Butterworth and Sam Mendes on The Ferryman, Front Row', *BBC Radio 4*, 22 June.

Cabinet Office (2007), *Security in a Global Hub: Establishing the UK's New Border Arrangements*, London: Cabinet Office.

Calhoun, Craig (2007), *Nations Matter: Culture, History, and the Cosmopolitan Dream*, London: Routledge.

Cameron, David (2011), Munich Security Conference, 5 February. Available at: https://www.gov.uk/government/speeches/pms-speech-at-munich-security-conference.

Cameron, David (2013), *Speech on the Future of Europe*, London: Bloomberg, 23 January.

Cameron, David (2015), 'Interview'. *ITV News*, 30 July.

Campbell, Siobhán (2017), *Heat Signature*. Bridgend: Seren.

Carey Sean (2002), 'Undivided Loyalties: Is National Identity an Obstacle to European Integration?' *European Union Politics* 3 (4): 387–413.

Carr, Garrett (2017), *The Rule of the Land: Walking Ireland's Border*, London: Faber & Faber.

Carroll, Roy (2018), 'Karen Bradley Admits Ignorance of Northern Irish Politics', *The Guardian*, 7 September. Available at: https://www.theguardian.com/politics/2018/sep/07/karen-bradley-admits-not-understanding-northern-irish-politics.

Castro-Martín, T. and C. Cortina (2015), 'Demographic Issues of Intra-European Migration: Destinations, Family and Settlement', *European Journal of Population* 31 (2): 109–25.

Cecil, Nicholas (2016), Brexit Poll: '11 Per Cent of People Want London to Become a Separate Country', *Evening Standard*, 11 July. Available at: https://www.standard.co.uk/news/politics/eleven-per-cent-of-people-want-london-to-become-a-separate-country-after-brexit-vote-a3292701.html.

Centre for Cross Border Studies (2016), 'The UK Referendum on Membership of the EU: Citizen Mobility', EU Referendum Briefing Papers, Briefing Paper 4.

Chakelian, Anoosh (2017), 'Chris Patten Says Theresa May is Creating "Millwall" Britain', *The Guardian*, 30 March. Available at: https://www.newstatesman.com/politics/uk/2017/03/chris-patten-says-theresa-may-creating-millwall-britain-no-one-likes-us-we-don-t.

Chakrabortty, Aditya (2016), 'Burning Anger in the Land of Nye Bevan: Why a Labour Heartland is Backing Brexit', *The Guardian*, 7 June. Available at: https://www.theguardian.com/politics/2016/jun/07/nye-bevan-labour-heartland-backing-brexit-south-wales.

Chaney, Paul (2017), 'Europe, Brexit and Welfare: Why Minority Nationalist Parties' Views Matter', Cardiff University, 16 May. Available at: https://blogs.cardiff.ac.uk/brexit/2017/05/16/europe-brexit-and-welfare-why-minority-nationalist-parties-views-matter/.

Cheah, Pheng (2008), 'What Is a World? On World Literature as World-Making Activity', *Daedalus* 137 (3): 6–38.

Churchill, Winston (1950), 'Conservative Mass Meeting: A Speech at Llandudno', 9 October 1948, in *Europe Unite: Speeches 1947 & 1948*, London: Cassell.

Ciesla, Robert (2006), 'The Sharp Edge: John King Interviewed by Robert Ciesla', 6 November. Available at: http://laurahird.com/newreview/johnkingreview.html.

Clarke, Harold D. (2017), *Brexit: Why Britain Voted to Leave the European Union*, Cambridge: Cambridge University Press.

Cleese, John and Connie Booth (1975), [TV programme] 'The Germans', *Fawlty Towers*, Series 1 Episode 6, BBC1, 24 October.

Coe, Jonathan (2019), 'The Brexit Referendum Tells the Story of the Radicalisation of Middle England', *The New Statesman*, 29 March. Available at: https://www.newstatesman.com/politics/brexit/2019/03/brexit-referendum-tells-story-radicalisation-middle-england.

Colley, Linda (2014), *Acts of Union and Disunion*, London: Profile.

Connelly, Tony (2018a), *Brexit and Ireland: The Dangers, the Opportunities, and the Inside Story of the Irish Response*, London: Penguin.

Connelly, Tony (2018b), 'Has Brexit Reopened Old Wounds on Both Sides of the Irish Border', *The New Statesman*, 16 January. Available at: https://www.newstatesman.com/2018/01/how-brexit-has-reopened-old-wounds-both-sides-irish-border.

Conservative Party (2010), 'Invitation to Join the Government of Britain', Election Manifesto.

Cook, Robin (2000), 'Stronghold at the Heart of Europe: Supporting the EU Should Be the Natural Reaction of Patriotic British Citizens', *Financial Times*, 13 November.

Cowley, Jason (2016), 'Michael Sandel: "The Energy of the Brexiteers and Trump is Born of the Failures of Elites"', *The New Statesman*, 13 June. Available at: https://www.newstatesman.com/politics/uk/2016/06/michael-sandel-energy-brexiteers-and-trump-born-failure-elites.

Crawford, Robert ([1982] 2000), *Devolving English Literature*, 2nd edn, Edinburgh: Edinburgh University Press.

Creative Industries Federation (2016), EU Referendum Response, 8 June. Available at: https://www.creativeindustriesfederation.com/news/federation-eu-referendum-response.

Crumbie, Alex (2018), 'Anthony Burgess, Europe and Brexit', The International Anthony Burgess Foundation, 7 September. Available at: https://www.anthonyburgess.org/blog-posts/anthony-burgess-europe-brexit/.

Curtice, John (2016), 'Why Did Scotland Vote to Remain', *The UK in a Changing Europe*, 24 October. Available at: https://ukandeu.ac.uk/why-did-scotland-vote-to-remain/.

Curtice, John (2018), 'Polls Reveal Many Scottish Independence Voters Happy in the UK', *Scotsman*, 20 November. Available at: https://www.scotsman.com/news/politics/john-curtice-poll-reveals-many-scottish-independence-voters-happy-uk-208996.

Curtice, John and Anthony Heath (2009), 'England Awakes? Trends in National Identity in England', in Frank Bechhofer and David McCrone (eds), *National Identity, Nationalism and Constitutional Change*, 41–63, Basingstoke: Palgrave Macmillan.

Dahlgreen, Will (2016), 'Rhodes Must Not Fall', *YouGov*, 18 January. Available at: https://yougov.co.uk/topics/politics/articles-reports/2016/01/18/rhodes-must-not-fall.

Daily Mail (2016), 'Who WILL Speak for England?', *Daily Mail*, 4 February. Available at: https://www.dailymail.co.uk/debate/article-3430870/DAILY-MAIL-COMMENT-speak-England.html.

Dallison, Paul (2019), 'Donald Trump Jnr: "Brexit and My Father's Election Are One and the Same"', *Politico*, 19 March. Available at: https://www.politico.eu/article/donald-trump-jr-brexit-election-comparison/.

Dardanelli, P. (2003), Ideology and Rationality: The Europeanization of the Scottish National Party, 8th EUSA International Conference, Nashville, USA, 27–29 March.
Datta, Ayona and Katherine Brickell (2009), '"We Have a Little Bit More Finesse, as a Nation": Constructing the Polish Worker in London's Building Sites', *Antipode: A Radical Journal of Geography* 41 (3): 439–64.
Davey, Kevin (1999), *English Imaginaries: Six Studies in Anglo-British Modernity*, London: Lawrence & Wishart.
Davies, Thom et al. (2017), 'Violent Inaction: The Necropolitical Experience of Refugees in Europe', *Antipode* 49 (5): 1–22.
Davies, William (2017), 'What Is "Neo" About Neoliberalism?', *New Republic*, 13 July. Available at: https://newrepublic.com/article/143849/neo-neoliberalism.
Davies, William (2020), 'The Great British Battle: How the Fight Against Coronavirus Spread a New Nationalism', *The Guardian*, 16 May.
de Carmoy, Guy (1971), Britain and the Common Market, The European Institute of Business Administration.
de Gaulle, Charles (1963), Press Conference, 14 January.
de Vries, Catherine E. (2018), *Euroscepticism and the Future of European Integration*, Oxford: Oxford University Press.
Deacon, Russell and Alan Sandry (2007), *Devolution in the United Kingdom*, Edinburgh: Edinburgh University Press.
Dennison, James and Matthew Goodwin (2015), 'Immigration, Issue Ownership and the Rise of UKIP', *Parliamentary Affairs* 68 (1): 168–89.
Denny, Neill (2019), 'London Book Fair: Ian McEwan Leads Writers Against Brexit', *Publisher's Weekly*, 13 March. Available at: https://www.publishersweekly.com/pw/by-topic/international/london-book-fair/article/79512-london-book-fair-2019-ian-mcewan-leads-writers-against-brexit.html.
Dewey, Robert F. (2009), *British National Identity and Opposition to Membership of Europe, 1961–63: The Anti-Marketeers*, Manchester: Manchester University Press.
Dinan, Desmond (1999), *Ever Closer Union: An Introduction to European Integration*, 2nd edn, Basingstoke: Palgrave.
Dix, Hywel (2013), 'Devolution and Cultural Catch-Up: Decoupling England and Its Literature from English Literature', in Clare Westall and Michael Gardiner (eds), *Literature of an Independent England: Revisions of England, Englishness and English Literature*, 188–201, London: Palgrave.
Docherty, Thomas (2018), 'Brexit: Thinking and Resistance', in Robert Eaglestone (ed.), *Brexit and Literature: Critical and Cultural Responses*, 181–95, London: Routledge.
Domínguez, César and Theo D'haen (2015), *Cosmopolitanism and the Postnational: Literature and the New Europe*, Leiden: Brill Rodopi.
Dorling, Danny and Sally Tomlinson (2017), *Rule Britannia: Brexit and the End of Empire*, London: Biteback Publishing.
Drabble, Margaret (1995), *Angus Wilson: A Biography*, London: Secker & Warburg.
Drabble, Margaret, ed. (2006), *The Oxford Companion to Literature*, Fifth edn, Oxford: Oxford University Press.
Duffy, Carol Ann (2016), 'Poets on Tour: "The UK has been Torn in Two Like a Bad Poem"', *The Guardian*, 24 June. Available at: https://www.theguardian.com/books/2016/jun/24/poets-on-tour-part-five-carol-ann-duffy.
Eade, John, Stephen Drinkwater and Michal Garapich (2006), 'Class and Ethnicity: Polish Migrants in London', Research report for the ESRC, University of Surrey. Available

at: http://www.surrey.ac.uk/Arts/CRONEM/polish/POLISH_FINAL_RESEARCH_R EPORT_WEB.pdf.

Eaglestone, Robert (2018), 'Cruel Nostalgia and the Memory of the Second World War', in Robert Eaglestone (ed.), *Brexit and Literature: Critical and Cultural Responses*, 92–104, London: Routledge.

Eagleton, Terry ([1983] 2008), *Literary Theory: An Introduction*, Minneapolis: University of Minnesota Press.

Easton, Mark (2018), 'The English Question: What Is the Nation's Identity?', *BBC*, 3 June. Available at: https://www.bbc.co.uk/news/uk-44306737.

El-Enany, Nadine (2017), 'Things Fall Apart: From Empire to Brexit Britain', *IPR*, 2 May. Available at: http://blogs.bath.ac.uk/iprblog/2017/05/02/things-fall-apart-from-empire-to-brexit-britain/.

Elgot (2016), 'JK Rowling Condemns "Ugly" Rhetoric of EU Referendum Campaign', *The Guardian*, 20 June. Available at: https://www.theguardian.com/books/2016/jun/20/jk-r owling-eu-referendum-campaign.

Elkins, Amy E. (2019), 'Has Art Anything to Do with Life?: A Conversation with Ali Smith on "*Spring*"', *Los Angeles Review of Books*, 3 September. Available at: https://la reviewofbooks.org/article/has-art-anything-to-do-with-life-a-conversation-with-ali -smith-on-spring/.

Encounter, Going into Europe I, December 1962, 56–65.

Encounter, Going into Europe II, January 1963, 53–64.

Encounter, Going into Europe – Again? A Symposium, June 1971, 3–17.

Enright, D. J., ed. (1955), *Poets of the 1950's: An Anthology of New English Verse*, Tokyo: Kenyusha Ltd.

Eriksen, T. H. (2015), 'Rebuilding the Ship at Sea: Super-Diversity, Person and Conduct in Eastern Oslo', *Global Networks* 15 (1): 1–20.

Etheridge, Bill (2014), *The Rise of UKIP*, Epsom, Surrey: Bretwalda Books.

European Commission (1997), *Our Cultural and Architectural Heritage*, London.

European Commission (2003), 'European Citizens and Freedom, Security and Justice: Qualitative Survey of Citizens of the 15 Member States and the 13 Applicant Countries'. Available at: europa.eu.int/comm/justice_home/doc_centre/intro/docs/eurobaro_qu alitatif_ en.pdf.

European Commission (2007), 'Attitudes Towards the EU in the United Kingdom', Flash Eurobarometer. Available at: https://ec.europa.eu/commfrontoffice/publicopinion/flas h/fl_318_en.pdf.

European Parliament (2015), 7 October. Available at: www.europarl.europa.eu/sides/g etDoc.do?pubRef=//EP//TEXT+CRE+20151007+ITEM013+DOC+XML+V0//EN.

Evans, Daniel John (2018), 'Welsh Devolution as Passive Revolution', *Capital & Class* 42 (3): 489–508.

Evans, Geoffrey and Anand Menon (2017), *Brexit and British Politics*, Cambridge: Polity Press.

Evans, Geoffrey and James Tilley (2017), *The New Politics of Class: The Political Exclusion of the British Working Class*, Oxford: Oxford University Press.

Evaristo, Bernardine (2018), 'Broken Identity', *TLS*, 2 February. Available at: https://www .the-tls.co.uk/articles/broken-identity-afua-hirsch-british/.

Farage, Nigel (2013), Speech to the Party Conference, 20 September.

Farage, Nigel (2016), 'Nigel Farage Says Leave Win Marks UK Independence Day', *BBC*, 24 June, Available at: https://www.bbc.co.uk/news/uk-politics-eu-referendum-36 613238.

Faulkner, Peter (1980), *Angus Wilson: Mimic and Moralist*, London: Secker & Warburg.
Fenton, Siobhan (2018), *The Good Friday Agreement*, London: Biteback Publishing.
Ferguson, Donna (2019), 'From Epic Myths to Rural Fables, How Our National Turmoil Created "Brexlit"', *The Guardian*, 27 October. Available at: https://www.theguardian.com/books/2019/oct/27/brexlit-new-literary-genre-political-turmoil-myths-fables.
Ferguson, Niall (2004), 'Eurabia?', *New York Times*, 4 April. Available at: https://www.nytimes.com/2004/04/04/magazine/the-way-we-live-now-4-4-04-eurabia.html.
Ferriter, Diarmaid (2019), *The Border: The Legacy of a Century of Anglo-Irish Politics*, London: Profile.
Fetzer, Thiemo (2018), 'Did Austerity Cause Brexit?' Warwick Economics Research Papers Series 1170 (Unpublished). Available at: https://warwick.ac.uk/fac/soc/economics/research/workingpapers/2018/twerp_1170_fetzer.pdf.
Fisher, Mark (2009), *Capitalist Realism: Is There No Alternative?*, Winchester: Zero Books.
Fisher, Mark (2014), *Ghosts of My Life: Writings on Depression, Hauntology and Lost Futures*, Winchester: Zero Books.
Fitzgibbon, John (2015), 'Eurosceptic Civil Society', in Karine Tournier-Sol and Chris Gifford (eds), *The UK Challenge to Europeanization: The Persistence of British Euroscepticism*, 172–90, Basingstoke: Palgrave Macmillan.
Flood, Alison (2019), 'John le Carré and Neil Gaiman Join Writers Warning Brexit is "Choosing to Lose"', *The Guardian*, 21 May. Available at: https://www.theguardian.com/books/2019/may/21/john-le-carre-and-neil-gaiman-join-writers-warning-brexit-is-choosing-to-lose.
Ford, Robert and Matthew Goodwin (2014), *Revolt on the Right: Explaining Support for the Radical Right in Britain*, London: Routledge.
Forster, Anthony (2002), *Euroscepticism in Contemporary British Politics: Opposition to Europe in the British Conservative and Labour Parties Since 1945*, London: Routledge.
Foster, Nigel G. (2002), *EC Legislation 2002–2003*, Oxford: Oxford University Press.
Fowles, John ([1964] 1998), 'On Being English but Not British', in Jan Relf (ed.), *Wormholes: Essays and Occasional Writings*, 79–88, New York: Holt.
Freedland, Jonathan (2016a), 'Post-Truth Politicians Such as Donald Trump and Boris Johnson are No Joke', *The Guardian*, 13 May. Available at: https://www.theguardian.com/commentisfree/2016/may/13/boris-johnson-donald-trump-post-truth-politician.
Freedland, Jonathan (2016b), 'A Warning to Gove and Johnson – We Won't Forget What You Did', *The Guardian*, 2 July. Available at: https://www.theguardian.com/commentisfree/2016/jul/01/boris-johnson-and-michael-gove-betrayed-britain-over-brexit.
Future of England Study (2018), Centre on Constitutional Change, 8 October. Available at: https://www.centreonconstitutionalchange.ac.uk/news_opinion/press-release-mays-precious-union-has-little-support-brexit-britain.
Gaitskell, Hugh (1962), Annual Labour Party Conference, 3 October.
Gallup, George H. (1976), *The Gallup International Public Opinion Polls: Great Britain 1937–1975*, New York: Random House.
Gambaudo, Sylvie (1999), 'Europeans: Foreigners in their Own Land', in Susanne Fendler and Ruth Wittlinger (eds), *The Idea of Europe in Literature*, 225–39, London: Palgrave Macmillan.
Gamble, Andrew (1998), 'The European Issue in British Politics', in David Baker and David Seawright (eds), *Britain For and Against Europe*, 11–30, Oxford: Clarendon Press.
Ganteau, Jean-Michel (2018), 'Diffracted Landscapes of Attention: John McGregor's *Reservoir 13*', *Études britanniques contemporaines*, 55.

Gardiner, Michael (2004), *The Cultural Roots of British Devolution*, Edinburgh: Edinburgh University Press.
Gardiner, Michael (2005), *Modern Scottish Culture*, Edinburgh: Edinburgh University Press.
Gardiner, Michael (2007), 'Literature, Theory, Politics: Devolution as Iteration', in Berthold Schoene (ed.), *The Edinburgh Companion to Contemporary Scottish Literature*, 143–50, Edinburgh: Edinburgh University Press.
Gardiner, Michael (2009), 'Arcades – the 1980s and 1990s', in Ian Brown and Alan Riach (eds), *The Edinburgh Companion to Twentieth-Century Scottish Literature*, 181–93, Edinburgh: Edinburgh University Press.
Gardiner, Michael (2012), *The Return of England in English Literature*, Basingstoke: Palgrave Macmillan.
Gardiner, Michael (2018), 'Brexit and the Aesthetics of Anachronism', in Robert Eaglestone (ed.), *Brexit and Literature: Critical and Cultural Responses*, 105–17, London: Routledge.
Gardner, Philip (1981), *Kingsley Amis*, New York: Twayne Publishers.
Garry, John (2016), 'The EU Referendum Vote in Northern Ireland: Implications for our Understanding of Citizens' Political Views and Behaviour', Northern Ireland Assembly, Knowledge Exchange Seminar Series.
Geddes, Andrew (2005) 'Europe', in Kevin Hickson (ed.), *The Political Thought of the Conservative Party since 1945*, 113–32, Basingstoke: Palgrave Macmillan.
Geddes, Andrew (2013), *Britain and the European Union*, London: Palgrave Macmillan.
George, Stephen (1998), *An Awkward Partner: Britain in the European Community*, Oxford: Oxford University Press.
Gibson, Robert (2011), *Best of Enemies: Anglo-French Relations Since the Norman Conquest*, Exeter: Impress.
Gifford, Douglas (2007), 'Breaking Boundaries: From Modern to Contemporary in Scottish Fiction', in Ian Brown (ed.), *The Edinburgh History of Scottish Literature, Vol III: Modern Transformations, New Identities (from 1918)*, 237–52, Edinburgh: Edinburgh University Press.
Gildea, Robert (2019), *Empires of the Mind: The Colonial Past and the Politics of the Present*, Cambridge: Cambridge University Press.
Gillingham, John (2018), *The EU: An Obituary*, London: Verso.
Gilroy, Paul (2004), *After Empire: Melancholia or Convivial Culture?*, London: Routledge.
Gilroy, Paul (2005), *Postcolonial Melancholia*, New York: Columbia University Press.
Gilroy, Paul (2013), 'Postcolonialism and Cosmopolitanism: Towards a Worldly Understanding of Fascism and Europe's Colonial Crimes', in Rosi Braidotti, Patrick Hanafin and B. Blaagaard (eds), *After Cosmopolitanism*, 111–31, Oxford: Routledge.
Gindin, James (1962), *Postwar British Fiction: New Accents and Attitudes*, Cambridge: Cambridge University Press.
Glencross, Andrew (2016), *Why the UK Voted for Brexit: David Cameron's Great Miscalculation*, London: Palgrave.
Goldfarb, Michael (2019), 'Brexit has been Driven by England's Nostalgia for an Imagined Past', *The National*, 4 February. Available at: https://www.thenational.ae/opinion/comment/brexit-has-been-driven-by-england-s-nostalgia-for-an-imagined-past-1.821625.
Goodhart, David (2017), *The Road to Somewhere: The Populist Revolt and the Future of Politics*, London: Hurst & Company.

Goodwin, Matthew (2018), 'Britain's Populist Revolt', *Quillette*, 3 August. Available at: https://quillette.com/2018/08/03/britains-populist-revolt/.

Goodwin, Matthew and Oliver Heath (2016a), 'The 2016 Referendum, Brexit and the Left Behind: An Aggregate-level Analysis of the Result', *Political Quarterly* 83 (3): 323–32.

Goodwin, Matthew and Oliver Heath (2016b), 'Brexit Vote Explained: Poverty, Low Skills and Lack of Opportunities', 31 August, Joseph Rowntree Foundation. Available at: https://www.jrf.org.uk/report/brexit-vote-explained-poverty-low-skills-and-lack-oppor tunities.

Goodwin, Matthew and Caitlin Milazzo (2015), *UKIP: Inside the Campaign to Redraw the Map of British Politics*, Oxford: Oxford University.

Goodwin, Matthew and Caitlin Milazzo (2017), 'Taking Back Control: Investigating the Role of Immigration in the 2016 Vote for Brexit', *The British Journal of Politics and International Relations* 19 (3): 450–64.

Gowland, David and Arthur Turner (2000), *Reluctant Europeans: Britain and European Integration 1945–1998*, Essex: Longman.

Griffiths, Niall (2007), 'Wales: England's Oldest Colony', *The New Statesman*, 23 April. Available at: https://www.newstatesman.com/politics/2007/04/welsh-language-wales -england.

Grob-Fitzgibbon, Benjamin (2016), *Continental Drift: Britain and Europe from the End of Empire to the Rise of Euroscepticism*, Cambridge: Cambridge University Press.

Gui, Weihsin (2015), 'Transnational Forms in British Fiction', in David James (ed.), *The Cambridge Companion to British Fiction Since 1945*, 224–38, Cambridge: Cambridge University Press.

Haffenden, John (1985), *Novelists in Interview*, London: Methuen.

Hague, William (1999), Identity and the British Way, Speech to the Centre for Policy Studies, 19 January.

Hames, Scott, ed. (2012), *Unstated: Writers on Scottish Independence*, Edinburgh: Word Power.

Hames, Scott (2019), *The Literary Politics of Scottish Devolution: Voice, Class, Nation*, Edinburgh: Edinburgh University Press.

Hamid, Mohsin (2017), 'There's a Real Fear of the Future Right Now', *The Irish Times*, 11 March. Available at: https://www.irishtimes.com/culture/books/mohsin-hamid-t here-s-a-real-fear-of-the-future-right-now-1.3002735.

Hammond, Andrew (2016), *The Novel and Europe: Imagining the Continent in Post-1945 Fiction*, London: Palgrave Macmillan.

Hammond, Andrew (2017), 'The Reluctant Europeans: British Novelists and the Common Market', *Literature and History* 26 (2): 213–30.

Harris, John (2016), 'Britain is in the Midst of a Working-Class Revolt', *The Guardian*, 17 June. Available at: https://www.theguardian.com/commentisfree/2016/jun/17/britai n-working-class-revolt-eu-referendum.

Harrison, Melissa (2019), 'Harrison Wins EU Prize for Literature', *The Bookseller*, 23 May. Available at: https://www.thebookseller.com/news/harrison-triumphs-uk-winner-eu -prize-literature-1011041.

Haseler, Stephen (1996), *The English Tribe: Identity, Nation and Europe*, Basingstoke: Palgrave Macmillan.

Hassan, Gerry and Russell Gunson, eds (2017), *Scotland, the UK and Brexit: A Guide to the Future*, Edinburgh: Luath Press.

Hastings, Selina (1986), *Nancy Mitford: A Biography*, London: Papermac.

Hawes, James (2004), *Half Welsh*, London: Bloomsbury.

Hawkes, Steve (2017), 'PUT EU HANDS UP: Germany Wants Britain's Unconditional Surrender in Brexit Talks, Claims German Official', *The Sun*, 16 November. Available at: https://www.thesun.co.uk/news/4932392/angela-merkel-want-theresa-may-surrender-on-brexit/.

Head, Dominic (2002), *The Cambridge Introduction to Modern British Fiction, 1950–2000*, Cambridge: Cambridge University Press.

Heaney, Seamus (1980), 'Englands of the Mind', in Seamus Heaney, *Preoccupations: Selected Prose 1968–1978*, 150–69, London: Faber & Faber.

Heath, Edward (1998), *The Autobiography of Edward Heath: The Course of My Life*, London: Hodder and Stoughton.

Heidemann, Birte (2020), 'The Brexit Within: Mapping the Rural and the Urban in Contemporary British Fiction', *Journal of Postcolonial Writing* 56 (5): 676–88.

Hennig, Benjamin and Danny Dorling (2016), 'In Focus: The EU Referendum', *Political Insight*, September, 20–1.

Herrschaft-Iden, Marlene (2020), 'EU Enlargement and the Freedom of Movement: Imagined Communities in the Conservative Party's discourse on Europe (1997–2016)', in Ina Habermann (ed.), *The Road to Brexit: A Cultural Perspective on British Attitudes to Europe*, 69–86, Manchester: Manchester University Press.

Hewison, Robert (1987), *The Heritage Industry*, London: Methuen.

Higgins, Charlotte (2018), 'Fiction Is a Way of Telling the Truth', *The Guardian*, 21 August. Available at: https://www.theguardian.com/books/2019/mar/23/ali-smith-spring-young-generation-brexit-future.

Hirsch, Afua (2018), *Brit(ish): On Race, Identity and Belonging*, London: Vintage.

Hitchens, Peter (2018), *The Abolition of Britain: From Winston Churchill to Theresa May*, London: Bloomsbury.

Hobsbawm, Eric and Terence Ranger (1983), *The Invention of Tradition*, Cambridge: Cambridge University Press.

Hobsbawm, Eric J. (1992), *Nations and Nationalism since 1780: Programme, Myth, Reality*, Cambridge: Cambridge University Press.

Hogan, Jackie and Kristin Haltinner (2015), 'Floods, Parasites: Immigration Threat Narratives and Right-Wing Populism in the USA, UK and Australia', *Journal of Intercultural Studies* 36 (5): 520–43.

Hooghe, Liesbet and Gary Marks (2005), 'Calculation, Community and Cues: Public Opinion on European Integration', *European Union Politics* 6 (4): 419–43.

Hooghe, Liesbet and Gary Marks (2009), 'A Postfunctionalist Theory of European Integration: From Permissive Consensus to Constraining Dissensus', *British Journal of Political Science* 39 (1): 1–23.

Hoops, Joshua F., Ryan J. Thomas and Jolanta A. Drzewiecka (2016), 'Polish "Pawns" Between Nationalism and Neoliberalism in British Newspaper Coverage of Post-European Union Enlargement Polish Immigration', *Journalism: Theory, Practice & Criticism* 17 (6): 727–43.

Hopper, Paul (2007), *Understanding Cultural Globalization*, Cambridge: Polity Press.

Horne, A. (1989), *Macmillan, Vol. II 1957–1986*, New York: Viking.

Hubble, Nick (2018), 'Respectability, Nostalgia and Shame in Contemporary English Working-Class Fiction', in Ben Clarke and Nick Hubble (eds), *Working Class Writing: Theory and Practice*, 269–88, Cham: Palgrave Macmillan.

Hughes, Brian M. (2019), *The Psychology of Brexit: From Psychodrama to Behavioural Science*, Cham: Palgrave Macmillan.

Hughes, Michael (2018b), 'The Irish Border Question – Who's Going to Blink First?', *The Big Issue*, 15 August. Available at: https://www.bigissue.com/opinion/the-irish-border-question-whos-going-to-blink-first/.

Hughes, Michael (2018c), 'Where Do I Stand on Ireland? That's a Difficult Question', *The Guardian*, 22 July. Available at: https://www.theguardian.com/commentisfree/2018/jul/22/where-do-i-stand-ireland-difficult-question-border.

Hughes, Sarah (2019), 'These People are Trying to Live Their Lives – as Things Imperceptibly Become Darker', *inews*, 3 May. Available at: https://inews.co.uk/culture/books/linda-grant-brexit-novel-stranger-city-interview-287482.

Humphreys, Richard (2018), *Beyond the Border: The Good Friday Agreement and Irish Unity After Brexit*, Newbridge: Merrion Press.

Hunt, Jo and Rachel Minto (2017), 'Between Intergovernmental Relations and Paradiplomacy: Wales and the Brexit of the Regions', *The British Journal of Politics and International Relations* 19 (4): 647–62.

Hunt, Joanne, Rachael Minto and Jayne Woolford (2016), 'Winners and Losers: The EU Referendum Vote and Its Consequences for Wales', *Journal of Contemporary European Research* 12 (4): 824–34.

Hutcheon, Linda (2000), 'Irony, Nostalgia and the Postmodern', in Raymond Vervliet and Annemarie Estor (eds), *Methods for the Study of Literature as Cultural Memory*, 189–208, Amsterdam: Rodopi.

Hutchinson, John (2005) *Nations as Zones of Conflict*, London: Sage Publications.

Hutton, Clare (2019), 'The Moment and Technique of Milkman', *Essays in Criticism* 69 (3): 349–71.

Ibrahim, Yasmin and Anita Howarth (2018), 'Review of Humanitarian Refuge in the United Kingdom: Sanctuary, Asylum, and the Refugee Crisis', *Politics and Policy* 46 (3): 348–91.

Ingersoll, Earl G. and Mary C. Ingersoll (2008), *Conversations with Anthony Burgess*, Jackson: University Press of Mississippi.

Introna, Arianna (2020), 'Nationed Silences, Interventions and (Dis)Engagements: Brexit and the Politics of Contextualism in Post-Indyref Scottish Literature', *Open Library of Humanities* 6 (1): 12, 1–31.

IOM (2015), 'IOM and Unicef Data Brief: Migration of Children to Europe', 30 November. Available at: https://www.iom.int/sites/default/files/press_release/file/IOM-UNICEF-Data-Brief-Refugee-and-Migrant-Crisis-in-Europe-30.11.15.pdf.

IPPR (2013), 'Euroscepticism in England is English Not British', 8 July. Available at: https://www.ippr.org/news-and-media/press-releases/euroscepticism-in-england-is-english-not-british.

Ipsos MORI (2015), 'April 2015 Issues Index', *Ipsos MORI*. Available at: https://www.ipsos.com/ipsos-mori/en-uk/economistipsos-mori-april-2015-issues-index.aspx.

Ishiguro, Kazuo (2016), 'Kazuo Ishiguro on his Fears for Britain After Brexit', *Financial Times*, 1 July. Available at: https://www.ft.com/content/7877a0a6-3e11-11e6-9f2c-36b487ebd80a.

Ishiguro, Kazuo (2017), *My Twentieth-Century Evening and Other Small Breakthroughs: The Nobel Lecture*, London: Faber & Faber.

James, Andrew (2013), *Kingsley Amis: Antimodels and the Audience*, London: MQUP.

Jamieson, Sophie (2018), 'Brexit Vote was "Driven by Nostalgia" for a World Where "Faces were White", Sir Vince Cable Claims', *The Telegraph*, 11 March. Available at: https://www.telegraph.co.uk/politics/2018/03/11/brexit-vote-driven-nostalgia-world-faces-white-sir-vince-cable/.

Jennings, W., G. Stoker and I. Warren (2018), 'Towns, Cities and Brexit', *The UK in a Changing Europe*. Available at: https://ukandeu.ac.uk/towns-cities-and-brexit/.

Jessop, Bob (2017), 'The Organic Crisis of the British State: Putting Brexit in its Place', *Globalizations* 14 (1): 133–41.

Johnes, Martin (2019), 'Why Wales Needs to Talk About Independence', *Wales Online*, 8 March.

Johnson, Boris (2002a), 'If Blair's So Good at Running the Congo, Let Him Stay There', *The Telegraph*, 10 January. Available at: https://www.telegraph.co.uk/comment/personal-view/3571742/If-Blairs-so-good-at-running-the-Congo-let-him-stay-there.html.

Johnson, Boris (2002b), 'Africa Is a Mess, But We Can't Blame Colonialism', *The Spectator*, 2 February. Available at: https://www.spectator.co.uk/article/the-boris-archive-africa-is-a-mess-but-we-can-t-blame-colonialism.

Johnson, Boris (2002c), 'I'm No Longer Nasty, But Please Stop Lying About Nice', *The Telegraph*, 17 October. Available at: https://www.telegraph.co.uk/comment/personal-view/3582944/Im-no-longer-Nasty-but-please-stop-lying-about-Nice.html.

Johnson, Boris (2013), 'The Aussies are Just Like Us, So Let's Stop Kicking Them Out', *The Telegraph*, 25 August. Available at: https://www.telegraph.co.uk/news/politics/10265619/The-Aussies-are-just-like-us-so-lets-stop-kicking-them-out.html.

Johnson, Boris (2016), 'The EU Wants a Superstate, Just as Hitler did', *The Telegraph*, 15 May. Available at: https://www.telegraph.co.uk/news/2016/05/14/boris-johnson-the-eu-wants-a-superstate-just-as-hitler-did/.

Johnson, Boris (2018a), 'Brexit is not about Migration, it's about Who Calls the Shots', *The Telegraph*, 18 April. Available at: https://www.telegraph.co.uk/politics/2018/04/18/boris-johnson-brexit-not-migration-calls-shots/.

Johnson, Boris (2018b), 'The Rest of the World Believes in Britain: It's Time that We did too', *The Telegraph*, 15 July. Available at: https://www.telegraph.co.uk/politics/2018/07/15/rest-world-believes-britain-time-did/.

Johnson, Simon (2016), 'France: EU Will Not Help Nicola Sturgeon "Dismantle" the UK', *The Telegraph*, 1 July. Available at: https://www.telegraph.co.uk/news/2016/07/01/france-eu-will-not-help-nicola-sturgeon-dismantle-the-uk/.

Jones, David Martin (2020), 'Brexlit and the Decline of the English Novel', *The Critic*. Available at: https://thecritic.co.uk/issues/january-2020/brexlit-and-the-decline-of-the-english-novel/.

Jones, Moya (2017), 'Wales and the Brexit Vote', *French Journal of British Studies* XII-2: 1–10.

Jordan, William (2013), 'Immigration and Europe Key to UKIP Success', *YouGov*, 3 May. Available at: https://yougov.co.uk/topics/politics/articles-reports/2013/05/03/immigration-and-europe-give-ukip-appeal.

Judah, Ben (2016), 'England's Last Gasp of Empire', *New York Times*, 13 July. Available at: https://www.nytimes.com/2016/07/13/opinion/englands-last-gasp-of-empire.html.

Kaiser, Wolfram (1994), 'Using Europe and Abusing Europeans: The Conservatives and the European Community, 1957–1994', *Contemporary Record* 8 (2): 381–99.

Kaufmann, G. L. (2018), 'A Hard Fall'. Available at: https://www.ahardfall.uk/.

Kay, Jackie (2016), 'Poets on Tour: Reeling After the Referendum', *The Guardian*, 2 July. Available at: https://www.theguardian.com/books/booksblog/2016/jul/02/poets-tour-reeling-after-the-referendum.

Keating, Michael (2018), 'Brexit and Scotland', in Patrick Diamond, Peter Nedergaard and Ben Rosamond (eds), *The Routledge Handbook of the Politics of Brexit*, 40–8, London: Routledge.

Kellaway, Kate (2016), 'If I'm a Storyteller it's Because I Listen', *The Guardian*, 30 October. Available at: https://www.theguardian.com/books/2016/oct/30/john-berger-at-90-interview-storyteller.
Kennedy, Joe (2018), *Authentocrats: Culture, Politics and the New Seriousness*, Londoner: Repeater Books.
Kenny, Michael (2014), *The Politics of English Nationhood*, Oxford: Oxford University Press.
Kenny, Michael and Nick Pearce (2018), *Shadows of Empire: The Anglosphere in British Politics*, Cambridge: Polity Press.
King, John (2015), 'The Left Wing Case for leaving the EU', *The New Statesman*, 11 June. Available at: https://www.newstatesman.com/politics/2015/06/john-king-left-wing-case-leaving-eu.
King, John (2016b), 'The People Versus the Elite', *Penguin*, 17 May. Available at: https://www.penguin.co.uk/articles/2016/john-king-on-the-football-factory-20-years-on.
King, John (2018), 'The Old Stars', *Artists for Brexit*, 24 November. Available at: https://www.artistsforbrexit.com/single-post/2018/11/24/The-Old-Stars.
King, John (2019), 'John King on the Brexit Vote', *Artists for Brexit*, 3 March. Available at: https://www.artistsforbrexit.com/single-post/2019/03/03/The-Full-Brexit-Launch-of-the-Transforming-Britain-After-Brexit-Tour.
Kingsnorth, Paul (2009), *Real England: The Battle Against the Bland*, London: Portobello Books.
Kingsnorth, Paul (2015b), 'Rescuing the English', 13 March. Available at: http://paulkingsnorth.net/2015/03/13/rescuing-the-english/.
Kingsnorth, Paul (2016), 'Brexit and the Culture of Progress', 3 November. Available at: http://paulkingsnorth.net/2016/11/03/brexit-and-the-culture-of-progress/.
Kingsnorth, Paul (2017), 'The Lie of the Land: Does Environmentalism Have a Future in the Age of Trump?', *The Guardian*, 18 March. Available at: https://www.theguardian.com/books/2017/mar/18/the-new-lie-of-the-land-what-future-for-environmentalism-in-the-age-of-trump.
Kirchick, James (2017), *The End of Europe: Dictators, Demagogues, and the Coming Dark Age*, New Haven: Yale University Press.
Kirkup, James and Robert Winnett (2012), 'Theresa May Interview: 'We're Going to Give Illegal Migrants a Really Hostile Reception', *The Telegraph*, May 25. Available at: https://www.telegraph.co.uk/news/uknews/immigration/9291483/Theresa-May-interview-Were-going-to-give-illegal-migrants-a-really-hostile-reception.html.
Knight, Jonathan, Robin Niblett and Thomas Raines (2012), *Hard Choices Ahead: The Chatham House-YouGov Survey 2012 – British Attitudes towards the UK's International Priorities*, London: Royal Institute for International Affairs.
Korte, Barbara (2020), 'Glimpses of a Divided Kingdom in Zadie Smith's Short Stories of the 2010s', in Barbara Korte and Laura Lojo-Rodríguez (eds), *Borders and Border Crossings in the Contemporary British Short Story*, 21–38, Basingstoke: Palgrave Macmillan.
Krastev, Ivan (2017), *After Europe*, Philadelphia: University of Pennsylvania Press.
Kruger, Hans Christian (1998), Plenary Session of the Council for Cultural Co-operation, Council of Europe, 21 January.
Kumar, Krishan (2003), *The Making of English National Identity*, Cambridge: Cambridge University Press.
Kwarteng, Kwasi, Priti Patel, Dominic Raab, Chris Skidmore and Elizabeth Truss (2012), *Britannia Unchained: Global Lessons for Growth and Prosperity*, London: Palgrave Macmillan.

Kymlicka, Will (2010). 'Citizenship in an Era of Globalization', in G. Wallace Brown and David Held (eds), *The Cosmopolitan Reader*, 435–43, Cambridge: Polity Press.
Laing, Olivia (2016), 'It's a Pivotal Moment . . . A Question of What Happens Culturally When Something Is Built on a Lie', *The Guardian*, 16 October. Available at: https://www.theguardian.com/books/2016/oct/16/ali-smith-autumn-interview-how-can-we-live-ina-world-and-not-put-a-hand-across-a-divide-brexit-profu.
Laing, Olivia (2018b), 'Charlottesville, Brexit, and Trump: From News Cycle to Novel', *Literary Hub*. Available at: https://lithub.com/charlottesville-brexit-and-trump-from-news-cycle-to-novel/.
Lanchester, John (2012a), 'ArtsBeat: John Lanchester on *Capital*'. Available at: https://artsbeat.blogs.nytimes.com/2012/06/13/a-microcosm-of-london-john-lanchester-talks-about-capital/.
Lanchester, John (2012b), 'Open Book', *BBC Radio 4*, 26 February. Available at: https://www.bbc.co.uk/programmes/b01cj83r.
Lanchester, John (2016), 'Brexit Blues', *LRB*. Available at: https://www.lrb.co.uk/v38/n15/john-lanchester/brexit-blues.
Le Carré, John (2017b), 'John le Carré Likens Donald Trump to Rise of 1930s Fascism: "Something Seriously Bad is Happening"', *The Telegraph*, 8 September. Available at: https://www.telegraph.co.uk/books/authors/john-le-carre-likens-donald-trump-rise-1930s-fascismsomething/.
Le Carré, John (2020), 'John le Carré on Brexit: "It's Breaking My Heart"', *The Guardian*, 1 February. Available at: https://www.theguardian.com/books/2020/feb/01/john-le-carre-breaking-heart-brexit.
Leconte, Cécile (2010), *Understanding Euroscepticism*, Basingstoke: Palgrave Macmillan.
Lee, Stewart (2019), *March of the Lemmings: Brexit in Print and Performance 2016–2019*, London: Faber & Faber.
Leith, Murray Stewart and Daniel P. J. Soule (2012), *Political Discourse and National Identity in Scotland*, Edinburgh: Edinburgh University Press.
Lewycka, Marina (2018), 'Born in a Refugee Camp, I Came to Britain a Child in the 1950s – Here's What it was Like', *Huffington Post*, 19 June. Available at: https://www.huffingtonpost.co.uk/entry/refugee-week_uk_5b27dbe8e4b0f9178a9fbcb4.
Linkon, Sherry Lee (2014), 'Men Without Work: White Working-Class Masculinity in Deindustrialization Fiction', *Contemporary Literature* 55 (1): 148–67.
Linkon, Sherry Lee (2018), *The Half-Life of Deindustrialization: Working-Class Writing about Economic Restructuring*, Ann Arbour: University of Michigan Press.
Littler, J. and R. Naidoo (2004), 'White Past, Multicultural Present: Heritage and National Stories', in Helen Brocklehurst and Robert Phillips (eds), *History, Nationhood and the Question of Britain*, 330–41, Basingstoke: Palgrave Macmillan.
London (2012), Olympic Games Opening Ceremony Media Guide (2012), LOCOG.
Longley, Edna (1994), *The Living Stream: Literature & Revisionism in Ireland*, Newcastle upon Tyne: Bloodaxe Books.
Lubbers, Marcel (2008), 'Regarding the Dutch 'Nee' to the European Constitution: A Test of the Identity, Utilitarian and Political Approaches to Voting No'. *European Union Politics* 9 (1): 59–86.
Lusher, Adam (2016), 'Aberystwyth: Welcome to the Most Europhile Place in Britain', *Independent*, 5 March. Available at: https://www.independent.co.uk/news/uk/home-news/aberystwyth-welcome-to-the-most-europhile-place-in-britain-a6913001.html.

Lynskey, Dorian (2019), 'Let's Stop Pretending There are Two Sides to the Brexit Argument', *inews*, 25 September. Available at: https://inews.co.uk/culture/books/ian-mcewan-cockroach-interview-brexit-uk-publication-date-343206.
Macmillan, Harold (1962), Conservative Party Political Broadcast, 24 January.
MacShane, Denis (2019), *Brexiternity: The Uncertain Fate of Britain*, London: I. B. Tauris.
Maguire, Kevin (2016), 'Nigel Farage Wants Second Referendum If Remain Campaign Scrapes Narrow Win', *Mirror*, 16 May. Available at: https://www.mirror.co.uk/news/uk-news/nigel-farage-wants-second-referendum-7985017.
Mahon, Derek (1985), *Antarctica*, Dublin: Gallery Press.
Mair, Peter (2013), *Ruling the Void: The Hollowing of Western Democracy*, London: Verso.
Mance, Henry (2016), 'Britain has had Enough of Experts, Says Gove', *Financial Times*, 3 June. Available at: https://www.ft.com/content/3be49734-29cb-11e6-83e4-abc22d5d108c.
Marchese, David (2016), 'Alan Moore on Why Superhero Fans Need to Grow Up, Brexit, and His Massive New Novel', *Vulture*, 12 September, Available at: https://www.vulture.com/2016/09/alan-moore-jerusalem-comics-writer.html.
Marquand, David (2018), 'England, Ireland, Scotland, Wales – Time for All to Jump in the Debate', *Open Democracy*, 22 June. Available at: https://www.opendemocracy.net/en/opendemocracyuk/england-ireland-scotland-wales-time-for-all-to-jump-in-to-debate/.
Marr, Andrew (2000), *The Day Britain Died*, London: Profile.
Marr, Andrew (2018), 'This Contest Isn't About Theresa, But Margaret', *The Times*, 16 December. Available at: https://www.thetimes.co.uk/article/this-contest-isn-t-about-theresa-but-margaret-mjvvv7q0m.
Matthews, Sean (2009), '"I'm Sorry I Can't Say More": An Interview with Kazuo Ishiguro', in Sean Matthews and Sebastian Groes (eds), *Kazuo Ishiguro: Contemporary Critical Perspectives*, 114–25, London: Continuum.
May, Adrian (2011), *Myth and Creative Writing*, Harlow: Longman.
May, Theresa (2015), 'Speech to The Conservative Party Conference', Central Convention Complex, Manchester, 6 October. Available at: https://www.independent.co.uk/news/uk/politics/theresa-may-s-speech-to-the-conservative-party-conference-in-full-a6681901.html.
May, Theresa (2016a), 'European Council October 2016: Prime Minister's Press Statement'. Available at: https://www.gov.uk/government/speeches/european-council-october-2016-prime-ministers-press-statement.
May, Theresa (2016b), Conservative Party Conference, The ICC Birmingham, 2–5 October.
May, Theresa (2017a), 'Brexit Speech', 17 January. Available at: https://time.com/4636078/theresa-may-hard-brexit-single-market/.
May, Theresa (2017b), Scottish Conservatives Conference, 3 March, Glasgow.
McDermott, John (1989), *Kingsley Amis: An English Moralist*, London: Macmillan.
McDowell, Frederick P. W. (1972), 'An Interview with Angus Wilson', *The Iowa Review* 3 (4): 77–105.
McDuff, Phil (2017), 'Enough of the Patronising Myths About the "White Working Class"', *The Guardian*, 7 September. Available at: https://www.theguardian.com/commentisfree/2017/sep/07/myths-white-working-class.
McEwan, Ian (2019b), 'Brexit, the Most Pointless, Masochistic Ambition in Our Country's History, is Done', *The Guardian*, 1 February. Available at: https://www.theguardian.com/politics/2020/feb/01/brexit-pointless-masochistic-ambition-history-done.

McEwan, Ian (2019c), 'Cockroach', 27 September. Available at: http://www.ianmcewan.com/books/cockroach.html.
McEwen, Nicola (2018), 'Brexit and Scotland: Between Two Unions', *British Politics* 13 (1): 65–78.
McGarvey, Darren (2017), *Poverty Safari: Understanding the Anger of Britain's Underclass*, Edinburgh: Luath Press.
McGee, Harry (2017), 'Key to UK's Future Lies in Dublin, Says Tusk', *The Irish Times*, 2 December. Available at: https://www.irishtimes.com/news/politics/key-to-uk-s-future-lies-in-dublin-says-tusk-1.3312870.
McGlone, Jackie (2017), 'Review: The Lie of the Land', *The Herald*, 16 June. Available at: https://www.heraldscotland.com/arts_ents/15351326.review-the-lie-of-the-land-by-amanda-craig/.
McGrath, Dominic (2017), 'No Surrender: Bad Blood at 30', *University Times*, 5 February. Available at: http://www.universitytimes.ie/2017/02/no-surrender-bad-blood-at-30/.
McGregor, Jon (2017b), 'I'm Allergic to Trying to Make Points in Fiction', *The Guardian*, 7 April. Available at: https://www.theguardian.com/books/2017/apr/07/jon-mcgregor-reservoir-13-novel-interview.
McHarg, Aileen and James Mitchell (2017), 'Brexit and Scotland', *The British Journal of Politics and International Relations* 19 (3): 512–26.
McIlvanney, Liam (2002), 'The Politics of Narrative in the Post-War Scottish Novel', in Zachary Leader (ed.), *On Modern British Fiction*, 181–208, Oxford: Oxford University Press.
McLaren, L. M. (2012), 'The Cultural Divide in Europe: Migration, Multiculturalism and Political Trust', *World Politics* 64: 199–241.
McLean, Duncan (1999), 'Poets' Parliament', *Edinburgh Review*, 100.
Meek, James (2019), *Dreams of Leaving and Remaining*, London: Verso.
Mergenthal, Silvia (2002), 'England's Finest—Battle Fields and Football Grounds in John King's Football Novels', in Barbara Korte and Ralf Schneider (eds), *War and the Cultural Construction of Identities in Britain*, 261–8, Amsterdam: Rodopi.
Merkel, Angela (2016), 'Merkel: Germany Should Play Bigger Role on World Stage', *DW*, 2 March. Available at: http://www.dw.com/en/merkel-germany-should-play-bigger-role-on-world-stage/a-19088542.
Miéville, China (2017), 'China Miéville: Author, Activist, Revolutionary?', *Varsity*, 10 May. Available at: https://www.varsity.co.uk/culture/12902.
Miles, Robert and Paula Cleary (1993), 'Migration to Britain: Racism, State Regulation and Employment', in Vaughan Robinson (ed.), *The International Refugee Crisis: British and Canadian Responses*, 57–75, Basingstoke: Palgrave Macmillan.
Mills, Edward and Chris Colvin (2016), 'Why Did Northern Ireland Vote to Remain?', *Queen's Policy Engagement*, 18 July. Available at: http://qpol.qub.ac.uk/northern-ireland-vote-remain/.
Mishra, Pankaj (2017), 'What Is Great About Ourselves', *LRB*, 21 September. Available at: https://www.lrb.co.uk/the-paper/v39/n18/pankaj-mishra/what-is-great-about-ourselves.
Mitchell, James (2009), *Devolution in the UK*, Manchester: Manchester University Press.
Mitchell, Sebastian (2007), 'Dark Interpreter: Literary Uses of the Brocken Spectre from Coledridge to Pynchon', *Dalhousie Review* 87 (2): 167–88.
Mitford, Nancy (1988), 'Rome Is Only a Village', in Charlotte Mosley (ed.), *Nancy Mitford, A Talent to Annoy: Essays, Journalism, and Reviews 1929–1968*, Oxford: Oxford Paperbacks.

Mitropoulos, Angela and Brett Neilson (2006), 'Exceptional Times, Non-Governmental Spacings, and Impolitical Movements', *Vacarme* 34. Available at: https://vacarme.org/article484.html.
Monbiot, George, *The Guardian*, 29 June 2016.
Mondal, Ashuman (2018), 'Scratching the Post-Imperial Itch', in Robert Eaglestone (ed.), *Brexit and Literature: Critical and Cultural Responses*, 82–91, London: Routledge.
Moore, Michael Scott and Michael Sontheimer (2005), 'I Remain Fascinated by Memory', *Spiegel Online*, 5 October. Available at: www.spiegel.de/international/spiegel-interview-with-kazuo-ishiguro-i-remain-fascinated-by-memory-a-378173.html.
Morace, Robert A. (1989), *The Dialogic Novels of Malcolm Bradbury and David Lodge*, Carbondale: Southern Illinois University Press.
Morley, Sheridan (1990), 'Ripe Comedy Sprouts in Brussels', *The Times*, 28 June.
Morrow, Duncan and Jonny Byrne (2017), 'Northern Ireland: The Promise Broken', in Gerry Hassan and Russell Gunson (eds), *Scotland, the UK and Brexit: A Guide to the Future*, Edinburgh: Luath Press.
Moss, Sarah (2018b), 'On Prehistorical Fictions'. Available at: https://www.sarahmoss.org/2018/06/.
Moss, Sarah (2019), 'Sarah Moss on Brexit, Borders, Bog Bodies, and the "Foundation Myths of a Really Damaged Country"', *Longreads*. Available at: https://longreads.com/2019/01/09/interview-with-sarah-moss/.
Moss, Sarah (2020), 'Sarah Moss and Her Editor Discuss Her Novel Summerwater, Brexit Anxieties and the Strangeness of Holidays', 31 August. Available at: https://www.panmacmillan.com/blogs/literary/sarah-moss-on-writing-summerwater
Mota, Miguel (2009), 'Boys Will Be Hooligans: History and Masculine Communities in John King's England Away', *Critique: Studies in Contemporary Fiction* 50 (3): 261–75.
Mould, Oli (2017), 'The Calais Jungle', *City: Analysis of Urban Trends, Culture, Theory, Policy, Action* 21 (3–4): 388–404.
Mullen, Tom (2019), 'Brexit and the Territorial Governance of the United Kingdom', *Contemporary Social Science* 14 (2): 276–93.
Mullin, Chris (2019b), 'Chris Mullin's Novel Projects Britain's Post-Brexit Woes', *NPR*, 20 April. Available at: https://www.npr.org/2019/04/20/715393936/chris-mullins-novel-projects-britain-s-post-brexit-woes.
Murphy, Mary C. (2018), *Europe and Northern Ireland's Future: Negotiating Brexit's Unique Case*, Newcastle: Agenda.
Mycock, Andrew and Chris Gifford (2015), 'Beyond the English? The UK's Pluri-National Euroscepticism', in Karine Tournier-Sol and Chris Gifford (eds), *The UK Challenge to Europeanization: The Persistence of British Euroscepticism*, 51–72, Basingstoke: Palgrave Macmillan.
Nairn, Tom ([1977] 2003), *The Break-Up of Britain: Crisis and Neo-Nationalism*, Altona: Common Ground.
Nicholls, Robert (2019), *The British Political Elite and Europe, 1959–1984: A Higher Loyalty*, Manchester: Manchester University Press.
The Nobel Prize (2012), The Nobel Peace Prize 2012. Available at: https://www.nobelprize.org/prizes/peace/2012/summary/.
The Nobel Prize (2017), The Nobel Prize in Literature 2017. Available at: https://www.nobelprize.org/prizes/literature/2017/summary/.
Nora, Pierre (1989), 'Between Memory and History: Les Lieux de Memoire', *Representations* 26: 7–24.

Norris, Pippa (2016), 'The Problems of Populism: Tactics for Western Universities', *Times Higher Education*. Available at: https://www.timeshighereducation.com/features/the-problems-of-populism-tactics-for-western-universities.

Norris, Pippa and Ronald Inglehart (2019), *Cultural Backlash: Trump, Brexit and Authoritarian Populism*, Cambridge: Cambridge University Press.

Nowicka, Magdalena (2018), 'Cultural Precarity: Migrants' Positionalities in the Light of Current Anti-immigrant Populism in Europe', *Journal of Intercultural Studies* 39 (5): 527–42.

Nussbaum, Martha C. (2010), 'Patriotism and Cosmopolitanism', in G. Wallace Brown and David Held (eds), *The Cosmopolitan Reader*, 155–62, Cambridge: Polity Press.

Ó Beacháin, Donnacha (2019), *From Partition to Brexit: The Irish Government and Northern Ireland*, Manchester: Manchester University Press.

O'Brien, Phil (2015), 'An Interview with Anthony Cartwright', *Contemporary Literature* 56 (3): 398–420.

O'Brien, Phil (2018), 'The Deindustrial Novel: Twenty-First-Century British Fiction and the Working Class', in Ben Clarke and Nick Hubble (eds), *Working Class Writing: Theory and Practice*, 229–46, Cham: Palgrave Macmillan.

O'Brien, Phil (2020), *The Working Class and Twenty-First Century British Fiction: Deindustrialisation, Demonisation, Resistance*, Abingdon: Routledge.

O'Carroll, Lisa (2018), 'Ireland Condemns Kate Hoey's "Reckless" Good Friday Agreement Remarks', *The Guardian*, 20 February. Available at: https://www.theguardian.com/politics/2018/feb/20/ireland-kate-hoey-good-friday-agreement-remarks.

O'Connor, Siobhan (2020), 'Brexit and the Tudor Turn: Philippa Gregory's Narratives of National Grievance', in Ina Habermann (ed.), *The Road to Brexit: A Cultural Perspective on British Attitudes to Europe*, 179–96, Manchester: Manchester University Press.

O'Hagan, Andrew (2017), 'Scotland, Your Scotland', *Edinburgh Literary Festival*, 16 August. Available at: https://senscot.net/scotland-your-scotland/.

O'Hagan, Ellie May (2016), 'Wales Voted for Brexit Because it has Been Ignored by Westminster for Too Long', *Independent*, 25 June. Available at: http://www.independent.co.uk/voices/brexit-wales-eu-referendum-vote-leave-uk-ignoredby-westminster-a7102551.html.

O'Hara, Mary (2015), *Austerity Bites: A Journey to the Sharp End of Cuts in the UK*, Bristol: Policy Press.

O'Keeffe, Alice (2019), 'Bookshops Pass on Anything to the Right of Tony Blair: Are Publishers Failing Leave Voters?', *The Guardian*, 11 November. Available at: https://www.theguardian.com/books/2019/nov/11/bookshops-pass-on-anything-to-the-right-of-tony-blair-are-publishers-failing-leave-voters.

O'Rourke, Kevin H. (2019), *A Short History of Brexit: From Brentry to Backstop*, London: Pelican.

O'Toole, Fintan (2018a), *Heroic Failure: Brexit and the Politics of Pain*, London: Head of Zeus.

O'Toole, Fintan (2018b), 'The Paranoid Fantasy Behind Brexit', *The Guardian*, 16 November. Available at: https://www.theguardian.com/politics/2018/nov/16/brexit-paranoid-fantasy-fintan-otoole.

O'Toole, Fintan (2019), *The Politics of Pain: Postwar England and the Rise of Nationalism*, New York: Liveright.

O'Toole, Fintan (2020), *The Brexit Chronicles: Three Years in Hell*, London: Head of Zeus.

Oakeshott, Michael (1962), *Rationalism in Politics and Other Essays*, London: Methuen Publishing.

Office for National Statistics (2018), 'Migration Statistics Quarterly Report'. Available at: https://www.ons.gov.uk/peoplepopulationandcommunity/populationandmigration/internationalmigration/bulletins/migrationstatisticsquarterlyreport/february2020#non-eu-immigration-to-the-uk.

Offices of the Houses of the Oireachas (2017), Brexit and the Future of Ireland: Uniting Ireland and its People in Peace and Prosperity, August.

Okri, Ben (1995), *Birds of Heaven*, London: Phoenix.

Oliver, Craig ([2016] 2017), *Unleashing Demons: The Inside Story of Brexit*, Hodder & Stoughton.

Oltermann, Philip (2019), 'German Sci-Fi Fans Lap Up Dystopian Tales of Brexit Britain', *The Guardian*, 30 June. Available at: https://www.theguardian.com/world/2019/jun/30/german-scifi-fans-reading-dystopia-brexit-britain.

Orwell, George ([1938] 2000), *Homage to Catalonia*, London: Penguin.

Orwell, George ([1941] 2018), *The Lion and the Unicorn: Socialism and the English Genius*, London: Penguin.

Orwell, George (1968), *The Collected Essays, Journalism and Letters, Volume I*, London: Secker & Warburg.

Orwell, George (1970), *The Collected Essays, Journalism and Letters, Volume III*, London: Penguin.

Osmond, John (1995), *Welsh Europeans*, Bridgend: Seren.

Osmond, John (2017), 'Wales Feels Powerless in Face of Brexit', *InFacts*, 14 March. Available at: https://infacts.org/wales-feels-powerless-face-brexit/.

Owen, Erica and Stefanie Walter (2017), 'Open Economy Politics and Brexit: Insights, Puzzles, and Ways Forward', *Review of International Political Economy* 24 (2): 179–202.

Oxford Languages (2016), 'Word of the Year 2016'. Available at: https://languages.oup.com/word-of-the-year/2016/.

Parker, George (2016), 'David Cameron Rejects Idea of Brexit "Neverendum,"' *Financial Times*, 17 May 2016. Available at: https://www.ft.com/content/139a0c5e-1c25-11e6-a7bc-ee846770ec15.

Parks, Tim ([1998] 2011), *Adultery and Other Diversions*, New York: Arcade.

Parks, Tim (2010), 'Europe Needs a Change of Heart', *The Guardian*, 26 December. https://www.theguardian.com/commentisfree/2010/dec/26/europe-change-of-heart-vision.

Parks, Tim (2016), 'Brexit or Not, is it Time for Me to Become an Italian?', *The Guardian*, 22 June. Available at: https://www.theguardian.com/commentisfree/2016/jun/22/brexit-or-not-time-to-become-italian.

Parrinder, Patrick (2006), *Nation and Novel: The English Novel from Its Origins to the Present Day*, Oxford: Oxford University Press.

Patten Report on Policing (1999), 9 September, HMSO.

Patterson, Glenn (2019a), *Backstop Land*, London: Head of Zeus.

Patterson, Glenn (2019b), 'Here's to Bandit Country: The Irish Border, Writing's New Frontier', *The Guardian*, 11 June. Available at: https://www.theguardian.com/books/2019/jun/11/writing-the-irish-border-ireland-northern-ireland-brexit.

Paxman, Jeremy ([1998] 1999), *The English: A Portrait of a People*, London: Penguin.

Peddie, Ian and Niall Griffiths (2008), 'Warmth and Light and Sky: Niall Griffiths in Conversation', *Critical Survey* 20 (3): 116–27.

Peston, Robert (2017), 'I Don't Appear to be Living in the Same Britain as Much of the Rest of the Country', *The Telegraph*, 29 October. Available at: https://www.telegraph.co.uk/men/thinking-man/robert-peston-dont-appear-living-britain-much-rest-country/.

Peyrefitte, Allan (1994), *C'était de Gaulle, Vol. 1*, Paris: Fayard.

Phillips, Caryl ([2001] 2002), *A New World Order*, London: Vintage.
Phillips, Mike (2004), 'Art, the Myth of Culture and the Struggle for British Identity', in Barbara Korte and Claudia Sternberg (eds), *Bidding for the Mainstream: Black and Asian British Film Since the 1990s*, 211–18, Amsterdam: Rodopi.
Pireddu, Nicoletta (2017), 'Europe at the End of the Chunnel: Malcolm Bradbury's and Tim Park's Eurosceptic Albion', *English Studies* 98 (6): 624–48.
Priestley, J. B (1962), *The Shapes of Sleep*, London: William Heinemann.
Priestley, J. B. (1977), *Instead of the Trees: A Final Chapter of Autobiography*, London: Heinemann.
Priestley, J. B. (2015), 'J. B. Priestley on Why Britain Would be Better Off Out of the Common Market', *The New Statesman*. Available at: https://www.newstatesman.com/politics/2015/04/archive-j-b-priestley-why-britain-would-be-better-out-common-market.
Pringle, John Douglas (1962), 'Re-winding the Clock', *Encounter* 18 (1–6): 9–10.
Prosser, Chris, Jon Mellon and Jane Green (2016), 'What Mattered Most to You When Deciding How to Vote in the EU Referendum?', British Election Study News, 11 July. Available at: http://www.britishelectionstudy.com/bes-findings/what-mattered-most-to-you-when-deciding-how-to-vote-in-the-eu-referendum.
Reynolds, David (2019), *Island Stories: Britain and its History in the Age of Brexit*, London: William Collins.
Ridley, Nicholas (1990), Interview, *The Spectator*, 14 July.
Robertson, James (2005), *Voyage of Intent: Sonnets and Essays from the Scottish Parliament*, Edinburgh: Luath Press.
Robertson, James (2012), *Republics of the Mind: New and Selected Stories*, Edinburgh: Black and White Publishing.
Rose, Richard (1982), *Understanding the United Kingdom*, London: Longman.
Rosello, Mireille and Stephen Wolfe (2017), 'Introduction', in Johan Schimanski and Stephen F. Wolfe (eds), *Border Aesthetics: Concepts and Intersections*, 1–4, New York: Berghahn.
Rosie, Michael and Ross Bond (2008), 'National Identities and Politics After Devolution', *Radical Statistics* 97: 47–65.
Ruane, Kevin (2002), 'Agonizing Reappraisals: Anthony Eden, John Foster Dulles and the Crisis of European Defence', 1953–54. *Diplomacy & Statecraft* 13 (4): 151–85.
Rukeyser, Rebecca (2015), 'Kazuo Ishiguro: Mythic Retreat', *Guernica*, 1 May. Available at: https://www.guernicamag.com/mythic-retreat/.
Rumford, Chris (2007), 'Introduction', in Chris Rumford (ed.), *Cosmopolitanism and Europe*, 1–15, Liverpool: Liverpool University Press.
Rygiel, Kim (2011), 'Bordering Solidarities: Migrant Activism and the Politics of Movement and Camps at Calais', *Citizenship Studies* 15 (1): 1–19.
Samuel, Raphael (1989), *Patriotism: The Making and Unmaking of British National Identity*, London: Routledge.
Saunders, Robert (2018), *Yes to Europe: The 1975 Referendum and Seventies Britain*, Cambridge: Cambridge University Press.
Saunders, Robert (2019), 'The Myth of Brexit as Imperial Nostalgia', *Prospect Magazine*, 7 January. Available at: https://www.prospectmagazine.co.uk/world/the-myth-of-brexit-as-imperial-nostalgia.
Sayer, Derek (2017), 'White Riot—Brexit, Trump, and Post-Factual Politics', *Journal of Historical Sociology* 30: 92–106.
Schmitt, Mark (2018), *British White Trash: Figurations of Tainted Whiteness in the Novels of Irvine Welsh, Niall Griffiths and John King*, Bielefeld: Transcript Verlag.

Schnapper, Pauline (2015), 'The Dilemma of Pro-European Parties in the UK: The Case of Labour and the Liberal Democrats Since 2010', in Karine Tournier-Sol and Chris Gifford (eds), *The UK Challenge to Europeanization: The Persistence of British Euroscepticism*, 117–33, Basingstoke: Palgrave Macmillan.

Schoene, Berthold, ed. (2007), *The Edinburgh Companion to Contemporary Scottish Literature*, Edinburgh: Edinburgh University Press.

Schoene, Berthold (2008), 'Cosmopolitan Scots', *Scottish Studies Review* 9 (2): 71–92.

Schofield, Emma (2014), 'Everything Must Change: Regenerating National Identity in Post-Devolution Anglophone Welsh Writing', *Wales Art Review*, 14 August. Available at: https://www.walesartsreview.org/the-gregynog-papers-6-everything-must-change-regenerating-national-identity-in-post-devolution-anglophone-welsh-writing/.

Scruton, Roger (2000), *England: An Elegy*, London: Continuum.

Scully, Roger (2017), 'I Spent a Year Researching Why Working-Class Welsh People in the Valleys Voted for Brexit, and This is What I Found', *Independent*, 26 October. Available at: https://www.independent.co.uk/voices/south-wales-valleys-brexit-vote-leave-a8021051.html.

Seidler, Victor J. (2018), *Making Sense of Brexit: Democracy, Europe and Uncertain Futures*, Bristol: Policy Press.

Seldon, Anthony and Peter Snowden (2015), *Cameron at 10: The Inside Story 2010–2015*, London: William Collins.

Sellars, Simon (2006), 'Rattling Other People's Cages: The J. G. Ballard Interview', 29 September. Available at: http://www.ballardian.com/rattling-other-peoples-cages-the-jg-ballard-interview.

Shaffer, Brian W. (2006), *Reading the Novel in English, 1950–2000*, Malden, MA: Blackwell.

Shamsie, Kamila (2020), 'Introduction', in China Miéville, *The City & The City*, London: Picador.

Shaw, Katy (2018), *Hauntology: The Presence of the Past in Twenty-First Century English Literature*, Cham: Palgrave Macmillan.

Shaw, Katy and Sunjeev Sahota (2017), *Living by the Pen: In Conversation with Sunjeev Sahota*.

Shaw, Kristian (2017), *Cosmopolitanism in Twenty-First Century Fiction*, Cham: Palgrave.

Shaw, Kristian (2018a), 'BrexLit', in Robert Eaglestone (ed.), *Brexit and Literature: Critical and Cultural Responses*, 15–30, London: Routledge.

Shaw, Kristian (2018b), 'Globalization', in Daniel O'Gorman and Robert Eaglestone (eds), *The Routledge Companion to Twenty-First Century Literary Fiction*, 25–35, London: Routledge.

Shaw, Kristian (2019), 'Refugee Fictions: Brexit and the Maintenance of Borders in the European Union', in Barbara Korte and Laura Lojo-Rodríguez (eds), *Borders and Border Crossings in the Contemporary British Short Story*, 39–60, Basingstoke: Palgrave Macmillan.

Shaw, Kristian (2021), 'Black British and British Asian Fiction', in Bran Nicol (ed.), *The Cambridge Companion to British Postmodern Fiction*, Cambridge: Cambridge University Press.

Shaw, Kristian and Sara Upstone (2021), 'The Transglossic: Contemporary Fiction and the Limitations of the Modern'.

Sheers, Owen (2019), 'We Have Been Left Poorer, Divided and Scarred – We Need a New Brexit Vote', *Wales Online*, 22 March. Available at: https://www.walesonline.co.uk/news/politics/we-been-left-poorer-divided-16014602.

Sherratt-Bado, Dawn Miranda (2018a), 'Postmodernist Conflict: Brexit and the Irish Borderlands', *Honest Ulsterman*, 3 February. Available at: https://humag.co/features/postmodernist-conflict.

Sherratt-Bado, Dawn Miranda (2018b), '"Things We'd Rather Forget": Trauma, the Troubles, and Magical Realism in Post-Agreement Northern Irish Women's Short Stories', *Open Library of Humanities* 4 (2): 1–30.

Sherratt-Bado, Dawn Miranda (2018c), 'Cross-Talk: Brexit and the Good Friday/Belfast Agreement', Honest *Ulsterman*, June. Available at: https://humag.co/features/cross-talk.

Sherratt-Bado, Dawn Miranda (2019), 'Keep Her Country', Honest *Ulsterman*, February. Available at: https://humag.co/features/keep-her-country.

Shipman, Tim ([2016] 2017), *All Out War: The Full Story of Brexit*, London: William Collins.

Shipman, Tim (2017), *Fallout: A Year of Political Mayhem*, London William Collins.

Sierz, Aleks (2019), 'Dark Times: British Theatre After Brexit', 1 January. Available at: https://www.sierz.co.uk/writings/dark-times-british-theatre-after-brexit/.

Silk, Michael (2014), '"Isles of Wonder": Performing the Mythopoeia of Utopic Multi-Ethnic Britain', *Media, Culture & Society* 37 (1): 68–84.

Simms, Brendan (2016), *Britain's Europe: A Thousand Years of Conflict and Cooperation*, London: Penguin.

Smith, Ali (2017b), 'Ali Smith's Goldsmiths Prize Lecture: The Novel in the Age of Trump', *The New Statesman*, 15 October. Available at: https://www.newstatesman.com/culture/books/2017/10/ali-smith-s-goldsmiths-prize-lecture-novel-age-trump.

Smith, Ali (2019b), 'Ali Smith's Great Post-Brexit Novel', *PRI*, 30 April. Available at: https://www.pri.org/programs/studio-360/ali-smith-s-great-post-brexit-novel.

Smith, Ali (2020b), 'Before Brexit, Grenfell, Covid-19 . . . Ali Smith on Writing Four Novels in Four Years', *The Guardian*, 1 August. Available at: https://www.theguardian.com/books/2020/aug/01/before-brexit-grenfell-covid-19-ali-smith-on-writing-four-novels-in-four-years.

Smith, Zadie (2018), *Feel Free: Essays*, London: Hamish Hamilton.

Smith, Zadie (2019), *Grand* Union, London: Hamish Hamilton.

Smout, T. C. (1994), 'Perspectives on the Scottish Identity', *Scottish Affairs* 6: 101–13.

SNP (2017), 'If Scotland's Voice Can Be Ignored on Brexit, What Else Will the Tories Enforce on Us?', 27 February. Available at: https://www.snp.org/scotland-s-voice-on-brexit/.

Snyder, Timothy (2018), *The Road to Unfreedom: Russia, Europe, America*, New York: Crown.

Spiering, Menno (1988), 'Evil Europeans in Angus Wilson', in A. Boxhoorn, J. Th. Leerssen and M. Spiering (eds), *Britain in Europe: Yearbook of European Studies*, 27–58, Amsterdam: Rodopi.

Spiering, Menno (2015), *Cultural History of British Euroscepticism*, Basingstoke: Palgrave Macmillan.

Spiering, Menno (2020), '"I Don't Want to be a European": The European Other in British Cultural Discourse', in Ina Habermann (ed.), *The Road to Brexit: A Cultural Perspective on British Attitudes to Europe*, 126–42, Manchester: Manchester University Press.

Stacy, Ivan (2019), 'Looking Out into the Fog: Narrative, Historical Responsibility and the Problem of Freedom in Kazuo Ishiguro's *The Buried Giant*', *Textual Practice* 35 (1): 1–20.

Stewart, Dixi (2016), 'Front Row: The Cultural Response to Brexit', *BBC Radio 4*, 26 July. Available at: https://www.bbc.co.uk/programmes/b07m88y1.

Stonebridge, Lyndsey (2018), 'The Banality of Brexit', in Robert Eaglestone (ed.), *Brexit and Literature: Critical and Cultural Responses*, 7–14, London: Routledge.
Sturgeon, Nicola (2016), 'First Minister Statement on EU Referendum Result', 24 June. Available at: http://news.scotland. gov.uk/ Speeches-Briefings/First-Minister-EU-Ref erendum-result-25ae.aspx.
Swinden, Patrick (1984), *The English Novel of History and Society, 1940–1980*, London: Palgrave Macmillan.
Taylor, Graham (2017), *Understanding Brexit: Why Britain Voted to Leave the European Union*, Bingley: Emerald.
Thatcher, Margaret (1975), Speech in the Commons, Hansard 888, 11 March.
Thatcher, Margaret (1988), Speech to the College of Europe, Bruges, 20 September.
Thatcher, Margaret (1993), *The Downing Street Years*, London: HarperCollins.
Thatcher, Margaret (1999), Centre for Policy Studies, 21 December.
Thompson, M. K. (2019), 'Brexit, Scotland, and the Continuing Divergence of Politics', *The Midwest Quarterly* 60 (2): 141–60.
Thomson, Alex (2016), 'From "Renaissance" to Referendum? Literature and Critique in Scotland, 1918–2014', *Journal of Scottish Thought* 8: 63–87.
Thorpe, Adam (2014), 'The Wake by Paul Kingsnorth Review', *The Guardian*, 2 April. Available at: https://www.theguardian.com/books/2014/apr/02/the-wake-paul-kings north-review-literary-triumph.
Thorpe, Adam (2016), 'Hobblers Hole', *Little Toller*, 26 July. Available at: https://www.lit tletoller.co.uk/the-clearing/adam-thorpe-hobblers-hole/.
Thorpe, Adam (2018b), 'Adam Thorpe on Half a Lifetime as a Brit in France', *The Times*, 24 June. Available at: https://www.thetimes.co.uk/article/adam-thorpe-on-half-a-lif etime-as-a-brit-in-france-6hcqwtqkz.
Toly, Noah (2017), 'Brexit, Global Cities, and the Future of World Order', *Globalizations* 14 (1): 142–9.
Tomlinson, Alan and Christopher Young (2006), *National Identity and Global Sports Events: Culture, Politics, and Spectacle in the Olympics and the Football World Cup*, Albany: State University of New York Press.
Tomlinson, Sally (2019), *Education and Race from Empire to Brexit*, Bristol: Policy Press.
Torfing, Jacob (1999), *New Theories of Discourse: Laclau, Mouffe, and Zizek*, Oxford: Blackwell.
Tratt, Jacqueline (1996), *The Macmillan Government and Europe: A Study in the Process of Policy Development*, Basingstoke: Macmillan.
Turner, John (2000), *The Tories and Europe*, Manchester: Manchester University Press.
Tusk, Donald (2016), '40th Anniversary of European People Party (EPPP) Speech'. Available at: https://www.consilium.europa.eu/en/press/press-releases/2016/05/30/pec -speech-epp/.
UK Independence Party (2015), Believe in Britain, UKIP Manifesto 2015.
Upstone, Sara (2018), 'Do Novels Tell us How to Vote?', in Robert Eaglestone (ed.), *Brexit and Literature: Critical and Cultural Responses*, 44–58, London: Routledge.
Urban, Eva (2011), *Community Politics and the Peace Process in Contemporary Northern Irish Drama*, Bern: Peter Lang.
Vadde, Aarthi (2015), 'Narratives of Migration, Immigration, and Interconnection', in David James (ed.), *The Cambridge Companion to British Fiction Since 1945*, 61–75, Cambridge: Cambridge University Press.
Valluvan, Sivamohan (2019), *The Clamour of Nationalism: Race and Nation in Twenty- First-Century Britain*, Manchester: Manchester University Press.

Varoufakis, Yanis (2016), *And the Weak Suffer What They Must: Europe, Austerity and the Threat to Global Stability*, London: The Bodley Head.
Verkaik, Robert (2018), *Posh Boys: How English Public Schools Ruin Britain*, London: Simon & Schuster.
Vernon, Matthew and Margaret A. Miller (2018), 'Navigating Wonder: The Medieval Geographies of Kazuo Ishiguro's *The Buried Giant*', *Arthuriana* 28 (4): 68–89.
Virdee, Satnam and Brendan McGeever (2018), 'Racism, Class, Brexit', *Ethnic and Racial Studies* 41 (10): 1802–19.
Vorda, Allan and Kim Herzinger (1991), 'An Interview with Kazuo Ishiguro', *Mississippi Review* 20: 1–2.
Wahl, Peter (2018), 'Between Eurotopia and Nationalism: A Third Way for the Future of the EU', in Jamie Morgan and Heikke Patomaki (eds), *Brexit and the Political Economy of Fragmentation: Things Fall Apart*, 59–65, Oxford: Routledge.
Waites, Martyn (2018), 'The Old Religion: Martyn Waites Talks to Crime Time', *Crime Time*, 17 May. Available at: https://www.crimetime.co.uk/the-old-religion-martyn-wai tes-talks-to-crime-time/.
Wakefield, Mary (2001), 'Empire of the Slum', *The Spectator*, 18 August. Available at: http://archive.spectator.co.uk/article/18th-august-2001/23/empire-of-the-slum.
Walkowitz, Rebecca (2007), 'The Location of Literature: The Transnational Book and the Migrant Writer', *Contemporary Literature* 47 (4): 527–46.
Wall, Stephen (2008), *A Stranger in Europe: Britain and the EU from Thatcher to Blair*, Oxford: Oxford University Press.
Wallace, Gavin (2007), 'Voyages of Intent: Literature and Cultural Politics in Post-Devolution Scotland', in Berthold Schoene (ed.), *The Edinburgh Companion to Contemporary Scottish Literature*, 17–27, Edinburgh: Edinburgh University Press.
Walters, William (2008), 'Acts of Demonstration: Mapping the Territory of (Non-) Citizenship', in E. F. Isin and G. M. Nielsen (eds), *Acts of Citizenship*, 182–207. London: Zed Books.
Ward, Stuart and Astrid Rasch, eds (2019), *Embers of Empire in Brexit Britain*, London: Bloomsbury.
Warner, Alan (2014), 'Scottish Writers on the Referendum – Independence Day?', *The Guardian*, 19 July. Available at: https://www.theguardian.com/books/2014/jul/19/scot tish-referendum-independence-uk-how-writers-vote.
Watts, Duncan and Colin Pilkington (2005), *Britain in the European Union Today*, Manchester: Manchester University Press.
Wellings, Ben (2010), 'Losing the Peace: Euroscepticism and the Foundations of Contemporary English Nationalism', *Nations and Nationalism* 16 (3): 488–505.
Wellings, Ben (2014), *The Politics of English Nationhood*, Oxford: Oxford University Press.
Wellings, Ben (2015), 'Beyond Awkwardness: England, the European Union and the End of Integration', in Karine Tournier-Sol and Chris Gifford (eds), *The UK Challenge to Europeanization: The Persistence of British Euroscepticism*, 33–50, Basingstoke: Palgrave Macmillan.
Wellings, Ben (2018), 'Brexit and English Identity', in Patrick Diamond, Peter Nedergaard and Ben Rosamond (eds), *The Routledge Handbook of the Politics of Brexit*, 147–56, London: Routledge.
Wellings, Ben (2019), *English Nationalism, Brexit and the Anglosphere: Wider and Wider Still*. Manchester: Manchester University Press.

Wellings, Ben and Helen Baxendale (2015), 'Euroscepticism and the Anglosphere: Traditions and Dilemmas in Contemporary English Nationalism', *Journal of Common Market Studies* 53 (1): 123–40.
Welsh, Irvine (2013), 'Scottish Independence Will Allow Us to Become More British, Says Irvine Welsh', *The Guardian*, 10 January. Available at: https://www.theguardian.com/politics/2013/jan/10/scottish-independence-british-irvine-welsh.
Welsh, Irvine (2018b), 'Irvine Welsh: Return Journey', *Big Issue North*, 8 May. Available at: https://www.bigissuenorth.com/features/2018/05/irvine-welsh-return-journey/#close.
Wheatley, David (2018), 'Poetry in the age of Brexit', *The Irish Times*, 23 June. Available at: www.irishtimes.com/culture/books/poetry-in-the-age-of-brexit-1.3536218.
Wilson, Angus (1967), 'Evil in the English Novel', *The Kenyon Review* 29 (2): 167–95.
Wilson, Harold (1961), Parliamentary Debates, Commons, 5th series, vol. 645, 3 August.
Wincott, Daniel (2018), 'Brexit and State of the United Kingdom', in Peter Nedergaard, Christian Lequesne, and Patrick Diamond (eds), *The Routledge Handbook of the Politics of Brexit*, 15–26, London: Routledge.
Winterson, Jeanette (2016), 'We Need to Build a New Left: Labour Means Nothing Today', *The Guardian*, 25 June. Available at: https://www.theguardian.com/politics/2016/jun/24/we-need-to-build-a-new-left-labour-means-nothing-jeanette-winterson.
Wolff, Michael, ed. (1976), *The Collected Essays of Sir Winston Churchill, Vol. II*, London: Library of Imperial History.
Wood, James (2015), 'The Uses of Oblivion: Kazuo Ishiguro's "*The Buried Giant*"', *The New Yorker*, 23 March. Available at: http://www.newyorker.com/magazine/2015/03/23/the-uses-of-oblivion.
Worley, Will (2019), 'Brexit Arguments Causing Rifts Between Couples, Counsellors Say', *Independent*, 29 December. Available at: https://www.independent.co.uk/news/uk/home-news/brexit-anxieties-issue-troubled-couples-relationship-counsellors-experts-a7500876.html.
Wright, Colin (2007), 'Conserving Purity, Labouring the Past: A Tropological Evolution of Englishness', in Graham McPhee and Prem Poddar, *Empire and After: Englishness in Postcolonial Perspective*, 159–80, New York: Berghahn Books.
Wright, Patrick (1985), *On Living in an Old Country: The National Past in Contemporary Britain*, London: Verso.
Wyn Jones, Richard, Guy Lodge, Ailsa Henderson and Daniel Wincott (2012), 'The Dog that Finally Barked: England as an Emerging Political Community', London: Institute for Public Policy Research. Available at: https://www.ippr.org/files/images/media/files/publication/2012/02/dog-that-finally-barked_englishness_Jan2012_8542.pdf.
Wyn Jones, Richard, Guy Lodge, Charlie Jeffery, Glenn Gottfried, Roger Scully, Ailsa Henderson and Daniel Wincott (2013), 'England and Its Two Unions: The Anatomy of a Nation and its Discontents', London: Institute for Public Policy Research. Available at: https://www.ippr.org/publications/england-and-its-two-unions-the-anatomy-of-a-nation-and-its-discontents.
Wyn Jones, Richard (2016), 'Brexit Reflections – Why Did Wales Shoot Itself in the Foot in this Referendum', Centre on Constitutional Change, 27 June. Available at: https://www.centreonconstitutionalchange.ac.uk/opinions/brexit-reflections-why-did-wales-shoot-itself-foot-referendum.
Young, David (2016), 'A Step into the Unknown', *Belfast Telegraph*, 25 June.
Young, Hugo (1999), *This Blessed Plot*, New York: The Overlook Press.

Younge, Gary (2016), 'Brexit: A Disaster Decades in the Making', *The Guardian*, 30 June. Available at: https://www.theguardian.com/politics/2016/jun/30/brexit-disaster-decades-in-the-making.

Zielonka, Jan (2014), 'Is the EU Doomed?', *Foreign Affairs*, 18 August. Available at: https://www.foreignaffairs.com/reviews/2014-08-18/eu-doomed.

Zürn, Michael (2016), 'Opening Up Europe: Next Steps in Politicisation Research', *West European Politics* 39: 164–82.

Zweig, Stephan (2016), 'European Thought in Its Historical Development', in Will Stone (trans.), *Messages from a Lost World: Europe on the Brink*, London: Pushkin Press.

Index

Agamben, Giorgio   144–5
Amis, Kingsley   37–9, 42 n.3, 55 n.13, 56
  I Like It Here   38–40, 48, 51, 52
  One Fat Englishman   38
Anderson, Benedict   2, 14, 27, 34, 62, 65, 66, 184
Anglosphere   7, 9, 13, 37, 37 n.1, 38, 42, 61, 63, 73, 75, 76, 76 n.8, 100, 122
Anti-Common Market League (ACML)   11
Appiah, Kwame Anthony   38–9, 141
Arnott, Peter   121–2
  A Little Rain   122
Attlee, Clement   6, 75, 216

Ballard, J. G.   78–9
Barker, Nicola   89–90
Barnes, Julian   4, 29, 64, 67–8, 70, 98
  Cross Channel   63–4
  England, England   64–70, 75, 75 n.6, 77, 79, 193, 203
  The Porcupine   47
Baucom, Ian   59, 62, 67, 84, 186
Baxendale, Helen   7, 12
Beck, Ulrich   14, 97, 164, 168
Benn, Tony   11, 44, 171 n.4
Bentley, Nick   30, 36, 62, 66
Berlant, Lauren   44, 64–5, 67, 170 n.3
Bhabha, Homi K.   32, 65, 160, 218
Black, Jeremy   85, 115 n.16
Black Lives Matter movement   34, 212, 217
Blair, Tony   16, 17, 24, 44 n.4, 56, 59, 138 n.31
Board, Douglas   173, 197
  Time of Lies: A Political Satire   173–4
Bogdanor, Vernon   17, 30, 132, 138
borders   1, 14, 15, 21, 22, 32, 47, 53, 90, 91, 99, 116, 120, 122–5, 139, 141, 142, 144–7, 153–66, 168, 171, 173, 180 n.11, 201–3, 208, 209, 212, *see also* immigration; Northern Ireland

Bradbury, Malcolm   47–9, 49 n.6, 49 n.7, 53, 57
  Dr Criminale   47
  Rates of Exchange   47–51
Brexit, *see* European Union (EU), EU referendum
Brexlit   4, 34, 106, 125, 169, 196–7, 197 n.18, 219, *see also* Euroscepticism
  origins/definition   4, 4 n.3
  post-Brexit fictions   4, 4 n.3, 30–4, 84, 89, 120, 122, 125, 136, 164, 167–214
British National Party (BNP)   83, 85–7, 143, 146, 187
Brown, Glen James   189–90
Brown, Gordon   16, 18, 25, 74
Burgess, Anthony   46
Burns, Anna   135–6
Butterworth, Jez   79
  The Ferryman   134–5
  Jerusalem   79–81, 88
Byers, Sam   4, 177, 197
  Perfidious Albion   173, 175–7

Callaghan, James   11, 12
Cameron, David   9, 18–24, 26, 64, 71 n.2, 73 n.4, 76–7, 79, 86, 117, 122, 127, 133, 138, 141, 145, 156, 163, 163 n.12, 186, 206, 216
Campbell, Siobhán   133
Cartwright, Anthony   84, 85, 87–9, 107, 186, 189
  The Afterglow   84, 185 n.13, 186
  The Cut   84, 89, 183–9
  Heartland   84–7, 186
  How I Killed Margaret Thatcher   88
  Iron Towns   84, 87–9, 186
Churchill, Winston   6, 7, 12, 18, 27, 40, 57, 66, 71, 71 n.3
class   2, 3, 11, 17–18, 23, 26, 30, 34, 61, 73, 74 n.5, 76, 81, 83–9, 88 n.12, 96–7, 105 n.6, 110, 114, 119 n.19,

138, 142, 143, 147, 148, 151, 152, 153, 167, 173, 174, 176, 180, 183–90, 192, 196–8, 204, 207, 217, 219, 220
Coe, Jonathan   188, 191, 196, 197, 208
  Middle England   190–6, 208
  Number 11   180
Common Market, *see* European Economic Community (EEC)
Commonwealth   2, 6–9, 12, 27, 35–7, 42, 43, 56, 57, 61, 70, 73, 73 n.4, 75–7, 83, 165, 215
Conservative Party   6, 8, 10–12, 15–16, 18–27, 45, 52, 57, 69, 74, 99, 101, 106, 109, 112, 115, 116, 118, 121, 127, 130, 138, 141, 143–4, 168, 173, 174, 179, 180, 188, 190, 205, 207, 220
Corbyn, Jeremy   25, 170, 173
cosmopolitanism   1, 3, 4, 14, 38–9, 115, 119, 123, 142, 155, 159, 162–4, 168, 195, 197, 203, 208 n.23, 212–14, 220
  cosmopolitanization   63, 66, 70, 74, 97, 125, 144, 184–5, 188
  hospitality   99, 114, 124, 150, 157, 160, 163, 180, 209, 210, 213
Covid-19 pandemic   34, 125, 204–5, 212, 213, 217, 220
Craig, Amanda   182
  Hearts and Minds   190 n.15
  The Lie of the Land   182–3
Cummings, Dominic   66, 138 n.31, 212
Curtice, John   97, 117, 125

Dabydeen, David   97–8
De Gaulle, Charles   9, 10, 40, 60, 64
Deighton, Len   45
deindustrialization   18, 30, 47, 59, 84–9, 84 n.10, 88 n.12, 104, 106–7, 107 n.8, 111, 120, 178 n.8, 185–8, 192, 196
Delors, Jacques   13, 14, 55
Democratic Unionist Party (DUP)   24, 127, 129, 130
devolution   1, 2, 15, 30–1, 58, 59, 64, 68, 71, 74, 78, 98, 100–40, 175, 188, 211, 217
  England   118, 137–40

Northern Ireland   17, 23, 125–36, 140, 213
Scotland   17, 23, 31, 103, 110–25, 140, 213, 219
Wales   17, 101–11, 140, 213
Dewey, Robert F.   5–6, 8, 64
Dorling, Danny   73, 190, 213
Drabble, Margaret   38, 44, 169
Duffy, Carol Ann   122
  My Country: A Work in Progress   170 n.2

Eaglestone, Robert   44, 197, 197 n.18
Eden, Anthony   6, 40
Englishness   3, 15, 20, 25–6, 29, 30, 31, 36, 55, 57, 59–100, 117–18, 120, 138, 152–3, 168, 181, 190–5, 200–4
  crisis of   18, 31, 64
  English sublime   62, 73–4, 80, 94–5, 95 n.14, 98, 149–50, 194, 210
  muscular   62, 78–90
  vampiric   74
English Votes for English Laws (EVEL)   31, 138–9
European Economic Community (EEC)   3, 6–14, 24, 36, 38–40, 42, 42 n.3, 43–4, 44 n.4, 45, 47 n.5, 48–9, 49 n.6, 49 n.7, 77, 82 n.9, 84, 91, 109, 111, 111 n.11, 126, 134
  1975 referendum   11–12, 23–5, 30, 89, 103, 111, 126
  Common Agricultural Policy (CAP)   10, 91
  Treaty of Paris   4, 6, 93–4
  Treaty of Rome   6, 21, 51, 64, 68, 93–4
European Free Trade Association (EFTA)   6–7
European Union (EU)   1, 2, 4–6, 8–10, 12, 14–34, 42, 45, 47, 50–61, 63, 66–70, 73–7, 79, 81–4, 86, 87, 89–91, 93, 95–7, 99, 101, 101 n.1, 102, 103, 105 n.6, 106–10, 111–12, 115–17, 119–21, 123, 125–9, 131, 132, 134, 137–9, 141–56, 158–63, 165, 165 n.14, 167 n.1, 168, 170, 171–5, 176 n.7, 177, 179, 181, 183, 184, 187, 190–3, 196–200, 205,

207, 209, 210 n.24, 213, 215, 216, 217 n.1, 218, 220
Economic and Monetary Union (EMU)   13, 14, 16, 49
enlargement   17–18, 24, 32, 47, 51, 142–3, 142 n.3, 148, 149, 152, 166, 192
European Coal and Steel Community (ECSC)   2, 5, 6, 28, 39–40, 42
European Commission   11 n.4, 13, 14, 47, 51 n.9, 52–3, 57, 61, 89, 131, 142 n.3, 175, 197
European Defence Community (EDC)   6, 28, 39–40
European Parliament   16, 45, 50–1, 54, 55, 145
Exchange Rate Mechanism   12, 13, 15–16, 47
EU referendum   1, 2, 4, 4 n.3, 11, 12, 15, 20–7, 29, 29 n.6, 30–4, 36, 44 n.4, 55–7, 60, 61, 63, 64, 66, 70, 71, 71 n.2, 73 n.4, 76, 79–81, 86, 87, 90, 95, 97–9, 101, 103, 104, 108–11, 114–18, 120–2, 124–30, 133, 134, 136, 138, 141–6, 149, 151–4, 156, 162, 165, 167–2, 177, 179, 180, 182, 183, 186–90, 191–3, 195, 195 n.17, 196, 197, 198 n.20, 199, 201, 202, 204, 206, 208, 209, 211, 213, 215–20
Maastricht Treaty   13–15, 21, 28, 50, 51, 53, 56–9, 63, 73, 78, 98, 137, 141, 143
Schengen Agreement   15, 21, 32, 142, 143, 145, 154, 155, 161, 162
Single European Act   12, 13, 28, 47, 160
Treaty of Amsterdam   16, 52, 145
Withdrawal Agreement   2, 33, 34, 136, 169, 219
Europeanization   14, 17, 45–6, 50, 54, 56, 57, 63, 80, 123 n.21
Euroscepticism   4, 5, 7, 8, 10–16, 18–24, 27, 29, 29 n.6, 30–2, 34, 35, 38, 40, 41, 45, 49, 52, 55, 56, 58–61, 73, 77, 82, 83, 118, 126, 127, 130, 133, 138, 139, 143, 143 n.4, 145, 153, 155, 163, 167, 168, 169, 171, 173, 174, 181, 182, 198, 215, 216, 218, 220
in British fiction   3, 4, 28, 32, 34–58, 72, 82–3, 87–9, 97–9, 109, 164, 173, 176–8, 214
Evaristo, Bernardine   98, 146, 159

Farage, Nigel   15, 20, 22, 26, 27, 45, 66, 146, 174, 176, 179, 190, 205
financial crisis   18, 144, 151–3, 187, 190 n.15, 216
Fisher, Mark   67
Ford, Robert   14, 83, 86, 186
Fowles, John   29, 62 n.1
Freedland, Jonathan   165, 170, 217

Gaitskell, Hugh   8
Gardiner, Michael   31, 72, 80, 85 n.11, 99, 102, 112, 115 n.16, 137–40, 219
Geddes, Andrew   9, 28
Gibraltar   42, 136–7
Gilroy, Paul   67, 72, 75, 150, 167, 186, 194–5
Glencross, Andrew   11, 12, 24, 32
globalization   1, 26, 33, 59, 63, 73, 84, 92, 153, 162, 184, 188, 195, 203, 216
Goodhart, David   144, 181–2, 184 n.12, 188–90
Goodwin, Matthew   14, 19, 41, 51, 62, 83, 86, 87, 106, 141, 141 n.1, 144, 167, 184, 186, 187, 190 n.14, 198 n.20
Gowland, David   2 n.1, 6, 7, 9, 15, 16
Grande, Edgar   97, 164, 168
Grant, Linda   181
  A Stranger City   181–2
Gray, Alasdair   112–14, 114 n.15
Gregory, Philippa   91
Griffiths, Niall   104, 105, 111, 205, 206
  Broken Ghost   197, 205–8
  Grits   105 n.7
  Sheepshagger   104–6, 113
Guo, Xiaolu   98

Hall, Sarah   116, 125
  The Wolf Border   116–17
Hames, Scott   112, 112 n.12, 114, 114 n.15, 115, 115 n.16, 116, 118, 125 n.23
Hamid, Mohsin   4, 162
  Exit West   162–3
Hammond, Andrew   44, 50, 58
Harris, Robert   45
Harrison, Melissa   201
  All Among the Barley   199–201, 204
Hawes, James   71, 74, 77, 98, 103 n.2
  Speak for England   71–8, 203

Heath, Anthony   97, 106, 141 n.1, 184, 190 n.14
Heath, Edward   10, 84
Hein, Christoph   164 n.13
Herd, David   156, 159
  Refugee Tales I   157–8
  Refugee Tales II   159
  Refugee Tales III   159
Hirsch, Afua   97, 147
Holmes, Annie, *see* Popoola, Olumide
Hughes Michael   133–4

immigration   16–19, 21, 22, 25–7, 32, 36, 61, 75, 76, 78, 87, 89, 99, 109, 122–5, 127, 129, 141–66, 168, 173, 176, 180, 187, 188, 190–2, 201, 202, 210
  EU   15, 21, 23–4, 32, 53, 123, 183
imperialism   4, 8, 10, 13, 24, 32, 41, 59–60, 64–74, 74 n.5, 75, 77, 78–9, 85, 91, 97, 112, 136, 137, 146, 150, 156, 159, 161, 200–2, 215, 217
  imperial nostalgia   29, 61, 71, 74–6, 89, 99, 186, 194, 200–1, 209
Inglehart, Ronald, *see* Norris, Pippa
Ishiguro, Kazuo   4, 66, 92, 95
  The Buried Giant   92–6
  The Remains of the Day   66

Johnson, Boris   26, 27, 45, 56, 66, 67, 69, 70, 73, 76, 77, 83, 89, 132, 170, 171, 174, 178, 193, 211, 212, 215–16

Kaufmann, G. L.   178
Kay, Jackie   113, 159–60, 169, 169 n.2
Kennedy, A. L.   130, 138 n.30, 169, 180, 188
Kenny, Michael   12, 13, 63, 73, 74, 76, 100, 137
King, John   57, 58, 81, 84
  England Away   81–4
  The Liberal Politics of Adolf Hitler   56–8
Kingsnorth, Paul   84, 91, 137, 138
  The Wake   91–2, 203
Kumar, Krishan   5, 90
Kunzru, Hari   160
  Red Pill   161
  Transmission   160–1, 164
Kymlicka, Will   174, 220

Labour Party   6, 8, 10–11, 11 n.4, 12, 16, 17, 19, 22–6, 31, 36, 44, 44 n.4, 50, 56, 59, 64, 74, 77, 83, 85, 86, 102, 104, 108, 119, 138, 143, 144, 169, 170, 173, 189, 196
Laing, Olivia   170 n.3, 197
Lanchester, John   151, 166, 183, 216
  Capital   151–3, 190 n.15
  The Wall   163–5
Le Carré, John   178, 179
  Agent Running in the Field   178
  A Legacy of Spies   178–9
'Lewycka, Marina   151, 166, 179
  The Good, the Bad and the Little Bit Stupid   196
  Two Caravans   149–51
Linkon, Sherry Lee   84–5, 185
Lodge, David   45
London   18, 25, 26, 33, 59, 74, 80, 81, 84, 89, 104, 109, 111, 118 n.18, 123, 131, 142, 143, 148, 151, 153, 154, 165, 173, 175, 179–82, 179 n.10, 183–7, 188, 189, 193, 197
  2012 London Olympic Games   193–5, 208
  London riots   191, 192, 207
Lovegrove, James   95 n.14

McEwan, Ian   169, 172
  Cockroach   171–3
  The Innocent   78
  Machines Like Me   171 n.4
McGregor, Jon   199
Macmillan, Harold   6–9, 60
McQueer, Chris   121
MacShane, Denis   25–6, 169
Marr, Andrew   1, 6, 25, 61, 99, 101, 170
May, Theresa   21, 24–7, 101, 102, 111, 118, 119, 130–2, 143–5, 154, 157, 159, 165, 168, 173, 179, 215, 220
Meek, James   94, 220
Menasse, Robert   51 n.9
Miéville, China   162
Milazzo, Caitlin   19, 51, 62, 87, 141, 141 n.1, 144, 184, 187, 198 n.20
Mitford, Nancy   39–40
Monnet, Jean   46, 57, 64
Moore, Alan   84, 169

Moss, Sarah   4, 202, 205
  Ghost Wall   202–4
  Summerwater   204–5
Mullin, Chris   170–1
multiculturalism   20, 26, 74, 87, 97, 113, 144, 163, 165, 181, 190, 194–6
Murphy, Mary C.   126, 130
Myers, Benjamin   90

Nairn, Tom   75, 101
nationalism   1–5, 18, 22, 26, 32, 33, 43–4, 46, 48, 50, 51, 82 n.9, 92, 94, 97–8, 101–3, 123, 142, 143, 143 n.4, 144, 155, 161, 161 n.10, 163, 164, 168, 170, 172, 178, 181, 183, 184, 203–4, 206–11, 214, 220
  English   15, 19, 20, 29, 30, 59–63, 65, 66, 72, 76, 77, 79–96, 99–100, 118, 132, 134, 137–9, 140, 186, 187, 193, 201
  ethnonationalism   31, 74, 78, 83, 96, 98, 146, 147, 158, 182, 219
  Northern Irish   127–30, 134, 140
  Scottish   103, 111–12, 114, 118, 119, 121, 122 n.20, 140
  supranationalism   13, 46, 213
  Welsh   106, 108–11, 140
Nicholls, Robert   5, 11
Nora, Pierre   65, 193
Norris, Pippa   173, 174, 220
Northern Ireland   12, 17, 23, 24, 27, 30, 31, 74, 100–2, 110, 111, 118, 119, 125–37, 139, 140, 171
  Assembly   127, 128, 130
  Good Friday Agreement   17, 24, 31, 63, 126–35, 128 n.24, 135 n.28
  Irish border   24–5, 110, 125–9, 131–4, 133 n.27, 135–6, 162, 171
  Troubles   123, 126–9, 128 n.24, 131, 134–6
Northern Powerhouse   139, 185

O'Brien, Phil   86, 187–8
O'Hagan, Andrew   121–2
Orwell, George   57, 61, 71, 72, 78, 84, 121
Osmond, John   108–11
O'Toole, Fintan   25, 29, 31, 33, 55, 56, 76, 100, 125, 129, 133, 137, 144, 183, 195, 215, 216, 218

Parks, Tim   51, 53, 63, 96, 218
  Europa   49–55, 53 n.11
Patterson, Glenn   126, 127, 131
Paxman, Jeremy   61, 62, 153
Pearce, Nick   12, 13, 73, 74, 76, 100
Phillips, Caryl   97–9
Pincus, Anna, *see* Herd, David
Plaid Cymru   103, 104, 109, 110, 111 n.11, 138
Popoola, Olumide   154–7
populism   1, 76 n.8, 95 n.14, 169, 170–1, 174–5, 181, 188, 220
  sadopopulism (*see also* Snyder, Timothy)
postcolonial melancholia, *see also* Gilroy, Paul
post-truth   23, 33, 57, 66, 79, 122, 123, 138 n.31, 167, 170–8, 192, 208, 211
Priestley, J. B.   4, 36

race/racism   1, 15, 20, 22, 27, 32, 38, 45, 50, 74, 74 n.5, 79, 83, 85, 89, 90, 96, 99, 123, 144, 148, 149 n.8, 151, 152, 156–60, 165, 178, 179, 181, 192, 197–9, 201, 206, 217
refugee   22, 32, 76, 99, 123, 142–5, 150, 154–60, 164, 180, 199
  Calais refugee camp   154–6
  Syrian refugee crisis   20–2, 32, 145–6, 153, 157, 162–6, 168, 181, 199, 201, 208, 209
Roberts, Andrew   44
  The Aachen Memorandum   55–6
Robertson, James   113, 115 n.17, 120
  And the Land Lay Still   115

Saunders, Robert   24, 126
Schmitt, Mark   83, 84, 106
Schoene, Berthold   114, 114 n.14, 119
Scotland   12, 17, 20, 21, 30–1, 68, 74, 75, 101 n.1, 102, 103, 108, 111–25, 137–9
  2014 Independence referendum   20, 31, 110, 112, 115–17, 119, 120–2, 128, 138, 140, 175
  Parliament   63, 101, 113, 114, 181
  Scottish Brexit vote   23, 27, 30, 100, 116–20, 122, 123

Scottish National Party (SNP)   12, 20, 21, 103, 111, 111 n.11, 112, 115–19, 119 n.19, 121, 122, 130, 138
Scruton, Roger   61, 69, 99, 195
Sebald, W. G.   53 n.11
Second World War   5, 16, 40, 44, 45, 51, 66, 72, 79, 81, 83, 98, 145
Shaw, Fiona   122–3, 125
Shaw, Kristian   4, 145, 213
Sherratt-Bado, Dawn Miranda   128, 128 n.24, 131, 133
Sinn Fein   130, 138
Smith, Ali   4, 123–5, 157, 158, 197, 208, 208 n.22, 211, 212
   Autumn   208–9, 212
   Spring   123–5, 124 n.22, 211–12
   Summer   212–13
   Winter   209–11, 212
Smith, Zadie   129, 169, 179–80, 188
   The Embassy of Cambodia   180
   Grand Union   180–1, 180 n.11
   NW   88 n.12, 180
Snyder, Timothy   176–7, 187
Spallen, Abbie   128
Spiering, Menno   2, 38, 43, 90, 163
Sturgeon, Nicola   118–20, 123

Thatcher, Margaret   10, 12–13, 15, 16, 47, 49, 88, 106, 109, 111, 112, 119, 144, 147, 190, 192, 216
Thomson, Rupert   139
Thorpe, Adam   78, 92, 197, 198
   Missing Fay   197–9
Tomlinson, Sally   73, 74 n.5, 190, 213
transglossic   213
Tremain, Rose   147–9, 166
Trezise, Rachel   107, 111

Trump, Donald   4, 27, 76 n.8, 77, 170, 172, 174, 179, 209, 210
Turner, Arthur, *see* Gowland, David
Tusk, Donald   130, 131

United Kingdom Independence Party (UKIP)   15, 18, 18 n.5, 19–22, 24, 63, 73 n.4, 81, 83, 86–8, 118, 127, 138, 141 n.1, 143, 146, 158, 168, 173, 174, 176, 183, 186, 187
Upstone, Sara   60, 89, 213

Valluvan, Sivamohan   44, 71, 96–7

Waites, Martyn   183
Wales   12, 17, 30, 68, 74, 75, 101, 102–11, 122, 137–9, 184, 205–8
   Assembly   17, 63, 103, 103 n.2, 104, 104 n.3, 105, 107, 108, 109, 111
   devolution   102, 103, 107 n.8, 107 n.9, 111, 140
   Welsh Leave vote   23, 30, 103, 104, 105 n.6, 106, 110, 146
Wellings, Ben   2, 7, 12, 17, 29, 55, 63, 76 n.7, 137
Welsh, Irvine   105, 113, 120
   Dead Men's Trousers   120–1
Wilson, Angus   40–1, 43, 44
   The Old Men at the Zoo   40–5, 56 n.14
Wilson, Elizabeth   49–50
Wilson, Harold   9–12, 46, 89
Winterson, Jeanette   178, 219
Wright, Patrick   65, 69, 72, 78, 85, 191–2, 194
Wyn Jones, Richard   31, 60, 97, 102, 103

xenophobia, *see* race/racism

www.ingramcontent.com/pod-product-compliance
Lightning Source LLC
Chambersburg PA
CBHW062126300426
44115CB00012BA/1826